THE SEVENTH DIVISION

Histed.

MAJOR-GENERAL SIR T. CAPPER, K.C.M.G., C.B., D.S.O.

[*Frontispiece*

THE
SEVENTH
DIVISION

1914 – 1918

By
C.T. ATKINSON,
LATE CAPTAIN, OXFORD UNIVERSITY O.T.C.

PUBLISHED BY
THE NAVAL & MILITARY PRESS

Dedication

TO THE MEMORY OF THOSE OFFICERS

AND MEN OF THE DIVISION

WHO GAVE THEIR LIVES FOR THEIR COUNTRY

PREFACE

THIS account has been put together mainly from the War Diaries kept by the Division and its component units and now in the keeping of the Historical Section of the Committee of Imperial Defence. I am very much indebted to Brigadier-General J. E. Edmonds, Director of the Military Branch of the Section, for access to those diaries and to the Staff of the Section, who have put every facility at my disposal. In addition to this official information I have derived much help from the criticisms and corrections of the numerous officers who have read parts of this work in type ; the information they have supplied has filled in a good many gaps in the story and thrown a lot of light upon the conditions under which the Division worked and fought. To mention and thank all who have helped in this way would take a great deal of space, to single out one or two who have been particularly helpful would be invidious, but their help has been invaluable. Of published sources, other than the Official History, I am chiefly indebted to *The Defeat of Austria as seen by the Seventh Division* (by the Reverend E. C. Crosse, formerly Senior Chaplain to the Division, published by Messrs. H. F. W. Deane & Son), which gives an admirable account of the last of the Division's battles.

In preparing the maps, which are to be taken rather as approximations to the facts than as claiming absolute accuracy, I have naturally been much assisted when dealing with the operations of 1914 by being able to refer to the case of maps attached to Vol. II of the Official History, and I have been also greatly helped for the operations of 1915 by seeing advance copies of those in preparation for

Vols. III and IV of that History. The others are nearly all copied or adapted from maps in the Diaries.

The appendixes giving the changes in the Staff and in the command of units are as nearly correct as it has been possible to make them, but it is not claimed that absolute accuracy has been attained. Diaries do not always record changes in command or the departure and arrival of a new Staff Officer. Temporary changes due to absence on leave or at courses have not been noticed.

In conclusion I would like to express my thanks to the Divisional History Committee for their forbearance over the time it has taken to produce this story and in particular to the Secretary of the Committee, Colonel the Hon. M. Wingfield, for his ready and unfailing help.

C. T. A.

November 1926.

CONTENTS

vii

viii CONTENTS

LIST OF ILLUSTRATIONS

LIST OF MAPS

x   LIST OF MAPS

THE SEVENTH DIVISION

CHAPTER I

MOBILIZATION AND ANTWERP[1]

AFTER the departure for France of the Sixth Division, the last portion of the " striking force " provided by the reorganization begun in 1907, there remained in England of Regular troops only three regiments of Household Cavalry,[2] five battalions of infantry, three of them Guards, seven batteries of Royal Horse Artillery, and five brigades of R.F.A., besides training and draft-finding units. If the " striking force," now rechristened " British Expeditionary Force," was to receive any substantial additions, they must clearly come from some other source than the Regulars on the Home Establishment. The Territorials had been mobilized and were beginning that six months' intensive training which they were officially supposed to require before they could take the field. They could hardly be expected to be ready to be thrown into the fighting line straight away, especially as their organization had been somewhat upset by their being invited to undertake foreign service instead of the " home defence " for which they had been raised. The " New Armies " had responded in wonderful style to the call to arms, but these magnificent improvizations lacked not only training but arms, equipment, uniforms, and almost everything except zeal and devotion : many months must elapse before they could attain even to the stage of readiness of the Territorials. In this desperate state of affairs there was, however,

[1] Cf. Maps 1 and 2.
[2] Each of these had contributed a squadron to a " Composite Regiment " in the 4th Cavalry Brigade.

one resource on which the Empire could fall back—the Regular troops stationed overseas, the Colonial garrisons, and the Army in India. At the very outbreak of the war the Colonies and Dominions had ranged themselves alongside the Mother Country ; South Africa in particular, the only self-governing colony still garrisoned by Regulars, had declared its readiness not only to undertake its own defence, but to tackle German South-West Africa, thereby releasing the garrison, over 6,000 strong, for service in Europe. The defended ports in the Mediterranean could not take over their own protection as South Africa could, nor was it possible to denude Egypt of its garrison, but the ready response of the Territorials to the invitation to volunteer for service overseas allowed of relieving the Regulars at these stations by less highly trained troops, and before the first clash between British and Germans at Mons measures for organizing another Division were on foot.[1]

The Seventh Division therefore came into existence with the assembly at Lyndhurst in the New Forest of the units assigned to it from the Regulars remaining in England.[2] These included the 1st Grenadier Guards from Warley, the 2nd Scots Guards from the Tower, the 2nd Yorkshire Regiment from Guernsey, the 2nd Border Regiment from Pembroke Dock, " C " Battery R.H.A. from Canterbury, " F " from St. John's Wood, the XXXVth Brigade R.F.A. from Woolwich, and the 54th Field Co. R.E. from Chatham. To these were added during September the 2nd Royal Scots Fusiliers and 2nd Wiltshires from Gibraltar, the 2nd Royal Warwickshires and 1st Royal Welch Fusiliers from Malta, the 2nd Gordon Highlanders from Egypt, and the 2nd Queen's, 2nd Bedfordshires, and 1st South Stafford-shires from the Cape, whence came also the XXIInd Brigade R.F.A. and the 55th Field Co. R.E.

[1] Some such measure had been previously contemplated, the Secretary of State, in introducing the Army Estimates in 1912, having referred to it as a plan that might be adopted.

[2] Some units had gone into camp on Baddesley Common, near Southampton, before the end of August, but moved to Lyndhurst early in September.

The R.H.A. batteries took the place of the third brigade
of 18-pounders that should normally have formed part of the
Division, while as neither field howitzers nor 60-pounders
were forthcoming it was provided with two Heavy Batteries,
armed with the none too reliable 4·7-inch guns, the " cow-
gun " of the South African War, a thoroughly inadequate
substitute, but all that the unprepared country could produce. No Regular cavalry being available, a whole
Yeomanry regiment, the Northumberland Hussars, took
the place of the usual Divisional squadron, a cyclist company being formed from the infantry units, as had been
done in the original " B.E.F." The Divisional Ammunition Column, the Heavy Batteries, and the Signal Company were also improvized, and the three Field Ambulances and the Divisional Train had to be specially brought
together.

Command of the Division was given to Major-General
T. Capper, C.B., D.S.O.,[1] who was holding the appointment
of Inspector of Infantry, having recently relinquished
command of the 13th Infantry Brigade at Dublin. With
him came Colonel H. M. Montgomery as G.S.O.I. ; the
C.R.A. was Brigadier-General H. K. Jackson, and as
C.R.E. Colonel A. T. Moore was appointed.[2]

As commanders of the infantry brigades there were
appointed Brigadier-Generals H. G. Ruggles-Brise, H. E.
Watts, and S. T. B. Lawford. General Ruggles-Brise,
himself an old Grenadier Guardsman, was given the 20th
Brigade, which comprised the two Guards battalions together with the Gordons and the Borders. The two battalions from Gibraltar together with the Yorkshires and
Bedfords formed the 21st Brigade under General Watts, the
two from Malta with the Queen's and South Staffords from
South Africa making up General Lawford's 22nd Brigade.
But though some of the units were not strangers to each

[1] General Capper's appointment was dated August 27th, which may therefore be taken as the official beginning of the existence of the Division.

[2] For the full list of the Staff, see Appendix 1, Order of Battle.

other or to some of their staff—Captain James, for example, the Brigade Major of the 22nd Brigade, had held the same post in the Pretoria garrison—the Division as a whole had to start at the beginning to gain that coherence and corporate spirit which the first six Divisions had acquired from working together in peace. The Division was fortunate in having as its first commander a man of great energy, driving power, and much experience as a trainer of troops. It was fortunate also in that most of its units, coming from stations overseas, were on a higher establishment than units at home and contained none but men who had completed their recruit training and were over 19 years of age. They had not to leave a third of their men behind and to fill up to war establishment by incorporating about 50 per cent of Reservists, who, if trained and mature men, needed some time to get back to the habits and conditions of Army life and to revive their knowledge of their work. The four battalions on the Home Establishment of course contained a high percentage of Reservists,[1] but these had been back with the Colours since the beginning of August, and had had ample time to shake down into their places. The units from overseas were completed to establishment by drafts from the Reserve, but these did not amount to more than 100 or 130 men per battalion, a proportion easily assimilated. The Queen's, for example, were joined by three Special Reserve officers and a draft of 253 men from the 3rd Battalion, some of them serving soldiers, but mostly Reservists, a hundred of whom were detailed as the " first reinforcements." Most battalions had a few officers from the Reserve of Officers or Special Reserve ; thus the Grenadiers had five, the Bedfords four, the Wiltshires three. The 55th Field Company, again, which came home with 4 officers and 150 men, was brought up mainly with Reservists to its establishment of 6 officers and 212 other

---

[1] The Grenadiers, who had sent off drafts to their 2nd Battalion, were nearly two-thirds Reservists, while the Scots Guards had 748 Reservists among 1,122 men.

ranks, and the Divisional Ammunition Column contained a large proportion of Reservists.

Mobilization was a difficult process, especially for the later arrivals, while one or two changes in the Staff did not tend to assist its progress. With the large demands which the maintenance in the field of the original six Divisions was making on the Ordnance, with the New Armies—not to mention the Territorials—clamouring for equipment, it was hard to obtain for the units of the Seventh Division all the transport, horses, and other items they needed. The mobilization of the Artillery was much delayed by troubles over farriers' stores and fuses for the Heavy Batteries. But Quartermasters are a resourceful race, and there were stories of local bakers' carts bought up, painted regulation colour, and figuring as " carts, Maltese, Medical Officer for the use of." Anyhow, by one expedient and another, the various needs were met. The 55th Field Company, for example, had four "civilian" carts instead of the regulation forage carts, and two more in place of a cook's cart and a G.S. wagon. The South Staffords, though about the last unit to arrive, distinguished themselves by being the first battalion reported ready for service. Mobilization, however, was not the Division's only occupation during this time. With characteristic energy and zeal General Capper started Brigade and even Divisional training directly units could be got together. There were repeated field days and constant route-marches ; indeed before orders to move arrived the Division had, as one officer put it, " marched close on three hundred miles about the New Forest by way of hardening the men who had come off foreign service." These exercises did give commanders and units some chance of getting to know each other, but, nevertheless, the Division was still rather a " scratch " team when it embarked for Flanders.

While the Division's mobilization had been going forward the military situation on the Continent had undergone a considerable change. The first arrivals at Lynd-

hurst had coincided with the end of the Retreat and with
the throwing back of the Germans in the battle of the
Marne. On that had followed the struggle on the Aisne,
in which the British had only missed a great success by the
narrowest of margins, the besiegers of Maubeuge having
arrived and filled the gap in the German line just as the
First Corps was about to penetrate through it. Then,
while the B.E.F. was enduring its first experience of that
" trench warfare " for which it was so singularly ill-pre-
pared in equipment, there had developed the " race to the
sea," in which the French left and the German right
continually outflanked each other in turn. As the Northern
ends of the opposing lines drew steadily nearer to Flanders
the situation in Belgium naturally became of increasing
importance. When October came the Belgian Field Army
was still within the fortified camp of Antwerp, to which it
had withdrawn just as the B.E.F. had started its move to
Mons. For some time the Germans had observed rather
than molested it, but on September 9th orders had been
issued to reduce Antwerp, and the end of the month saw
the German pressure on that position already becoming
serious.

Antwerp was, in effect, an isolated position echeloned on
the left in front of the Allied line running Northward from
the Aisne, the outer flank of which had by now reached
the neighbourhood of Lens. Between Lens and Antwerp
stretched a No Man's Land of the greatest importance
economically as well as strategically, for it included the
great manufacturing area about Lille and Roubaix, and
the important coalmines round Lens. To link Antwerp
up with the French left would be of the utmost value ; it
would not only preserve all this rich district from German
occupation, but would keep the Germans back from the
Belgian coast and retain in Belgian possession the portion
of West Flanders on the left of the Scheldt. However,
while it was easy to see what important results might
follow from linking up the French and Belgian armies, to

achieve this desirable object was more difficult. General
Joffre was sufficiently hard pressed already to thin out the
right and centre of his long line and find troops to prolong
his left Northward and continue the effort to outflank the
Germans. Accordingly the approaching completion of
the Seventh Division's mobilization and the arrival at
Marseilles of the first instalments of the forces which the
Indian Empire was contributing to redress the balance of
Europe were of special importance, as holding out the prospect that British troops might before long be available
for this purpose. Moreover, many reasons, those connected
with supply and administration no less than the political
and strategical, urged the transfer of the B.E.F. back to
its original position on the French left. More particularly,
if additional British Divisions would soon become available
for operations in Flanders, it would be absurd to have them
operating apart from Sir John French's original six.
Accordingly it was decided that the B.E.F. should be
extracted from the Aisne, where it was embedded amidst
French armies, and on October 1st its transfer to Flanders
was begun, the Second Corps being withdrawn from the
line and moved Westward before entraining for Abbeville.
The Third was to follow forthwith, and the Cavalry at the
same time started to move by road, the First Corps remaining some little time longer, largely in order to conceal from
the Germans the fact that the British would soon be upon
them in Flanders.

Meanwhile the situation at Antwerp was developing
rapidly, and the developments were most unsatisfactory to
the Allies. The fortifications, at one time reputed among
the finest in Europe, were in 1914 far from up to date, and
shortly after the Germans undertook systematic siege
operations it became evident that the fall of Antwerp could
not be long delayed. On October 2nd it was decided that
the Belgian Court and Government should withdraw from
the city, and the removal of the Field Army was also taken
into consideration. For various reasons, in which political

2

and even sentimental motives seem to have predominated, the British Government attached enormous importance to preventing the fall of Antwerp, and mainly at its instance it was decided to prolong the resistance, to reinforce the garrison with the brigade of Marines already in Flanders since September 20th and the two newly raised brigades which with it constituted the "Royal Naval Division," to retain the Belgian Field Army at Antwerp, and to collect a Franco-British force to attempt to raise the siege. To this force the Seventh Division was allotted, and on October 4th orders were issued for its embarkation, while General Capper proceeded to the War Office to receive verbal instructions from the Secretary of State.

When the embarkation orders were received, mobilization had fortunately just been completed,[1] though the 3rd Cavalry Division, also allotted to the relieving force, was still far from completely mobilized. The orders were so unexpected that several battalions had let the men off duty on the completion of the day's work—it was a Sunday—and had hastily to summon them back from Lyndhurst. The Queen's got their orders at 3 p.m. to be ready to move at 3.45, an impossible task in the circumstances. They were ready, however, at 5.30, and other units were not less prompt, though several officers who were out of camp on short leave returned only just in time. One battalion met the problem by sending the buglers up to any high ground near camp and bidding them blow the "Assembly" for all they were worth, thereby bringing the men tumbling back in double-quick time. Within four hours of the receipt of the order to move the first units were on the road to Southampton. Embarkation was begun before midnight and proceeded rapidly, ships leaving the docks as loaded and proceeding up Channel to Dover. There was some uncertainty as to the naval situation : German submarines were believed to be about,

---

[1] The XXIInd Brigade R.F.A. and the two Heavy Batteries were only reported as having completed their mobilization that very day.

and the transports, which sailed in two groups, did not at
first proceed beyond Dover, where the first group spent
most of October 5th before crossing to the Belgian coast,
its destination having been at the last moment altered
from Boulogne and Dunkirk to Zeebrugge.

Thanks to the efficient protection afforded by the Navy
the first instalment of the Division arrived at Zeebrugge
without mishap early on October 6th, and about 6.30 a.m.
disembarkation began. As the troops landed they were
moved to Bruges, 15 miles away, dismounted men going
by train, mounted men and vehicles by road. Pressure
was put upon General Capper by the local Belgian military
authorities to entrain at once for Antwerp ; but as special
emphasis had been laid, both by Lord Kitchener and by
Sir Charles Douglas, the C.I.G.S., on the paramount
importance of not getting shut up in that town, he firmly
refused to take such a step, and was supported in his
decision by receiving orders from Sir Henry Rawlinson, the commander of the Fourth Corps, of which the
Seventh Division formed the principal part, to proceed to
Bruges and remain there until the Division could be concentrated. By 9 p.m. on the 6th all troops who had dis-
embarked were in billets at Bruges, but several battalions
were incomplete, only one of their half-battalions having
arrived. Meanwhile the second group of transports was
on its way. A certain liveliness attended its passage ; the
escorting destroyers reported German submarines about
and claimed to have sunk one ; but whether this claim
was well founded or not, the convoy made Zeebrugge at
3.30 a.m. on October 7th, and at 6 o'clock the ships came
alongside the quays and disembarkation started. The
previous day's procedure was repeated, and by 5 p.m.
practically the whole Division was concentrated round
Bruges, where it received the warmest of welcomes, though
the urgent demands for " souvenirs " proved highly
detrimental to the uniforms of the troops, cap and collar
badges and buttons being torn off freely.

By this time the military situation had become clearer, though not any more satisfactory. The promised French Territorial Division had not appeared, nor were there any signs of the brigade of French Marines who should have arrived. The Royal Naval Division, or rather the three infantry brigades without artillery, engineers, transport, or ambulances who were known by that name, was already shut up in Antwerp, so that the force available for the projected stroke at the besiegers' heavy guns was reduced to the 18,000 men of the Seventh Division and—when it should arrive—the 3rd Cavalry Division, about 4,000 strong. The offensive was obviously out of the question, and, although the officers and men of the Seventh Division knew nothing of it, the situation at Antwerp was becoming worse so rapidly that not even the most optimistic amateur strategist could have entertained any hopes of seriously postponing the inevitable fall of the town. It was now a question how much of the Belgian Field Army could extricate itself from an entanglement from which it might have withdrawn with much greater ease a couple of days earlier ; indeed the task before the Division was now not to relieve Antwerp but to rescue the Belgian Army.[1] However, before this could be attempted the Division had another task. The 3rd Cavalry Division, which had left Southampton on October 7th, was to disembark at Ostend, as Zeebrugge had been found unsuitable for a base, and this process had to be covered, as reports had come in that large German forces, mainly cavalry, had concentrated at Lille and were moving Westward. Accordingly, by the orders of General Rawlinson, the Division moved on October 8th towards Ostend and took up a position on an arc of 4 miles from that town to cover the landing of the cavalry. The 13-mile march, a trying performance for men who were making their first acquaintance with the Belgian pavé roads, under a hot sun and with a full active

---

[1] Actually the Belgian Field Army had been moved to the West of the Scheldt on October 6th and began its retreat on Bruges next day.

service load on their backs, was completed by 4 p.m., but lack of wharf accommodation and other difficulties delayed disembarkation; midnight came before the cavalry were all ashore, and meanwhile a crisis had been reached at Antwerp—the forts had been lost, the inner line of defence broken, and the decision reluctantly taken to evacuate the city.

Accordingly General Rawlinson decided to move two brigades with some artillery to Ghent to support the French Marines, who had now arrived there, in covering the withdrawal from Antwerp. The movement, which was begun early on October 9th, the troops going by rail, took some time ; for though the distance was only 40 miles, there was much confusion and congestion on the railway, everything having to be extemporized with a temporary railway staff. As troops arrived at Ghent an outpost line was thrown out East and South, with the French Marines at the S.E. corner of the road to Alost, the direction from which danger was now most to be feared, as the enemy was reported in strength near that town.

Despite this the night of October 9th/10th passed without the Seventh Division getting touch with the enemy. It was a miserable night, the rain poured steadily down, no fires or lights were allowed, and a hot meal was impossible for those in the trenches or in bivouac. One battalion solved the rations question by an issue of German sausage purchased locally, but it was a depressing start to the campaign. There was some firing during the night on the French Marines' front, and they reported in the morning that they had repulsed an attack and had inflicted 200 casualties on the Germans ; but the British outposts had nothing to fire at, and during the night the entrainment of the Division was pushed on, the 21st Brigade, 12th and 25th Batteries R.F.A., Divisional Ammunition Column, and Heavy Batteries moving by road to Bruges, where the 3rd Cavalry Division was concentrating. The Wiltshires were left to cover Ostend and protect the disembarkation of stores and supplies, so the 21st Brigade was short by one battalion.[1]

October 10th was a day of inaction for the bulk of the Division. About noon orders were received that, as the Belgians were now clear of Ghent, the Division should withdraw in such time as to reach Aeltre, ten miles to the S.W., by daylight. However, in the afternoon it became clear that the Belgian movement was not far enough advanced to allow of this, so the Division was ordered to remain in position for another night, while the 3rd Cavalry Division pushed out one brigade to Thorout and the other to Ruddervoorde, the 21st Brigade and other details at Bruges also shifting before nightfall to Beernem, being much delayed by the congestion of the roads by Belgian refugees.

The night of October 10th/11th was not without excitement for the troops at Ghent. There were many reports of Germans in the near neighbourhood, especially to the S.E., and both French and Belgian outposts indulged in spasmodic bursts of firing. These constant bursts of firing naturally kept the outpost line on the alert, and few officers or men got any rest or sleep. With morning, patrols were pushed out in all directions and some encounters with German cavalry took place ; the Scots Guards claiming "first blood" for the Division by inflicting several casualties on a patrol of Uhlans, while the Northumberland Hussars did excellent work, showing considerable enterprise and initiative. The information which came in seemed to indicate that the Germans were moving towards Ghent, rather than endeavouring to follow the Belgian retreat ; but although both brigades reported contact with snipers and small parties of enemy, no attack developed, and about 4 p.m. General Rawlinson issued

---

[1] The entrainment was not actually completed till the afternoon of October 10th ; it had taken 36 hours to entrain two brigades of infantry with two of artillery and details.

orders to withdraw from Ghent after nightfall and to make
for Thielt, eight miles beyond Aeltre. The troops moved
in two columns, the 20th Brigade, the R.H.A. Brigade, and
the 58th Battery R.F.A. taking the Northern road by
Mariakerke and Somerghem, the 22nd Brigade and the
XXIInd Brigade R.F.A. with Divisional Headquarters
moving by Tronchiennes and Hansbeke to the South. The
Grenadiers and the South Staffords with the Yeomanry
squadrons formed the rear-guards of their respective
columns. Orders were issued that the march was to be
made in strict silence, and that if the enemy was encountered he was to be tackled with the bayonet.

It was 9 p.m. before the march was started, and with
the troops already somewhat tired by their shiftings to and
fro and two trying nights on outposts, while many of them
were rather " soft " after a long sea voyage, it proved most
exhausting. The night was bitterly cold, the men found
the pavé very hard on the feet, and the congestion of
the roads caused many delays. Shortly after daybreak
the Canal du Lys was reached ; the troops had done 16
miles since leaving their outpost line and were not sorry
to halt, most of the men finding billets in Hansbeke, Somerghem, and Aeltre, covered by rear-guards along the canal.
Of the enemy nothing was seen, though they were reported
as advancing in force from Ghent, and soon after midday
the retirement was resumed on Thielt, the French Marines
leading, the Seventh Division following. It was another
toilsome affair, much delayed by the crowding of the roads,
and it was nearly midnight before the rear-guards at last
crawled into Thielt. The men had covered over 26 miles [1]
in the last 24 hours, most of them being short of sleep and
food, and were greatly exhausted ; however, the extrication of the Belgian Field Army had been safely accomplished
and the Division was now available for other work.

Of this there was plenty in immediate prospect. On
the day the Division moved to Ghent the Second Corps

---

[1] Some units had done as much as 30 miles.

had completed its concentration in Flanders, and that night it had begun moving N.E. towards Béthune to prolong to the North the line of the French Xth Army, then heavily engaged with the enemy between Lens and Vermelles. It had soon encountered German cavalry and Jagers in some force, but pushed them steadily back towards the Aubers Ridge S.W. of Lille ; on its left the 3rd Corps, having completed its concentration round Hazebrouck, began to come into line on October 13th, while the British cavalry under General Allenby pushed forward farther to the left again. There was a chance that if the enemy's cavalry held on too long they might be intercepted by the Fourth Corps, and in any case it was desirable to establish touch between this detached force and the British main body at the earliest possible moment.

Accordingly on October 13th the Division resumed its march for Roulers, the transport being sent on ahead at an early hour, though the main body's start was delayed till nearly noon to rest the tired infantry. The distance to be covered was only 10 miles, but matters were not improved by heavy and persistent rain ; the roads where not pavé became deep in mud, out of which the weary men had often to pull carts and wagons ; moreover, delays were frequent, partly because reports that the Germans were close at hand caused a covering position to be taken up, and it was already dark when the main column got into Roulers, while the 21st Brigade, which had moved from Beernem to Coolscamp on the previous day and now rejoined the main body, did not come in till 9 p.m. The Wiltshires, having completed their duties at Ostend by covering the re-embarkation of the remnants of the R.N.D., had arrived by train rather earlier. There had again been no serious contact with the Germans, though in the morning a hostile aeroplane flying over Thielt had been brought down by rifle fire, while the 3rd Cavalry Division, which had pushed on to Ypres and then taken up a protective line on the way to Menin, had met and accounted for various patrols.

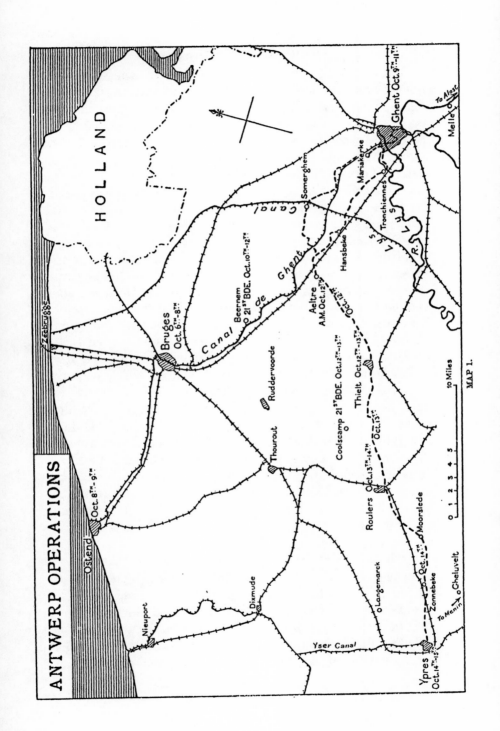

ANTWERP OPERATIONS

HOLLAND

Ostend Oct. 8TH.-9TH.

Zeebrugge

Bruges Oct. 6TH.-8TH.

Beernem
21ST BDE. Oct.10TH.-12TH.

Canal de Ghent Canal

Somerghem

Mariakerke

Ghent Oct. 9TH.-11TH.

To Alost

Melle

Tronchiennes

R. LYS

Hansbeke

Aeltre
A.M. Oct.12TH.

Oct.12TH.

Thielt Oct.12TH.-13TH.

Ruddervoorde

Coolscamp 21ST BDE. Oct.12TH.-13TH.

Oct.13TH.

Thourout

Roulers Oct.13TH.-14TH.

Oct.13TH.

Nieuport

Dixmude

Moorslede

Langemarck

Zonnebeke

To Menin

Cheluvelt

Yser Canal

Ypres
Oct.14TH.-15TH.

0 1 2 3 4 5   10 Miles

MAP 1.

October 14th saw the first phase in the Division's operations completed. At 6.15 a.m. it was on the march again, making for Ypres—some 15 miles away—in three columns, over bad roads, and in steady rain. The transport and the Divisional Ammunition Column led, and strong rear- and flank-guards covered the movement. As before there was no interruption from the enemy, and Ypres was reached without incident, but as the billeting parties were proceeding about their duties they found themselves in contact with Germans, some who had apparently slipped into Ypres just before the Seventh Division arrived. The billeting parties had some lively moments. The Yorkshires' Quartermaster distinguished himself by his promptitude in bagging a Uhlan, and the surviving Germans soon cleared off, some 20 of them taking refuge in a wood, which the 10th Hussars surrounded, forcing them to surrender. To cover Ypres an outpost line was put out to the S.E.,[1] roughly from St. Eloi to Zillebeke, being continued from Zillebeke to Wieltje by the French, whose 87th Territorial Division had arrived and connected up the Division with the forces farther North. In putting out the outposts the Gordons had a sharp brush with some Uhlans, engaging and destroying a strongish patrol. Meanwhile the 3rd Cavalry Division, which had moved back to Ypres early in the morning, was pushing out again to the Southward towards Kemmel and Wytschaete, clearing off before it a good number of German cavalry and establishing touch with the 2nd Cavalry Division, who were making for the Lys.

With this establishment of connexion with the British main body the Fourth Corps finished its independent rôle. It had been unable to do anything for Antwerp, but its presence in Belgium and its rather risky advance to Ghent had undoubtedly contributed to the extrication of the Belgian Field Army from the dangerously prolonged entanglement of Antwerp. It had been a difficult and

[1] Cf. Map 2.

anxious period for those in command, confronted with an
obscure and constantly changing situation, torn between
the desire to do something effective to assist the Belgians
and their express orders not to compromise the safety of
their force.   It had, as already mentioned, been a strenuous
and exhausting period for the troops, who had had little
rest or sleep, and not too much food, and had made toilsome marches.   The men arrived at Ypres tired : their
movements had seemed somewhat aimless, and they had
not had the satisfaction of a serious encounter with the
enemy and of seeing Germans fall under their rifle fire,
such as the original B.E.F. had enjoyed at Mons.   Whether
the Seventh Division's first week in Flanders had been
spent to the best purpose was not a question which can
have much concerned its officers and men.   They had had
their orders and had carried them out ; but for the demonstration towards Melle, of the strength of which the Germans
were ignorant, they might have pressed more vigorously
after the retreating Belgians and impeded their arrival.
Still it may be asked whether the Division might not have
been much more effectively employed but for Antwerp.
Had the two British Divisions been directed through
Ypres on Lille directly they landed in Flanders they could
hardly have failed to influence materially the operations
of the Second and Third Corps.   The threat to the flank
and rear of the opponents of Generals Smith-Dorrien and
Pulteney which such an advance would have constituted
must have shaken the German defence ; it might even
have enabled the British to reach Lille, to secure the
Aubers Ridge, and to turn the La Bassée position before
the arrival of the German reinforcements who actually
checked the Third Corps just outside Lille and drove the
Second off the Aubers Ridge into the mud flats at its foot.
That any useful purpose was served by prolonging the
defence of Antwerp it is hard to believe.   That it delayed
the German thrust through Ypres at the Channel Ports
seems most unlikely ; that thrust was carried out not by

the besiegers of Antwerp—who were engaged with the Belgians along the Yser—but by the new Reserve Corps improvised since the beginning of the war, now hurriedly thrown into the fight. There is no reason to think that the resistance of Antwerp affected in the least the preparation and dispatch to the front of these units. Had the Belgians withdrawn two days earlier their retreat might have been accomplished in better order and with less loss ; they might even have held a line farther East than that of the Yser. Possibly, but for the wish to save Antwerp, the Seventh Division might not have been allowed to leave England as early as it did, but consideration of what it might have accomplished in closer and earlier cooperation with the main British force in Flanders does suggest that an opportunity for effective action was not fully utilized.

CHAPTER II

THE Division's arrival at Ypres was followed by a few days
of relative quiet : the Fourth Corps, though in touch with
the British main body, was ahead of it, and there was no
purpose to be served by an unsupported advance, especially
as there was great uncertainty as to the strength of the
German forces which had followed up the retirement from
Antwerp and Ghent. For these days, therefore, the situation was governed by the instructions issued by G.H.Q.
on October 15th that the Cavalry should establish themselves on the right bank of the Lys between Armentières
and Menin, and then move East, covering the Third Corps'
advance down the Lys, while the Second Corps also pushed
forward. The Fourth, with the 3rd Cavalry Division on
its left connecting it with the Belgians, was to advance
between Courtrai and Roulers, keeping a look-out to the
N.E. for any attack against the Belgians ; but could not
start until the Third Corps came up level with it. Accordingly the Seventh Division was directed to establish an
outpost line covering the approaches to Ypres from the
E. and S.E., while the 3rd Cavalry Division extended this
line past Poelcappelle and in front of Houthulst Forest.
Before the final orders reached him General Capper had
already on October 15th given directions for the occupation
of a defensive line from Vormeezeele on the right to Zillebeke with outposts pushed well forward, the 21st Brigade
being on the right, the 20th on the left, and the 22nd in
reserve. The occupation of this line had been accompanied
by much activity. The woods S. and S.E. of Ypres swarmed
with German patrols and snipers, and the Northumberland

---

[1] Cf. Maps 2, 3, and 4.

Hussars encountered enemy on all the roads leading towards Menin; while the scouts of the Border Regiment were particularly successful near Zillebeke, " accounting," as one Diary says, " for some twenty over-curious Teutons " without losing a man. Several prisoners were taken and useful identifications thereby obtained, but beyond a report that 20,000 Germans were advancing on Courtrai no very explicit information was received. When in the afternoon the Corps orders arrived, the 20th Brigade took over the whole line originally allotted to the Division, the 21st relieving the French between Zillebeke and Wieltje. The 22nd Brigade meanwhile shifted back to Ypres from its original reserve position near Kruistraathoek.

The night of October 15th/16th passed quietly, apart from a little sniping. Very early next morning in accordance with orders issued overnight an advance was made ; the 20th Brigade pushed out to Zandvoorde and entrenched a line running Eastward to Gheluvelt, whence the 21st Brigade carried it on in a Northerly direction past Reutel, the 22nd moving up on the 21st's left and continuing the line beyond Zonnebeke. The movement was almost unopposed, though the Yorkshires, the advanced guard of the 21st Brigade, encountered some German cavalry near Gheluvelt and drove them off, inflicting over a dozen casualties, while " B " Company of the Wiltshires, which reconnoitred as far forward as Becelaere, also encountered Uhlans in some force. It appeared also that a whole regiment of Germans had evacuated Zonnebeke just before the Welch Fusiliers, the 22nd Brigade's advanced guard, got there. The country people were full of rumours of the advance of large bodies of Germans, and the 3rd Cavalry Division reported several encounters with hostile patrols and the presence of the enemy in force a little to the Eastward. Accordingly the troops started to entrench the position, a terribly long front for one Division with less than the normal complement of artillery. From Zandvoorde it was nearly eight miles to the left of the 22nd

Brigade, flung back N.W. of Zonnebeke across the road
to Passchendaele ; indeed the Division's position was no
more than an outpost line, for there was only one battalion
in Divisional reserve.   By this time, however, the whole
First Corps had left the Aisne and both the Second and
Third had made substantial if slow progress, while as yet
such news as had come in did not seem to point to the
presence in Flanders of much more than the force which
had besieged Antwerp, though on the British right nearer
La Bassée infantry were already reinforcing the cavalry
hitherto opposing Generals Smith-Dorrien and Pulteney.

The rest of the line was not yet far forward enough to
warrant an advance by the Fourth Corps, so the Division's
orders for October 17th were to remain in the position held
overnight.   During the night of October 16th/17th there
was some firing on the 21st Brigade's front in which the
Division suffered its first officer casualty, Captain Magor
of the Wiltshires being killed ; but it did not appear—
despite some rather alarmist reports from sentries—that
the enemy were anything more than patrols.   During the
day the Division was spasmodically and somewhat
innocuously shelled from the direction of a farm known as
" America " ; there was some sniping and several brushes
with German patrols—the Scots Fusiliers, for instance,
drove about 60 cavalry out of Becelaere, getting an identification of the 20th Uhlans.   The chief incident was that,
partly to drive back the snipers, two companies of the
Scots Guards pushed forward and occupied Kruiseik, a
position on which their commander, Major Fraser, reported
unfavourably as a salient and very difficult to defend [1] : he
was to be justified in his criticisms only too well before
many days were out.   Most battalions were mainly occupied in improving their trenches and clearing their fields of
fire, while the gunners endeavoured, without much success,
to find satisfactory positions for their batteries.   In the
evening Corps orders were received for an advance next

[1] Kruiseik village straggled along the road for about 300 yards.

day to the line Kortewilde–Terhand–Waterdamhoek. The
3rd Cavalry Division would cover the left flank ; on the
right touch had already been established with the 2nd
Cavalry Division, who were all along the left bank of the
Lys from Warneton downwards, but had as yet failed to
secure the passage of the river.

The advance to the new line encountered little opposition, though the 21st Brigade, in swinging its left forward to
the line Kilo. 10 on the Ypres–Menin road-Terhand, met
heavy rifle fire and was sharply shelled as it came over a
rise. The Bedfords had nearly 30 casualties, mainly from
artillery fire, but pushed on, however, and, with the Scots
Fusiliers on their left, entrenched themselves on the spur
running South from Terhand, the Germans clearing off
before their advance.[1] The Gordons also, who advanced
almost to " America," were heavily shelled from Wervicq,
but escaped more lightly. Their position was none too
good ; the line bent very sharply back from " America "
to Zandvoorde, forming a pronounced salient, with thick
woods a little distance away in which the enemy could
mass unseen for an attack.[2]

The Division had not, however, advanced as far as
G.H.Q. desired, and about midday a liaison officer from
G.H.Q. arrived at General Capper's headquarters and
expressed surprise that the Division was not conducting
an attack in force on Menin.[3] The Divisional Commander
was equally surprised to find that he was regarded as being
" backward in advancing," especially as his orders gave no
indication that anything more than a slight gain of
ground was expected. That he should proceed independently to attack Menin had never entered into

---

[1] On the left the advance covered over two miles.

[2] The 22nd Brigade advanced to a line running North from Becelaere,
having the Queen's about a mile and a half in front, acting as flank-guard on
the left rear of the 21st Brigade.

[3] G.H.Q. had used the word " move " of the Fourth Corps, " attack " of
the Second : General Rawlinson had, therefore, cautioned General Capper
against moving too far forward.

his mind in view of the Division's already advanced
position, the known presence of considerable hostile forces
at Courtrai and Wevelghem, and the necessity for co-ordinating his movements with those of the troops on his flanks.
The liaison officer went off to report General Capper's views

MAP 2.—OPERATIONS OCTOBER 15TH-18TH, 1914.

at G.H.Q., with the result that during the afternoon various
important officers turned up at Divisional Headquarters
who pooh-poohed the idea that the concentrations reported
at Courtrai and Wevelghem amounted to anything sub-
scantial, and seemed quite taken aback to find that the
Divisi)n was not well advanced on the road to Menin.

3

Eventually a specific order to attack Menin was received from G.H.Q., but too late to allow of an advance that day, and G.H.Q. had to be contented with the issue of orders for the attack to be started at 6.30 a.m. on the 19th.

The move was to be carried out in three phases, the first an attack from the North on Kleythoek by the 22nd Brigade. This was to be followed by the other two brigades attacking Gheluwe, till then they were to remain in concealment near Kruiseik and Terhand ; finally all three were to press forward on Menin. The attack was to be supported by the XXIInd Brigade R.F.A. from just East of Terhand and by the XXXVth Brigade R.F.A., who were on their right, with the 112th Heavy Battery just in rear W. and S.W. of Terhand, while the XIVth Brigade R.H.A. and the 111th Heavy Battery on the Kruiseik knoll supported the 20th Brigade and kept down fire from Wervicq. The Northumberland Hussars were to cover the left of the 22nd Brigade, keeping connexion with the 3rd Cavalry Division, which was to ward off any interruption from the Roulers direction. The attack was arranged on the principle of refusing the right flank, which was likely to be enfiladed from Wervicq where the enemy was entrenched and had some guns. The left was therefore to lead, and though it certainly appeared that it would be " in the air," the assurances of G.H.Q. led General Capper to believe that the 3rd Cavalry Division would easily provide all the protection needed and that on the other flank the 2nd Cavalry Division would effectually keep the enemy round Wervicq occupied.

One great difficulty about the attack was that the undulating and thickly wooded country presented a nasty problem to the artillery, who found observation most difficult and could give the infantry little effective support, being unable to locate accurately either the enemy trenches or gun positions. However, the 22nd Brigade moved off well up to time and advancing by Strooiboomhoek to Dadizeele deployed there. The Royal Warwick-

shires were on the right, directing, with their left on the
Menin–Roulers road, the Welch Fusiliers being on the left,
beyond the road, the South Staffords in support, and the
Queen's in reserve. The actual advance began about 9 a.m.
and at first made good progress, though the Northumberland Hussars almost at once came into contact with the
enemy near Ledeghem. This caused a little delay, as
a company of the Welch Fusiliers had to be sent to their
assistance, but on the arrival of the 6th Cavalry Brigade
the Germans cleared off and the detached company
rejoined the main body. However, two companies of
the Queen's under Major Bottomley were now detailed
as flank-guard, and soon afterwards, the brigade having
inclined to its right, the remaining companies of the
Queen's, "A" and "D," prolonged the Welch Fusiliers' line
to the left. It was then about 10.30, and after that the
attack was vigorously pressed, the Welch Fusiliers distinguishing themselves by the mixture of dash and steadiness which characterized their advance. "Things went
splendidly," writes one officer; "the attack was going just
like the drill-book." Some parties of Germans cleared
off as the troops pushed forward, and the machine-guns
covered the advance admirably, silencing rifle fire from
behind a hedge which was threatening to check the Fusiliers. On the right "B" Company of the Warwickshires
got on specially well, making good use of favourable
ground. The leading companies had been reinforced by
nearly all the supports, and by 1 p.m. the firing-line was
almost within assaulting distance of the German position,[1]
when the Brigadier received urgent orders from the
Division to break off the attack at once and withdraw
under cover of the 21st Brigade.

The cause of this sudden change was the unfavourable
situation which had suddenly developed on the left. Here
the 3rd Cavalry Division had soon met enemy North of

---

[1] The trenches at Kleythoek appear to have been held by the right of the
German XIIIth Corps.

Ledeghem and East of Moorslede. At first these enemy were pushed back, but before long the Royals and 10th Hussars found infantry attacks developing against them from Rolleghemcapelle and were soon hard pressed ; simultaneously the 7th Cavalry Brigade on their left encountered the enemy in force [1] and was driven back to Moorslede. Heavy pressure was also developing against the French and Belgians farther North, and it was clear that the enemy were in much greater force than G.H.Q. had anticipated. The actual order to General Capper to break off his advance was based on the air reports which had reached G.H.Q. ; these showed that large columns, each of a division at least, were moving from Courtrai and Thielt on Gulleghem and Pitthem.

But with the Welch Fusiliers and Warwickshires close up to the enemy's trenches at Kleythoek,[2] to break off the engagement was far from easy, especially as the artillery were finding it so hard to give the infantry adequate support. The Queen's too were in close contact with the enemy ; " B " and " C " Companies had pushed through Ledeghem and had nearly reached Moorseele which they found held in some force ; while " A " and " D," who were covering the flank of the Welch Fusiliers, came under artillery fire at fairly close range. Some of the South Staffords too had been pushed up into line between the Welch Fusiliers and the Queen's, and about a platoon had got well forward. However, the task was successfully accomplished. The Queen's went first, " A " and " D " falling back to a position N.W. of Dadizeele which the South Staffords had entrenched, though " B " and " C " did not get their orders till about 3 p.m. and on retiring towards Ledeghem found Germans coming into the village in force. However, a small party gallantly pushed into the village to engage the enemy, and, thus covered, Major Bottomley got his

---

[1] Apparently the 53rd Reserve Division, the right column of the 27th · Reserve Corps.

[2] These were about 4,000 yards from Menin.

men away South and West of Ledeghem. Meanwhile the Welch Fusiliers had followed " A " and " D," their steadiness in the difficult work of retiring when so closely engaged being as conspicuous as their dash in the advance. The Warwickshires then went back to some high ground near Kezelberg, covered by their "A " Company, whose shooting apparently effectually discouraged the Germans from crossing .the Menin road in pursuit. Two batteries of the XXIInd Brigade R.F.A. also lent useful support after moving back to a position on the left rear of their original line. The retirement was steadily but rather innocuously shelled, the shells mostly bursting too high, and the Germans quite failed to press the retreat ; ultimately the 22nd Brigade retired in good order past the left of the 21st, the Wiltshires doing good work in covering the movement. For a time the 22nd Brigade halted on the line Terhand–Strooiboomhoek, in readiness for the expected German advance, but as the cavalry had had to evacuate Moorslede owing to the withdrawal of the French, orders were issued to continue the retirement, and for the 20th and 21st Brigades to conform, the Division reoccupying the position entrenched on the night of October 16th/17th. The 20th Brigade, as before, was on the right, holding Zandvoorde and Kruiseik, but evacuating the unsatisfactory advanced position at " America " occupied on the 18th ; from the 10th Kilometre on the Ypres–Menin road the 21st Brigade continued the line Northwards, past the Eastern edge of Polygon Wood, facing Becelaere ; on their left the 22nd Brigade's line extended to the Broodseinde cross-roads, 800 yards East of Zonnebeke, whence it was thrown back across the railway to face N.E. Farther North the line was held by the 3rd Cavalry Division, who connected up with the French near Passchendaele. The 20th Brigade had the Grenadiers and Borders in line, the Scots Guards and Gordons being in reserve ; the 21st Brigade had the Yorkshires, Scots Fusiliers, and Wiltshires in line from right to left, with the Bedfords in reserve. In the 22nd

Brigade the South Staffords were on the right, the Welch Fusiliers in the centre, covering the Broodseinde cross-roads, the Queen's on the left, with their flank thrown back North of Zonnebeke, while the Warwickshires formed the

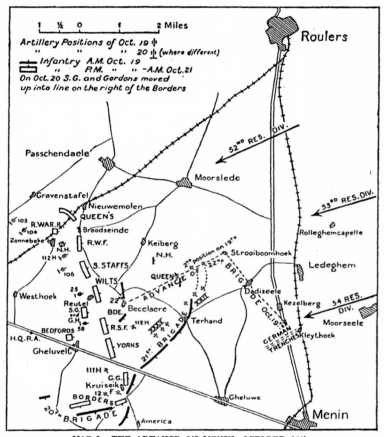

MAP 3.—THE ADVANCE ON MENIN, OCTOBER 19th.

brigade reserve.   The R.H.A.[1] covered the 20th Brigade's front ; the XXXVth Brigade R.F.A. was dug in behind

---

[1] The 12th Battery R.F.A. was detached from its brigade, and placed under the orders of the R.H.A. Brigade, to replace " C " Battery, transferred to the 3rd Cavalry Division.

Reutel, the XXIInd Brigade R.F.A. and the two Heavy
Batteries supporting the left from positions behind the
ridge running N.W. past Zonnebeke.[1] The total casualties
had been not far short of 300, more than half being in the
Welch Fusiliers, who had 2 officers killed, 5 wounded
and 1 missing, with over 150 casualties among rank and
file.[2] But the promptitude with which action had been
taken, the steadiness and discipline of the troops, and the
skill with which the retirement had been conducted had
enabled the Division to extricate itself from a most awkward predicament.

This check to the advance on Menin did not, however,
mean the breaking off of all offensive movement by the
British forces. Actually both Second and Third Corps
had reached the Eastern limits of their advance, and the
Second in particular was hard pressed to maintain its
position, but the whole First Corps was now at hand,
and Sir John French intended to use it in a vigorous thrust
Eastward from Ypres, which he hoped would turn the
German right and thereby complete the outflanking movement which the Allies had been aiming at ever since the
deadlock had set in on the Aisne. The Seventh Division
had, therefore, to be prepared to hang on until the First
Corps could deliver its blow. That the Germans were
about to attack in unsuspected strength was of course quite
unknown ; Sir John French indeed persisted in an optimistic view of the situation some time longer, hardly attach-
ing sufficient importance to the reports of his highly efficient
Intelligence Service, which showed that the Germans
were in unexpected force. But it must be admitted that
the persistent, if none too successful, efforts of the British
to advance contributed appreciably to the discomfiture

---

[1] The withdrawal of the two Heavy Batteries was a difficult task owing to
the mud.

[2] The Warwickshires had lost about 60, including three officers killed or
missing, and the Queen's about 20. The 20th Brigade had only a few casualties, and the 21st had also escaped very lightly. A good many of the farthest
forward of the wounded could not be got away.

of the Germans, who could not imagine that the British could be undertaking an offensive without having large reserves behind them.   No German commander would have dreamt of persisting in the attack in face of such odds as the British encountered East of Ypres ; and the Germans, paying Sir John French and his army the compliment of crediting them with what they themselves would have done in like circumstances, could not believe that only three British Divisions stood between themselves and Ypres or that the Seventh Division's eight-mile front was anything but an outpost line to cover the massing of many concealed Divisions for a counter-stroke.

On October 20th, however, neither G.H.Q. nor the Seventh Division had any conception of what the future had in store for the troops then East of Ypres, and the Division's orders were to push out strong reconnaissances to the Eastward to ascertain the enemy's strength, and at the same time divert his attention from the 3rd Cavalry Division,[1] on whom heavy pressure had developed on the previous day.   The reconnaissance took the form of an advance towards Gheluwe, carried out by the Scots Guards and Gordons, assisted by the Northumberland Hussars and Divisional Cyclists, and supported by " F " Battery R.H.A. The advance started about 10.50 a.m., the Scots Fusiliers and Wiltshires, accompanied by the 25th Battery R.F.A., simultaneously moving out through Becelaere along the Terhand spur to protect the left flank.   Little opposition was encountered, except for shell fire from Wervicq, and by midday the Scots Guards were within half a mile of the enemy's infantry, while the Wiltshires had cleared the Germans out of Becelaere and were close to Terhand, despite several casualties from shell fire.   However, by this time heavy attacks had developed against the 3rd Cavalry Division, and had extended to the 22nd Brigade's front.

---

[1] The 3rd Cavalry Division was now back on the line Nieuwemolen–Passchendaele–Westroosebeke, with the French beyond it still East of Houthulst Forest.

Indeed, the Welch Fusiliers and Queen's had come under artillery fire even before the reconnaissance started, though it was some time before infantry came forward in force against them. Obviously no purpose would be served by pushing the reconnaissance home, so orders were issued for a retirement, which was successfully accomplished, the enemy making no attempt to pursue the 20th Brigade,. though the Wiltshires were more closely pressed. Their leading company, " C," had got within 200 yards of the German trenches, and " D " Company was getting into action when the retirement was ordered. " C " found it hard to extricate itself, but " D " covered its retirement successfully, despite heavy shelling, and the battalion withdrew in good order to its old trenches North of Reutel, having had 60 casualties. The Scots Fusiliers on their right had scarcely been engaged and got back without incident.

It was just as well that the reconnaissance had not been pressed home, for about midday the situation took an unexpected turn for the worse owing to the sudden retreat of the French cavalry. Byng's 3rd Cavalry Division, till then quite comfortable, now found its left flank altogether " in the air," and had to retire to the line Zonnebeke–St. Julien–Poelcappelle, leaving Passchendaele and Westroose-beke to the Germans, who before long followed them up and began attacking the new position. The cavalry's retreat naturally affected the 22nd Brigade. The enemy had begun to bombard its position fairly early, but had not developed any really serious infantry attack. After the capture of Passchendaele, however, he began to press forward in greater force, and by 2 p.m. the brigade was heavily engaged. Earlier in the day the Queen's had moved forward, pivoting on their right and bringing their left up to the level crossing near Nieuwemolen, 1½ miles North of Zonnebeke Station, in order to keep touch with the cavalry. Though much exposed by the retreat of the troops on their flank and heavily shelled, the Queen's retained

their position until after dark, when they received orders
to fall back to their old trenches parallel to and North of
the Zonnebeke–Langemarck road, " C " Company occupying some trenches which the Warwickshires had dug more
to the right, between the railway and the Passchendaele
road. The Welch Fusiliers also had maintained their
position unflinchingly, despite heavy shelling. Dead
ground in front allowed the enemy's infantry in
places to get up within 150 yards, but a well-placed
machine-gun on the battalion's left enfiladed the dead
ground, and though the Germans established themselves
in a wood close up to the line, their efforts to debouch from
it only resulted in heavy casualties. They managed,
however, to occupy some of the cottages scattered about
in front and sniped with some success from their roofs
and upper windows. The South Staffords likewise, though
suffering from the shelling, held on firmly and did not
allow the enemy's infantry to get within 500 yards of their
line. Effective assistance was given by the 104th Battery,
in action half a mile West of Zonnebeke, which caught German infantry advancing in mass. Thus the 22nd Brigade
ended the day with every reason to be satisfied ; only one
company of its reserve battalion, the Warwickshires, had
had to be used, and though the Welch Fusiliers had had
rather heavy casualties the other battalions had escaped
lightly, the South Staffords reaping the reward of their
energy in digging themselves in.

The 21st Brigade, to whose front the afternoon attack
had also extended, had been equally successful. About
3.45 p.m. a strong advance had begun to develop from
Becelaere, coming mainly against the Scots Fusiliers and
Wiltshires, though the Yorkshires' machine-guns took full
advantage of some admirable targets. The Wiltshires
were quite hard pressed, but the enemy were beaten off
every time with heavy losses, the XXXVth Brigade R.F.A.
co-operating effectively and catching the Germans as they
came over the ridge ; the Scots Fusiliers, though less

severely pressed, caught a company working forward along
the edge of a wood and drove it into the trees in disorder,
besides getting effective fire at German infantry crossing
their front from right to left through some turnip-fields
about 1,200 yards away. Farther to the right the Yorkshires were hardly attacked, and against the 20th Brigade
the Germans made little serious effort, though about 3 p.m.
both the Grenadiers, who were East of Kruiseik, and the
Borders on their right reported that the enemy were
advancing and were within 800 yards. That, however,
was their limit, thanks to the rifle fire which greeted them
and to the splendidly accurate shooting of " F " Battery
R.H.A. and the 12th Battery R.F.A. These batteries,
firing at 1,400 yards' range, with fuses set to clear the crest
and just catch the German infantry, did magnificent work,
as was warmly acknowledged by the C.O. of the Grenadiers,
and in this quarter any inclination of the enemy to advance
was completely repressed.[1] However, the German attacks
continued till nightfall, and even after dark there was
desultory firing, the Yorkshires dealing most effectually
with attempts to tamper with the wire and other obstacles
they had put up. There were various alarms during the
night, and some promiscuous and rather unnecessary firing ;
indeed the Division had an exciting rather than a restful
time, the precursor of many exhausting nights.

But while the Seventh Division had held its ground
satisfactorily, October 20th had nevertheless marked a
definite turn in the fight. It had seen the beginning of
great German counter-attacks : farther South both Second
and Third Corps had been very hard pressed, and both had
lost ground, while between the Third Corps' left and the
Fourth's right Allenby's cavalry had also had to yield
ground to superior numbers. Thus the Division's line had
become more than ever the point of a salient, both faces
of which were exposed both to frontal and to enfilade fire.

[1] The remaining battalions of the 20th Brigade came up on the right of the
Borders, continuing the line Westward past Zandvoorde.

On the other hand, the Second Division had come up behind
Byng's cavalry, and before evening the 2nd Coldstream of
the 4th (Guards) Brigade arrived near Zonnebeke behind
the left of the 22nd Brigade. The First Division too had
completed its detraining, and was moving forward past
Poperinghe towards Elverdinghe ; there was, therefore,
some hope that the next day might see the tables turned
and the advancing Germans thrust back, for as yet the
great strength which their attack was about to develop had
not been revealed.

G.H.Q.'s orders for October 21st reflected strongly this
expectation. The First Corps was to press forward N.E.
towards Roulers, Byng's cavalry on its right connecting
it with the Seventh Division, which was to hold its line
but be in readiness to throw forward its left if the First
Corps' advance fulfilled expectations. However, soon after
daybreak it became clear that, whatever might happen
on its left, the Seventh Division was in for a hard day.
The German guns were at it early, beginning soon after
daybreak to shell the whole line with great severity and
considerable effect. As they " shot themselves in," as
one account puts it, their fire became more accurate,
making movement in the open dangerous, inflicting much
damage on the trenches, and causing many casualties among
the defenders. The Welch Fusiliers were soon in sore
straits ; their position was enfiladed from the left, the sandy
soil made good trenches hard to construct,[1] while about
the worst result of the bombardment was that the sand
tended to get into rifles and machine-guns and put them
out of action. By 9 a.m. both the battalion's machine-
guns had been disabled and the heavy shelling made it
extremely difficult to keep the firing-line supplied with
ammunition. The Warwickshires sent up their machine-
gun section to replace the disabled guns and did some

---

[1] There was also a shortage of picks and shovels ; many had been lost
through the repeated moves and changes, and it had been found difficult to
replace them from local supplies.

effective work until they in turn were put out of action. There was no relaxation in the German pressure, and they concentrated their bombardment on "A" Company's trenches astride the road to Moorslede only too successfully. Farther to the left (North of the cross-roads) they tried to work round the flank. To counter this move Lieutenant Wodehouse led a charge from a trench on the left rear, only to be driven back, though the Germans who stood up to shoot at his men exposed themselves to destructive covering fire from another party. "A" Company also made a gallant but not very successful counter-attack against the wood on their front in which the Germans were collecting, few of those who reached the wood ever getting back.[1]

Meanwhile, about 10 a.m., the Queen's centre company, "B," in obedience to a mistaken or possibly bogus order, began to withdraw to a ridge in rear, parallel to the Zonnebeke–Langemarck road. The Germans were not slow to take advantage of the gap thus created, but though they promptly occupied the vacated trenches, "A" Company on the left maintained its position for nearly three hours, and then only fell back because it was enfiladed. Even then "C" Company, in the trenches just West of the Broodseinde–Passchendaele road, held on unflinchingly and never went back all day. Some relief was given to the Welch Fusiliers when about noon the Warwickshires sent up several platoons to reinforce them. As the reinforcements approached the Fusiliers opened rapid fire, and covered by this the Warwickshires crossed the open ground behind the trenches almost without casualties. Their arrival helped the Fusiliers to maintain their resistance despite increasing odds and the great difficulty of keeping their rifles free from sand. The South Staffords, however,

---

[1] The attackers at this point seem to have belonged to the 52nd Reserve Division, which had the 53rd on its left with the 54th farther South, opposite Gheluvelt and Kruiseik, the 3rd Cavalry Division attacking the Southern face of the salient held by the Division.

on the right of the Welch Fusiliers fared better than their neighbours. They were constantly attacked and the attacks were supported by heavy artillery fire, but nevertheless they held on, and thanks to the good cover afforded by their deep and narrow trenches—the battalion contained many miners and prided itself on its digging—their casualties were low, while they had the satisfaction of inflicting heavy losses on their opponents, especially with the machine-guns, well handled by Sergeant Bytheway after the machine-gun officer, Lieutenant Holmes, had been killed. Luckily the German artillery fire, though very heavy, mostly just went over the trenches; indeed more trouble was caused by snipers in a farm-house on the right, and by unlocated machine-guns. On the left the Germans got within about 300 yards, but found it impossible to advance farther in face of the battalion's musketry, and a field battery which came forward boldly into the open to shell the Welch Fusiliers at short range gave the Staffords' left company a target of which it promptly availed itself.

Meanwhile the 21st Brigade was being scarcely less vigorously attacked. On its left, however, the Wiltshires held their own against heavy odds with conspicuous success. Their trenches were on a plateau which rose slightly to a crest line which afforded a good aiming point, and the field of fire, though obstructed by trees and hedges, was quite good except on the left. The enemy came on with great resolution and in close formation, line upon line, not once but several times, and the battalion took full advantage of its chances. Even " A " Company, with the worst field of fire, brought the Germans to a standstill some distance away, being admirably controlled by Captain Timmis and shooting straight and steadily though rifles jammed and extractors broke. Splendid work was done by ammunition-carriers from the reserve trenches, who again and again crossed the fire-swept zone behind the fire-trenches in response to the repeated demands for cartridges. Evening found the Wiltshires exhausted but triumphant ; the ground in front of them was heaped with German dead and wounded, a testimony at once to the battalion's musketry and to its opponents' determination and devotion.   On the right the Scots Fusiliers had been fully as hard pressed.   Here the left company, " C," had only about a 200-yards' field of fire, but others were more fortunate.   The line was heavily bombarded from about 6.30 a.m., and during the hours of darkness there had been several attacks.   As the morning wore on these continued, the Germans seeking persistently to find a gap in the line. With a long and thinly held front, and in country as yet little damaged by war, so that buildings, hedges, and woods provided excellent cover, it was impossible to keep every line of approach under effective fire, and about noon Germans managed to penetrate between the Yorkshires and the Fusiliers' right company, "D," whose trenches were in front of Poezelhoek hamlet.   They pushed a machine-gun up into the gap, and its enfilade fire forced " D " back to the Château grounds.   The Germans then tried to press on against " B " Company in the centre, but some of " A " reinforced " B " and by their aid this attack was stopped.   " C," North of the Reutelbeck, was also attacked in great force, but it also held on and punished the enemy severely, an attempt to outflank its line being checked by effective cross fire from a section near the bridge over the Reutelbeck.   Thus despite the loss of " D's " trenches the Scots Fusiliers had no reason to be dissatisfied : while against the Yorkshires the Germans were even less successful, for that battalion, though severely pressed, beat off all their efforts to turn its left.   However, the pressure on the 21st Brigade was enough to cause the Division to order the 20th Brigade to send half a battalion to their help.   General Ruggles-Brise had already had to put half the Scots Guards into line on his right to secure the connexion with the cavalry at Zandvoorde and had sent the rest of that battalion off as Divisional Reserve ; but though all his trenches had reported the Germans as advancing the pressure was nowhere really severe, and he promptly sent two companies of the Grenadiers off towards Reutel. They reached General Watts about midday, only to find the Yorkshires' line intact and the situation well in hand.

It was fortunate that it was so, for the 21st Brigade was without reserves, the Bedfords having been hurried off to Zonnebeke to help the 22nd Brigade. When the Bedfords reached Zonnebeke, however, the situation had been relieved by the arrival on the left of the Irish Guards, the flank battalion of the Second Division, whose advance was already making itself felt. This enabled General Lawford to send the Bedfords back to Gheluvelt and to relieve the Queen's, who with the help of a company of the Warwickshires and two squadrons of Household Cavalry had successfully maintained the position to which they had fallen back. But there was work, not rest, in store for the Queen's. The pressure on the Welch Fusiliers had been getting steadily worse, some of their trenches had been rendered quite untenable, especially on the left, and their surviving occupants were rallying on a ridge in rear. Accordingly the Queen's, after hastily reorganizing, started off towards the Broodseinde cross-roads. It was dark by this time and very hard to discover the exact situation, but the battalion seems to have made its way to Moulin Farm, and thereby recovered touch with its " C " Company, who had held on between the railway and the Broodseinde–Passchendaele road, although dangerously exposed and isolated. Not only had the rest of its battalion fallen back on its left, but the troops on its right also— the left company of the Welch Fusiliers—seem to have been overpowered by the Germans about an hour before dark, possibly a little earlier. But if the lack of continuity in the line opened the door to the outflanking and destruction of isolated units, it sometimes entailed the compensation that units held on in ignorance of and unaffected by disaster elsewhere.

The exact sequence of events on the front of the Welch Fusiliers is hard to establish with any certainty : it seems pretty clear that rather before 4 o'clock the defenders of their left centre trenches [1] became aware that their flank was in the air, that the Germans were trying to work round it and had secured the Broodseinde cross-roads. They held on, however, keeping the enemy in their immediate front at bay, and getting occasional effective bursts of rapid fire at Germans who were trying to work across their front to the left. Eventually, somewhere about 7 o'clock if any reliance can be placed upon the times in the different accounts, Germans got right behind this part of the line and its surviving defenders were forced to surrender. They had fired away all their ammunition and their position was hopeless. Even then the rest of the battalion maintained its ground till about midnight, and when finally ordered to withdraw was the last battalion to go, covering the others so successfully that the Germans made no effort to follow up the retirement. The battalion had made a memorable and magnificent defence : outnumbered, with a long line to hold which it had had no time to prepare properly for defence against shell fire, let alone for a bombardment of such weight and intensity, greatly handicapped by the clogging sand, which rendered rifles useless, they had maintained a stubborn defence with splendid steadiness. Their losses had been very heavy, 5 officers were killed, 3 wounded, 6 missing, and there were over 300 casualties among the men.

Meanwhile General Lawford, realizing that the Broodseinde position had become quite untenable, had arranged with the Divisional Commander for a withdrawal to a new line, thrown back so as to run N.W. and S.E. from the level crossing West of Zonnebeke in the depression made by one of the tributaries of the Hannebeck. To this line the brigade withdrew in good order shortly after midnight,

---

[1] These included the trenches reached by the reinforcing platoons of the Warwickshires.

General Lawford and Major James themselves guiding the battalions into position. The Warwickshires were on the left next the level crossing, then the Queen's, with the South Staffords on the right, reaching to some cottages known in later years as Helles. The South Staffords had till then maintained their position intact, but to have hung on to it any longer would have been to court disaster ; as it was the battalion transport which attempted to get back by way of the Broodseinde cross-roads was captured, though the battalion retired most successfully across country, its move being covered by a small party which was left to fire rapid till the battalion was well away. The Welch Fusiliers, the last battalion to withdraw, were placed in reserve. In the new position the field of fire was very limited, but there was the compensating advantage that the dip in the ground gave cover against artillery fire.

The 22nd Brigade's gallant defence had cost it dear. The Welch Fusiliers had left only their C.O., Lieut.-Colonel Cadogan, and the Adjutant, Lieut. Dooner, with four other officers and about 300 men ; the four platoons of the Warwickshires who had reinforced the Fusiliers had been practically wiped out, and the Queen's also had lost nearly 200, though the South Staffords had fared much better, losing only 2 officers and under 50 men. Neither of the other brigades had suffered anything like as heavily ; the Wiltshires and Scots Fusiliers had had appreciable casualties, but the Bedfords and Yorkshires got off almost scot-free, while the 20th Brigade's total was barely 150. Attacks had developed against both Grenadiers and Borders in the course of the afternoon, but both battalions had checked their opponents easily enough. The Scots Guards also had been heavily shelled, and one company had lost its commander and several men. Apart from these losses and the throwing back of the 22nd Brigade's line behind Zonnebeke, the Seventh Division had grounds for satisfaction over the day's work. Though attacked by

at least two of the new Reserve Divisions,[1] and by a Cavalry
Division, it had maintained the greater part of its line and
had inflicted on its opponents losses which without exaggeration may be called tremendous. It had been difficult for
the British gunners to do very much against the numerous
and well-concealed German guns, though they had searched
and swept for them, firing by the map. But the German
infantry had not been concealed, and of them the British
artillery had taken an ample toll; the XXIInd Brigade
R.F.A. in particular got into advancing infantry in the
afternoon with remarkable effect. On the right, where,
quite apart from the disadvantage of the salient, the shape
of the ground made observation difficult, a section of
" F " Battery in close support of the Gordons proved most
useful, though in places the enemy's snipers got too close
to our front line for the guns to get at them, and they had
to fire bursts at short range to catch the enemy's supports.
Splendid work was done in this quarter by the R.E., the
55th Field Company burning down some houses in which
snipers had found shelter quite close to our trenches.

Elsewhere the fighting of October 21st had resulted in
the holding up of the British effort to advance past the
left of the Seventh Division. Both First and Second
Divisions had encountered greatly superior numbers of
Germans, and though they had inflicted tremendous
casualties on their opponents, they themselves had been
unable to get on. But Sir John French did not readily
relinquish his hopes of an advance, as his orders for October
22nd showed. Once again the Seventh Division was to
maintain its eight-mile front while the First Corps sought
to gain ground. This object, however, the First Corps
could not achieve ; indeed a day of fluctuating fighting
saw it ousted from one or two untenable salients, though
at a disproportionately heavy cost to the Germans.

For the Seventh Division October 22nd was less eventful

---

[1] The 53rd and 54th, while the 52nd was engaged with the 22nd Brigade as
well as with the Second Division.

than its predecessor. The German bombardment started again about 7 a.m. and was maintained intermittently all day, the British guns [1] replying, though with due regard to the necessity—already becoming urgent—of husbanding the none too plentiful ammunition. During the night two attempts were made to assault the Wiltshires' position, but these were repulsed, and the Scots Fusiliers got some good targets in Germans whom the light of a burning house exposed. Elsewhere the night was quiet, and in the earlier part of the day the German infantry were little in evidence, except for the inevitable snipers ; their machine-guns were more troublesome, some near "America" proving a special nuisance to the Borders at the apex of the Kruiseik salient, and the 106th Battery was moved over from the left to Zandvoorde to give additional artillery support. One particular machine-gun was effectively dealt with by "F" Battery. It was in a house which gave it good protection from rifles and machine-guns, so the gun detachments drew a 13-pounder forward by means of drag ropes over several hundred yards of rough country and had it in position quite close to the house ready to open fire with the first streak of dawn. Directly the target became visible, rapid fire was opened and the house was quickly breached and the machine-gun silenced, a successful exploit being crowned by the withdrawal of the gun before the Germans could locate it. In contrast to its experiences of the previous day the 22nd Brigade was but little troubled, the enemy making no attempt to exploit his occupation of Zonnebeke. On its right there was found to be a gap of 600 yards separating the South Staffords from the 21st Brigade, although the Wiltshires, on hearing from Brigade H.Q. of the 22nd Brigade's retirement, moved half their

[1] The artillery dispositions had been altered in consequence of the pushing back of the left. The XXIInd Brigade R.F.A. had fallen back to new positions about midway between Zonnebeke and Westhoek, the two Heavy Batteries were South of Westhoek with one gun detached to support the right flank by firing on Gheluwe, the XXXVth Brigade R.F.A. had the 25th Battery North and the 58th South of the Menin road just East of Veldhoek.

reserve company across to the left rear of " B " Company, where they dug in facing about North. The Northumberland Hussars and the Divisional Cyclists were promptly pushed up to help fill the gap, and held on under considerable shelling till evening, when a company of the Scots Guards replaced them. This battalion had been relieved at Zandvoorde by the cavalry, so that for the moment General Capper actually had a battalion in Divisional Reserve. Being in reserve, however, did not mean much rest, for the battalion was first hurried across to the N.E. corner of Polygon Wood, and after one company had been posted on the left rear of the Wiltshires two others, under Major Fraser, were recalled to Kruiseik by an alarm that the 20th Brigade was being severely pressed. Actually it was only against the 21st Brigade that a serious attack developed.[1]

The Germans had bombarded its trenches mercilessly all the morning, and early in the afternoon heavy columns of infantry advanced from Becelaere. The guns were promptly turned on, and with good effect, but the Wiltshires had a strenuous experience. The enemy's fire had now become more accurate and the trenches were terribly knocked about, men being buried and rifles put out of action. The destruction of the reserve trenches increased the difficulty of keeping the firing-line supplied with ammunition ; there had been no time to dig communication trenches and parties bringing ammunition up by hand lost heavily in crossing the open. However, when the Germans attempted to advance from the woods where they had massed they were met by such a storm of fire from guns and rifles that their dead were literally piled up in heaps. Nothing could have exceeded the determination and gallantry with which these new levies [2] came on, but for all their resolution they were unable to establish them-

[1] On this day, during an attack on part of the 20th Brigade's line, a sergeant and five sappers of the 55th Field Company went calmly on cutting down trees and making an entanglement when an attack was in progress against the next trench but one.

[2] They were the 54th Reserve Division, a Würtemberg formation.

selves within 400 yards of the Wiltshires. Opposite the Scots Fusiliers the Germans were equally unsuccessful, and the Yorkshires' machine-guns, firing obliquely across their front, contributed effectively to the German repulse. Towards evening the Fusiliers attempted to recover the trenches evacuated on the previous day, and " A " Company and part of " D " counter-attacked down the Poezelhoek road, clearing the houses of snipers. One big house in the centre of the village was stubbornly defended and Captain Fairlie of " D " Company was killed heading an attack on it, but the house was quickly surrounded, whereupon its occupants surrendered. Beyond the Poezelhoek-Reutel road, however, the counter-attack failed to penetrate, for as it reached the Shrine Germans were met advancing in force in the open. There was a sharp fight, bayonet-work, charges, and counter-charges, but a whole battalion came up to reinforce the Germans, and in the end the Scots Fusiliers withdrew to their starting-point, bringing with them some 30 prisoners.

Even a day of relative " quiet " like October 22nd was a severe strain on the endurance of the Division. Practically every officer and man was in the firing-line or in close support, and few got any chance of sleep or rest. One officer writes of this time : " It is very difficult to differentiate between day and night. With only occasional lulls the terrific din of firing went on without ceasing. Shells, guns, and rifles all going at once made one's recollections of the Boer fire seem like crackers at a picnic. And all the time the Boche coming on, rows on rows of cannon fodder ; four or five to one, perhaps more, but as we were in good trenches we had only slight losses at first." The Germans, too, had taken to shelling the roads leading from Ypres to the fighting-line, thereby making the task of bringing up the ammunition, water, and rations both dangerous and difficult. Meals, therefore, were uncertain and scrappy ; those who had managed to stuff some biscuits or hard chocolate into their pockets might count themselves lucky,

and an occasional hot meal was an incident of note. To
wash or shave was out of the question for the majority of
officers and men, and the strain on all ranks was enormous.
Casualties were mounting up steadily, and the German
bombardment was tending to increase in volume and
vehemence rather than to diminish. It did not actually
open on October 23rd until after 9 a.m., for till that hour
a thick mist prevented both sides from using their artillery,
but it then developed with special intensity against the
Kruiseik salient and the point of junction between the
21st and 22nd Brigades. The attack hardly extended to
the 22nd's front, which was so little troubled that detachments of the Queen's, the Warwickshires, and the Welch
Fusiliers tried to re-enter Zonnebeke, which was believed
to be unoccupied, in order to rescue any wounded still in
the village, bury the dead, and collect equipment. However, the village proved to be held in force : a heavy
fire was opened, whereupon the detachments fell back
at once, without losing many, the enemy making no effort
to pursue.

Far otherwise was it with the 21st Brigade. About daybreak " C " Company of the Bedfords, the Brigade reserve,[1]
went up to try to recover the lost trench of the Scots Fusiliers, " D " Company of that battalion assisting them. The
attack was gallantly pressed : the Fusiliers got within 100
yards of the trench, but were then enfiladed and forced
back ; the Bedfords after a gallant attempt to charge a
German gun had also to withdraw. The Germans then
started attacking in their turn, pressing very hard
against the Yorkshires and bombarding the Wiltshires
with exceptional vehemence. Both battalions suffered
severely but held on gallantly. The increased severity
and accuracy of the German fire was very noticeable. The
trenches were so badly blown in that the men often had to
lie out in the open, while the houses in rear of the line
were nearly all destroyed, and their wells being put out of

---

[1] One company, " A," had already reinforced the Yorkshires.

action, difficulties over getting water were added to the defenders' other troubles. One advance against the Wiltshires established itself in some buildings just short of the battalion's line, but was then shelled by its own guns, " A " Company having the satisfaction of catching the enemy thus dislodged and bowling over many of them. Another company of the Bedfords, " B," which went up later in the day to help the Yorkshires, lost heavily, but nevertheless made its way to that battalion's left trenches. This reinforcement was the more welcome because the Germans had just previously penetrated into a wood in the gap between the Yorkshires and the Scots Fusiliers and had begun working to the right. The Yorkshires' reserve company, however, was rushed across from the right, and cleared the wood in splendid style, losing three officers and many men, but taking some prisoners. " The tenacity of this battalion," says the diary of the 21st Brigade, " was most remarkable ; though subjected to heavy artillery fire and constant infantry attacks, it held on stoutly and never wavered." The Scots Fusiliers were fiercely attacked in the afternoon, and " C " Company, whose trenches were on a forward slope, had two officers hit and many other casualties from shell fire, but all infantry attacks were quickly and effectively stopped. The Wiltshires, too, maintained their ground successfully, useful help being given to their left by half a company of the South Staffords which Capt. Dunlop brought up, retaking with the bayonet a trench which the enemy had just occupied. Some platoons were forced to shift their position as their trenches had been completely destroyed, and this apparently caused various alarming rumours about lost trenches to reach Brigade Headquarters. General Watts, however, on visiting the battalion that evening found it exhausted but confident in its capacity to hold on. After dark two platoons of " F " Company of the Scots Guards reinforced the battalion, one under Lieut. Lord Garlies going into the line just North of Reutel, the other, under Lieut. Orr, being

farther to the left.[1]   On the other flank of the Brigade also
the situation was improved by bringing up the rest of the
Bedfords, who linked up the Yorkshires with the Scots
Fusiliers, their line being astride the light railway from
Gheluvelt to Becelaere.

The 20th. Brigade also maintained its position in the
advantageous Kruiseik salient, the Grenadiers on the left
facing East, the Borders and the Gordons[2] South.   They
owed a good deal to " F " Battery and the 12th Battery,
both of which pushed a section forward to give close
support, and at the cost of several casualties[3] stopped
a threatening attack.   " F " Battery, which was in action
just West of Kruiseik about 600 yards behind the Grenadiers' front line, was greatly assisted by the intrepidity of
the Signal Officer of the Grenadiers, Lieut. Hope, who was
indefatigable in his efforts to locate the enemy's machine-
guns, usually by drawing their fire on himself, and in
indicating accurately to the gunners the precise position
of their targets.   By keeping in close personal touch with
the battery commander he enabled him to turn his information to good account.   Half No. 4 Company of the
Grenadiers posted in a gap between the 20th and 21st Brigades was attacked in great force,[4] but held on though both
platoon commanders were killed and the trenches practically
obliterated.   That evening the Right Flank company of
the Scots Guards went up to Kruiseik and took over the
Borders' left trench and the two right trenches of the
Grenadiers[5] ; it thus became responsible for the actual
apex of the salient.

[1] The Left Flank company seems to have been echeloned on the left rear
of the Wiltshires, but accurate details as to this company are not available.

[2] Drummer W. Kenny of this battalion was awarded the V.C. for rescuing
wounded men under heavy fire and for gallantry in carrying messages in
dangerous circumstances.

[3] The 12th Battery's section had 1 officer and 9 men hit and lost 10 horses.

[4] These attacks seem to have been carried out by the 11th Landwehr Brigade
with Petersen's Jagers on its left nearer Zandvoorde.

[5] Both these units had had to shorten their lines owing to heavy casualties.

Thus the evening of October 23rd found the Division's position practically unchanged : it was still holding its eight miles of front, and except for the withdrawal behind Zonnebeke and the loss of advanced trenches, as at Poezelhoek, had not given ground although attacked by three times its numbers and outweighted heavily in artillery. It was welcome news therefore that during the night of October 23rd/24th French troops would relieve the Second Division between Zonnebeke and Langemarck, which would thus soon be free to take off some of the pressure on General Capper's hard-tried line. Relief by this time was badly needed ; officers and men were worn out for want of sleep and by the continual strain of the shelling and fighting. Men were so tired that they sometimes fell asleep in the act of firing, and the discomforts of existence were on a par with the dangers and hardships. Some units had been specially unlucky ; the South Staffords, for example, had lost all their transport on the night of October 21st, cookers, water carts, mess cart, G.S. wagons, and everything, officers and men being left with just what they stood up in.

The withdrawal of the Second Division into reserve was effected just in the nick of time, for October 24th saw the German attack renewed in special force. The night had been fairly quiet except that about 5 a.m. the Scots Fusiliers discovered that some Germans had worked round " C " Company's flank during the night and were in a position to enfilade the trench held by the M.G. section. A prompt counter-attack, however, removed all danger by disposing of this adventurous party, 40 of whom were taken. But with daylight the bombardment started again with the greatest fury, and torrents of shells came pouring down on the 20th and 21st Brigades. Communication between Brigade Headquarters and the firing-line was soon cut, and though about 8 a.m. a report reached Divisional Headquarters from General Watts that the Scots Fusiliers and Wiltshires were very hard pressed,

definite information became hard to obtain. A little later
the Scots Fusiliers reported that the enemy had penetrated
into Polygon Wood and were threatening to outflank their
left, though a line had been formed facing North of every
man not actually engaged in the front trenches, and the
Bedfords had sent a platoon to reinforce it. The 22nd
Brigade also discovered that things had gone wrong
beyond their right, for the enemy were in force in Polygon
Wood in the right rear of the South Staffords. Luckily
the Queen's had just extended to their left, relieving
the Warwickshires, and that battalion,[1] though much
reduced by casualties, was available. General Lawford
at once dispatched it to the danger spot together with
" B " Company of the South Staffords under Captain
Dunlop. Pushing into the wood from the North, the
Warwickshires were soon hotly engaged. About the same
time General Capper sent the Northumberland Hussars
forward from Hooge, where they had been forming his
only reserve, to counter-attack from the S.W. and cover
the Scots Fusiliers' left. The Yeomanry had been under
fire already, but this was their first serious action, indeed
the first time that any Territorial unit had been engaged in
more than skirmishing. The Hussars rose to the occasion
in style and not only checked the Germans but drove them
back some way, though neither they nor the Warwickshires
could clear the wood completely. The Warwickshires had
very heavy fighting, and were held up at a farm where a
large body of Germans offered a most desperate resistance,
using machine-guns with great effect. Colonel Loring
was killed in directing his battalion's attack on this farm,
and casualties were heavy.[2] But the Warwickshires were
not to be denied ; they stormed the farm taking several
prisoners with it, and then pressed on. Meanwhile the
Northumberland Hussars, pushing Eastward, had gained
touch with the Scots Fusiliers. This battalion was in sore

---

[1] It had lost 9 officers and over 250 men.
[2] The Royal Warwickshires had over 100 casualties.

straits. Its left company just South of Reutel had been heavily attacked again after its success in the small hours, and eventually was outflanked from the left. It put up a desperate fight, being reinforced by the remnants of " D " Company, but in the end numbers told, only Captain Whigham and a mere handful managing to cut their way back to the support trenches nearer Poezelhoek Château. These also were in danger of being outflanked by Germans who were working forward into Polygon Wood, but the hastily formed defensive flank on the Northern edge of the Château grounds had already checked the enemy. Here very fine work had been done by a platoon under Lieut. H. W. V. Stewart, who took post along a ride and caught the Germans in enfilade, the officer alone shooting down about sixty Germans and effectually putting out of action two machine-guns which were pushed forward within a short distance of the British line. The Germans sent up man after man to try to work the guns, but Lieut. Stewart continued to shoot steadily, and picked off one after another as they came forward. But if the main position of the Scots Fusiliers was intact—for its right company in front of Poezelhoek was keeping the enemy successfully at bay, while the Yorkshires farther South were holding on as tenaciously as ever, and North of Polygon Wood the South Staffords were quite happy—some misfortune had clearly befallen the Wiltshires. A few stragglers, mostly belonging to the right company, had arrived at the gun-positions in rear of Polygon Wood and reported that they believed the battalion had been rolled up from the left, and that they alone had managed to escape.

Though the Warwickshires and the Northumberland Hussars had not managed to complete the clearing of the wood, their prompt intervention had averted a greater disaster and the widening of the breach, and had given time for the 2nd Worcestershire and 1st H.L.I., the leading battalions of the 5th Brigade, to arrive from reserve

just East of Ypres about 11 a.m., having been ordered
forward by Sir Charles Monro directly he received
General Capper's appeal for help. They were at once put
into the wood, and counter-attacking with vigour swept
through it almost to the Eastern edge, driving the Germans
before them with the bayonet and inflicting many casualties
on them. The actual trenches of the Wiltshires on the
Reutel ridge were not recovered, the advance stopping
some hundreds of yards short of that. This counter-attack
resulted in an extraordinary admixture of units, Worcestershires and H.L.I. being sandwiched in by companies
between units of the Seventh Division ; but a more or less
continuous front was once more established and Polygon
Wood was clear of Germans.[1] However, the day's fighting
was anything but over. Severe fighting continued nearly
all the afternoon, the enemy attacking repeatedly and
pressing vigorously. The Scots Fusiliers were greatly
troubled by a wood in front of their line which they had
not had time either to clear or to entangle; it covered
the enemy's advance, and twice enabled them to reach
" B " Company's advanced trench. Each time they
were dislodged by a bayonet charge headed by Lieut.
Mackenzie, and though in the end Colonel Baird-Smith
decided to evacuate this trench, the battalion maintained its main position successfully and repulsed an
effort early in the evening to debouch from the wood.
Nor were the 21st Brigade alone in being hard pressed,
the attack extended to the 20th's front also. The
Scots Guards at the point of the salient had a rough
time : casualties were numerous, but the accurate fire

---

[1] The precise relation between these different counter-attacks seems to
defy all efforts at elucidation. Presumably the Warwickshires coming from
Zonnebeke cleared the N.E. portion of the wood, the Yeomanry coming from
Hooge cleared the Southern borders, and the two battalions of the 5th Brigade,
coming up rather later, swept through the wood from S.W. to N.E., going
right across the race-course. The company of the South Staffords seems to
have joined in with this attack, in the course of which it captured a house
in a clearing held by 60 Germans but lost its commander, Captain Dunlop.

of the company in the trenches prevented the Germans from getting within 150 yards of the British position. Both Borders and Gordons were attacked, but dealt quite successfully with their assailants.[1] The attack came also with special force on the cross-roads East of Gheluvelt where the 20th and 21st Brigades joined. Here sharp fighting had taken place earlier in the day, No. 4 Company of the Grenadiers under Major Colby having delivered a most dashing counter-attack on some Germans who had established themselves during the night quite close to the British line. The attack was handicapped by having to cross some tobacco-drying grounds, which presented what one account calls " ready-made wire entanglements on which the men's packs and accoutrements caught "; but despite these obstacles, enfilade machine-gun fire, and heavy casualties, No. 4 charged home and dislodged a greatly superior body of Germans. At the critical moment some salvos from " F " Battery had caught and checked the Germans, causing them to bunch and materially assisting the counter-attack to take them in flank. Their success cost the Grenadiers dear : Major Colby and one of his subalterns were killed, Captain Leathem was wounded, and over 100 men were hit, leaving the company with only one officer and under 80 men ; but the dislodging of the Germans had made an awkward bit of line secure.[2]

At intervals through the afternoon the Germans made attack after attack. Further reinforcements from the

---

[1] A sergeant of the Gordon Highlanders who was mortally wounded is recorded to have been bitterly disappointed at not having been able to kill 40 Germans before the 1st of January, which feat the C.O. had requested every man in the battalion to accomplish.

[2] It is typical of the difficulty of putting together an accurate story of these days of unending and complicated fighting that this incident is given as having occurred on different days and at different times in three separate diaries. What fixes it as the 24th are the messages reporting casualties given as appendixes to the Divisional diary. But the discrepancies in the fragmentary and disjointed stories which do duty for materials for history are certainly hard to reconcile.

5th Brigade had to be called for, and a company of the
Connaught Rangers came up between the Grenadiers
and Yorkshires, the Oxfordshire L.I. taking up a
position in support of the last-named ; while later on a
company of the Queen's[1] went up to support the
Grenadiers. On the way up this company came across
a party of Germans who had penetrated through a
gap in the line and established themselves in the woods.
At the cost of several casualties the Queen's disposed
of this party. Two companies of the Scots Guards and
one of the Gordons were sent forward on the strength
of an unfounded report that the Germans had broken
through the Borders and were so unlucky as to lose
nearly 50 men from shell fire.

Nightfall, however, found the 20th Brigade's position
intact, despite a trying and anxious day, but Northwards
the Division's line was much altered, the 22nd Brigade
having been relieved and the 21st Brigade's front in-
dented by the loss of the Wiltshires' trenches, while the
admixture of units from the Gheluvelt cross-roads Northwards was really remarkable, 5th, 21st, and 22nd Brigades
being almost inextricably intermingled. It had been a
day of heavy losses for the Division ; the Wiltshires had
practically ceased to exist, " F " Company of the Scots
Guards had been virtually wiped out, and the infantry
alone had little short of 1,500 casualties. Exact details
of what had happened to the Wiltshires were not forthcoming at the time, none of the officers were left, and when
all the stragglers had been collected and had joined the
details with the battalion transport the battalion consisted of the Quartermaster, Sergeant-Major, half a dozen
sergeants, and about 200 men. It was not till the repatri-
ation of the surviving officers after long captivity in
Germany that the details of the battalion's fate could be

[1] The 22nd Brigade had been relieved on the Zonnebeke–Helles line by
the 6th Brigade of the Second Division and was being concentrated at
Veldhoek.

gathered. It then appeared that the enemy had attacked in great force about 5.30 a.m., had been beaten off with heavy losses, but had renewed the attack with increased vigour and persistence, and had eventually succeeded in penetrating through gaps in the long and thinly held line. Thus the two platoons on the right, South of Reutel, had been taken in flank somewhere about 8 a.m. and rolled up, the Scots Guards' platoon under Lieut. Lord Garlies soon after suffering a like fate. The Germans then pressed on into Reutel, occupied it, and after massing in force in the re-entrant near by attacked each company in turn from the rear, while it was busily engaged with enemy in its front. Thus "A" Company had been overwhelmed before its peril was realized by "C," about the same time other Germans had made their way round the battalion's left and before long the whole firing line had been over-powered, the Colonel, senior Major, and several other officers being taken with 450 men, many of them wounded. The survivors on their way through their captors' lines had the satisfaction of seeing that the enemy's trenches were full of dead and that corpses were stacked in heaps in the copses, and of learning that two whole regiments had been needed to make the final and successful assault upon them. They were also warmly congratulated on their resistance by the commander of the 54th Reserve Division which had taken them.

With the evening of October 24th the first stage in the Division's share in the struggle for Ypres may be said to have ended. Direct help had now been given to it by other portions of the British Army and it was no longer attempting to defend single-handed its eight miles of front. Though it was still responsible for a frontage from Reutel to Kruiseik and thence nearly to Zandvoorde of over four miles, quite enough for its already greatly diminished numbers,[1] the shortening of his line enabled General Capper

---

[1] Its infantry casualties had already amounted to about a quarter of the original strength.

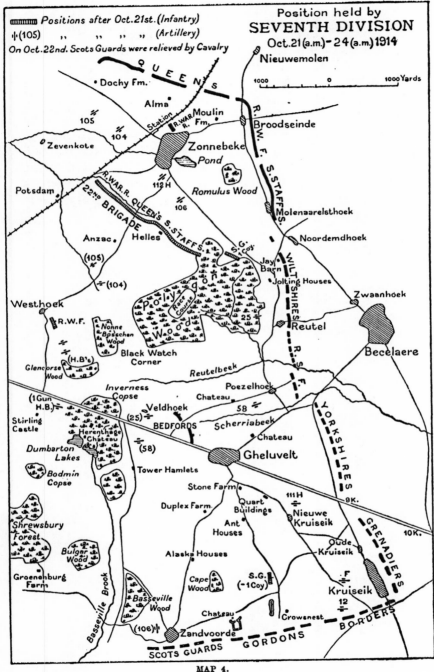

Positions after Oct.21st.(Infantry)
‖(105) ,, ,, ,, ,, (Artillery)
On Oct.22nd. Scots Guards were relieved by Cavalry

Position held by
SEVENTH DIVISION
Oct.21 (a.m.) – 24 (a.m.) 1914

Nieuwemolen

1000   0   1000 Yards

Dochy Fm.

Alma

Moulin Fm.

Broodseinde

R.WAR.R.

Station

105

104

Zevenkote

Zonnebeke

Pond

112 H

Romulus Wood

Molenaarelsthoek

Potsdam

22ND BRIGADE

R.WAR.R.

QUEEN'S

S.STAFFS.

106

Noordemdhoek

Anzac

Helles

S.G.
Co.

Jay Barn

Jolting Houses

Zwaanhoek

(105)

(104)

Westhoek

R.W.F.

Nonne Bosschen Wood

Race Course

Polygon Wood

25

Reutel

Becelaere

WILTSHIRES

(H.B's)

Black Watch Corner

Glencorse Wood

Reutelbeek

Poezelhoek

Inverness Copse

Chateau

58

(1 Gun H.B.)

Veldhoek

(25)

BEDFORDS

Scherriabeek

YORKSHIRES

Stirling Castle

Herenthage Chateau

(58)

Chateau

Dumbarton Lakes

Gheluvelt

Bodmin Copse

Tower Hamlets

Stone Farm

111 H

9 K.

Duplex Farm

Quart Buildings

Nieuwe Kruiseik

GRENADIERS

Shrewsbury Forest

Ant Houses

10 K.

Bulgar Wood

Alaska Houses

Oude Kruiseik

Groenenburg Farm

Cape Wood

S.G. (–1 Coy)

Kruiseik

Basseville Wood

Chateau

12

Crowsnest

BORDERS

(106)‖

Zandvoorde

SCOTS GUARDS

GORDONS

Basseville Brook

MAP 4.

5

to form a small reserve and the guns could be redistributed so that each individual battery had not quite so extensive a front to cover. But the battle was only beginning ; the demands on the tenacity, endurance, and discipline of the Division were far from having reached their maximum, and only to a small fraction of it did the shortening of the line bring even a small measure of relief. The majority of its officers and men had to remain in the positions they had already been defending for nearly a week, weary, unwashed, unshaven, short of sleep and sometimes of food, but grimly resolute.

CHAPTER III

THE heavy fighting which had lasted almost without intermission throughout the day of October 24th died down sufficiently after nightfall to allow of considerable readjustment on the left of the Division's line. With some difficulty the tangle in Polygon Wood was straightened out, units sorted out, and those of the Seventh Division extricated from the new line of the Second, which took over as far South as Reutel, the Scots Fusiliers now becoming the left battalion of the Seventh. The 22nd Brigade was concentrated in reserve near Veldhoek, the two detached companies of the Scots Guards, " F " and the Left Flank,[2] rejoined their battalion in support to the 20th Brigade, while the survivors of the Wiltshires were taken right back to Ypres to reorganize. The artillery positions were slightly modified, the XXIInd Brigade R.F.A. taking up a new position in the woods just West of the ridge running from Gheluvelt to Zandvoorde with the 104th Battery about 800 yards farther forward than the other two.

The chief incident of the night of October 24th/25th was a gallant but unsuccessful attempt by the Divisional Cyclists to capture a house in front of the Gordons' trenches from which machine-guns were being used with much effect. The Germans were on the alert and received the Cyclists with a hot fire ; Captain Peel of the Yorkshires, the company commander, was killed and nearly half the men became casualties. Elsewhere little of note happened; some very good work was done by the R.E. in putting up wire and improving the trenches, but they were sadly

---

[1] Cf. Map 5.

[2] Both had suffered severely, " F " being reduced to a mere handful.

handicapped by lack of materials, and in the sandy soil good defences were far from easy to construct. One diary notes with appreciation that this night saw a ration of rum issued, and to most of the troops in the trenches this was no doubt its most memorable incident.

For October 25th the orders were that the Second Division was to attack Becelaere, and the 21st Brigade to co-operate by swinging forward its left as the Second Division advanced. But there was much delay before the Second Division could start its advance, and all through the morning and early afternoon the 21st Brigade had to hold on under a heavy shell fire which got more destructive as the German gunners got the range more accurately. However, this did not prevent a small party of the Scots Fusiliers, under C.-S.-M. Evans, from going out, armed with shovels only, to bury Captain Fairlie and the other dead lying near the cross-roads. While so employed it was fired on from one of the houses, but promptly engaged its occupants with the shovels, laying about to such good effect that the Germans, an officer and 19 men, surrendered. About 3 p.m. the Second Division began to advance, but its right made little progress, and though about 5 p.m. the Bedfords endeavoured to push forward they soon had to suspend their efforts as the enemy were attacking the Yorkshires, who were pinned to their trenches, and a successful advance would have brought them ahead of the Second Division. Farther to the right the 20th Brigade had had a rather troubled night, the Germans keeping up an almost continuous rifle-fire,[1] though such attacks as they attempted were all repulsed, and the 12th Battery R.F.A. moved three guns forward into the open, one under Lieut. Lee just West of Kruiseik in the Borders' section of the line, the other two under Lieut. Woodhouse in front of the Gordons' trenches. At dawn on the 25th these opened fire at close range on houses from which machine-guns had been firing, and by demolishing them

---

[1] One officer writes of " sheets of lead going over our heads all night."

gave the infantry distinct and most welcome relief,[1] though
the Kruiseik salient got its usual dose of heavy shelling
and casualties were heavy.

In the evening the enemy began to show signs of developing an attack, and about 6 p.m. " D " Company of the
Queen's reinforced the Yorkshires, close to where the road
to Becelaere crosses the Ypres–Menin road. The Grenadiers, supported by " D " Company of the South Staffords,
were on the Yorkshires' right, then at the point of the
salient came " G " Company of the Scots Guards under
Captain Paynter, which had relieved the Right Flank
Company on the previous evening, the rest of the battalion
being behind Kruiseik village. Beyond this company
were two of the South Staffords who had relieved two of
the Borders,[2] the latter moving back to their battalion
headquarters, 1,000 yards in rear. " A " and " B "
Companies of the Borders continued the line Westward,
while on the right were the Gordons, connecting with the
cavalry at Zandvoorde. The line, however, was not
continuous, companies and even platoons being sometimes
separated by considerable gaps ; moreover the continuous
shelling had not only damaged the trenches badly and
inflicted many casualties, but had completely prevented
any digging of communication trenches.

The exact sequence of events on the night of October
25th/26th is even more than usually difficult to ascertain.
Apparently a German attack developed about sunset and
was vigorously pressed under cover of the darkness. The
Grenadiers' right was specially hard beset : while Germans
penetrated the line farther to the right, and got into some

---

[1] Sergt. Spain of " F " Battery R.H.A. was awarded the D.C.M. for bringing a single gun forward close up to the Gordons' trenches, though exposed to
a very heavy fire at a short range : this gun did most valuable work and
was of great assistance to the infantry.

[2] " C " Company of the South Staffords went up first about 7 p.m., and
rather before midnight Major Welchman took up " A " also, which on the
way up to the trenches encountered and captured several Germans who had
worked through the gaps in the line.

houses behind the right platoon's trench. Reinforcements from No. 3 Company came up from reserve, cleared most of the houses, taking several prisoners, and recovered touch with the front line. These Germans would seem to have belonged to a large party which had rushed the Scots Guards' left trench and pushed on into Kruiseik village. But though they thus had Germans right behind them, Captain Paynter and his company held on to their trenches, keeping the enemy out. It was nearly midnight when the news reached General Ruggles-Brise, and Major Fraser was at once sent up with two companies of the Scots Guards to counter-attack. After establishing touch with Capt. Paynter he began moving up the village street from the South to clear the Germans out. About the middle of the village a cinder track ran off Eastward at right angles, with the lost trench at its far end. A preliminary move down this track by Major Fraser and some 40 men was unsuccessful, the Major and most of his party being shot down. However, Major Lord Dalrymple and Capt. Fox had better success in attacking a large house standing just off the road, about midway between the lost trench and the village. This Lord Dalrymple attacked from the Westward, and as the Germans streamed out of the house to meet him a platoon under Capt. Fox enfiladed them effectively from the Southward. A bayonet charge quickly settled matters, and seven German officers and nearly 200 men gave themselves up as prisoners.[1] The Left Flank Company promptly marched them off to Brigade Headquarters, where it handed them over to a company of the Queen's and then returned to the front to complete their brilliant success by retaking the lost trench. It proved to be full of dead and wounded Germans, but it was found necessary to re-dig it and most of the other trenches which the two companies now occupied. This allowed of the relief of Capt. Paynter's men, who,

[1] They belonged to the 233rd and 242nd Reserve Regiments, units respectively of the 51st and 53rd Reserve Divisions.

though repeatedly attacked, had held on tenaciously, repulsing not only direct attacks, but the more insidious attempts of the enemy to represent themselves as friends. Their determined courage in sticking to their trenches all night, though quite cut off from all other units and with enemy all round them, in rear as well as in front, was worthy of the highest traditions of the Brigade of Guards.

To the left of the Scots Guards the Grenadiers had maintained their ground all night, no less than 50 dead Germans being counted in front of their right platoon alone when morning came.   They had been vigorously supported by " D " Company of the South Staffords, which had cleared a good many Germans out of the Northern end of Kruiseik on its way up to the trenches but had had the misfortune to lose its commander, Capt. Ransford, killed in reconnoitring the way.   Part of the company under Lieut. Riley occupied the Grenadiers' right trench, next to that which the Scots Guards had lost and recovered ; the rest were along the line to the left.   On the other face of the salient both Borders and Gordons had been kept busy all night, but had beaten off every attack, the Gordons having one particularly vigorous onset to meet, so that once again morning found the line of the sorely tried 20th Brigade still intact, though all ranks were almost exhausted.

However, despite the failure of their night attacks, the Germans meant to have Kruiseik, and soon after daybreak they resumed their bombardment with increased intensity and effect.   The trenches at the point of the salient suffered particularly ; many officers and men were buried, and though several were dug out in time, others were suffocated.   The British guns did their best to reply, but the enemy had the advantage both in number of guns and in the supply of ammunition ; moreover, they further succeeded in locating " F " Battery R.H.A. and the 12th Battery R.F.A. and forced them to withdraw first to just North of Zandvoorde and then farther West.   The 104th Battery was also ousted from its position and driven back

behind the ridge connecting Veldhoek and Zandvoorde ;
so that altogether the gunners had a very trying time.
However, from its new position " F " Battery put in some
very satisfactory shooting at Germans moving forward
from Kruiseik ; it was able to take full advantage of the
" remarkable " targets which they offered it, and one of
its officers has written of the colossal losses which the
" magnificent brigade " it was supporting, with " its Regular
Army 1914 shooting capacity," inflicted on the enemy.

In the intervals of the bombardment the German infantry
made determined efforts to break through. For some
time they were kept at bay. The Scots Guards, though
they had only a 300-yards' field of fire on the right—to the
left it was nearly double that—and though both sides of
their salient were enfiladed, managed to prevent any
attacks from developing, Lieut. Gladwin's machine-guns
at the apex of the salient doing particularly effective work.
But the line was too long for the reduced numbers available
for its defence, the Germans were fresher and in great force,
and ultimately their persistence was rewarded by success,
and they broke through gaps in the thinning line. The
South Staffords' two companies between the Scots Guards
and the Borders seem to have been overwhelmed somewhere
before 11 a.m.[1] The survivors fell back towards their
battalion headquarters, with the Germans hard on their
heels, but they managed before long to rally and to check
their pursuers. " A " and " B " Companies of the Borders
had been attacked in force from about 9 o'clock by enemy
who had concentrated in large numbers in the woods in
front, but had till now maintained their ground. They
were now taken in flank, and only about 70 survivors
managed to get away, though their battalion headquarters
with the assistance of the battalion scouts, the machine-
gun section, and other details successfully defeated the

---

[1] The last reserves, two platoons of " B " Company, were taken up by
Lieut. Hume to reinforce the firing-line about 10 a.m., and this apparently
was some time before the Germans broke through.

enemy's efforts to pursue their advantage.[1] The Scots
Guards fared even worse ; their very success in holding
their line made it all the easier for the Germans to cut off
their retreat and to roll them up from the right, taking the
trenches one by one. The defenders of the left trenches
might perhaps have got away, but held on resolutely in
strict obedience to their orders ; and not till 2 p.m. were
the survivors taken, among them Colonel Bolton, the C.O.,
Lord Dalrymple, and Capt. Fox.[2] This left the Grenadiers'
right hopelessly exposed, more especially as the orders,
which General Ruggles-Brise had issued, to fall back to a
line across the base of the Kruiseik salient, somewhat S.E.
of Gheluvelt, never got to the firing-line till the rest of the
battalion had fallen back. It was only by forcing their
way with the bayonet through the Germans, who were
already in occupation of Kruiseik, that the bulk of the
King's Company under Major Weld Forrester extricated
themselves from their desperate plight. Even then one
platoon with another from No. 3 Company farther to the
left were unable to get away and were overwhelmed by
numbers.

It was largely the resistance of these isolated detachments in the firing-line which delayed the German advance [3]
and gave time for General Ruggles-Brise to rally the
remnants of the 20th Brigade and South Staffords on the
Western slopes of Kruiseik Hill. The Gordons on the

[1] The Borders' casualties this day came to over 250, including nine officers,
the great majority being " missing." The South Staffords fared even worse,
being reduced to under 500 of all ranks, although until this day their casualties had not been heavy.

[2] That evening only 12 officers and 460 men were present with the battalion,
including all details at the transport lines.

[3] The captured Scots Guards had the satisfaction of seeing the ground to
their front " paved with German dead," and of learning from their captors
that they had not been taken until a cavalry division had been specially
brought up to attack them, after all the efforts of the infantry on their front
had been beaten off. A Landwehr brigade of five battalions, a Jager brigade
of four, and a regiment of the 51st Reserve Division all seem to have been
engaged in the attack on Kruiseik.

right had not budged,[1] and the new line ran N.E. from
their left flank. Meanwhile, about 2 p.m., orders had
reached the 22nd Brigade near Veldhoek to go to the
assistance of the 20th, and General Lawford moved S.E.
past Gheluvelt with the Welch Fusiliers on the left, the
Warwickshires on their right, and the Queen's [2] in support.
The brigade came under heavy shell fire as it crossed the
Gheluvelt–Zandvoorde road, and when nearly a mile S.E. of
Gheluvelt heard about 4 p.m. that the 20th Brigade had
been compelled to retire again. This meant that the 22nd
Brigade must conform, so it fell back a little way and proceeded to entrench a position South of Gheluvelt and
extending Westwards to the road to Zandvoorde. What
seems to have happened was that about 3.30 p.m. "F"
Battery R.H.A. and the 12th Battery R.F.A. had fallen
back to new positions West of the Basseville brook, the
Grenadiers going back at the same time in readiness to
cover the rest of the brigade should the enemy press on.
But the enemy had apparently had enough and did not
make any real effort to push on. However, after nightfall General Ruggles-Brise, finding his position isolated
and dangerously exposed, gave orders for a retirement
behind the Basseville brook, which was carried out in good
order,[3] despite the great fatigue of the troops. The 20th
Brigade was thus facing East with the 22nd on its left at
right angles to it and facing South. The line thus formed
a pronounced re-entrant in place of the salient it till then
had presented.

There was, however, a gap between the left of the 22nd

---

[1] This battalion, though several times heavily attacked, had been fortunate
so far in having very few casualties. Even with those of October 26th included
the total was not much over 150.

[2] One company (" C ") and a platoon of another (" D ") were not with
the battalion, having taken over trenches near the cross-roads half a mile
East of Gheluvelt, where they were rather mixed up with the Yorkshires.
They remained here till the morning of October 28th.

[3] The Gordons conformed to this move, evacuating the position which they
had till now so successfully maintained.

Brigade's new line and the right of the 21st's, which remained as before stationary, astride the Menin road near the cross-roads at the 9th kilometre stone. The 21st had had a much less eventful day than the 20th ; its orders had been as before to support the Second Division's advance on Becelaere, and the latter's failure to achieve any substantial advance had meant that the 21st Brigade had merely stuck to its trenches and endured another day of heavy shelling, the enemy making no attempt to profit by his success in driving back the 20th Brigade to take the 21st in flank. The Bedfords were greatly worried by snipers and lost two officers thereby, one of whom, Lieut. Bastard, had distinguished himself considerably by gallantry and good leadership ; but the Germans could make no advance by daylight, though just before relief the Scots Fusiliers were attacked but beat their assailants off without difficulty.

The Germans had not attempted to follow the 20th Brigade, and General Capper determined to see if he could not recover some of the evacuated ground. During the afternoon the 1st Brigade of the First Division had arrived, and after dark it took over the 21st Brigade's line from the Menin road Northward, placing that brigade—which moved back behind Veldhoek on relief—at the Divisional Commander's disposal. General Capper therefore determined to go on with his intention of advancing, and during the night the 22nd Brigade pushed forward practically unopposed to the approximate line on which the 20th had first rallied across the base of the Kruiseik salient. This it now reoccupied, having the South Staffords on the right, then the Queen's,[1] then the Warwickshires, the Welch Fusiliers being in reserve. Between the Warwickshires and the Camerons on the right of the First Division there was a gap of nearly 900 yards, General Lawford's force being much too weak to cover the very extended front assigned to it, but this was eventually filled by the First

---

[1] The position taken up by the Queen's seems to have been near Epines.

Division. The move was much delayed by the darkness
and the difficulty of finding all the units concerned. It
had been intended that the 3rd Brigade should relieve the
22nd, but daylight had come before the relieving battalions
could arrive, so the 22nd Brigade had to spend another
day (October 27th) in the line.

All these movements, naturally enough, had greatly
hindered the work of improving the trenches, though the
R.E. did all they could and even put up some amount of
wire.[1] Fortunately October 27th brought a lull in the
storm. The 22nd Brigade was but little shelled and was
never really attacked, though there was constant sniping
and its supporting artillery did some effective shooting; the
20th actually spent the whole day in bivouac, reorganizing
and resting—it needed both sorely ; the 21st was almost as
fortunate, remaining quietly at Veldhoek till the evening,
when it moved forward to take over the line from the
Menin road to Zandvoorde, relieving the 22nd Brigade, who
withdrew to Klein Zillebeke. The Bedfords were on the
left next the road, with the Yorkshires beyond them and
the Scots Fusiliers farther to the right again towards the
château East of Zandvoorde, while the 22nd Brigade left the
South Staffords near Zandvoorde to support the cavalry.[2]
The new position, though only inadequately entrenched,
represented a real improvement on the Kruiseik salient,
so tenaciously defended by the 20th Brigade for five days
of intense strain and shelling. A less satisfactory position
it is hard to imagine, and the defence made under such
disadvantageous circumstances was enormously to the
20th Brigade's credit. Kruiseik Hill, though only 50 feet
above the general level, was terribly exposed, subjected
to concentrated enfilade fire, and all units had fought most
stubbornly. "Special mention," says the Divisional

---

[1] On the night of October 26th Capt. McEnery, O.C. 54th Field Company,
was accidentally shot by a sentry when going round the trenches.

[2] The 25th and 58th Batteries had also to shift their positions, going back
to Hooge in reserve.

Diary, " is due to the Borders,[1] who had maintained their ground throughout this period, during which many of their trenches had been blown in."

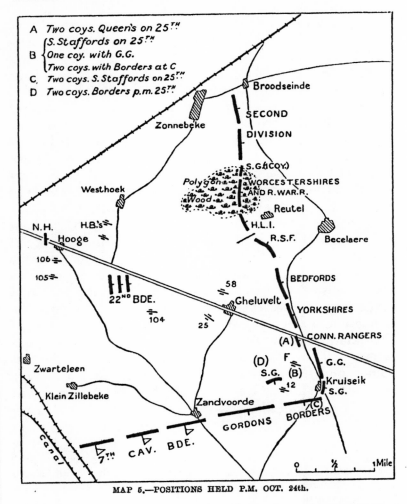

A *Two coys. Queen's on 25*[TH]
B {*S. Staffords on 25*[TH]
   One coy. with G.G.
   Two coys. with Borders at C
C. *Two coys. S. Staffords on 25*[TH]
D *Two coys. Borders p.m. 25*[TH]

MAP 5.—POSITIONS HELD P.M. OCT. 24th.

To be singled out for special praise in the Seventh Division was already a remarkable distinction. The length of its line, the severity of the shell fire to which it

[1] This battalion had been reduced to 12 officers and 538 other ranks.

had been exposed, the vigour and persistence of the German infantry attacks had all been out of the common, and the Division's losses testified to the ordeal it had gone through. By October 27th its infantry had already lost over 43 per cent. of their officers and 37 per cent. of their men. The 20th Brigade had been reduced to 70 officers and 2,480 men, the 21st to 61 officers and 2,600 men, the 22nd to 55 and 2,230.[1] In the other arms the casualties had been much lower, but the Artillery had lost several officers, mostly when forward as " observing officers," and the R.E., who had done splendid work not only at their own special tasks, but in helping the infantry to beat off attacks,[2] had by no means come off scatheless. Artillery and R.E. had alike had a tremendous amount to do, and were scarcely less exhausted than the infantry ; but though the relief of the First Corps on the Zonnebeke– Langemarck front by French troops had allowed the First and Second Divisions to take over about two-thirds of the Seventh's original line, there was no question of relief for that Division. Later in the war an ordeal such as the Seventh had endured and a casualty list of equal length would have earned a Division a respite from the trenches and some degree of real rest : in the autumn of 1914 there was no prospect of rest for anyone who could carry a rifle or serve a gun : twenty-four hours " in reserve," and that well within range of the German heavy guns, was the utmost a shattered unit could hope for. The Seventh had indeed not much over two miles of front to hold now, but most of the line had been but hastily

---

[1] Only the Bedfords, Yorkshires, and Gordons had had under 200 casualties, while the Scots Guards, Welch Fusiliers, and South Staffords were all reduced below 500 of all ranks, and the Wiltshires for the time being had been withdrawn for reconstruction.

[2] On October 21st, for example, the 55th Field Company was employed as infantry in support of the Grenadiers, on the 25th it had one officer killed when taking part in a counter-attack, and both companies when engaged on their own work in the firing-line had often to lay down their tools and pick up rifles to assist in repulsing attacks.

entrenched, there had been hardly any time to put up
wire, still less to provide dug-outs or communication
trenches ; some trenches actually faced the wrong way,
many were little more than mere scratches, and the line
as a whole was barely defensible. It says volumes for
the stubbornness with which it was defended that the
German official account should describe it as " a veritable
fortress."

The contraction of its front, which made it no longer
responsible for anything North of the Menin road, was not
the only change which October 27th had brought to the
Seventh Division. It now came under the direct orders
of Sir Douglas Haig, commanding the First Corps, as the
G.O.C. Fourth Corps had returned to England to assist
in preparing the Eighth Division for the field. As already
stated, the Division's line had now been entrusted to the
21st Brigade. The other two infantry brigades—or rather
their survivors, for both had lost most severely—spent the
28th getting as near to a rest as Klein Zillebeke and Hooge
could afford. It was not a very active day even for those
in the front line. For the moment their opponents had
shot their bolt and were being replaced by more experienced
troops from a quiet sector of the line. There was some
shelling and snipers were active enough. The Bedfords
got the worst of such bombardment as there was, one
platoon of their right company having its trenches blown
in and suffering severely. The XXIInd Brigade R.F.A.
too came in for some extremely severe shelling, Brigade
Headquarters receiving special attention ; but the
British guns, though outnumbered and compelled to
exercise great care about ammunition expenditure, replied
quite effectively, and the Scots Fusiliers reported that
the fire of the XIVth Brigade R.H.A. had done much
damage to the German trenches facing them and had
kept the artillery fire down, even if it could not be completely silenced. The Fusiliers also did some effective
shooting at Germans who were shelled out of houses only

300 yards away, and got good targets in German infantry who exposed themselves when digging trenches.

Sir John French had not yet relinquished his hopes of a successful offensive, and his orders for October 29th prescribed a fresh attempt to advance North of the Menin road, in which the Seventh Division was to be ready to co-operate, though until the moment for the advance came it was to remain on the defensive. To assist in this General Capper sent the 20th Brigade up to take over the left of the 21st's line, and on the evening of October 28th the Grenadiers relieved the Bedfords from the cross-roads S.E. of Gheluvelt to a point about 400 yards to the S.W. of them. The Gordons came into line on their right, relieving the Yorkshires, while the Scots Guards and Borders were placed in support just East of Gheluvelt. This allowed the 21st Brigade to shorten its line, but the Bedfords shifted across from left to right and put two companies [1] into the line between the 7th Cavalry Brigade, which was holding Zandvoorde, and the Scots Fusiliers, who retained their position. For this part of the line the Yorkshires just N.E. of Zandvoorde provided the reserves, the South Staffords doing the same for the cavalry at Zandvoorde, while the remainder of the 22nd Brigade, 1,600 [2] all told, were back at Klein Zillebeke.

The comparative quiet of October 28th was deceptive. Actually the newly formed " Army Group Fabeck " was moving up to replace the Jagers, Landwehr and dismounted cavalry hitherto in action against the Southern face of the Ypres Salient and the frontage running thence to Messines. The Seventh Division, few of whose units had had more than a fleeting moment of rest since landing in Belgium, while as yet it had received only a handful of

---

[1] The other two were in support.

[2] The Queen's mustered 19 officers and 716 men, the Royal Warwickshires and R.W.F. were both under 500, though the Fusiliers had just received their " first reinforcements," 100 strong, with 7 officers, mostly Special Reserve or newly Gazetted.

reinforcements,[1] was about to be attacked in greater force
than ever by troops who came from comparatively quiet
sectors and at any rate in comparison with the exhausted
Seventh Division could be reckoned as fresh.

Before evening on October 28th Corps Headquarters
circulated a warning that a German wireless message had
been intercepted ordering a general attack on the Seventh
Division's front at 5.30 next morning. However, owing
to the late hour at which the reliefs were completed, the
exhausted state of the troops, and the scanty supplies of
material available, little could be done to make any
special preparation to meet the expected attack. The
Division was so reduced that even with its shortened
front the only reserves available were the Northumberland Hussars, the Cyclists, and three battalions of the
22nd Brigade, two of them together barely equal to a
full battalion.

Soon after 5 a.m., October 29th, the German bombardment opened, but for some time no infantry action followed;
indeed the reserve battalions of the 20th Brigade which had
moved up closer to the Gheluvelt cross-roads during the
night were sent back towards Veldhoek about daybreak to
avoid exposure to the bombardment and to get food, for
it had been found impossible to get the wagons with their
rations as far forward as the support trenches. Soon
after this the bombardment increased in vigour and
the Germans advanced to the attack.

The morning was foggy, while the lie of the ground
made it hard anyhow for the Grenadiers to see what was
going on just to their left;[2] indeed almost their first
intimation of the attack was that about 5.30 a.m. rifle
fire was opened upon them from their left rear. Colonel
Earle promptly ordered the King's Company, his only

---

[1] Not more than 400 reinforcements in all had as yet joined the Division.

[2] Their trenches were on lower ground than those North of the road, and
the houses, gardens, and orchards, which had not yet been swept away, interfered greatly with the view.

reserve, to be ready to counter-attack. But the Colonel was badly wounded and disabled and the Germans came on so hard that although an attempt was made to throw back the battalion's left flank and so prevent the rolling up of the line, the two left companies were thrust back to their support trenches. On the right No. 4 held on in the front line and kept its opponents at bay, while beyond its flank the Gordons successfully withstood repeated German efforts to advance. The attack had now developed against the 21st Brigade, who were soon very hard pressed, especially the Scots Fusiliers. But the left had to meet the main strength of the German thrust and here the danger was greatest. It was pretty clear that the First Division's line had been penetrated, for Germans were swarming forward along the road to Gheluvelt in strength. They came on shoulder to shoulder, presenting splendid targets of which the Grenadiers took ample advantage, though the support trenches proved a mere snare, being so deep that the men had to get out into the open to fire. Still, even when the King's Company had been brought up by Major Stucley, the second in command, the Grenadiers were too few to stay the advance of such overwhelming masses. Major Stucley led one counter-attack which thrust the enemy back, but they surged forward again, and in heading a second he was killed and most of his men went down. The pressure increased every minute ; Capt. Lord R. Wellesley was killed in a counter-attack on the right, and before long No. 4 Company was forced back from the front trenches to a brickyard in rear. Here a brief stand was made, but finally the remnants of the battalion recoiled to a wood some distance back. Most of the officers were down now ; only Captain Rasch, the Adjutant, and a few subalterns were left, and the position was all but desperate. Luckily the Gordons were faring better and could spare their reserve company ; and when this was brought up by Captain Burnett and Lieut. Brooke Captain Rasch rallied

the Grenadiers for a desperate counter-attack. The first
rush drove the Germans from the brickfields but was
checked and driven back by reinforcements ; however,
Gordons and Grenadiers were not to be denied and a
second charge swept the Germans back through the brickfields. It was an astonishing success for such a mere
handful, but the very audacity of the attack tended to
magnify its strength in the minds of the Germans—they
could not believe that there was nothing more behind
and in consequence failed to make full use of their advantage in numbers.

The stubborn resistance of the overmatched 20th
Brigade had at least prevented the Germans South of
the Menin road from keeping level with their progress
North of the road. Here their attack, delivered in even
greater force and with even more success, had broken the
1st Brigade's right : and some of them pressing forward
had nearly reached Gheluvelt, while others turning right-
handed had rolled up the thinly held line from the flank.
Company after company when hotly engaged to its front
was taken in flank and rear and overpowered. However,
the reserves of the First Division were quickly thrown in,
and the 3rd Brigade, advancing S.E. past Gheluvelt
North of the road, before long checked and thrust back
the leaders of the German advance. At the same time
General Capper was striving to restore the situation with
his own scanty reserves. Behind the 20th Brigade's
front line he had the Scots Guards, 6 officers and about
350 men,[1] and the Borders, about 100 stronger. These
two battalions were ordered forward from Veldhoek and
eventually counter-attacked South of the Menin road.
The Borders were the first to get into action. Deploying
to their right they made for the windmill, South of the
8th kilometre stone. Their advance brought a welcome
help to the remnants of the Grenadiers, now about due
South of Gheluvelt, with the Gordons on their right

[1] Exclusive of transport and details out of the line.

front. As they crossed a crest line the Borders met a tremendous storm of fire from guns, rifles, and machine-guns. Colonel Wood was wounded, several other officers were hit, and the casualties were heavy, but they pressed on and effectively checked the Germans.

In the later stages of their advance the Borders benefited from the fact that the 2nd Queen's, who had been detached from the 22nd Brigade to the assistance of the 20th, were also pushing forward S.E. of Gheluvelt, apparently filling a gap between the Borders and the Menin road. Their leading company, " A," at first lined the track from Ghelu-velt to Kruiseik, facing N.E., and replied effectively to the rifle fire coming from the Menin road. Part of the company reached a farm just South of the windmill, but here encountered enemy in force, and not till two more companies came up on their right could any progress be made.[1] A little later the Scots Guards also came up, so that South of the Menin road the situation was beginning to look decidedly less unfavourable. The Gordons were still holding on, and from their left there was something like a continuous line almost as far as the Menin road, though in places Germans still remained behind the line. But these were mainly leaderless parties, more concerned to make their way back to their friends than to give trouble to their enemies.

Meanwhile the First Division's counter-attack North of the road was making itself felt, and by a curious coin-cidence it was the 1st Queen's who were the right unit in this advance and consequently got into close touch with the left of the Seventh Division, their own 2nd Battalion. The two battalions not only fought side by side, but got quite mixed up ; some of the 1st, for example, joined up with Major Bottomley's company of the 2nd, " B," which pushed right forward and ultimately retook

---

[1] It seems that the Queen's advanced across the central track of the three which go South from Gheluvelt, that towards Tenbrielen, and occupied some farms West of Nieuwe Kruiseik.

some trenches quite near Kruiseik. With this assistance
the 20th Brigade eventually recovered quite a lot of ground,
taking two machine-guns, although the advance stopped
some way short of the front trenches held by the Grenadiers in the morning ; the new line running from the
Menin road about level with the windmill to the old line
about 600 yards West of Kruiseik, where the Gordons
were still in position. This battalion had put up a
remarkable resistance and had taken a toll of the enemy
which was something to set off against the brigade's
losses : it had inflicted terrible punishment on the efforts
to overrun its trenches, and in front of one platoon only
of the right company, Captain B. G. R. Gordon's, some
240 German corpses were counted. The Gordons' resistance, indeed, had played no small part in enabling
the Division to recover much of its lost ground and re-
establish a more or less consecutive line.

The 20th Brigade may have met the greatest strength
of the German attack, but the 21st had been sufficiently
severely tried. The day had begun for it with a vigorous
early morning attack, which it had decisively repulsed.
Thereupon had followed other attacks, which met with
the same fate. However, when the Germans broke
through the 20th Brigade " B " Company of the Scots
Fusiliers suddenly found itself enfiladed as well as attacked
in front, but held stoutly on, however, not a little assisted
by some German howitzers which shelled their own men
at the critical moment, while the Gordons' machine-guns,
concealed in a hollow behind the Fusiliers' left, did
tremendous execution, bowling over nearly 200 Germans
and altogether stopping the attack. " C " Company of the
Yorkshires had already been sent up to reinforce, and
until almost noon the position was maintained, the Bedfords and the 7th Cavalry Brigade also dealing successfully
with all attacks on them. Effective help was afforded
by the artillery ; the 106th Battery in action about the
point afterwards known as Tower Hamlets, 1,000 yards

S.W. of Gheluvelt, took on and silenced a German battery which ventured into the open S.E. of Zandvoorde. But about noon the enemy had established themselves well in rear of the Scots Fusiliers' firing-line [1] and accordingly orders were issued to fall back. The bulk of the battalion began to retire therefore towards battalion headquarters, but the order never reached "B" Company, which remained in its position; indeed Major Burgoyne, its commander, was so far from feeling disposed to retire that he sent back word to this effect and to ask for reinforcements. Largely owing to this company's retention of its position, the Germans failed to exploit the retirement of the other companies, who rallied along the Gheluvelt–Zandvoorde road, and when Colonel King brought up two companies of the Yorkshires from reserve the enemy were checked.

By this time the remaining battalions of the 22nd Brigade were coming to the help of General Watts, and on their arrival a counter-attack was launched from the Gheluvelt–Zandvoorde road towards Kruiseik.[2] In this the Yorkshires were on the left along with those of the Scots Fusiliers who had been driven from their front trenches : two companies of the Bedfords came next, then the Warwickshires, South Staffords, and Welch Fusiliers. This effort, which apparently coincided with the 20th Brigade's last attempt to get forward, was met and somewhat checked by heavy fire, especially from machine-guns, but the Bedfords' machine-guns did most effective work in keeping down this fire and in helping the advance forward.[3] In the end the attack recovered much of the ground which had been lost and regained

[1] It was very foggy, and as the line was not continuous it was possible for the Germans to get round the flank of a unit although the trenches of the next one on that side, in this case the right of the Gordons, were still untaken.

[2] The 54th Field Company shared in this counter-attack, acting as infantry, and had several casualties including one officer killed.

[3] When the Bedfords counter-attacked, Lieut. Osborne and five men of the Signal Company pushed forward and rescued a cable-wagon which had had to be abandoned.

touch with Major Burgoyne's company and with those
of the Bedfords who had retained their places in the
firing-line.   Casualties were heavy, however, some machine-
guns which were left behind in concealed positions when

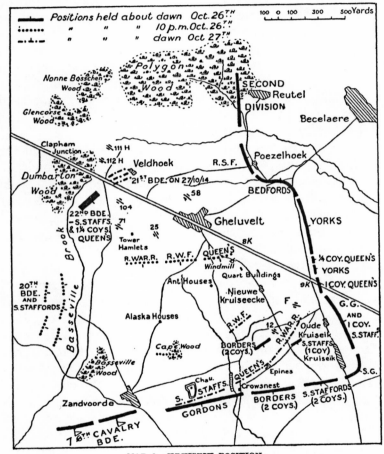

MAP 6.—KRUISEIK POSITION.

the German infantry were driven back doing much damage.
The Bedfords had 8 officers hit and the Yorkshires 7,
while the Scots Fusiliers were reduced to 300 of all ranks.
The 22nd Brigade had fared better; the Queen's had

100 casualties, but the other units got off more lightly, their counter-attack having encountered little resistance. The 20th Brigade's losses, however, had been very serious. The Grenadiers, in the morning a strong battalion as units went in the B.E.F. at this time, had lost 10 officers and over 400 men and were left with only 6 officers and 250 men. The Borders' losses, well over 200, had reduced them below 300, the Scots Guards, diminished by another 100 casualties, being even weaker; so that only the Gordons, who had got off with the loss of 7 officers and about 100 men, mainly in the reserve company that went to the aid of the Grenadiers, could still put into the field a reasonably strong battalion.[1]

The new line ran from a farm [2] near the junction of the Gheluvelt–Kruiseik and Gheluvelt–Zandvoorde roads to the cross-roads N.W. of Kruiseik and thence to the old line about 600 yards West of Kruiseik, so that the net loss of ground was about 500 yards. Much readjustment was necessary, and in the end the 20th Brigade was withdrawn to Veldhoek. Unluckily the Scots Guards, who had got farther forward than the rest of the line, were mistaken for enemy when falling back and were fired upon by another unit, only too effectively. The line as finally taken up was held on the left by the 2nd Queen's, who were in touch on their left with their own 1st Battalion, from whom they were eventually disentangled. On their right came the Scots Fusiliers in their old trenches with the Yorkshires beyond them, and the Welch Fusiliers linking up the 21st Brigade with the cavalry nearer Zandvoorde.[3] The Warwickshires and South Staffords and the remnant of the 20th Brigade were in reserve. The Division was thus holding its old line on the right and

---

[1] Lieut. Brooke, who was among their killed, received a posthumous V.C. for his gallantry and good leadership in the counter-attack of the reserve company. It was the battalion's second V.C. in the campaign.

[2] Apparently the one later known as Stone Farm.

[3] They took over the trenches which the Bedfords had been holding, that battalion going into support behind the Scots Fusiliers.

centre, but its sharply bent back left formed a fresh indefensible salient about West of Kruiseik.[1]

Without question October 29th had been a bad day : the heavy casualties and the exhaustion of the surviving officers and men were really the most disquieting feature in the situation, more serious even than the loss of ground, though this meant that once again new trenches had to be dug and that the work of the previous days had to be begun all over again. Each day that a line could be held gave more chance of strengthening it and adding to its defences, of making dug-outs and communication trenches, so that each loss of ground meant the loss of the results of past days' work. The driving back of the infantry, moreover, necessitated the shifting of gun positions and fresh labour for the gunners in digging new gun-pits, so that they too had little chance of rest.

The strain was telling heavily by now on officers and men. They had been fighting almost continuously for ten days : they had been far from fresh when they started fighting ; they were now shorter of sleep than ever, few had had the chance of a wash or a shave, meals had been scanty and irregular, and though as yet no really bad weather had been experienced, life in the open at the end even of a fine October was no picnic. If the strain perhaps fell heaviest on the infantry in the trenches the other arms felt it heavily enough. The gunners were continually in action, even if the limited supply of ammunition meant that there were often long intervals in the actual firing. The R.E., in addition to their own labours, strenuous enough when so many new lines had to be taken up and made defensible at short notice and in face of a great scarcity of materials, had had more than once to be used as infantry. The R.A.M.C. found themselves fully occupied

[1] The artillery dispositions had also had to be altered: " F " Battery R.H.A. and the 12th Battery were now back near Klein Zillebeke, the 106th was dug in South of Gheluvelt with the 104th and 105th behind the Veldhoek–Zandvoorde road, the Heavy Batteries remaining near Westhoek and the rest of the XXXVth Brigade R.F.A. in reserve at Hooge.

in tending the large numbers of wounded, whose collection from the forward zone under the almost incessant German shelling and rifle fire was both difficult and dangerous.

On the Divisional and Brigade staffs the strain was of the heaviest. With the line constantly shifting, with communications with the scattered battalions and companies constantly interrupted—indefatigable as was the Signal Company in its efforts to maintain them—with scanty reserves no sooner scraped together than they had to be thrown in to strengthen the breaking line or fill a dangerous gap, the task of controlling the fight was almost beyond them. But General Capper was full of confidence and vigour, constantly up in the fighting line to exhort and encourage the weary men, to instil into them something of his own unflinching determination to endure to the bitter end. He was well backed up by his staff and his brigadiers, and the men responded splendidly to his exhortations. It was really remarkable how companies and even platoons, isolated in the front trenches by the forcing back of the units to right and left, hung on nevertheless and by their bold front and stubborn resistance imposed upon the Germans, prevented them from exploiting their advantages and opportunities, and gave time for the assembly of reserves and the launching of counterattacks. Half the infantry of the Division were down by now, but the grit and toughness of the British soldier were never more strikingly in evidence than in the Seventh Division's stand between Zandvoorde and the Menin road.

CHAPTER IV

FIRST YPRES (*concluded*)
ZANDVOORDE AND ZILLEBEKE [1]

THE evening of October 29th had left the Seventh Division holding only a fraction of its old line, a frontage of under 3,000 yards from just East of Zandvoorde, where the right of the Welch Fusiliers was in touch with the cavalry, to a point on the Gheluvelt–Tenbrielen road about South of the 8th kilometre stone. Here the two battalions of the Queen's had been for the moment mixed up together, but during the night they were sorted out, the 2nd Battalion taking up a line facing roughly N.E., while the 1st on its left faced almost S.E. Between the two battalions of the 22nd Brigade were the Royal Scots Fusiliers and the Yorkshires with the Bedfords in support.

The night of October 29th/30th allowed of much readjustment and re-arrangement, if not of much rest or of doing much to prepare the new line for defence against the attack which the morning was certain to bring. Had there been time to entrench and wire the line properly, to clear the country sufficiently to allow for mutual support, and to establish satisfactory communications, the position might have been maintained despite the nasty salient on its left which the previous day's fighting had created. But the Germans were not going to give the weary Seventh the chance either to improve its position or to snatch a scrap of rest. Soon after daybreak on October 30th they were at it again, shelling the whole line with renewed fury and devoting special attention to Zandvoorde and the ridge on which it stands. This was held by the Household Cavalry, and it was on them that the brunt of the bombardment

[1] Cf. Maps 6 and 7.

fell, though about 8 a.m. the 54th Reserve and 30th Divisions attacked the Seventh Division's line only to be beaten back. The Household Cavalry hung on valiantly, but their trenches were practically obliterated by the bombardment, and when at length the German infantry pressed forward to the assault there were but few defenders left to meet it. The ridge and village seem to have passed into German hands rather after 8 a.m., and almost immediately the Welch Fusiliers, already well employed in keeping off the German infantry in their front, found themselves enfiladed from the right. They still held on stubbornly, but the Germans brought a battery right forward which came into action on the Zandvoorde ridge itself and did terrible execution among the Fusiliers, whose trenches had already been badly mauled by the storm of shells which descended upon them. These guns were engaged by a section of the 105th Battery, S.W. of Alaska Houses ; four guns of the 106th also turned on to them from the woods round Herenthage Château, and, catching them in enfilade at about 1,200 yards' range, forced their detachments to bolt for shelter, repeating the dose successfully whenever they came forward to try to reopen fire.

Directly General Capper heard of the loss of Zandvoorde, realizing the critical situation of the Welch Fusiliers, he threw into the fight the scanty reserves he possessed. Of the 22nd Brigade the South Staffords and Warwickshires were available, being bivouacked about three quarters of a mile in rear of the Welch Fusiliers, and about 8 a.m. General Lawford had brought them forward into a position East of the Basseville brook, which now became the front line. The Gordons also were ordered to advance on their right and endeavour to regain Zandvoorde by co-operating with the reserves of the cavalry. This battalion pushed on through the woods, but met the enemy in force, and though it brought the Germans to a standstill West of the Basseville brook it could not get anywhere near Zandvoorde. It held on for some hours, though under heavy

fire from a wood on its left flank, but was eventually forced
to fall back about 2.30 p.m., having lost very heavily, the
C.O., Colonel Uniacke, being among the wounded. The
German pressure continued unabated, and before long the
South Staffords found Germans in their right rear. " D "
Company was promptly deployed in the open to face this
party, and covered by its fire the rest of the battalion
withdrew to a better position a little farther back, to which
the survivors of " D " retired a couple of hours later.
This was about North of Zandvoorde and faced about
due South, the Warwickshires on the left facing about
S.W. and maintaining touch with the 21st Brigade. Meanwhile help was being sent up by Sir Douglas Haig from the
scanty reserves of the First and Second Divisions, and the
Royal Sussex and Northamptons of the 2nd Brigade,
under Brigadier General Bulfin, were thrown in between
the Gordons and South Staffords about half an hour after
midday. This reinforcement was most timely, for
though it could no more recover Zandvoorde than could
the Seventh Division and cavalry, it stopped the danger
of a further extension of the German advance, and a new
line was formed about 500 yards North of Zandvoorde,
beyond which the Germans failed to penetrate.[1] Effective
help was also given by the 12th Battery R.F.A., which
came forward to the edge of a wood East of Klein Zillebeke,
only to find itself almost in line with the infantry and
under very heavy fire. Three of its officers were hit,
including its C.O., Major Christie, together with Colonel
Lambert, the Brigade commander; three guns were completely disabled and the others silenced by their detachments being shot down. The other two batteries of its
brigade, the 25th and 58th, also came forward almost in
line with the 12th, but fell back to Zwarteleen to avoid
its fate, though the 25th pushed up again later on and did
excellent service in a rather dangerously exposed position.

[1] When the Gordons fell back, they took post on the left of the Northamptons.

The section of the 105th Battery also had been heavily shelled by howitzers and forced to quit its position, but did so with only a few casualties, being concealed by the smoke from a burning haystack to which the battery's C.O., Major Hill, had set fire.

Long before this, however, the Welch Fusiliers' gallant resistance had come to an end. They had fought stubbornly on, the hopelessness of their position notwithstanding, and had thereby greatly delayed the German advance. But, taken in flank and rear, enfiladed and hard pressed in front, their destruction was only a question of time. Of the 12 officers and rather over 400 men to which the battalion had been brought up only 86 men were present at the end of the day.[1] Colonel Cadogan, his Adjutant, Captain Dooner, and the great majority of the officers and men were killed, only four officers and about fifty men being reported later on as prisoners, and most of them wounded.

The overwhelming of the Welch Fusiliers put the Scots Fusiliers in considerable danger. They had been vigorously attacked by infantry in front from about 6 a.m., and about 8 some of " C " Company were driven from their trenches, but were promptly rallied and taken back to the line to find that the Germans had failed to seize the chance ; the rest of " C " were still in possession and their officer, Lieut. Whitton, was doing excellent practice with his rifle, " shooting at helmets." Their line now came under enfilade fire both from rifles and from field-guns which were pushed forward to within quite close range of Brigade Headquarters, whence they opened an accurate fire upon the Scots Fusiliers, besides enfilading the Bedfords who were in close support. A company of the Bedfords and half the 54th Field Company attempted to establish themselves on a spur facing Zandvoorde to cover the Fusiliers' right, but the German fire was too hot. There was no

---

[1] These details were attached to the 2nd Queen's until after the relief of the Division.

alternative but to fall back, for the brigade's line now formed a pronounced salient on both flanks, and about 1 p.m. orders were issued for this by the brigade. The retirement was covered by the Bedfords, and by about 40 Scots Fusiliers, who took post to the right rear of the original line. Thanks to their efforts a line of sorts was formed across the Zandvoorde–Gheluvelt road and facing towards the Eastern end of the Zandvoorde ridge ; and here also the further advance of the enemy was at last stayed, a German battery which had ventured into the open being effectually silenced.

To this the dogged resistance of the left companies of the Scots Fusiliers contributed not a little. The order to retire never reached them and Major Burgoyne with Captains Le Gallais and Fleetwood and about 200 men held on till evening. They beat off all the German efforts to roll them up, though both flanks were " in the air " and the enemy were also right behind them. At nightfall Major Burgoyne gave orders to try to cut a way back to the new line of the brigade, but though Captain Le Gallais and about 100 men got through successfully the Major and the rest of the survivors were intercepted near where their battalion headquarters had been and all killed or taken.

On the Scots Fusiliers' left the Yorkshires had found themselves to start with in a pronounced salient, and their position was made worse when the Germans got forward beyond Zandvoorde, especially as the Queen's, after helping to repulse the earlier German attacks, had been withdrawn by order. Their retirement was carried out under heavy fire from guns S.W. of Kruiseik and from infantry near the Kruiseik cross-roads, but companies retired steadily in succession, covering one another, and re-formed just before reaching the Veldhoek–Zandvoorde road, being placed in reserve and digging in at the corner of a wood East of the Basseville brook.[1] The whole battalion, however, had not gone back, for Major Bottomley's detachment, already

---

[1] This was some distance South of " Tower Hamlets."

mentioned, remained in its advanced position though repeatedly attacked, beating off all the German advances and ultimately rejoining its main body. This isolated party was no doubt partly responsible for the failure of the Germans to do more against the Yorkshires, who held on unshaken for nearly 3 hours after the order for the retirement of the 21st Brigade had been issued. They were severely shelled and lost heavily, including their C.O., Colonel King, and several other officers, but they were not dislodged. About 1 p.m. the right platoon reported the advance of some 500 Germans against its line : it had, however, fired on them with such effect that they had dropped into some trenches and stopped there. When the belated order to withdraw was received, somewhere about 3.30 p.m., the situation seemed almost hopeless ; but Captain Blundell, now in command,[1] decided to make the attempt, and effectively covered by the fire of his right platoon got the battalion away with the loss of only 10 men, a great tribute to the respect which the British musketry had established among the Germans.

Indeed, reduced in numbers as were the battalions of the Seventh Division, they were all trained men, able to fire their 15 aimed rounds a minute as long as ammunition held out and rifles remained free from the clogging sand and mud. It was noticed, moreover, that the troops of the 15th Army Corps, who were now carrying out the attacks South of the Menin road, did not show that dash and devotion displayed by the less experienced men of the new Reserve Corps, to whom the Seventh Division had at first been opposed. With them inexperience had been largely discounted by zeal and reckless bravery—they had no doubt incurred avoidable losses by their want of tactical skill and training ; but the Seventh Division might well be thankful that the more experienced units of Von Fabeck's Group had not been inspired by their energy and

---

[1] The second in command, Major Alexander, had been wounded on the previous day when Major Walker had been killed.

dash. It was extraordinary that the Germans should have failed to make better use of openings like the capture of Kruiseik and of Zandvoorde. The stubbornness of the Seventh Division's resistance no doubt imposed on them, concealing by its audacity the numerical weakness which the Germans ought to have been able to exploit more effectively ; the broken character of the country also was partly responsible. If the woods and copses and hedge-rows interfered with observation and intercommunication and with the transmission of orders and intelligence, making it hard for one part of the line to know what was happening at another, they tended thereby to conceal from the defenders the dangers which surrounded them and from the attackers the chances which were within their grasp ; moreover, when attacks were broken up and officers could not exercise effective control over more than tiny handfuls of men, the calls on the initiative, tactical knowledge, and resourcefulness of the rank and file were greatly increased, a test to which the German infantry with all their devotion and good discipline were not exactly equal.

October 30th had thus ended with a loss of valuable ground, heavy losses in irreplaceable officers and men, with another battalion practically wiped out and with the survivors, wearier than ever, still indomitably patching up yet another new line to meet the certainty of renewed attacks in the near future.

Among the indomitable was certainly to be included the commander of the First Corps, for his orders for October 31st actually laid down that the offensive was to be taken against the Germans holding the line from Zand-voorde across the canal to Hollebeke. In this a French detachment which had been placed under Sir Douglas Haig's orders would be on the right, the left being formed by General Bulfin's force.[1] As General Bulfin's battalions

---

[1] This included, besides his own two battalions, three of the Second Division whom Lord Cavan had just brought down from nearer Polygon Wood. These were farther to the right nearer Klein Zillebeke.

advanced, the Gordons, whom the previous day had left
sandwiched in among them, were to close to their flank and
gain touch with the 22nd Brigade. From the exhausted
Seventh Division nothing in the nature of a counter-attack
could be expected. There were only three fragments of
battalions in reserve, the Grenadiers, Scots Guards, and
Borders,[1] and of the units in the front line more than one
was little stronger than a full company.

During the night of October 30th/31st a successful effort
was made to recover the 12th Battery's guns, and the
battery reassembled at Hooge to refit. Efforts were also
made to strengthen the new line, but the task was the more
difficult because it had been found necessary to utilize the
R.E. as infantry, and the 54th Field Company in particular
had had many casualties. On the Seventh Division's left
the 3rd Brigade was now holding the line in front of Gheluvelt, having the 1st Queen's at the point of the salient angle
where the line turned West, and detachments of the 2nd
K.R.R.C. and Loyal North Lancashires of the 2nd Brigade
on their right. Next came 100 Scots Fusiliers, and beyond
them the Bedfords, who were in touch with the Royal
Warwickshires, another handful doing duty as a battalion.
The South Staffordshires, who mustered rather under 400,
were on the Warwickshires' right and beyond them came
General Bulfin's force with the Gordons in the middle of its
line. About 80 Scots Fusiliers were in support nearer
Gheluvelt together with the Yorkshires, the 2nd Queen's
being in reserve to the 22nd Brigade on the Veldhoek–
Zandvoorde track about half a mile South of the Menin
road.

General Bulfin's attack was to start as soon as the French
on his right got level, but, somewhere about 7 a.m. on
October 31st, the Germans developed a tremendous bombardment. The French were soon checked, and fell back,
compelling " F " Battery R.H.A., which was in support of
them, to retire through Klein Zillebeke to Sanctuary Wood,

[1] These units dug in South of the Menin road a little to the East of Veldhoek.

though one section was left in action on the mound later
famous as " Hill Sixty." The result of the French retirement was that Bulfin's men, instead of advancing, found
the enemy attacking in force. The 25th Battery R.F.A.,
which had moved forward to support an attack, thus
found itself right up in the firing-line and under very heavy
fire. It was splendidly fought and did invaluable service,
but at a heavy cost ; and eventually about 4 p.m. machine-
gun fire at short range made its position quite untenable :
only by great skill and gallantry could the guns be extricated, the wagons having to be left behind until dark.
Much the same experience befell the 58th Battery, which
also had got right forward and came under very heavy fire
in consequence. But thanks largely to the help of the
artillery Bulfin's battalions were able to hold on all morning
and to check the German efforts to advance, though these
were vigorously pressed and supported by a great weight
of artillery.

The fighting on the right of the Division, West of
the Basseville brook, was heavy enough ; on the Division's left nearer Gheluvelt the situation was, if possible,
even more critical. Before the German bombardment
started the Scots Guards and Borders of the 20th Brigade, more than half the available reserve, had been
brought forward to entrench a second line behind the 21st
Brigade on the Eastern edge of the wood later on known as
Herenthage Wood. They found the shelling quite terrific :
" the amount of ammunition used by the Germans must
have been something colossal," writes one account ; " only
the very stoutest troops could have stood such a severe
bombardment." That the exhausted remnants of battalions in the front line should have stuck so tenaciously to
apologies for trenches is enormously to their credit, for
stick on they did against overwhelming odds. The Germans had brought up still more fresh troops and were
determined to force their way through, and the infantry
attacks were pressed with great vigour, especially up the

main road against Gheluvelt. The details, still more the
exact sequence, of the fight can hardly be established with
any accuracy; it is fairly clear that somewhere before noon
the Germans broke the line on both flanks of the 1st Queen's
and, pressing forward, isolated and overwhelmed that
battalion, which was cut to pieces, making a splendid
stand. The penetration of the line to the right of the 1st
Queen's brought disaster to the handful of Scots Fusiliers
in the front line who were taken in flank and rear and overwhelmed. A similar fate overtook about half of " C "
Company of the Bedfords under Captain Lemon, who were
holding a small fir-wood 200 yards in advance of the line.
Quite early on Germans were seen trying to push past both
flanks of this wood, which covered a dangerous gap, and
a heavy toll was taken of them. But when, about 1 p.m.,
orders were received from Brigade Headquarters for the
Bedfords to fall back to the support line, this party could
not be withdrawn. Some of the battalion achieved this
but losses were heavy; Major Traill, the C.O., and Major
Stares, the second in command, were both killed in holding
on to the front trenches while seven other officers were
casualties.[1] At the support line a stand was made while
the Yorkshires, who now found themselves in front line,
held on till after dark, doing great execution among the
German infantry and giving another of the many examples
of small detachments whose steadfast resistance, when
isolated and in apparently hopeless straits, contributed
greatly to break up the German attacks and to prevent
them exploiting to the full their successes and opportunities.
If the German leadership seems at times to have been indifferent, that so many such stands were successfully made is a
great tribute to the steadiness, tenacity, coolness, and resolution of the " serving soldiers " of the Seventh Division.
    When the left of the 21st Brigade was overwhelmed the

---

[1] The battalion was now left with its Adjutant, Transport Officer, and
Quartermaster, with one newly arrived Special Reserve subaltern attached
from another regiment.

Germans seem to have pushed forward South of Gheluvelt
and fallen upon the other detachment of the Scots
Fusiliers, that under Colonel Baird-Smith, which was in
second line about S.W. of Gheluvelt. This party put up
a fine fight, but it was attacked in front, from its left
rear, and also from the right, where the Germans had
got in between it and the Bedfords. Somewhere about
2 p.m. the resistance of this handful seems to have been
overcome, and it was then that the Germans, pressing
on West and simultaneously streaming forward in force
from Zandvoorde, pushed back the front line of the
22nd Brigade, which till then had maintained its position
despite all attacks. The Warwickshires, finding their
left flank and rear exposed by the falling back of the
21st Brigade, tried to cover that flank by occupying
some trenches facing about East ; their new trenches
were shallow and bad and their field of fire was poor,
but they held on long enough to allow a field battery just
behind them to be successfully got away. Then, their
ammunition being exhausted and the enemy already well
behind them, the survivors tried to cut their way through,
but came under a terrific fire and were either shot down or
intercepted and taken. A similar fate overtook many
of the South Staffords farther to the right ; they found
Germans working round their outer flank and were compelled to retire to avoid being cut off. Thus just North
of Zandvoorde there seemed nothing to check the German
advance. However, the 22nd Brigade did not retreat
far. By tremendous efforts, in which the Divisional Commander, who had just come up to see General Lawford,
also took a conspicuous part, the Brigadier and his staff [1]
soon rallied it, and thanks to their exertions the remnants of the front line battalions came forward again,[2]

[1] Captain Barker, the Staff Captain, who did fine work at this time, was
killed later in the day.

[2] R.-S.-M. Baker of the South Staffords got the D.C.M. for splendid work in
rallying and reorganizing the survivors of his battalion.

though now a mere handful with hardly any officers. Unluckily their right flank was much exposed as General Bulfin's left had also been forced back to a position on the Eastern edge of the wood afterwards known as Shrewsbury Forest. The 22nd Brigade was therefore unable to maintain the ground it had regained and fell back once more.

The thrusting back of the 22nd Brigade's front line naturally exposed the 2nd Queen's who formed its supports. That battalion had dug in during the night on the Eastern slope of the Basseville valley just West of the Veldhoek–Zandvoorde road ; fairly early in the morning these positions were made quite untenable by the fury of the bombardment, and their defenders were withdrawn into the Herenthage woods in rear, where they dug in afresh near the line on which the 20th Brigade was entrenched, and covering some guns of the 104th and 105th Batteries which had been pushed forward to give close support to the infantry. Some men under Major Crofts, however, held on to the first position, despite the shelling ; they could see Germans crossing the brook away to their right rear and in consequence already well behind them, but they maintained their ground nevertheless for some time till, after Major Crofts had been disabled, they too were forced back. The rest of the battalion, however, held on in its second position despite the heavy shelling, and actually counter-attacked, pushing forward across the Veldhoek–Zandvoorde road, to allow the guns to get away. Colonel Coles was wounded in leading this advance, but his men held on till dusk, when they were withdrawn to Herenthage Château, having materially helped to check the German advance.

Equally effective work was being done meanwhile by the 20th Brigade nearer to the Menin road. The overwhelming of the 21st Brigade and the German success in capturing Gheluvelt had left the Borders and Scots Guards as the only obstacle to the continued advance

of the enemy through the woods just South of the
Menin Road. They were now attacked in great force,
the Germans swarming forward in such overwhelming
numbers that, despite the effective fire which Borders
and Scots Guards poured into them, it seemed hopeless
to arrest their advance.

To reinforce these two battalions, or rather to prolong
their line to the right, the 200 survivors of the Grenadiers
were now brought forward by General Ruggles-Brise
just in time to meet the Germans streaming forward
from the Gheluvelt–Zandvoorde road towards that from
Zandvoorde to Veldhoek. The Grenadiers had advanced
through a regular storm of shells and many of them had
fallen, but the survivors opened a most effective fire,
doing tremendous execution on the extraordinarily fine
targets presented to them. The Germans came on in
dense masses, but with conspicuous absence of leading
or direction, their advances being unorganized and disjointed. Those who came forward directly against the
20th Brigade were checked by its accurate and destructive
rifle fire, and few got within three hundred yards
of the line : those who pressed forward beyond the
right flank of the Grenadiers, though heavily punished
by enfilade fire, made no attempt to turn right-handed
and roll up the line from the right, but crossed the
Veldhoek road and the brook and disappeared into the
woods beyond.

The position of the 20th Brigade seemed hopelessly
compromised, but there was no question of retiring.
Captain Brooke, General Ruggles-Brise's Staff Captain,
promptly went off to find Divisional Headquarters and
tell General Capper what was happening. He arrived
to find that the General had already got into touch with
General Bulfin, that the latter was advancing to counter-
attack, and that the Gordons, who had been sent back
to prepare a position farther to the rear, had been recalled
to join in the stroke. The Northumberland Hussars,

almost the only reserves under General Capper's control, were put in to support this effort; the Royals and 10th Hussars of the 3rd Cavalry Division also came up on the left, the 26th Field Company and half the Oxfordshire L.I. joined in on the right, linking up Lord Cavan's battalions with General Bulfin's right. Still the total force employed cannot have nearly equalled the Germans in front of them, for the enemy had put in the whole 39th Division [1] of their 15th Corps, and it was almost fresh, having only come into the line on the previous day.

Disparity in numbers notwithstanding, the 39th Division failed altogether to stem Bulfin's attack or to hold on to the gains it had made. The Gordons had lost heavily that day, but in the final counter-stroke they had the satisfaction of taking a full vengeance for their losses. When General Bulfin saw them coming up, led by their giant Adjutant, Captain Stansfeld, now the senior officer present, he ordered them to form a single line and to push forward through the wood, cheering and making as much noise as possible, so as to make the Germans think a big force was coming up. Directly they started cheering the firing-line was to open rapid fire, and when the Gordons reached the front the Sussex and Northamptons were to join in the charge.

The plan worked admirably: when 300 yards away from the firing-line the Gordons started cheering. On that there came a burst of rapid fire from the firing-line, a "mad minute" at the rate of 18 rounds such as the Germans had never dreamt of, and as the Highlanders reached the firing-line all rose up together and went for the Germans. The latter turned and ran, pursued hotly by Bulfin's men. There was not much taking of prisoners, but the flying Germans were bayoneted and shot in

[1] The other half of the 15th Corps, the 30th Division, had carried out the attack on the 21st and 22nd Brigades, and the 4th Bavarian Division was in action against the French between Klein Zillebeke and the Canal,

hundreds,[1] and the counter-stroke was carried forward
to a depth of over half a mile, when it was within 100
yards of the original line of the morning. Here along
the Eastern edge of Shrewsbury Forest it halted[2] and the
men dug in, little disturbed by the Germans, while later
on various rallied stragglers of the Seventh Division came
up to reinforce on the left.

This successful counter-stroke not only restored the
position between the Basseville brook and Klein Zillebeke,
it enabled the advanced parties of Yorkshires and Bedfords
to be extricated and drawn back to the new position
which the Division was trying to entrench. This started
from a point about 200 yards S.E. of Veldhoek cross-roads,
where it joined the right of the First Division, ran South
and a little West to cross the Basseville brook about
1,500 yards N.W. of Zandvoorde, whence it continued
West of Klein Zillebeke, Bulfin's force taking over from
the Seventh Division about 500 yards West of the stream.
The left of this line was held by the 21st Brigade, in other
words by the Yorkshires and Bedfords,[3] for the Scots
Fusiliers were now reduced to little over 100 men, mainly
the transport party and other details who had not been
in line. The Yorkshires were on the left, the Bedfords,
flung back almost at right angles, being astride the Basseville brook and facing South along the edge of the Herenthage woods. The 20th Brigade, well under 1,000 all
told,[4] continued the line Westward to join up with Bulfin's

---

[1] The Gordons alone were said to have killed about 300.

[2] It was then rather after 5 p.m.

[3] The Bedfords, who mustered 4 officers and rather over 350 men, were
reinforced next day by a welcome draft of 2 officers and 96 men. The total
strength of the brigade was under 1,000, though a certain number of men who
had got detached and had joined up with other units turned up during the
next few days.

[4] The figures given in the Brigade Diary are: Grenadiers, 5 officers and
200 men ; Scots Guards, 5 and 250 ; Borders, 5 and 270 ; Gordons, 3 and
200—a total of 18 officers and 920 men, which of course includes the four
Quartermasters, the transport detachments, orderly room and battalion
headquarter staffs, so that it does not mean anything like 900 rifles in the line.

force. This left the remnants of the 22nd Brigade, about 500 bayonets, as the only reserve.[1]

During the night of October 31st/November 1st there was not a little movement, readjusting the line to get it into conformity with that held by General Bulfin. Units were shifted about ; the Scots Guards and Borders, for example, who had been relieved by the 21st Brigade, moved over to the right of the new line, while the Grenadiers went back to dug-outs at Herenthage Château. As they withdrew they came across two apparently abandoned field-guns close behind the old trenches of the 22nd Brigade, with their detachments lying around them, having been one and all shot down at their post. These guns the Grenadiers and Scots Guards, with the help of some Bedfords, man-handled back into safety and handed them over to their battery, the 105th. A section of the 106th Battery also had been in action near the " Tower Hamlets," and had maintained a heavy fire on the woods South of Gheluvelt, reducing the range as the enemy came on, till at last it had been silenced by machine-gun fire and shelling at close range,[2] and had passed for a time into German hands ; the German advance past Gheluvelt going beyond this position. However, in retiring after the 2nd Worcestershire retook the village, the Germans had failed to carry off these prizes, and in the evening the teams were brought up and got the guns away.[3]

October 31st is usually reckoned the most critical day in the whole struggle to keep the Germans out of Ypres,

[1] Every one of the twelve battalions in the Division had by now lost its C.O. Colonels King, Cadogan, Loring, and Major Traill had been killed; Colonels Earle, Bolton, Baird-Smith, and Forbes were prisoners; the other four had been wounded.

[2] The detachments being practically wiped out, the subaltern in charge managed to remove the breech-blocks and dial-sights but had to leave the guns.

[3] Three D.C.M.'s were awarded to this section, to Sergt. Warr, Gunner Laley, and Corporal Holmes, who had continued to work the guns though all the rest of the detachments had been knocked out.

though the most celebrated incidents of the day had taken
place North rather than South of the Menin road.   Still,
the Worcestershire's famous counter-attack, the fine
defence of Gheluvelt Château by the South Wales
Borderers, and the stubborn resistance of the 1st Brigade
and Second Division farther to the North, would have been

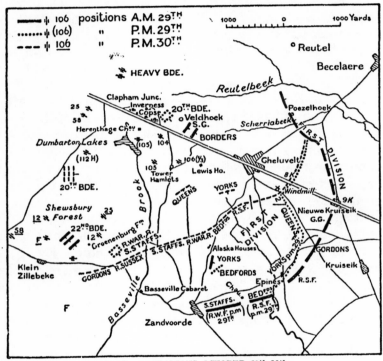

MAP 7.—OPERATIONS OCTOBER 29th-30th.

of no avail had the 15th Corps managed to overrun the
Seventh Division and the troops co-operating with it on
its right.   The Germans did overwhelm the scanty detachments scattered along its front line, they ought to have
easily rolled up the slender reserves which then interposed
between them and the guns, but they had failed to utilize
their chances and had in the end allowed themselves to be
thrust back and yet another new line to be somehow

patched up by their resolute and tenacious opponents.
Once again the very audacity of the little force which
presumed to hold a position out of all proportion to its
actual strength against greatly superior numbers of fresher
troops had imposed on the Germans, who could not credit
any troops with attempting to achieve impossibilities
and therefore pictured the Seventh Division as having
behind it vast reserves. The success of General Bulfin's
counter-attack was in part due to the Germans expecting
it and believing that here at last the British were bringing
into action their long and carefully concealed reserves.

Luckily for the much-tried Seventh Division the first
few days of November saw some relaxation in the intensity
of the strain. The battle continued, but the 15th Corps
did not display any marked anxiety to press in against
the Seventh Division. On both its flanks there were
important incidents and critical moments, but the Division
itself was less severely tried, though the exhausted fragments of its infantry were sufficiently strained by merely
holding on in hastily dug trenches which were none too
well sited and very far from complete. They had their
share of fighting, too. The French were now arriving in
force and taking over the line between the right of the
First Corps and the left of Allenby's cavalry, and it was
still hoped that they would manage to recover some of the
lost ground S.E. of Ypres. But their advance on November
1st between Klein Zillebeke and the canal came to an early
standstill ; Bulfin's men, who were to have fallen on the
flank of the Germans as the French pushed them back,
had therefore no chance of carrying out their part in the
programme, and on the contrary the Germans themselves
attacked, first against Bulfin's battalions, and then against
the 20th Brigade, till finally the attack spread all along
the line, involving the 21st Brigade also. The shelling
developed into quite a serious bombardment. However,
when the infantry attacks were delivered, they lacked
vigour and determination, and, weak and exhausted as

were the remnants of the Seventh Division, they repulsed
every advance without much difficulty. The 20th Brigade
did not have to call up the Grenadiers from their dug-outs
in the Herenthage woods ; the 22nd Brigade, too, remained
undisturbed in reserve, and the chief incident was that
Lieut. Lamb, the Borders' machine-gun officer, caught a
German battalion crossing his front from one wood to
another at about 800 yards range. He opened fire with
tremendous effect, shooting them down in scores, barely
60 escaping, and though this drew heavy fire on the Borders
which knocked out the machine-gun and its team, the
battalion's 20 casualties were but a fraction of those it had
inflicted. Opposite the 21st Brigade the Germans massed
in the woods, but were too effectively fired on to achieve
any advance, and the day ended with the Division's line
intact ; indeed one battalion notes in its diary that the
R.E. actually managed to put up some wire. What was
even more satisfactory was that drafts appeared for one
or two battalions, while some units found their scanty
numbers slightly increased by the collecting together of
various small parties and isolated individuals who had
got separated during the fighting. It proved necessary,
however, to reorganize the 22nd Brigade as two battalions,
one under Captain Alleyne of the Queen's consisting of
that battalion and about 80 survivors of the R.W.F., the
other of the South Staffords and the Warwickshires with
four officers attached from the Queen's, who alone had
any to spare, under Captain Vallentin of the South
Staffords.

The next day (November 2nd) saw rather more serious
fighting on the left flank, where the Germans, pressing
forward from Gheluvelt up the Menin road, scored a success
over the 1st K.R.R.C. and threatened the left of the 21st
Brigade. So serious was the situation at one time that
more than half the 22nd Brigade had to be put in to assist
the 21st to maintain its position. This, however, it
continued to do, the Bedfords getting effective enfilade

fire into enemy who were collecting to attack the Scots Guards, while the supporting artillery,[1] notably the XXIInd Brigade R.F.A., fired to no small purpose, nipping German attacks in the bud. Actually it was the right battalion of the Division, the Borders, who came in for the heaviest fighting. About 11 a.m. the Northamptons, the left battalion of Lord Cavan's [2] force, were shelled out of their left trenches and fell back a little way, uncovering the Borders' right. For some time the Germans made no advance.; then about 1 p.m. they suddenly pressed forward into the gap and at the same time advanced against the Borders' front. The attack was heralded by a tremendous blowing of bugles, but this merely served to warn the British reserves to move up, and, when the Germans came on, the Borders held their fire till the advance was close to the wire which they had managed to put up. Then they let fly with devastating effect, knocking over from 200 to 300 Germans and driving the rest back into the sheltering woods. Here they rallied and came on again. The same scene was again enacted, but that the withdrawal of some troops on the right allowed the Germans to push on past the Borders' flank. There was a perilous moment in which the battalion seemed about to be outflanked and rolled up, but Sergeant Booth averted the danger by rushing up two platoons from reserve ; these reoccupied the vacated trenches in the nick of time and kept the enemy at bay until help came up in the shape of the 2nd Worcestershire, now acting as General Capper's Divisional Reserve, along with the Cyclists and the Northumberland Hussars. When that night the Borders were relieved by the Grenadiers and taken back into reserve

[1] The guns had now been moved back to new positions, the XIVth Brigade R.H.A. being three-quarters of a mile S.W. of Hooge, the XXIInd Brigade R.F.A. close to Hooge, and the 25th and 58th Batteries of the XXXVth Brigade near Zillebeke Lake, the 12th Battery being still out of action but refitting. The Heavy Batteries were near Westhoek.

[2] He was now in command of all General Bulfin's battalions, as that officer had been wounded on November 1st.

they received special praise and congratulations on their
tenacity from General Capper. They had had over 50
casualties, but had inflicted many times that number.
The Scots Guards, who had also been attacked, but only
in front, had dealt quite successfully with their opponents,
but the Brigadier, General Ruggles-Brise, was among the
day's casualties.[1] He was succeeded temporarily by the
Brigade Major, Major Cator, the only field officer left in
the Brigade.

By this time the line was becoming a trifle more defensible. Some wire had been put out, and something had
been done towards deepening and improving the trenches
and making them continuous. The R.E. had worked
indefatigably and were beginning to erect strong points
and redoubts in rear, intended to break up any attack
which might penetrate the line. But neither on November
3rd or November 4th did any attack look like achieving as
much. On the first of these days the Germans maintained
a steady bombardment, but their only real advance,
against the 21st Brigade's left in the early afternoon, was
so effectively discouraged by guns and rifles directly their
men emerged from the shelter of the woods that it withered
away at once. Much the same thing happened in front of
the 20th Brigade, for the guns were turned on so promptly
and effectively when the first signs of a German concentration in the woods were discovered that it never
developed into a serious attack. The artillery, too, with
the assistance of the R.F.C., who successfully located
several German batteries, did some very satisfactory
shooting, silencing the opposing guns or at least forcing
them to change their positions. The 12th Battery, which
had had such a bad time on October 30th, contrived to
get three of its guns into action again on the 3rd, and these
along with the 25th Battery and " F " Battery R.H.A.
lent very effective support to Lord Cavan's battalions,

---

[1] Captain Douglas, the G.S.O. 3 of the Division, was also wounded on this
day ; he subsequently died of his wounds.

while the arrival of over 700 reinforcements for the infantry
was very welcome. Desultory shelling in the morning of
the 4th developed into a regular bombardment in the
afternoon, but though about 2 p.m. German infantry tried
to advance against the junction of the 20th and 21st
Brigades, the Scots Guards and Bedfords soon sent them
back, and the Division could even send off a company of
the Queen's to help the right of the First Division, where
pressure was reported severe. But the day was marked
by a serious loss to the Division, and indeed to the whole
Army, Captain James, General Lawford's Brigade Major,
being killed by shell fire. An officer of exceptional promise,
he had done splendid work throughout the operations and
would have gone far had he lived. The 22nd Brigade's
Staff had indeed been unlucky ; the Staff Captain, Capt.
Barker, had been killed on October 31st, the Interpreter
had been wounded, Lieut. O'Connor, the Signalling Officer,
had been disabled by an accident, and General Lawford
alone was left ; while two subalterns of the Queen's who
were appointed to officiate as Brigade Major and Staff
Captain were both knocked out on November 5th
when in billets in Ypres, which the Germans were then
bombarding.

November 5th brought renewed heavy shelling in the
morning—" The Fifth well kept, a rare shelling and some
trenches blown in," is one officer's account—and some of
the trenches of the 20th Brigade were evacuated by order
to reduce casualties, but directly the Germans tried to come
forward these trenches were reoccupied and the enemy's
advance was promptly checked. In front of the Gordons
the Germans tried to bring a field-gun up to close quarters,
but the Gordons' musketry was equal to stopping the gun
before it could get within 800 yards of the trenches, the
team being all shot down and the gun kept out of action
all day. As before, the Division's guns did much to help
Lord Cavan's infantry, who were having a bad time.
Some more drafts turned up, but even more welcome was

the news that the Division, or rather its infantry, was about
to be relieved. The Indian Corps had by this time taken
over the Givenchy–Neuve Chapelle line from the Second
Corps and this set free a composite force of two brigades
to replace the Seventh Division, whose relief was begun
on the night of November 5th/6th, the 20th Brigade being
relieved by the 7th, which included the 1st Gordons, the
21st Brigade by the 15th, in which the 1st Bedfords were
serving. Neither of these units, however, actually took
over from its own 2nd Battalion.

The whole Division did not obtain a relief. All the
artillery except the XXXVth Brigade R.F.A. was left
behind, along with the 55th Field Company and some of
the Signal Company, while the 22nd Brigade, now increased
by drafts to nearly 1,200 strong, was left at Dickebusch
as Corps Reserve to the First Corps, the 20th [1] and 21st,
who moved to Meteren and Bailleul on November 6th,
becoming General Reserve. Not for some days therefore
did the Seventh Division's share in the defence of Ypres
come to an end. The artillery continued to support Lord
Cavan until relieved [2] on November 13th, and though the
22nd Brigade had been sent back to rest some days earlier
it had had one very sharp action with heavy casualties.

This was on November 7th and formed a fitting conclusion to the Division's services in the great struggle for
Ypres. The brigade had been held in reserve and on
November 6th found itself in bivouac at a cross-roads 1½
miles S.E. of Dickebusch, when news was received that a
violent attack had driven in the French and thus enabled
the Germans to force back Lord Cavan's right. The
situation had been partially restored by a counter-attack
of the Household Cavalry, but it was essential to push the

---

[1] The 20th Brigade now mustered 24 officers and 1,381 other ranks.

[2] It had been very busily employed in the meantime, November 6th, 7th,
and 11th being all days of special activity and heavy firing. Great difficulty
was experienced in locating hostile guns in such thickly wooded country, and
the proximity of the opposing trench lines made it very hard indeed to give
our infantry as much support as might have been desired.

8

Germans further back. Accordingly, the 22nd Brigade, 14 officers and 1,100 men all told,[1] set off from its bivouac about 6 p.m., reached Zillebeke about 10 p.m., and spent the night near the farm which served as Lord Cavan's headquarters rather more than a mile farther East. About 5 a.m. next day it moved forward again to the chosen position for deployment.

This was in rear of a slight rise in the ground just where there was a narrow clearing in the woods, the front German trench being on the edge of the woods about 300 to 400 yards away. By 6 a.m. the brigade was formed up with the Queen's in front, the South Staffords supporting them and the handful of the Warwickshires in reserve. At 6.15 a.m., just as it was beginning to get light, the signal was given and the troops dashed forward. Directly they topped the rise they were met by a sharp fire from rifles and machine-guns, but the Queen's were not to be stopped. They carried the front German trench with so impetuous a rush that they swept forward on the heels of the flying enemy to another trench 100 yards farther on. This, too, they carried, taking three machine-guns and inflicting considerable losses on the enemy. However, so weak a force could do little more once the enemy recovered from his surprise ; for the Germans, who had yet a third line of trenches 150 yards deeper into the wood, which was thick here and full of undergrowth, proved to be in considerable force, and before long their counter-attacks forced the troops back to the first line of trenches which they had carried on the edge of the wood. In this retirement the Queen's lost heavily, their commanding officer, Captain Alleyne, being wounded and taken prisoner, and the Adjutant, Lieut. Haigh, killed ; but at this German front line they rallied, assisted by the South Staffords [2] and the Warwickshires ;

---

[1] This excludes the few details with the transport.

[2] Captain Vallentin of the South Staffords, who was killed, received a posthumous V.C. for his gallant leading in this action : he had already distinguished himself by repeated acts of courage.

some of the 2nd Royal Sussex and details of the 3rd Brigade came up in support on their flanks and all the German efforts to push them farther back were successfully held up. The position was a bad one, however, forming a pronounced salient, as the rather belated French efforts to get forward on the right had met with no success ; it was decided therefore in the evening to bring the troops back to their starting line. But their effort had not been in vain. It had prevented the Germans from exploiting their previous day's success; it had allowed much to be done in improving and consolidating Lord Cavan's line ; and, like many other counter-attacks by small bodies, it contributed to impress the Germans with the idea that they had large forces opposed to them. The audacity— it may well be called the impudence—of these counter-attacks by handfuls was an important factor in the successful defence of Ypres, and it was highly appropriate that the Seventh Division's last exploit in that defence should have taken this shape.

The 22nd Brigade had suffered severely enough in this effort. The Queen's had lost six officers and about 100 men, the South Staffords had lost equally heavily, the total in the brigade coming to 10 officers and 304 men, so that when it rejoined the Division its strength was less than the establishment of one battalion and it had only four combatant officers with it.

The Seventh Division's share in the defence of Ypres stands out as the most memorable of its exploits in the war, much as it was to accomplish in the succeeding years— at Loos, on the Somme, at Ecoust and Bullecourt, at Ypres again in 1917, and in Italy. The Division was plunged suddenly into the fiery trials of Ypres almost before it had had time to get together and to acquire cohesion and unity. It was called on to withstand a series of attacks by fresh troops in numbers greatly superior to its own. Inadequately supplied with artillery, without howitzers and modern heavy guns, very scantily provided with ammunition, it had to face bombardments of exceptional severity in trenches which it had had the scantiest of time to dig and prepare for defence. It had to hold a length of line out of all proportion to the guns and rifles available. Its officers and men were in action continually with the briefest and most inadequate opportunities for rest. The First and Second Divisions may have been engaged in the struggle for a longer period than the Seventh : neither of them had quite the same length of line to defend single-handed. The units of the Second Corps who replaced the Seventh Division came into the Salient exhausted and weakened after a fortnight's bitter fighting round La Bassée ; but though they had much to endure and deserve the greatest credit for an important share in keeping the Germans back from the Channel Ports, the edge had been to some extent taken off the German attacks before they came in, and in the last ten days of the battle the German pressure was distinctly diminished. To bring out fully what individuals and units endured, to describe a tithe of the deeds that deserve to be remembered, is out of the question ; partly from lack of space, even more from lack of material. The records of the fighting that have survived are scanty, imperfect, often inaccurate and confused, often hard to reconcile with one another. There was little time or opportunity to note them down at the moment : sterner and more pressing calls had to be met. Many of those who survived fell later in the war without having contributed what they might have brought to the collecting of records ; those who have survived not only First Ypres but the other murderous struggles which followed it have often but hazy recollections. But besides the deeds of which some record survives there are all the unrecorded and often unwitnessed things that were happening all along the line—isolated stands by little parties, individuals fighting to the last with their backs to the wall, a platoon sticking grimly to its battered trench till the last man was hit. Any attempt to tell the story must

necessarily therefore fall very far short of what one would
like to make it, but it has been well said that the Seventh
Division left the Salient "a mere wreck . . . its fighting
power nearly exhausted, but its fame secure for all time,"
and with that the Division may well be content.   It owed
much to its commander, whose energy and resourcefulness
were untiring, who never despaired, who was happiest when

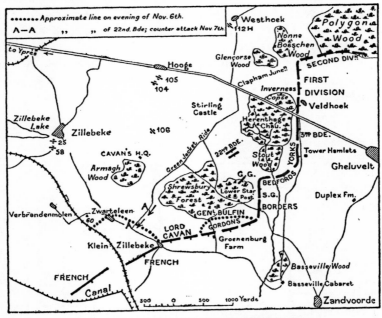

MAP 8.—OPERATIONS OCTOBER 31st-NOVEMBER 6th.

up in the front trenches in the thickest of the battle.   It
was fortunate in its brigadiers, who seconded their commander splendidly, doing their utmost with their scanty
reserves to fill gaps in the thinning line, always on the
look out to lend any help they could to other portions of
the line.   All arms worked together splendidly, and the
Division, improvised formation though it was, fell but
little short in cohesion and co-operation of those six who
composed the original "Striking Force."   It had often

been remarked that, if one wanted to see the British Army properly, one ought to see not its units at home, but those on service abroad. The Seventh Division was mainly composed of units from abroad, full of fully-grown and fully-trained men : it contained but few young soldiers just out of the recruit stage and not many Reservists, rather rusty and out of touch with military life, and to that, too, it owed much : its splendid stand does substantially bear out the claim that has been made for these units on the Indian and Colonial establishments. It is not claimed for the Seventh Division that its performance in any way surpassed the achievements of its six predecessors, but it suffered from special disadvantages from which they were free.[1]

[1] YPRES CASUALTIES

	Killed.		Missing.		Wounded.		Total.	
	Officers.	Men.	Officers.	Men.	Officers.	Men.	Officers.	Men.
Staff . . .	2	13	1	7	7	26	10	46
R.A. . . .	3	31	—	23	13	185	16	239
R.E. and Signals .	3	11	—	11	1	62	4	84
Northumberland Hussars . .	—	3	—	1	6	17	6	21
Cyclists . .	—	1	1	9	—	20	1	30
Grenadier Guards .	6	83	—	315	14	277	20	675
Scots Guards . .	6	41	8	529	8	204	22	774
Borders . . .	9	79	—	253	11	259	20	591
Gordons . . .	7	88	2	161	21	289	30	538
Bedfords . . .	9	75	2	151	18	324	29	550
Yorkshires . .	8	104	—	153	17	374	25	631
R. Scots Fusiliers .	3	91	8	488	15	288	26	867
Wiltshires . .	5	53	19	574	2	116	26	743
Queen's . . .	3	75	—	283	25	441	28	799
R. Warwickshires .	7	88	12	342	9	357	28	787
R. Welch Fusiliers .	7	72	15	724	15	228	37	1,024
S. Staffords . .	6	25	5	742	17	97	28	864
Train . . .	—	1	—	6	—	1	—	8
R.A.M.C. . . .	1	1	4	28	3	2	8	31
Total . . .	85	935	77	4,800	202	3,567	364	9,302

CHAPTER V

EXHAUSTED as was the Seventh Division when it left the " Salient " with which its name will always be associated, reduced to fragments as were its infantry units, only the briefest period of rest could be allowed it. There were other dangerously weak places in the British line where reinforcements were urgently needed, notably opposite Rouges Bancs where the right of the Sixth Division joined the Indian Corps. The Sixth had not had as much or as heavy fighting as had fallen to the other Divisions of the B.E.F., but it had held a much longer stretch of line and had been in trenches practically without intermission or relief ever since the middle of October. It was imperative to shorten its line enough to allow some of its units to be relieved. Accordingly the Seventh Division could only be given an altogether insufficient time for the rest and reconstruction it so badly needed before it had to return to the trenches.

Its need for rest and reconstruction was of the greatest. A few reinforcements had arrived just before it left the Ypres Salient, but of the 225 officers and 8,486 men reported as present on November 7th the infantry—normally two-thirds of the Division's establishment—accounted for under a third of the officers and a bare half of the men.[2] The weakness in officers was the worst feature of the situation— few battalions had enough for the necessary administrative

---

[1] Cf. Maps 9 and 10.

[2] The actual figures were: 20th Brigade, 30 officers and 1,728 men; 21st Brigade, 24 and 1,606; 22nd Brigade, weakened by its losses in its attack at Klein Zillebeke, 10 and 921. The Bedfords with 9 officers and 550 men were easily the strongest battalion, the Grenadiers, Scots Guards, and Yorkshires could show between 450 and 500 all told, the Borders and Gordons over 400.

work or for imparting to the newly arrived drafts the instruction which so many of them needed, to say nothing of commanding them in action. The Gordons with five officers to over 400 men were the worst off, and reorganization was much delayed by the shortage of officers.[1]

As one means of supplying the deficiency it was decided to attach to each battalion four " probationary 2nd Lieutenants " taken from the Artists' Rifles and this experiment was not slow to justify itself. The Artists, like other crack Territorial units, were full of good material for officers, many of whom had joined up in the ranks at once rather than wait about for a commission, and the first batch of probationers who came to the Seventh Division contained several who were to distinguish themselves, though many were to be prematurely cut off within the next few months.

Reinforcements on the extensive scale required by the Division were not to be found in a moment. Of its infantry units only the Yorkshires and Borders had not got a sister-battalion already serving in the B.E.F., and in some cases, notably the Queen's, whose 1st Battalion had been wiped out at Gheluvelt on October 31st, and the Wiltshires, whose 1st Battalion had lost very heavily indeed in defending Neuve Chapelle against overwhelming odds, the other battalion's demands on the draft-finding powers of its Special Reserve unit equalled those of the battalion in the Seventh Division. Losses in the B.E.F. had altogether outstripped the calculations of those responsible for framing establishments and organizing the replacement of casualties. Most 3rd Battalions had

---

[1] A return of November 18th, 1914, gives the officers present with the infantry units and shows the respective figures of Regulars, Reserve of Officers, and Special Reserve to be as follows: Grenadiers, 2, 8, 5; Scots Guards, 11, 6, 5; Borders, 6, 0, 2; Gordons, 4, 0, 2; Bedfords, 5, 0, 5; Yorkshires, 4, 0, 5; Scots Fusiliers, 7, 1, 2; Wiltshires, 3, 0, 0; Queen's, 8, 0, 2; Royal Warwickshires, 5, 0, 1; R.W.F., 7, 0, 1.

Many of these Regulars were newly Gazetted officers from the R.M.C. or recently promoted from the ranks, and several were attached from other regiments. Each unit had also four " probationers " from the Artists.

already shipped off to France nearly all the young soldiers left behind to complete their training, with practically all the Regular Reservists and many of those serving on the Special Reserve engagement. If they were full to overflowing it was with recruits who had joined since the declaration of war and whose training, conducted under great difficulties over equipment, housing, clothing, ammunition and weapons, was as yet far from complete. Any number of old soldiers whose Reserve time had been up long ago had hastened to re-enlist, and these formed a large proportion among the drafts which now replenished the shattered units of the Seventh Division. There were fine and experienced men among them, veterans who did most useful work, but they included also not a few who were quite unfit for the hardships of that trench warfare to which the Division was about to settle down. Life in trenches in mid-winter, especially in the low-lying valley of the Lys, where any depression tended to fill with water, was a severe trial even to the young and robust until systematic arrangements for washing and drying clothes, for bathing, for cooking in the trenches, and for making conditions more bearable could be devised, and the thousand-and-one things requisite in trench warfare supplied in adequate quantities : for the middle-aged and for those in any way affected by campaigns and service in tropical countries it was infinitely worse ; indeed the marvel was that the sick-rate was not much higher.

Shortage of material was another trouble which delayed the reconstitution of the Division. Only three battalions, the Scots Guards, South Staffords, and Wiltshires, possessed even one machine-gun : several had lost all or part of their transport, most batteries had had wagons destroyed or badly damaged, several had had guns put out of action or in need of repair. The R.E. companies had expended many of their tools and had long lists of stores required, and it did not make matters easier that most of the artillery and one Field Company had been left behind at

Ypres and did not rejoin the Division for several days.[1]
The two Heavy Batteries indeed were not relieved till the
French took over the Salient, and it was November 22nd
before the 112th came under the Division's orders again ;
it had then been in action for 32 days continuously without
relief.

Long before that the Division had gone into line.
General Capper on reaching Bailleul on November 6th
had been placed in command of the General Reserve, which
included several units of the Fifth Division besides his own
Division.   On November 9th he had to send off the 21st
Brigade to support the Third Corps at Ploegsteert, where
heavy fighting on November 7th had resulted in some loss
of ground.   The brigade did not actually go beyond the
support trenches and was not actively engaged, its casualties only amounting to a dozen ; but this interfered not a
little with the work of reconstruction and re-equipment.

This proceeded steadily nevertheless.   The gaps in the
Staff were soon filled, Brigadier-General Heyworth arriving
on November 14th to command the 20th Brigade, Major
Daly becoming A.A. & Q.M.G.   A Brigade Major for the
22nd Brigade was slower to appear : it was November
20th before Captain Thurlow joined.[2]   New commanding
officers arrived for several battalions—Major Brewis for
the Warwickshires, Major Gabbett, who had been wounded
on October 24th, for the R.W.F., Lieut.-Colonel Nicholson
for the XXXVth Brigade R.F.A.[3]   Major Corkran joined
the Grenadiers soon after the return to the line, when
also Major Denne took command of the Bedfords, and
gradually units began to look more like battalions again.

---

[1] The XIVth Brigade R.H.A. was relieved on November 14th and rejoined
the Division two days later, the XXIInd Brigade R.F.A. had been relieved a
day earlier, the XXXVth Brigade R.F.A. came out with the infantry.   The
55th Field Company was more fortunate, coming out on November 8th and
rejoining next day.

[2] Cf. Appendixes III and IV.

[3] The R.H.A. Brigade had already got a new C.O. before leaving Ypres,
Lieut.-Colonel Robinson having joined on November 6th.

The Yorkshires got a big draft of five officers and 513 men on November 15th, the Grenadiers one of 400 men on the 11th with another of 133 next day, while the Scots Guards, Queen's, Royal Warwickshires, Bedfords, and R.W.F. all received substantial reinforcements; the other battalions, however, remained very weak despite urgent appeals to the War Office for reinforcements,[1] and the South Staffords were detailed for temporary duty as Corps Troops, being replaced by the 8th Royal Scots, a fine Territorial battalion nearly 1,000 strong, which joined the 22nd Brigade at Merris on November 11th.

The Division had therefore to return to the line long before its reconstruction and re-equipment were complete. On November 14th it marched in three columns to Bac St. Maur (20th Brigade), Sailly (21st), and Croix du Bac (22nd), and that evening began relieving the Sixth Division on the line Rouges Bancs–Bridoux. The 20th Brigade went in on the right, the 22nd on the left, with La Boutillerie as their point of junction, the 21st remaining for the time as Corps Reserve, but eventually coming in in the centre, when the line was definitely divided into three sections, that on the right reaching from Rue Petillon to near La Cordonnerie Farm, the centre thence to just S.E. of La Boutillerie and the third to the Le Touquet–Bridoux road.

The line now entrusted to the Seventh Division could not from any point of view be described as good. It ran through the flat and water-logged valley of the Lys, more or less parallel to the slight rise in the ground glorified by the name of the Aubers Ridge, from which the Germans enjoyed considerable advantages in observation. It had been taken up accidentally rather than selected, much less planned; it contained not a few awkward salients and re-entrants, which registered the results of the fighting of

---

[1] At the end of November, when the Division had reached a total of over 15,000 of all ranks, four battalions were still much below strength, the Borders having only 16 officers and 431 men, the Wiltshires 15 and 502, the Scots Fusiliers 16 and 509, the Gordons 11 and 607.

October,[1] and had no tactical meaning or plan. It was practically continuous—till the wet weather came and rendered parts of it untenable, thereby isolating others. Communication trenches existed in some parts and had been begun in others, but were often too deep in mud and water to be much use. There was wire in places but nothing like enough, and the softness of the ground made revetting an urgent necessity. Behind the trenches there were still many undemolished buildings, and hedges and trees gave cover from view, while farther back there was a good variety and quantity of billets in which a fair degree of comfort could soon be obtained by those out of the line. A support line had been begun but was in a rudimentary stage, and it was easy to see that if the line was to be rendered defensible and habitable and in any degree satisfactory the Division must put in a prodigious amount of hard work, under very adverse conditions as regards drainage, supply of materials, and weather. Fortunately in these respects the Germans, whose lines were in places as near as 150 yards away, but elsewhere as much as 600, were no better off; and the Seventh Division soon found that little hostile interference with its work of trench-improvement was to be expected. Thus new-comers to the Division found themselves let in for far more labour than fighting. The Royal Scots note that they had to handle picks and shovels hard before ever they had occasion to use their rifles, and but little was seen of the enemy. There was occasional shelling, but the British guns were so strictly limited in their ration of shells that a brigade commander's sanction was almost necessary before even one could be fired, and the German artillery on their part were none too plentifully provided with ammunition and fired but seldom. German snipers were more active and occasionally were very troublesome—" quiet except for snipers " is a frequent

---

[1] The tendency had been to take advantage of dips in the ground which gave cover in fighting but which naturally were specially wet when the rain came.

entry in the Diaries of this period—but they sent out few
patrols and seemed to be anything but enterprising or
aggressive. The contrast after Ypres was startling to
those who had gone through that fearful ordeal, the
recollection of which was like a nightmare.

With the Germans thus inactive the Division could get

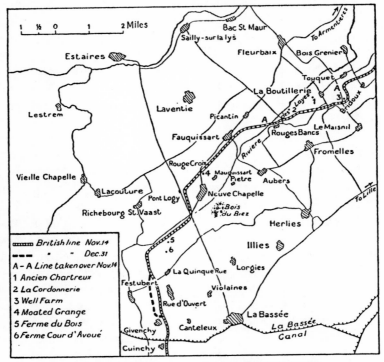

MAP 9.—POSITION IN LYS VALLEY WINTER 1914-15.

on with the all-essential strengthening of its line, while
units got a chance of shaking down quietly, of assimilating
the large drafts which had filled their depleted ranks, and
of recovering cohesion : the raw hands could be gradually
entered to war without being too severely tested at first,
and the strength of the Division was gradually built up
without any very heavy wastage from battle casualties.
Sickness was a severer drain—" trench-feet " began to

make their appearance, the result, it seemed, of having boots and puttees on continuously for days as well as of the wet and cold of the trenches. An unexpectedly early snap of cold and snow swelled the sick-rate, but was to some extent discounted by the issue of fur-clothing ; a large consignment of fur waistcoats is noted as having arrived on November 23rd, and braziers in the trenches with hot baths and dry clothing in billets helped to keep down the daily sick-returns. The daily issue of a rum ration was another useful innovation, proving a great restorative ; and if rations tended to be monotonous, consisting mainly of " bully beef " and Army biscuits with very rare issues of fresh meat, there was no shortage of them, tea, sugar, and potatoes being plentiful. But the conditions under which the men lived in the trenches were awful. A trench in which the water was less than ankle deep was exceptional ; little movement was possible in daylight, so that men were hard put to it to keep warm when there was little to be done except to sit. " Four miserable days in a drain with no shelter " is one summing up of a tour of duty. Night was a more active time than day. Under cover of darkness reliefs were carried out, ration parties came up, repairs and systematic improvement of the trenches could be undertaken, patrols and wiring parties were sent out. But even then there was the mud to contend against. It was everywhere, though at its worst in the so-called communication trenches, along which progress was always slow and often impossible, one leg at a time having to be pulled out of the mud and re-planted a little farther on to allow of the process being repeated with the other one. The mud had remarkable powers of suction—it could pull off boots and socks quite easily, and the Highland units in the Division came off very badly indeed. Shoes, spats, and hose could not compete with the mud and were drawn off wholesale ; at its worst the mud was rumoured to have disposed of kilts also.

Major operations at this time were clearly out of the question, both for reasons connected with the general situation on the Western Front and with the particular circumstances of the Seventh Division; but General Capper was not the sort of commander to let his troops become inactive or to be satisfied with a policy of "live and let live," and before long minor enterprises became fairly frequent. On the night of November 24th/25th, for example, a small party of Welch Fusiliers and R.E. successfully attacked a farm from which German snipers had been making themselves a nuisance, the farm being rushed and demolished without casualties; a few nights later a patrol of the Scots Guards carried out what may be regarded as the Division's first "raid" against the German trenches. The party included one officer, Lieut. Sir E. Hulse, and nine men: it went out down a ditch running towards the German lines, crossed No Man's Land, here a field of roots which delayed progress considerably, and got within ten yards of the German parapet undetected. On being challenged the party rushed forward to the parapet, and seeing a group of Germans clustering round a camp fire in the light of which they showed up clearly, blazed away and threw bombs, inflicting several casualties, while directly the party got home again, machine-guns and rifles opened heavy fire upon the German trenches, which were seen to be strongly manned; and the XXXVth Brigade R.F.A. chimed in, firing with the greatest accuracy and apparently considerable effect.

These activities and some vigorous patrolling did not greatly curtail the work of reconstructing trenches, which was steadily pushed on. As already indicated, the water problem was almost insoluble. The country was naturally apt to get water-logged in times of heavy rain, for the flatness made drainage slow, but the fighting had much increased the difficulties of draining, fallen trees and other debris had blocked natural channels, and the digging of trenches and building of breastworks made matters worse.

But, despite all difficulties, steady improvement was made, and the opening, albeit on a very restricted scale, of leave to England on November 29th was cheering, not only in itself but because it indicated that the Division's line was becoming reasonably secure.

December, at any rate its first fortnight, presented no new features. If the ground was getting more water-logged, much had been done to drain and improve the trenches. Steel loop-hole plates, issued before the end of November and found satisfactory, a limited supply of Hales grenades and Very lights, the arrival of the 55th Battery R.F.A., which provided the Division with the field-howitzers it had so long needed, all helped to improve matters. White smocks, first issued on November 19th, proved very useful for patrolling over snow-covered ground ; with the help of periscopes and of stalkers' field-glasses, provided by the National Service League, more could be done to keep down the sniper ; and by strict economy a small reserve of shells was built up for emergencies. The strength of the Division rose gradually, not only through the arrival of drafts, but from the addition of new units. During December 156 officers and 5,111 men joined the Division ; battle casualties came to 36 officers and 1,079 men and the total wastage to 77 officers and 2,775 men, a net gain of nearly 2,500 of all ranks. Of the weaker battalions the Borders had had a draft of 570 on December 2nd, the Wiltshires one of 300 on the 17th ; the South Staffords, who had rejoined the Division on the 13th, being then 470 strong, were more than doubled by a draft of 500 on the 21st ; but the Scots Fusiliers and Gordons continued much under their establishment. On December 5th the 6th Gordons had been added to the 20th Brigade, " T " Battery reinforced the R.H.A. Brigade on December 20th, while the Heavy Batteries were increased from four 4·7-inch guns each to six, though these ancient pieces were none too reliable in their shooting and were almost as likely to hit our own trenches as the enemy's. It was cruel to the gunners that they should be provided with such unsatisfactory weapons.

Of the battle-casualties of the month two-thirds occurred in a not very happily conceived enterprise undertaken on the night of December 18th/19th by orders from G.H.Q. With an optimism which did not indicate any very close acquaintance either with the state of the ground or with the general conditions in the front line, or any very accurate appreciation of the difficulties of attacking entrenched positions defended by modern rifles and machine-guns and protected by belts of barbed wire, the higher authorities of both the British and the French forces had decided upon resuming offensive operations, partly with the idea of profiting by the withdrawal, which had now become known, of several German divisions to the Russian front. The first stage in these operations was aimed at recovering the Messines Ridge. The Third Division attacked there in concert with the French on its left, but neither French nor British could make any serious progress, and General Joffre soon found himself compelled to abandon his offensive in Flanders, but decided to continue it North of Arras and begged Sir John French to do all he could to assist. Orders were therefore issued for local activities at various points in the British line to distract the attention of the Germans and, if possible, make small local gains. A year later these diversions would have taken the form of raids, but in December 1914 the raid had not yet been developed into a definite form of offensive, and in selecting objectives for his attacks General Capper had to think of retaining anything he reached.

Orders for greater activity on the part of the infantry in the trenches were issued by the Corps on December 13th, and at the same time the Divisional artillery indulged in such bombardments as its scanty ration of ammunition would allow. Thanks to the better organization for co-operation with the R.F.C. and to the practice which gunners and airmen were obtaining in combined work, it was

9

possible to get quite effective results from these bombardments, considering how little ammunition could be used. At the same time the Division's patrols developed considerable activity, bringing in plenty of information about the enemy's trenches and identifying their garrisons by capturing prisoners. A typical example of the patrol encounters which made such demands on the resource, daring, and initiative of officers and men occurred on the night of December 14th, when a party of the Queen's, 23 strong, under 2nd Lieut. Ramsay, left the British lines about 700 yards S.E. of La Boutillerie cross-roads to try to rush a German picquet which had previously been located. While a lance-corporal and six men moved straight forward towards the picquet with orders to divert its attention and draw its fire, the main body worked round to the right so as to get into position on the left rear of the picquet, intending to rush it from the flank as soon as it opened fire. On reaching the position he was aiming at 2nd Lieut. Ramsay noticed a small group of men between him and the picquet, and thinking it might be the rest of his party who had lost their way, sent an orderly to reconnoitre. Private Knowles, the orderly, crept forward and got right in among this party, when finding them to be Germans he shouted out, " Here they are ! Open fire." He was promptly bayoneted, but 2nd Lieut. Ramsay's party fired and followed up their volley with a charge, killing two Germans and wounding two others, one of whom was at once sent back to the British lines. A heavy fire was now opened from the main German trench, and as a prisoner had been taken and one of the objects of the enterprise thereby achieved, 2nd Lieut. Ramsay withdrew his party, covered by Corporal Lamond, who lay down and opened fire and then drew off in a different direction from the rest, thereby distracting the German attention. A messenger, Private Viney, was sent to warn the other party to withdraw, but approaching it from the direction of the German trenches he was mistaken for a German and shot : though mortally wounded he managed to deliver his message of recall before he died, thereby enabling the party to withdraw successfully. The battalion was warmly complimented on the success of the enterprise, and the information obtained from the prisoner proved most valuable, confirming an identification of the 55th Infantry Regiment of the 7th Corps as the immediate opponents of the Division.

The points finally selected for the Seventh Division's attacks were near La Boutillerie and Rouges Bancs. At the first the Warwickshires, supported by the Queen's, were to attack at 4.30 p.m. on December 18th ; their attack being preceded by a quarter of an hour's artillery bombardment—all the ammunition supply would permit.[1] It was to be followed at 6 p.m. by the 20th Brigade's attack, which was to dispense with a previous bombardment and to trust to surprise. In this both the Scots Guards and the Borders were to take part, and in case both attacks succeeded a third was to be made by the 21st Brigade with the Yorkshires leading.

The 22nd Brigade was attacking just West of the pronounced salient in its lines at Well Farm near La Boutillerie. The Warwickshires were to form up in these lines on a front of 200 yards and to advance on the close of the bombardment, the Queen's and South Staffords, who held the trenches to right and left, opening covering fire as they went forward. Two companies, " C " and " D," of the Queen's were to occupy the trenches vacated by the attackers and hold themselves in readiness to support them and open up communications with the position to be captured.

By 4.30 on a December evening it was practically dark, and for some time after the attack started it was impossible to make out what success had attended it. All that was known was that the Warwickshires had gone forward most

---

[1] 4·5-inch howitzers were limited to 20 rounds per gun, 4·7-inch guns and 18-pounders to 40 rounds, only the 13-pounders having an unrestricted supply.

resolutely in face of a very heavy fire from guns, rifles, and machine-guns and had been lost to sight in the dark. About 5 o'clock, however, a N.C.O. came back and reported that the battalion was held up just short of the German trenches, had lost heavily, and needed reinforcements, whereupon " C " Company of the Queen's and two platoons of " D " promptly went forward to their help. The bombardment had inflicted little damage on the German wire and had not prevented the Germans from manning their parapet in force and opening a heavy fire directly our troops got so near that our guns could not fire for fear of hitting their own men. Major Brewis was killed at the head of his Warwickshires within a few yards of the German wire, and several other officers were shot down close to him or in trying to work their way through the wire. One small party established itself in a small trench just outside the German parapet and held on there all night, only to have to surrender when the morning light revealed the hopelessness of their position. But the bulk of the attackers were either shot down on their way across No Man's Land or brought to a standstill outside the wire. The Queen's, though gallantly led by Captains Lee and Fearon, who continued to go forward although wounded, could do no more than reach the wire and reinforce the Warwickshires. Realizing that the attack had failed, the C.O. of the Queen's, Major Montague Bates of the East Surreys, decided not to use the Welch Fusiliers, of whom one company had just reached the front trench, to renew it, but issued orders for the survivors to get back as best they could. This they did, while stretcher-bearers went out and brought in many of the wounded, unimpeded by the Germans. The losses had been heavy : besides Major Brewis the Royal Warwickshires had 8 officers and over 300 men killed, wounded, and missing ; of the Queen's 8 officers and 90 men were casualties, more than half of them killed or missing. These casualties were the more felt because both battalions had barely been re-formed

after their losses at Ypres, but both the Brigadier and
Divisional Commander testified to their gallantry and
devotion : it was no fault of theirs that they had
failed—they had been asked to do what experience
was to show to be impossible in the conditions then
prevailing.

The 20th Brigade also, if more successful at first, could
make no lasting gain. It attacked on a front of 500 yards
from the Sailly–Fromelles road Eastward with two companies of the Scots Guards on the right, two of the Borders
on the left. Unluckily the Borders do not seem to have
heard the signal for the assault, which was given by whistle
by the Scots Guards, and the two battalions did not go
forward together. The Scots Guards, advancing with great
dash and enjoying the advantage of surprise—the absence
of the preliminary bombardment proved a real benefit,
for that which had preceded the 22nd Brigade's attack
had merely put the enemy on the alert—managed to effect
a lodgment, though their right ran into thick and uncut
wire and lost heavily from machine-guns. Elsewhere,
however, the wire, which varied greatly in strength, being
quite weak and thin in places, proved less of an obstacle,
and Captain Loder, who led the attack, was able to effect a
surprise, most of the defenders being bayoneted and others
shot down as they bolted. He promptly set to work to
consolidate his position in the German line, blocking the
ends of the portion taken, though there were gaps between
some of his parties where bits of stronger wire had held
up the attackers, and not all these could be connected
up. Unluckily, too, the great depth of the German
trenches made it impossible for the men to see to shoot
out of them, and they had to climb out and lie on the
parapet to get a fire position. Attacks were not slow
to begin, and the Scots Guards were soon hard beset
to maintain their ground. Efforts were being made by
Captain Paynter, their C.O., to get a communication
trench dug across No Man's Land, and some reinforce-

ments were sent across, but on the left flank the Borders had failed to get in and the Scots Guards were therefore quite isolated.

The Borders' failure to effect a lodgment was due mainly to the impossibility of hearing the signal for the starting of the assault. They went forward directly the sound of cheering on their right told them the Guards had started, but the delay, though short, was long enough to give the Germans the warning they needed and to let them man their trenches. The Borders went forward in face of a murderous fire which mowed most of them down within a very short time. Captain Askew, the commander of the attacking force, reached the German trenches and was killed there, using his revolver effectively. Some men seem to have got in with him and shared his fate, but a counter-attack drove most of the attackers back, not without a sharp fight, however, for when, during the armistice of December 25th–26th, many of the dead were buried, German bodies were found outside their wire and mixed up with the Borders' dead. A second advance which Major Warren organized proved ineffectual, and now that the Germans were fully on the alert it was recognized to be hopeless to continue the attempt. The survivors of the Borders were therefore withdrawn to the British lines.[1]

The effort of the Scots Guards to maintain themselves in the German line looked for a time like meeting with more success. Though strongly counter-attacked they held on stoutly, and though driven out from some points maintained a hold until long after midnight on the centre of the line taken. But it was evident that No Man's Land was too wide—nearly 200 yards—for a trench to be opened up across it in time, and shortly before daylight the last section

[1] Privates Acton and Smith of the Border Regiment were awarded the V.C. for their gallantry in going out under heavy fire on December 21st and bringing in wounded men who had been lying out ever since this attack. Private Mackenzie of the Scots Guards received the same honour for a similar act of gallantry on December 19th.

held was successfully evacuated, a wounded officer being
got safely away.[1]

Apart from this unsuccessful venture the Division's
activities were mainly confined to experimenting with
improvised trench-mortars and hand grenades, a Grenade
Company being formed in each brigade, and to the elimina-
tion wherever possible of salients and re-entrants by digging
new trenches. The existing salients were not to be abandoned, but were to be used as advanced posts, while

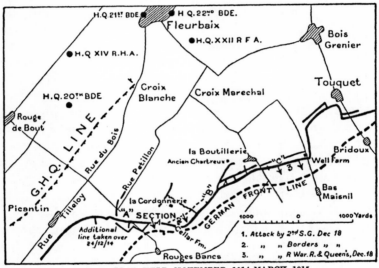

MAP 10.—LINE HELD NOVEMBER 1914-MARCH 1915.

in the same way re-entrants were to serve as support
trenches. In places saps were run out from the front line
and ultimately joined up so as to make a new front trench.
But this work was greatly impeded by trouble with water,
which was threatening to make some parts of the line
untenable, and the main interest of the closing days of the
month was the effort to keep the trenches dry. An informal

[1] The Scots Guards had 3 officers and 112 men killed and missing, 3
officers and 76 men wounded; the Borders 2 officers and 71 men killed and
missing, 2 officers and 40 men wounded.

armistice, started by mutual consent on the morning of December 25th and continued till the next afternoon, did not meet with approval in higher quarters and its repetition was peremptorily forbidden, but it afforded an opportunity for burying and identifying many of those killed in the attack of December 18th, for learning something about those still " missing," and for identifying the German units opposite the Division.

January saw little change in the situation except that the water problem grew increasingly serious. A violent storm on December 28th had flooded all the more low-lying trenches, in places to a depth of two feet and more, and many of the communication trenches were so bad with mud and water that men preferred to go above ground and risk being sniped. It was decided to start constructing posts on bits of high ground in rear for use in case floods should compel the evacuation of the front line. The flooding of the front-line trenches put a stop to sapping out towards the German lines, and all efforts had to be concentrated on keeping our own lines habitable and defensible. Trenches and dug-outs filled with water, and by the end of the first week in January quite half the original trenches had had to be abandoned. By damming short stretches of trenches and pumping vigorously it was possible to maintain garrisons in parts of the front line. By heightening the parapet and constructing wooden platforms above the water-level these garrisons could be kept more or less out of water, but on the whole the labour devoted to fighting the water was wasted and would have been better spent in taking earlier to the construction of breastworks, which proved on the whole satisfactory. These were formed by making retrenchments behind the fire-trenches and throwing up thick parapets with high command: the abandoned trenches then served as effective wet ditches. This necessitated much cutting of brushwood to make hurdles for revetting, but the breast-work line was certainly healthier and more comfortable

than swamped trenches. Redoubts were also constructed
as points d'appui in rear of the front system, and this
method was gradually extended into one of arranging for
" defended localities." Groups of houses were loop-holed
and prepared for defence, trenches and breastworks being
dug to connect them up and the hedges round them wired.
This plan was calculated to economize men and afford
equal or even greater security. But considerations of
security were not so much in the mind as usual because
the Germans enjoyed no immunity from the water trouble
and were also forced to abandon their front line in places.
The 21st Brigade was able, by damming up streams and
ditches which ran from our lines towards those of the
Germans—here on a slightly lower level—to divert water
from our trenches to theirs and had the satisfaction of
seeing them busy baling and pumping and of sometimes
getting a shoot at them when so employed. They too
were forced to build up high command parapets. When
patrols did manage to get across the swamp which No
Man's Land had become in many places they often reported
the Germans hard at work baling water out of their
trenches, and occasionally our machine-guns and rifles
got targets in Germans who were forced to expose themselves owing to the flooded state of their lines. But with
so much water about a serious attack was out of the question, and even patrol activity was much reduced. What
offensive action could be indulged in usually took the shape
of bombardments of the enemy's trenches or of houses and
villages in rear which he was believed to be using for billets.
Co-operation between the guns and the infantry had now
been systematized, and whenever the artillery devoted
some of their carefully doled-out shells to bombarding
houses in rear of the German lines our rifles and machine-
guns were warned to be on the look out for targets. Occasionally also working parties which our patrols had located
were effectively shelled or caught by machine-gun fire.

Considering the meagre quantity of ammunition available, what the guns did to assist the infantry by keeping down the German artillery fire was really remarkable. One gets such entries in the C.R.A.'s Diary as this : " Jan. 25th, a good day for us : we destroyed a sap-head (55th Battery), a mortar pit (106th), a M.G. emplacement (12th), and silenced another M.G. (12th). Very little reply from hostile artillery." Still, with an expenditure restricted to 76 rounds per 18-pounder for the whole month, just 5 rounds in two days, with the 4·5-inch howitzers only allowed half that amount, and the 4·7's and the 13-pounders of the Horse Artillery barely exceeding the 18-pounders' allowance, these opportunities were necessarily limited, and the month passed away without the Division attempting even a minor enterprise ; the casualty list, 2 officers and 68 men killed, 6 officers and 193 men wounded, and 1 officer missing, showed clearly the nature of the month's operations, while a sick-list of 33 officers and 1,613 men admitted to Hospital proved conclusively that the weather and the conditions of the trenches had caused more serious wastage than the enemy. Still, the sick-rate was really remarkably low and most creditable to those responsible for combating the possible causes of invaliding, especially " trench-feet " and frost-bite. Conditions in billets were getting better now, things like the washing and drying of clothes were getting organized, a Divisional shoemakers' shop had been set up and proved a great boon, repairing 2,000 pairs of boots in a month. The arrival of a special Sanitary Section was another step towards better conditions, and if the addition to the Division of a third Field Company of R.E.—the 2nd Highland Field Company (Territorial) joined on January 17th—was primarily an advantage from the military point of view, for each brigade and each section of the line now had its own Field Company attached, it was indirectly beneficial also in providing more skilled workmen for the multifarious requirements behind the line, all of which contributed to the greater comfort and better health of the Division.

February also left matters much as they were. There was rather more ammunition to expend and in consequence increased artillery activity, but the German guns also were somewhat more liberally supplied and could therefore retaliate. On both sides snipers were active, but there was less general rifle fire, the use of rifle grenades tending to discourage the enemy's activities in this line and to keep their snipers in hand. Water continued a serious problem, but, once the breastworks and support points had been completed, more could be done to drain and reclaim the old front line, especially as the weather became finer and drier. Something was done to improve the line ; the 20th Brigade, for example, dug a line from La Cordonnerie to where the Fromelles road crosses the Rivière des Layes, making a chord behind a very bad salient, and the construction of a two-foot-wide trench-tramway from the Rue Petillon to Cellar Farm proved most useful in saving labour and time in getting supplies of all kinds up to the front line and also provided an excellent footpath.

Infantry activity was as before much restricted, though on February 19th the Intelligence Summary notes that there had evidently been a change in the regiment facing the 21st Brigade, " the enemy shoot higher, give more chances to snipers, and don't keep their trenches so well " ; and occasionally the infantry got something to shoot at, though as a rule the main work of worrying the enemy was left to the artillery and to the trench-mortars which were now available, though still in an experimental stage and none too accurate. Casualties for the month were again low : 6 officers wounded, 72 men killed, 213 wounded, 2 missing, under 300 in all. The attachment of the G.O.C., C.R.A., C.R.E., and Brigadiers of a " New Army " Division, the Eleventh, for a period of instruction in " trench warfare " was an interesting incident, suggesting that before long the troops might hope to see appearing those New Armies of which rumour told so much and whose arrival was to usher in the much anticipated " push " in which the monotonous stalemate of trench warfare was to terminate. There had been much to endure in the winter of 1914-1915, discomfort, hardship, monotony, disappointment, toil ; men had seemed to be working continually only to have their labours swept away by a night of rain or a brief bombardment, there seemed little to show for the winter's work and for all that the Division had had to go through. Its lines had not advanced : the enemy's trenches still confronted them in the same place, rather stronger and more complete than when the Division had staggered out of the Ypres Salient into their new positions in November ; neither it nor the Germans were a yard nearer the Rhine. When therefore at the end of February a warning was received that the Division was about to be relieved by the recently arrived Canadians, the news was welcomed as indicating that the long period of inaction was likely to come to an end.

The relief actually began on the evening of March 1st, when two Canadian battalions took over the left sector from the 22nd Brigade, but the two battalions and a half of the brigade who were in support and reserve moved up at the same time and relieved the left brigade of the Eighth Division in what were known as " E " and " F " Lines. These were immediately on the right of the 20th Brigade's sector and stretched from just N.W. of Rouges Bancs nearly to a house known as the Moated Grange, about 1400 yards N.W. of Neuve Chapelle. On the following evening (March 2nd) another Canadian brigade relieved the 21st, which withdrew to the area Laventie–Estaires, and on March 3rd the relief was completed.[1] By 9 p.m. the 20th Brigade was on its way to billets round Vieux Berquin. As the Canadians were as yet very ill-supplied with such essential articles for trench warfare as bombs and periscopes, the Division left a good proportion of its store of these and similar objects behind with the new-comers :

[1] The Divisional artillery for the most part remained in position or shifted a little to its right to cover the new frontage.

some perhaps were sanguine enough to hope that before long they would have no more use for such weapons, emblematic of a stagnant type of warfare. For although no definite orders had as yet been issued, rumours were rife of a coming stroke. The shortening of the Division's line and the concentration of two of its brigades in rear of the new frontage certainly pointed in unmistakable manner in that direction.

The Division's withdrawal from the trench-line it had held for over three months ends a second phase in its story. It had reached that line in November shattered and broken : if it was still very different in March from the Division which had landed in Belgium in October, it had been built up to strength, had assimilated enormous drafts and welded them together into coherent and effective units. The losses incurred on December 18th had naturally retarded the process ; in February one of the battalions engaged in that attack had only one Regular Major and two Special Reserve Captains with a dozen subalterns, all newly commissioned and mostly Special Reserve, and other units were scarcely better off. But all the same much had been done and the progress had really been remarkable. Several more officers and men wounded in the autumn fighting had reappeared. Colonel Wood had rejoined the Borders in January, Colonel Uniacke was back with the Gordons ; and though there had been little active fighting and not too many opportunities for training owing to the needs of the trench-lines and other labours, the Division had had time to get together and settle down. It was a great thing for it that in Generals Watts and Lawford it still had two of its original brigadiers, and that in its G.O.C. it had a man of remarkable capacity as a trainer of troops, who had found the task of reconstructing the exhausted battalions work after his own heart. The Division had had no opportunities of distinction, but it had had unlimited hard work to weld it together, and the gradual establishment of a systematic and orderly trench routine

and of approved methods of annoying and upsetting one's
enemy was a process of great educational value. If in
March 1915 the proportion of veterans of " First Ypres "
in the ranks of the Seventh Division was only too low,
especially in the infantry units, enough had been done,
as the next few days were to show, to render the Division
once again an efficient and effective fighting unit.   These
months of dull monotony and toil had not been devoid of
value.

CHAPTER VI

NEUVE CHAPELLE [1]

THE offensive in which the Seventh Division correctly calculated it was about to be engaged had been resolved upon by Sir John French after considerable consultation both with the authorities at home and with General Joffre. Opinion at home inclined to the belief that the German lines in France could not be broken by a direct attack, but the British Commander-in-Chief did not share this view, and both he and General Joffre were anxious to take advantage of the diversion of German troops and guns to the Eastern Front to strike a blow in France, not only because they hoped to effect a break-through, but in order to assist the Russians. Various methods of carrying out these objects had been discussed between the two commanders, but the British were not yet ready to relieve one of the French Corps still in the Ypres Salient and without it the French Xth Army could not undertake its proposed offensive North of Arras, so no plan for joint action could be arranged. However, Sir John French was determined to make some movement; he was extremely anxious to foster in the troops the offensive spirit, for which the long period of trench warfare had given so few opportunities; moreover, to get his men out of the water-logged flats of the Lys valley on to the Aubers ridge was tactically most desirable, while strategically the capture of the ridge would serve as a useful basis for more ambitious operations whenever a joint major offensive by French and British might be possible.

The precise point to be attacked by the British was to some degree determined by the unsatisfactory state in which the autumn fighting had left the tactical position

[1] Cf. Maps 11, 12 and 13.

round Neuve Chapelle. By capturing that village the Germans had created a deep re-entrant in the British lines, and the long casualty list of the Eighth Division, who had held this sector since the middle of November, testified only too clearly to its disadvantages. The recapture of Neuve Chapelle was therefore the first object of the attack, which was to be begun by the Eighth Division on the left and by the Meerut Division of the Indian Corps on the right, but, Neuve Chapelle once taken, an advance was to be promptly made to the line Ligny le Grand–Haut Pommereau–Aubers. This would establish the First Army on the S.W. end of the ridge and open prospects of further exploitation. It was in this stage that the Seventh Division was to come into the fight, two of its brigades attacking Aubers, while the Eighth Division on their right moved against La Cliqueterie, covered on its right again by the Indian Corps. The remaining brigade of the Division would at first remain in occupation of the lines immediately North of those from which the Eighth Division was attacking, but as the attack went forward it was to advance, covering the left flank and taking the German trenches on the Fauquissart–Rouges Bancs–Bridoux front in flank and rear.

On March 6th the Corps Commander held a conference at which the plans were explained to the Divisional commanders and brigadiers. It was pointed out that a considerable force of artillery—according to 1915 standards, by those of 1917 or 1918 woefully inadequate—had been collected opposite the point to be attacked, that the ammunition so carefully husbanded during the past months had accumulated in sufficient quantities to allow of over half-an-hour's preliminary bombardment, that assembly trenches already dug in rear of the line would provide ample cover for the attacking troops, and that depôts of ammunition and for rations and R.E. stores had been formed in and near the trenches, so that the attack would start under favourable circumstances. Moreover, there

was credible information that the Germans had only one
regiment on the front to be attacked and that they did
not appear to have any considerable reserves at hand.

Definite orders for the attack were received from Corps
Headquarters two days later, whereupon Divisional orders

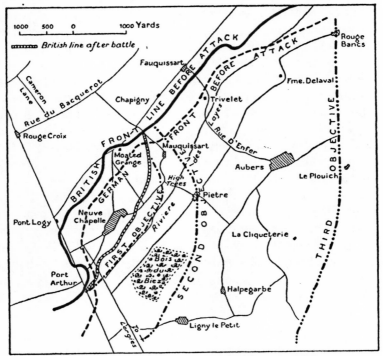

MAP 11.—NEUVE CHAPELLE: OBJECTIVES AND RESULT.

were issued. The 22nd Brigade was to remain in occupation of the Divisional trenches, having the Welch Fusiliers
in " E " Lines, the Queen's and the Royal Scots in " F,"
the South Staffords in Brigade Reserve, and the Royal
Warwickshires in Divisional Reserve. The 21st Brigade was
to assemble along the Rue Tilleloy, North of Pont Logy,
behind " B " Lines, and to occupy the Eighth Division's
support trenches as these became clear. It was ultimately
10

to advance through the Eighth Division's left brigade, the 23rd, and attack the line Pietre–Moulin du Pietre, having on its right the 24th Brigade, the Eighth Division's reserve.   The 20th Brigade was to assemble at Pont Croix and would occupy the 21st Brigade's trenches in succession as it moved forward.   But the Corps Orders were very explicit that the actual moment for the 21st Brigade to advance beyond the support trenches was to be decided by the Corps Commander.   Very little latitude was thus left to any subordinate commander, and success would depend largely on the rapid transmission to the Corps Commander of accurate information about the progress of the attack and on his orders reaching the Division promptly.

As already explained the artillery support available was looked upon as really considerable, and it was thought that recent economy in ammunition expenditure had allowed of the accumulation of a really adequate supply both for wire-cutting, to be done by the field-guns, and for the demolition of the trenches and strong points in rear, the task of the howitzers and heavy artillery.   The gunners of the Seventh Division, both Horse and Field, were included among the batteries detailed to form a belt of fire behind the lines to be attacked so as both to intercept the retreat of the defenders, should they try to escape, and to prevent the arrival of reinforcements ; in other words, to form a " barrage," of which this was practically the first example in the campaign.

March 10th, the day selected for the attack, began by being misty, but well before 7.30 a.m., the hour for the bombardment to open, it had cleared enough to make post-ponement unnecessary, and at the appointed hour a deluge of shells descended upon the German wire and trenches. Judged by the standards of later years it was an altogether inadequate " artillery preparation " for a serious attack, but in March 1915 the German defences were pale shadows of what they were to become, and when, 35 minutes later, the assaulting infantry went " over the top " most of them

found the wire well cut and the trenches and their garrisons
very much knocked about. The 25th Brigade on the
Eighth Division's right was rapidly and completely
successful; by 9 a.m. its men were into the ruins of Neuve
Chapelle and establishing themselves on their objective.
Unluckily, on the 23rd Brigade's frontage, about 200 yards
of the trench-line had escaped demolition, the batteries
detailed to shell it having arrived from England too late
to construct satisfactory gun platforms or to do any
registration. Not only was the left battalion, the 2nd
Middlesex, mown down almost to a man in No Man's Land,
but the left company of the Scottish Rifles on its right was
enfiladed and checked, so that only the extreme right of
the brigade managed to reach and capture the German
lines. It was promptly reinforced by the 2nd Devons, the
supporting battalion, but even so fell well behind the 25th
Brigade, not getting beyond the German support trenches
till some time later. Ultimately, after a fresh bombardment of the undamaged portion of the German front line,
its surviving defenders, who were being pressed from the
flank by bombers, surrendered, whereupon the 23rd
Brigade pushed on across the road running North from
Neuve Chapelle to the Rue Tilleloy,[1] and reached the
Smith Dorrien Trench,[2] some 150 yards farther East on
the right and nearly 400 yards away on the left. But it
was 1 p.m. before it was established on this line, and the
four hours thus lost were never made up. The 25th
Brigade, with its left flank " in the air," had to wait for the
23rd to come up and cover its left. Not only this, but the
24th Brigade, which was to have passed through the 25th,
was also delayed; one of its battalions was diverted to
link up the inner flanks of the 23rd and 25th and the others
remained halted.

[1] This joined the Rue Tilleloy just West of the ruins of " the Moated
Grange," formerly a substantial farm: it may for convenience be called
Moated Grange Road.

[2] The line round and East of Neuve Chapelle held by the Second Corps in
October when it fell back from the Aubers Ridge.

The 21st Brigade, meanwhile, had been affected by the check to the advance. At 8.30 a.m. the Scots Fusiliers on the right and Yorkshires on the left had moved forward into the rearmost assembly trenches of the 23rd Brigade, only to find them still blocked. Then followed a long and weary wait, with the troops cooped up in the crowded trenches and the precious minutes in which so much might have been done passing slowly away. There was a little shelling, and in moving across the open the brigade had had a few casualties from rifles and machine-guns, but not enough to have stopped it for a minute. The Germans had been completely surprised and only a few handfuls of men were in a position to oppose an immediate advance.

However, when General Capper telephoned to the Corps Commander that the 21st Brigade was ready to advance, a message came back about midday that the orchard South of the Moated Grange had not yet been taken and that till it was in our hands the Seventh Division could not go forward.

At length, however, at 1.19, the order came through for the 21st Brigade to cross No Man's Land and occupy the German front line. The move was promptly carried out, only for another wearisome wait to follow. The Indian Corps also, though successful elsewhere, had failed to take the extreme outer flank of its objective and was hung up while the untaken portion could be dealt with. This took much time, and as it was considered essential that both Corps should advance together to the second objective, the Fourth was delayed even after it had secured all its own objective by the need for co-operating to the minute with the Indians. The Germans had been prompt to rush up all available reserves to the incomplete second position about a mile in rear of their front system, and these troops, boldly and skilfully handled, made excellent use of the strong points which had been constructed at the bridge over the Rivière des Layes East of Neuve Chapelle, out of some cottages at a right-angled bend in the Neuve

Chapelle–Mauquissart road,[1] and at the hamlet of Mauquissart itself; still an immediate and vigorous advance by the 24th and 25th Brigades N.E. and E. from Neuve Chapelle would have found little in its front at any time up to the early afternoon.

When, about 2.15 p.m., the Scots Fusiliers and Yorkshires at last began their advance, they passed through the 23rd Brigade about 100 yards East of Moated Grange Road and, working steadily forward in the face of a little shelling[2] and rifle fire, were nearly 300 yards farther East when they were stopped by orders from the Brigadier, who had just heard that the 24th Brigade, with whom he had to co-operate, was not ready. The two battalions therefore lay down in the open where they were and another tedious wait occurred. The Wiltshires came up during this period and took up their position on the Yorkshires' left, among the German trenches just South of the Moated Grange, ready to clear these from the flank. Just before 3.30 orders were received for an advance to be begun at 3.30 p.m. with Moulin du Pietre as its objective; but though the firing-line tried to get forward this was impossible till our own guns should lift,[3] and as yet there was no sign of the 24th Brigade.

Thus in the end it was after 5 o'clock before the 24th Brigade was reported to be ready and the advance really started, and even then progress was slow. The evening was dark and cloudy, the country intricate and unfamiliar; trenches of all kinds, some disused, nearly all half full of water, intersected it in all directions; ditches, some of them quite serious obstacles, and hedges helped to make direction and connexion hard to keep. Rifles and machine-guns fired away freely, and while the Scots Fusiliers' left

---

[1] Shown on the map as The High Trees, there being a group behind the cottages which served as a landmark.

[2] The German guns were firing away vigorously, but as yet the defenders had been unable to bring up much additional artillery.

[3] The artillery were greatly handicapped all day by the difficulty of getting accurate information about the infantry's position.

company met heavy frontal fire from a road-bend midway between Mauquissart and the High Trees (" 88 " on map), " A " Company on the right found its flank " in the air " as the 24th Brigade was still behind, so had to face that way to cover this exposed point.   By 6 p.m. the battalion had come to a standstill, " A " Company just East of the Sunken Road, the other three about 200 yards from the road-bend.   The Yorkshires in the centre had to make their way through a maze of trenches and to rely mainly on bombs, but they made good progress, especially on their right, for on their left more opposition was encountered and the fire from a German redoubt kept the left company back behind the others.   On their left again the Wiltshires were actively engaged.   They had to work along the German lines to the N.E. of the portion already taken and parallel to the Rue Tilleloy.   Bombers pushed forward down the trenches, " C " Company heading the main advance.   As they pushed on Germans retiring before them gave targets to the Welch Fusiliers in " E " lines opposite who were thus able to co-operate effectively.   Many Germans, however, could not get away, and over 150 prisoners, mostly from the 13th Infantry Regiment, had surrendered to the Wiltshires, who pressed on until, about 100 yards beyond the Moated Grange, they came across a wide ditch [1] behind which their advance encountered a determined resistance.   Captain Hoare, who commanded " C " Company, was killed, as was 2nd Lieut. Spencer, who brought up the leading platoon of " D " ; but 2nd Lieut. Hunter rallied " C " when his commander fell and forced the Germans back another 50 yards to a slight rise in the ground.   It was dark now, and with all three battalions rather split up, to press forward in the dark into the maze of trenches without reorganizing would have been extremely risky, especially as the Germans seemed to be preparing a counter-attack, for the Scots Fusiliers had reported enemy moving forward farther to their right as though

[1] Apparently that between " 2 " and " 99."

about to attack. Accordingly, General Watts sent back
word to General Capper, who had sent a staff officer forward
to urge the 21st Brigade to press on, that a farther
advance was inadvisable, as until the 24th Brigade came
forward it would merely have exposed his right flank
and laid it open to be turned. The Divisional Commander

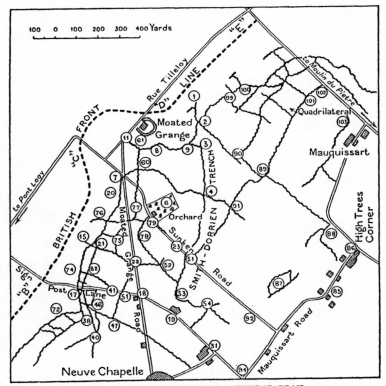

MAP 12.—NEUVE CHAPELLE: GENERAL PLAN.

concurred and ordered the 21st Brigade to consolidate
the ground gained, sent up the 2nd Highland Field
Company and three sections of the 55th to assist, and
directed the 20th Brigade, which had occupied the assembly
trenches when the 21st vacated them, to return to billets.

Thus the day ended without the break-through that had

seemed in the Seventh Division's reach.   The 21st Brigade
was some way short of the Mauquissart road, and though
it had not lost heavily [1] the amount of fire which it had
met indicated that serious resistance must be expected
when the advance was renewed.

The night passed quietly enough : the expected counter-
attack never developed, though rifle fire was almost continuous and the Scots Fusiliers beat off a weak attack,
probably only a strong patrol.   The position was considerably improved and units were reorganized while the Wiltshires, assisted by a company of the 2nd Gordons, dug a
trench across No Man's Land to connect up the captured
trenches with " D " lines.   Orders were issued during the
night for the continuation of the attack : the 21st Brigade
was to start it at 7.30 a.m., making N.E. for the line Rue
d'Enfer–Les Mottes Farm–Trivelet, the 20th Brigade would
come up on its right and attack Aubers from the S.W. in
conjunction with the Eighth Division.   To cover this
advance the artillery were to open fire at 6.45 a.m., the
Siege Batteries under the Seventh Division's orders and
the 31st Howitzer Battery bombarding the Mauquissart
road, while the 13-pounders and 18-pounders shelled zones
in rear.   The siege-guns were allotted five rounds a gun for
the first objective, the howitzers seven, the 18-pounders
and Horse gunners 15.   Unfortunately the morning was
misty and the gunners found it hard to give their fire the
requisite accuracy.   Moreover, the Germans had made only
too good use of the night and working most strenuously
had linked up the strong points in their rear line with a
continuous trench ; they had also brought up many more
machine-guns, and just when extreme accuracy of fire was
needed the British gunners found air observation impossible
and communication with our forward trenches extremely

[1] The Wiltshires had five officers hit, including their C.O., Capt. Gillson,
who was wounded, while the Bedfords, who had moved up behind the Scots
Fusiliers and entrenched in rear of them, about midway between the Orchard
and " 88," had about 60 casualties, mostly from " overs " aimed at the troops
in front, but the leading battalions had hardly lost as many.

difficult, for telephone lines were cut as quickly as laid and too constantly to be kept in repair. With the artillery blinded the infantry could do little, and the second day proved one of disappointment.

The battalions of the 21st Brigade in the front line had therefore the thankless task of holding on to their trenches under heavy fire without many opportunities of retaliating. They were occasionally shelled by their own guns,[1] and the heavy shelling and machine-gun fire which greeted every movement effectually prevented any advance against the German positions along the Mauquissart road. On the left in the tangle of support and communication trenches in which the Wiltshires and Yorkshires were established there was some sharp fighting, the bombers of the latter regiment doing splendid work and capturing several prisoners, but the line as a whole remained unchanged, an afternoon attempt by the Wiltshires to advance proving unsuccessful.

Meanwhile the 20th Brigade was on its way up to the front. It had moved off from Cameron Lane about 3.30 a.m., the Grenadiers leading, and following the trench tramway reached the Pont Logy–Fauquissart road breast-works under cover of darkness with only a few casualties from stray shrapnel. Here the 2nd Gordons, who had been at the 21st Brigade's disposal on the previous day, came under General Heyworth again. Orders to advance reached the brigade at 6.30, only just in time for a start at 7 a.m., when the leading battalions pushed forward, the Gordons on the left through and North of the Orchard, the Grenadiers South of it, with the High Trees Corner as their objective. Very heavy fire was opened at once and from the first the Grenadiers suffered severely ; they pressed on, however, crossed the Sunken Road and had nearly reached the Bedfordshires' trenches before Colonel Fisher-Rowe, seeing that until the enfilade fire of the German machine-guns could be neutralized further advance was impossible,

_____
[1] With the worn-out and inaccurate 4·7's it was impossible to avoid this.

halted the battalion in the shelter of some old trenches. To
have pushed on would have merely invited annihilation, and
the Grenadiers had to hang on all day under heavy fire,
displaying conspicuous steadiness under very trying circumstances. The Gordons had been able to do no more ;
taken in flank by fire from the left they had swung slightly
to that flank and ultimately dug in S.E. of the Moated
Grange and North of the Orchard. They had had nine
officers hit with heavy casualties among the men, but they
too held on and endured their punishment unflinchingly.

With the leading battalions checked, the supports were
also brought to a standstill, the Scots Guards' leading line
close behind the Grenadiers, their rear platoons in the old
German front line. The Borders on the left gradually
worked forward until their leading companies were up
level with the Gordons' left, between them and the Moated
Grange.[1] The 6th Gordons remained in reserve, though
not far enough back to escape about 30 casualties from
shell fire.

No unit of the 20th Brigade had thus even reached the
front line, much less managed to carry it forward, and there
was nothing to show for their casualties, in all nearly 500.
The 21st Brigade had scarcely fared any better. On the
conclusion of the first bombardment of the Mauquissart
road positions the troops attempted to advance but met
so heavy a fire that no ground could be gained : it was
clear that the bombardment had not achieved the results
required and that the German position was much stronger
than had been supposed. A fresh bombardment was
arranged, but it too was insufficient to let the infantry get
on. The Germans on their part plastered the ground with
shells and kept their rifles and machine-guns on the alert
for any movement, but never ventured on any serious
counter-attack. A small effort against the Scots Fusiliers
about 8 a.m. was easily repulsed, but though the Eighth
Division had now come up on the 21st Brigade's right, and

[1] Approximately between " 8 " and " 9 " on the map.

gained touch with the Scots Fusiliers, whose right company,
" A," found itself separated from the rest of its battalion
by the Northamptons, it could do nothing against the
German lines along the road from Neuve Chapelle to the
High Trees Corner. All that could be done was to
strengthen the position by improving the parapet rather
than by deepening the trenches, for directly one dug down
any depth one came to water. Some slight readjustments
were made, but the German fire was too heavy to allow of
any substantial body of troops moving by daylight.

With matters in this state it was recognized early in the
afternoon that no good could result from renewing the
attack till fresh arrangements could be made. Orders
were accordingly issued to withdraw the Grenadiers into
reserve and to shift the Borders to a position just behind
the junction of the Yorkshires and Wiltshires. The Scots
Guards were to take ground on their right, but for that
battalion to reach the required position involved a difficult
and roundabout move along communication trenches
waist-deep with water. It was only after dark, of course,
that these movements could be made. That evening also
the XXIInd and XXXVth Brigades R.F.A. moved forward
to new positions, the former N.E. of Laventie cross-roads,
the latter along the Rue de Bacquerot.

The orders for March 12th were that after half-an-hour's
bombardment the German positions along the Mauquissart
road should be assaulted at 8 a.m. by the Borders and Scots
Guards, who were to pass through the 21st Brigade. At
1 a.m., however, the attack was postponed till 10.30, which
was just as well, for it was obvious that the Scots Guards
could not get into position in time. However, long before
10.30 things had become exceedingly lively, not only on
the Seventh Division's front, but all the way to Port
Arthur, on the extreme right of the Indian Corps. The
Germans, profiting by the check to the British advance,
had brought up large reinforcements, including the whole
6th Bavarian Reserve Division and several battalions of

the XIXth (Saxon) Army Corps, besides concentrating
a considerable force of artillery to support the counter-
attack by which they expected to recover all their lost
ground.

The British got their first warning of what was coming
from an extremely heavy bombardment which opened
about 4.30 a.m. on March 12th, and went on with great
intensity for half an hour. Luckily the German guns had
had no time to register and it was much too early to allow
of accurate observation of fire : most of their shells therefore went clean over the British front line, which escaped
with little damage and few casualties, so that when at 5 a.m.
the Germans launched their attack a destructive fire
blazed out all along the line. On the left, where the network of old trenches provided good cover, the assailants
closed with the Wiltshires and ousted their advanced company, " C," from its position. This company's retreat
exposed the flank of " A," which was in turn dislodged and
driven off across No Man's Land into the old British line,
here held by the 4th Camerons. The third company, " D,"
just behind the broad ditch where there had been so sharp
a fight on the 10th, stood firm and effectually stopped the
German advance, while after daylight 2nd Lieut. Hunter
rallied " C " for a counter-attack. In this some bombers
of the Yorkshires who had hurried to the Wiltshires' help
did magnificent service. Corporal Anderson dashed forward with three men, bombed a party of Germans who were
advancing down a trench and then, having used up his own
bombs and those of his men, who had all been wounded,
opened rapid fire with such good effect that about 60 Germans surrendered.[1] Confused fighting went on at close
quarters for some time longer, the Germans being finally
driven back and most of the lost ground recovered.
Against the Yorkshires the Germans had no success whatever, although the darkness and mist allowed them to get
within 100 yards before they could be seen. Then the

[1] He was awarded the V.C.

Yorkshires let fly with rifles and machine-guns, doing tremendous execution in the thick lines approaching them. Hundreds of Germans were shot down, hardly a man got within 30 yards of the British trenches, and the attacking battalion was practically wiped out. Simultaneously another battalion advanced against the Scots Fusiliers, whose left and centre companies dealt with their opponents no less effectually than the Yorkshires had done. " B " Company, however, which had apparently advanced slightly in front of the general line and was holding a trench close to the road-bend at " 88," was not so successful. The attackers had less distance to cover here and managed to get right into the trench : " B," with all its officers down, was driven back and the Germans pressed forward after it. However, Private Reid, a machine-gunner, rose to the occasion and handling his weapon with great effect prevented the advance from penetrating any farther. The Bedfords, who were in support, promptly tried to retake the lost trench and came charging across the open headed by Major Denne, their C.O., and Captains Baird and Cumberbatch. But they had 150 yards to cover and the fire was so hot that only Captain Baird and a handful got in and they were too few to achieve their object ; the other officers were wounded and the Germans remained in possession of the trench. However, a fresh attempt to advance against the Scots Fusiliers' main position was repulsed with heavy loss, no Germans getting within 70 yards of the line. Another advance a little later was equally unsuccessful, and then Captain Foss of the Bedfords, with a party of bombers and a platoon in support, attempted the recapture of the lost trench. He worked forward along the Northamptons' trenches [1] and rushed the trench from the flank. A sharp fight followed ending in the surrender of the surviving Germans, an officer and about 50 men, whereupon a crowd of Germans rose up out of ditches and shell-holes in which

---

[1] These faced the Neuve Chapelle–High Trees road and ran roughly at right angles to the general line of the 21st Brigade.

they had taken refuge on the failure of their attacks, and put their hands up. About 60 of them came in to our trenches and surrendered, the rest endeavoured to make off and were for the most part shot down. The Bedfords promptly pushed up a company into the recaptured position and later on two machine-guns were also established there.[1]

By this time—about 9 a.m.—the Wiltshires had recovered their lost ground and the 20th Brigade was getting into position for the attack, the Borders in the assembly trenches which had been dug close behind the 21st Brigade's line, the Scots Guards being somewhat to their right and rear, the 6th Gordons in the old British lines near the Moated Grange, and the other two battalions farther back. All along the British front the German counter-attacks, which had been most gallantly pressed, had been decisively repulsed, and another favourable opportunity for an advance seemed within reach of the British. However, the mistiness of the morning had again seriously interfered with the artillery preparations, preventing the guns from ranging accurately on the key-positions in the German line, so orders were issued to postpone the bombardment for another couple of hours. Unluckily, owing to the two orderlies who were taking the message being killed on their way up, these orders did not get through to the Borders and Scots Guards in time, and at 10.30 a.m. they started forward only to come under a devastating fire. The Scots Guards made about 150 yards, in which Major Paynter and two other officers were hit with about 100 men: they then stopped, being about level with the Borders, whose advance Colonel Wood had stopped directly he realized that without more covering fire it must lead to the annihilation of his battalion.

About the same time a message reached General Hey-worth that the Wiltshires were in trouble, so he ordered up

---

[1] Captain Foss, who had already won the D.S.O. at Ypres, was awarded the V.C.

a detachment from the Brigade Bombing Company under
Captain Nicol of the Grenadiers, who arrived to play a
prominent part when, at 12.30 p.m., the long-postponed
attack at last started. It had been preceded by a most
effective bombardment of the Quadrilateral, the obstructing
redoubt West of the Mauquissart road. During its closing
stages the troops had crept forward so as to be close up to
the German trenches when the guns lifted, and when this
happened Borders and Scots Guards were into the Quadrilateral with the utmost promptitude. There was not much
resistance; the defenders seemed demoralized by the bombardment and surrendered wholesale; one of their officers
indeed complained bitterly that the bombardment wasn't
war, "it was carnage." Others retiring towards the road
were caught by the fire of the Yorkshires and Scots Fusiliers
and heavily punished. Simultaneously with the assault
on the Quadrilateral, indeed before the bombardment
ended, the Wiltshires, assisted by the bombers from the
20th Brigade, had begun to work forward through the network of trenches on the left. Lieutenant Morrison, who was
leading their advance, was hit, and the attack was checked
till Captain Makins worked forward round the next corner
and cleared about 40 yards, while two Grenadiers, Lance-
Corporal Fuller and Private Barber, distinguished themselves greatly. Barber pushed on ahead alone, bombing
the enemy with great effect and clearing a long stretch of
trench. When the rest of his party caught him up they
found him alone and surrounded with Germans who were
surrendering to him. Fuller, seeing some Germans making
off down a communication trench, ran forward to intercept
them and bombed them so effectually that 50 of them put
up their hands and surrendered.[1] Thus substantial progress was made along the German front line, the 22nd
Brigade co-operating by keeping the Germans under fire

---

[1] Both these men received the V.C., in Barber's case posthumously. Captain Nicol, who had handled his bombing company with great skill and courage,
received the D.S.O.

and taking advantage of the targets presented by Germans clearing off in front of the Wiltshires.[1] On the news of this success the reserve battalion of the 22nd Brigade, the Warwickshires, who had reinforced the Northamptonshire Yeomanry in " D " lines with one company, was now brought up and placed in the British lines between the Moated Grange and Chapigny in readiness to co-operate should the advance be renewed.

This, however, proved impossible. Both Borders and Scots Guards tried to press on against the Mauquissart road, but could not get far beyond the Quadrilateral. Some of them seem to have been captured in this effort, as about 1 p.m. a report, which proved inaccurate, reached General Capper that our troops were crossing the road. Apparently an artillery observing officer had seen British prisoners being marched to the rear. On this the 21st Brigade was ordered to push forward towards Rue d'Enfer and the 20th to make for Pietre, the Grenadiers and 2nd Gordons being ordered forward to join in. However, the trenches along the Mauquissart road had not been seriously damaged by the bombardment and the Germans had enough machine-guns in action to hold up the 21st Brigade ; indeed the Grenadiers, who moved forward about 1.30 p.m. with orders to come up on the right of the Scots Guards, suffered almost as badly as in the previous day's abortive advance. Major Trotter, the second in command, was wounded almost directly they left the breastworks behind which they were sheltering, and the leading company soon lost direction and swung to its left quite off its proper line. Those in rear in like manner lost direction in the confusing trenches, Colonel Fisher-Rowe was killed, and the Grenadiers never reached their proper position. The 2nd Gordons, who crossed No Man's Land by the trench dug by their " B " Company two nights earlier, eventually arrived in rear of the 21st Brigade's left but could go no farther ; nor could the 22nd Brigade,

---

[1] The Wiltshires now recovered touch with the portion of the battalion who had been driven off into the old British lines earlier that morning.

though, as before, taking advantage of such targets as presented themselves, achieve anything more. Two companies of the Royal Warwickshires had been ordered to push forward along the Mauquissart road, but though one platoon advanced and established itself in No Man's Land just to the left of the captured part of the German front line, the British trenches were congested with troops,[1]

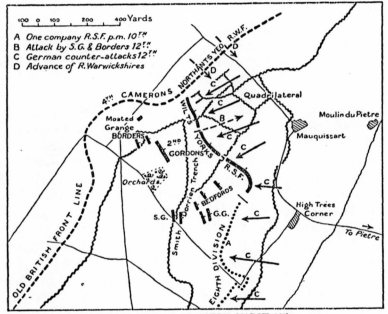

MAP 13.—NEUVE CHAPELLE, MARCH 12th.

and it was difficult to give adequate support to the advanced platoon. The Welch Fusiliers, who had already lost their Adjutant, Captain Wood, had both his substitute, Lieutenant Alston, and their acting C.O., Captain Minshull-Ford, wounded, but got some opportunities of effective fire at intervals. However, there was no prospect of the 22nd Brigade being able to carry out the work originally assigned

---

[1] Some Grenadiers seem actually to have found their way into this part of the lines.

11

to it, and at 11 p.m. orders were received for the Warwickshires and South Staffords to relieve the left of the 21st
Brigade. The net result of the day, therefore, was another
disappointment ; the capture of the Quadrilateral and the
Wiltshires' advance on the left beyond " 100 " were useful
gains, but fell far short of the desired break-through, and
the heavy punishment inflicted on the German counter-
attack was here as elsewhere the substantial asset of
the day.

During the night something was done to sort out the
troops, withdraw the most exhausted units, and reorganize
the line. It was a difficult task ; units were much split
up, the trenches already congested with troops as well as
with dead and wounded. General Capper, however, was
determined to make one more effort, and accordingly
General Heyworth set out about 11 p.m. to do what he
could to get his units into their appointed places. The
Borders were to be at the Quadrilateral, the 2nd Gordons to
come up on their left, relieving the Yorkshires, the 6th
Gordons to relieve the Scots Guards and support their 2nd
Battalion, the Grenadiers to move across to the right and
replace the Scots Fusiliers. This last move, however,
proved impossible, for the battalion had to be got together
and to cross 1,000 yards of most intricate country : daylight found only one company up with the Scots Fusiliers,
the rest being still out in the open, where they had therefore
to dig in as best they could and to hang on under heavy
fire from machine-guns and artillery of all calibres. It
was a trying ordeal, especially for a battalion which had
lost as heavily in officers and N.C.O.s as the Grenadiers
had, but the men showed a most creditable steadiness
and endurance.

March 13th, therefore, proved another day of disappointment and casualties, with nothing to show for them. As
before the bombardment failed to silence the German
machine-guns, which frustrated every attempt to advance.
The 6th Gordons, who had been brought up during the night

to the old German front line, made a most gallant effort,
which, however, cost them their C.O., Colonel Maclean, who
had fearlessly pushed across the open to get touch with the
2nd Battalion and find out the time for his battalion's
advance.   At 9.30 a.m. the battalion advanced in two lines,
and moving in good order but with great speed, despite a
heavy fire, got up into position on the left and 100 yards
ahead of their 2nd Battalion.   They had the satisfaction
of opening rapid fire on Germans who were retiring before
them, and a few men of both battalions got forward to a
trench another 50 yards ahead, but the German fire was too
severe to allow of further progress.   Colonel Uniacke of
the 2nd Gordons, who had gone sick on the previous day but
insisted on rejoining his battalion, was killed when reconnoitring the line of attack, his Adjutant, Major Stansfeld,
was wounded ; and with accurate artillery support difficult
to arrange and the Germans obviously in strength and little
shaken, it was clear that to attack would merely sacrifice
lives to no purpose.   The Scots Fusiliers had the satisfaction of beating back some small attacks from High Trees
Corner, but the reception their previous day's effort had met
with evidently deterred the Germans from trying another
counter-attack in force and they were content to maintain
their line.   On the extreme left there was some activity.
The Warwickshires' move across to the captured trenches
to relieve the Wiltshires had been considerably delayed
owing to the mistakes of the guides, and daylight found
their last companies crossing the open North of the Moated
Grange ; all they could do was to reach and remain in " D "
Lines, though the leading companies, " A " and " B," got
across to the old German front line.   During the morning
" A " Company started to advance, but its movements
drew such a heavy fire that it had to halt till after dark,
when it proved possible to connect the captured trenches
with the position seized on the previous day by the platoon
which had advanced beside the Bacquerot–Mauquissart
road.   The South Staffords remained in reserve, but were

ordered up in the evening to relieve the portions of the 21st
Brigade still in the front line.   During the day Sir Douglas
Haig had visited the Commander-in-Chief and discussed
with him the policy to be adopted in the immediate future.
It was obvious that it would be futile to attempt to extend
the salient already driven into the German lines : on that
front a deadlock had been reached.   Sir Douglas Haig was
anxious, however, to strike another blow from the Fauquissart–Tilleloy frontage, aiming at Trivelet and Ferme
Delaval, and proposed to use the Seventh Division to accomplish this and if successful to let the Canadians push on
against Aubers.   But, though Sir John French approved of
the idea, the expenditure of ammunition had altogether surpassed expectations and had so depleted the painfully
collected reserve that an early renewal of the offensive was
out of the question.   The production of ammunition in
England, despite all efforts, still fell sadly short not only
of requirements but of calculations, and it would take weeks
to replace the shells expended at Neuve Chapelle.[1]   Till
this could be done, however, it would be highly imprudent
to indent any further on the scanty reserve, and accordingly
all thought of an immediate resumption of the attack had
to be set aside.   In the meantime the 20th and 21st Brigades had been relieved, the Eighth Division taking over
the whole of the captured position and the 22nd Brigade
holding " E " and " F " Lines beyond their left.   The 20th
and 21st were placed in Corps Reserve to get a chance of
resting, refitting, and reorganizing.

The Division's losses, 138 officers and 2,666 men, though
not approaching those suffered in the long-drawn-out
struggle at Ypres, were heavy enough for a four days'
battle in which only two brigades had been seriously
engaged, one of which had suffered most of its casualties
before it reached the firing-line.   The 20th Brigade, indeed,
had suffered nearly half the Division's casualties, 70 officers

[1] At the current rate of production it would take ten days to replace the
18-pounder ammunition used in the first day's bombardment alone.

and 1,303 men, and its hardest-hit unit, the Grenadiers, had had least chance of effective retaliation on the enemy. Of its battalion commanders only Colonel Wood of the Borders was unhit, and it had lost heavily both in officers and N.C.O.s. The 21st Brigade, with only four battalions to the 20th's five, had lost proportionately almost as many, 53 officers and 1,021 men, the Yorkshires and Scots Fusiliers both having over 300 casualties. In the 22nd Brigade the Warwickshires alone had lost appreciably, and their 3 officers and 126 men came to nearly half the Brigade's total, though the Welch Fusiliers with 6 officers among 80 casualties might be reckoned very unlucky. The arm which had come off best was the artillery, whose total of 17 casualties for the four days was no more than it might have had in four days of " ordinary trench warfare," and testifies to the almost complete absence of German counter-battery work. But the casualties [1] had not been heavy

[1] The definite figures were :

	Killed.		Wounded.		Missing.	
	Officers.	O.R.	Officers.	O.R.	Officers.	O.R.
Northumberland Hussars . .	—	1	—	4	—	—
R.A.	—	2	1	14	—	—
R.E.	—	2	1	16	—	—
R.A.M.C.	—	1	3	7	—	—
20th Brigade H.Q. . . .	—	—	1	4	—	—
Grenadiers	8	36	8	242	—	54
Scots Guards	1	22	6	132	—	35
Borders	2	62	12	175	—	41
2nd Gordons	4	49	11	179	1	11
6th Gordons	5	24	11	225	—	12
Bedfords	—	33	8	144	—	19
Yorkshires	3	93	11	182	—	24
Scots Fusiliers	5	79	9	161	—	50
Wiltshires	6	55	11	164	—	57
Royal Scots	—	9	—	22	—	—
Queen's	1	2	—	19	—	—
Warwickshires. . . .	1	27	2	85	—	14
Welch Fusiliers . . .	2	16	4	55	—	—
S. Staffords	—	1	—	5	—	—

Total : 38 officers and   514 men killed.
          99   ,,   1,835 ,, wounded.
           1   ,,   317 ,, missing.

enough to counteract the legitimate satisfaction with which
the action could be regarded. If the results had fallen
short of what had seemed well within reach, Neuve Chapelle
had demonstrated that the German lines could be stormed,
that the spirit of initiative and daring had not been drowned
in the water-logged trenches in which the troops had endured
the winter, that despite the general inexperience of the
junior officers and men they could carry out an attack and
show resourcefulness, good leadership, and tactical skill.
More than one battalion commander in the Seventh Division
commented on this and could bring to notice examples of
good handling of companies and platoons by youthful
officers with but little training. Moreover, however heavy
their own losses, the troops had had the satisfaction of
inflicting heavy punishment on their enemies, of taking
many prisoners, of seeing Germans fall in heaps under their
fire and retiring in disorder before them. They could feel
themselves better men than their opponents. That the
battle had taught many lessons, had shown up things to be
avoided in future, had exposed unsuspected or underrated
difficulties—notably that of keeping the higher commanders
in rear accurately informed of the progress of the attack—
was obvious, but Neuve Chapelle was of the nature of an
experiment, and through experiments alone could the right
road to success be reached. "Next time we shall know
how to do it better" was the prevailing feeling, and there
was no reluctance to contemplate "next time." After all,
the great experiment about Neuve Chapelle had been in
the temper and capacity of the troops. Would the recruits
who had replaced the trained officers and men of 1914 be
equal to the tasks to be faced ? To no portion of the
attacking force did this question apply more urgently than
to the infantry of the Seventh Division. Not a battalion
but had had to be practically re-formed afresh after Ypres ;
one or two had been thrown back into the melting-pot by
their losses on December 18th. The proportion of veterans
of Ypres was but small; even with all the returned

wounded [1] it can hardly have reached 20 per cent. But if the delays in launching the Division to the attack—things quite beyond its control—had robbed it of a full chance of getting its own back on the Germans, it had gone forward with a spirit and a dash which showed that those who had fallen at Ypres had found worthy successors in whose keeping the reputation of the Seventh Division would not suffer.

[1] The Grenadiers had only two officers present at Neuve Chapelle who had been at Ypres, Lieut. M. A. Darby (killed) and Lieut. and Qrmr. J. Teece. The C.O.s of the Scots Guards, Borders, 2nd Gordons, Yorkshires, and Queen's had all been present in both actions. Unfortunately no Battalion Diary gives the lists of officers who went into action at Neuve Chapelle and not many give those who landed with their units in October 1914. Accurate statistics even for officers are therefore beyond the reach of the compiler.

CHAPTER VII

AUBERS RIDGE AND FESTUBERT [1]

THE weeks that followed Neuve Chapelle were for the Seventh Division marked by few outstanding incidents. Sir Douglas Haig's hopes of promptly following up Neuve Chapelle by a fresh attack at another point had had to be relinquished, as already explained, owing to the heavy expenditure of ammunition and the difficulty of replacing the rounds fired away. The ammunition question indeed dominated the situation. Though much had been done and was being done to accelerate production, much time was needed for the provision of the necessary plant, the collection of skilled workers, and other essential preliminaries to the rapid expansion of the ammunition output, and many vexatious delays retarded the fulfilment of the plans that had been set on foot. The British Army in France had to resign itself to a period of waiting, during which, as afterwards appeared, the chances of an effective blow at the Germans were steadily diminishing. Neuve Chapelle had at least shown that the German defences were not proof against even the limited bombardment of which the British ammunition supply had permitted; it had also warned the Germans that they must treat the prospect of a British attack more seriously than they had done hitherto. Accordingly they devoted all their energy to strengthening their lines and improving their defensive organization. They now reinforced their breastworks, rendering them proof against anything but heavy guns, and developed the plan of siting machine-guns at the ground-level in pits just in front of the breastworks. But the adoption of these devices took some time, and though in May, when the

[1] Cf. Map 14.

belated attack was at last delivered, the German defences proved unexpectedly formidable, it seems reasonable to think that if Sir Douglas Haig could have launched an attack in the last week of March it might have achieved more success than that of March 10th.

For the rest of March the Seventh Division continued to occupy the trenches parallel with the Rue Tilleloy roughly from its junction with the Mauquissart road to the right of its old lines. One brigade held the line at a time, which gave the others a much-needed chance of a little rest and of assimilating the large drafts which soon replenished their depleted ranks. The Grenadiers, for example, got a draft of 6 officers and 350 men, the Yorkshires one of 275 men, the Borders one of 4 officers and 273 men. By the end of March most units were up to establishment again,[1] and while most of the newly arrived officers and men were recruits the drafts included a good many recovered sick and wounded. Thus the Queen's got back four of their original officers, Major Stansfeld rejoined the Yorkshires, and several other officers made welcome reappearances. Colonel Corkran took command of the Grenadiers and Major Cator that of the Scots Guards, Major Alston replacing the latter as Brigade Major of the 20th Brigade, while on March 28th Colonel Hoskins was promoted to command the 8th Brigade, being succeeded as G.S.O.I. by Colonel Gathorne-Hardy. A little later Captain Wyatt rejoined the Indian Corps, Captain Crossman becoming Brigade Major to the 21st Brigade in his stead and Captain Minshull-Ford of the Welch Fusiliers Staff Captain.

" Comparative quiet " did not mean that vigilance in patrolling and in looking out for opportunities of inflicting losses on the enemy was in any way relaxed. He was

---

[1] The Scots Fusiliers and Wiltshires were exceptions, numbering respectively 21 officers and 631 men and 18 officers and 712 men on March 31st, while the 6th Gordons were down to 12 officers and 567 men, there being at this time special difficulty over finding drafts for T.F. battalions, as their " Second Line " units, originally formed for reserve and draft-finding purposes, were now being reorganized for service overseas.

working unusually hard at his trenches and in doing so gave chances to our rifles and machine-guns, and Diaries and daily trench summaries contain frequent references to opening fire on hostile working and carrying parties and to preventing the enemy from wiring. The Germans retaliated by greater activity in sniping, to which cause most of our casualties were due[1] ; their artillery, however, was little more active than our own guns, now even more severely restricted in their ammunition expenditure than before Neuve Chapelle. On our part activity was mainly concentrated on preparing assembly and communication trenches for the next offensive, while patrols brought in much valuable information as to No Man's Land and the means of negotiating the passage of the Rivière des Layes and other obstacles. Our lines were considerably improved, especially as regards drainage, and several gaps were filled up. As the days lengthened the weather improved and the ground began to dry up, so that conditions in the trenches became distinctly better ; while by this time the system of reliefs and facilities for washing clothes and bathing had been thoroughly well organized. However, the days passed on without the launching of the new offensive, and though it was hardly appreciated at the time the delay was of great moment.

April opened with an unlucky accident, the Divisional Commander being injured on the 1st by a premature explosion when watching some experiments with trench-mortars. At first the injury was not thought to be serious and though he went home on medical leave he was expected back in a few days. However, he proved to be more injured than had been thought and was forced very reluctantly to relinquish command. In his farewell order General Capper spoke with pride of the Division's achievements and its spirit, and expressed the hope that he might

---

[1] Among the officers killed in this way was 2nd Lieut. W. C. G. Gladstone of the Welch Fusiliers, a grandson of the Liberal leader and himself an M.P. : he had taken a Special Reserve commission in September 1914.

some day return to it.   Major-General Gough from the 2nd
Cavalry Division succeeded him, taking over command on
April 19th.   On April 8th the Division was augmented by
the transfer to the 21st Brigade of the 4th Cameron Highlanders, a fine Territorial battalion hitherto serving in the
Eighth Division.   This brought all three brigades up to
five battalions, but shortly afterwards the Divisional
mounted troops were reduced by the departure of two
squadrons of the Northumberland Hussars, as this regiment and the Northampton Yeomanry were relieving the
15th and 19th Hussars hitherto serving as Divisional
cavalry to the original six Divisions, thereby allowing a
new 9th Cavalry Brigade to be formed from those regiments.

About the middle of April parties of the recently arrived
West Riding Territorial Division [1] were attached to the
units in the trenches for introduction into the practice of
trench warfare, and orders were received for the 22nd
Brigade to relieve the Bareilly Brigade of the Meerut
Division on the frontage between Chapigny and Neuve
Chapelle, roughly the line secured by the Fourth Corps in
the fighting of March 10th/13th.   However, before this
move could be carried out there came the news of the German gas attack at Ypres (April 22nd), of the driving back
of the French and the consequent outflanking of the Fifth
Corps.   The intended relief was postponed, and General
Gough was ordered to have two infantry brigades, two
Field Companies, and any artillery who happened to be out
of the line ready to move at two hours' notice towards
Ypres.   At the moment the 20th Brigade was in the line,
together with all the artillery.   However, by arrangements
with the Eighth Division it proved possible to pull out both
the XXIInd and XXXVth Brigades R.F.A. as well as the
31st (Howitzer) Battery, which now came under the
Division's orders.   The 54th and 55th Field Companies
were also ordered to stand by.

The Division remained standing by for several days.   All

---

[1] Later numbered Forty-Ninth.

sorts of rumours were rife as to the progress of the fighting at Ypres. It was clear that things were going none too well there, and no one was surprised when on April 28th orders to move North were received. The day was warm and the march proved a hard trial to the men, who during the long months of trench warfare had had little chance of keeping up their marching. Some battalions were carrying as much as 220 rounds of ammunition, and though only ten miles had to be covered there was much straggling and the men reached their destinations, Strazeele and Pradelles for the 21st Brigade, Merris for the 22nd, very much exhausted. The R.E. were sent on to Ypres by train and promptly pushed forward, the 54th Field Company to Wieltje, the 55th to Verlorenhoek, to assist in constructing new defences [1] in rear of the salient in the British lines at Zonnebeke. They were kept busy there for nearly a week, supervising working parties of infantry and wiring, and having a few casualties from long-range fire, and then on May 4th were sent back to the First Army's front.[2] The R.E. had been the only portion of the Division to see Ypres again ; the remainder stood by for five days in G.H.Q. reserve and then (May 4th) received orders to return South. The British counter-attacks had stopped the Germans from pushing forward to Ypres and from cutting off the bulk of the Fifth Corps, which had seemed imminent at one moment ; but as the French had failed to recover the Pilckem Ridge from which the gas attack had driven them, the Twenty-Eighth and Twenty-Seventh Divisions could not possibly retain their advanced positions on the Broodseinde ridge and in front of Polygon Wood. Accordingly it was decided to abandon further efforts to recover the lost ground and to fall back to the second line which the Seventh Division's R.E. had helped to construct ; and the

---

[1] This was the line to which the Twenty-Eighth Division fell back on the night of May 3rd/4th.

[2] General Plumer, G.O.C. Fifth Corps, sent a special message of thanks for the good work the two companies had done.

troops borrowed from the First Army were now free to
return to its front. Here final preparations were being
made for the new offensive which, it was hoped, would
eclipse Neuve Chapelle entirely and more than compensate
for the Second Army's loss of ground at Ypres. To some
extent the diversion of troops from the First Army to Ypres
had interfered with and delayed these preparations—the
54th and 55th Field Companies, for instance, had been
hard at work on assembly trenches till called off North,
while the inroads which the Ypres fighting made on the
still none too ample ammunition supply were even more
serious drawbacks.

The 20th Brigade meanwhile, acting under the G.O.C.
Eighth Division, had carried out the relief of the Indian
Corps, but had had little out of the usual routine to report.
When the rest of the Division returned the 21st Brigade,
with two battalions of the West Riding Division attached,
relieved the Eighth Division and the 20th Brigade between
Neuve Chapelle and Rouges Bancs, General Gough assuming
command of this frontage at 6 a.m. on May 6th. The
artillery had already gone back into position, the XXIInd
Brigade R.F.A. at Rue du Bois and Rue de Quemes, the
XXXVth between Laventie and Rouge du Bout, and had
registered. The 20th Brigade on relief was held in readiness, as was the 22nd also, to exploit any success the Eighth
Division might gain.

The plan of the attack, which, after many postponements,
had been finally fixed for May 9th, was more ambitious
than that of March 10th. A double attack was being made :
by the Eighth Division backed up by the Seventh near
Fromelles, by the Indian Corps and the First Corps South
and West of Neuve Chapelle. The Eighth Division, if
successful in storming the trenches opposite it, was to
press on Southward, the Seventh co-operating on its right ;
the Indian Corps and First Corps would also push forward,
and it was hoped that the inner flanks of the attacks would
eventually obtain touch on the S.W. end of the Aubers

Ridge. The artillery available considerably exceeded that collected for Neuve Chapelle, and the highest hopes were entertained. It was believed that the reasons for the failure to achieve more complete success had been taken into account, and the causes of delay provided for, so that this time things would go better than at Neuve Chapelle.

It was because such high hopes were entertained that May 9th was so bitter a disappointment. The greatly increased strength of the German defences was an unpleasant surprise : instead of the attackers finding but few survivors of the garrison of the front trenches, and those mostly demoralized by the bombardment which had destroyed their lines, they were met by determined opposition and heavy rifle fire from behind little-damaged defences, while the German artillery's reply was much heavier and more effective than at Neuve Chapelle. On the Eighth Division's front only a handful of the right brigade, the 24th, managed to reach the German lines, and though on the left a substantial foothold was gained by the 25th Brigade, grazing fire from the well-concealed and protected machine-guns which swept No Man's Land from both flanks effectually prevented any exploitation of this success. The bombardment was renewed but with little effect, the machine-guns could not be located or silenced, and despite several gallant efforts no effective help could reach the troops in the German lines, and gradually, as they ran short of bombs and cartridges, they were overwhelmed or driven out by counter-attacks. Not only did the 20th and 22nd Brigades spend the whole day in inactivity, the 23rd, the Eighth Division's reserve brigade, got no farther than the British front trenches, which were too badly damaged by the counter-bombardment and too much congested with the casualties and the disorganized remnants of the attacking brigades for it to be possible to put the 23rd in for a fresh attack.

Practically the only portion of the Seventh Division to be actively employed on May 9th were the gunners. They

were busy enough, firing away according to the previously
arranged programme from 5 a.m. to 6.40 a.m., repeating
various phases of the programme to assist the later attempts
to advance, firing intermittently during the afternoon in
the hopes of keeping back the counter-attacks and assisting
the hard-pressed survivors of the first attack to maintain
their hold on the captured trenches. " F " and " T "
Batteries R.H.A. were mainly employed to form barrages to
prevent German supports from coming up, and fired
respectively 1,141 and 878 rounds.[1] In the XXIInd
Brigade R.F.A. the 104th Battery had an advanced section
up in the trenches for wire-cutting, which work was
effectively performed at many points, but unluckily more
than wire-cutting was needed. The XXXVth Brigade
R.F.A. fired altogether over 3,000 rounds of shrapnel and
313 of high explosive and the practice was reported to
be good, though the effect on the greatly strengthened
German parapets fell far short of expectations.

Evening found the 2nd Rifle Brigade with a few handfuls of other units clinging desperately to a short stretch
of the German lines. It had been proposed that as soon
as it was dark the Queen's should push across No Man's
Land and relieve them ; " D " Company indeed actually
moved forward in order to do so but was sent back by the
C.O. of the Rifle Brigade as the trenches were already
congested with troops. Still less was it possible to adopt
a proposal from the Fourth Corps that the Seventh Division
should relieve the Eighth and carry out on the 10th the
programme arranged for the 9th. Generals Gough and
Davies concurred in opposing this plan. The Eighth
Division was much too disorganized and mixed up for the
smooth carrying out of so difficult a relief, the routes to
the assembly places were much exposed to fire, the assembly

---

[1] One section of " T " Battery was detailed to accompany the Queen's who
were to lead the advanced-guard of the Seventh Division : it took part in the
initial stages of the preliminary bombardment and then came out of action,
joining the Queen's at their assembly position.

places themselves were badly knocked about, and the
trenches as a whole hopelessly congested.   Accordingly
the idea was abandoned and about midnight the remnants
of the Rifle Brigade evacuated the trenches they had so
tenaciously defended.

However, if the Seventh Division was not to renew the
unsuccessful attack at Rouges Bancs hard work was in
store for it.   Despite the double repulse of May 9th—for
the attacks beyond Neuve Chapelle had failed even more
completely—Sir John French was anxious to continue
the offensive, if only to assist the big French attack near
Arras by diverting German reserves to the British front.
It was therefore arranged that the First Corps should make
another attack S.W. of Neuve Chapelle, with which should
be combined an advance Eastward from Festubert on the
other flank of the salient formed by the German lines N.W.
of Ferme Cour d'Avoué.   For this operation the Seventh
Division was selected, being temporarily attached to Sir
Charles Monro's First Corps.

May 10th therefore saw the Seventh Division on the
move, not Eastward across the Aubers Ridge as many had
fondly hoped, but S.W. towards Béthune, where evening
found the 20th Brigade established, with the 21st round Le
Touret and the 22nd about Essars and along the Béthune–
Festubert road.   This was new ground for the Division.
It was flat country, in places marshy, intersected with
ditches, devoid of good artillery positions or facilities for
observation, little improvement on the water-logged
meadows with which the Division was so painfully familiar.

In the new offensive, a deliberate bombardment spread
out over several days was substituted for the " hurricane
bombardment " which had preceded the attack of May
9th.   It was hoped that this would allow of more accurate
observation of the effects produced, so that any sections
of wire uncut after the first day's bombardment could be
systematically tackled.   To delude the enemy as to the
exact hour of the assault there were to be feint bombard-

ments, followed not by an attack, but by a fresh burst of
fire which it was hoped would catch the enemy manning
his trenches in anticipation of the expected assault.
Between the Division's arrival in its new area and the
renewal of the attack five days elapsed, during which the
artillery programme was duly and, apparently, most
successfully carried out.   On the night of May 11th the
21st Brigade began relieving the Forty-Seventh (London
Territorial) Division on the frontage from which the
Seventh was to attack.   This ran from astride Prince's
Road to the road running N.E. from Festubert through
La Quinque Rue.   The Bedfords took the right and the
Yorkshires the left ; and were both kept busy with trying
to prevent the Germans repairing their damaged trenches
or mending the gaps in their wire by keeping them under
rifle and machine-gun fire.   The Germans on their part
retaliated quite vigorously, and the Yorkshires had the
misfortune to have their C.O., Colonel Alexander, killed on
the 14th, to the great loss and regret of his battalion.

On the evening of May 15th the two brigades told off for
the assault, the 20th and 22nd, moved out of their billets
towards the assembly position.   They were to " go over
the top " at 3.15. a.m. on May 16th, but the Second
Division and Indian Corps, with whom the Seventh was
co-operating, were to attack half an hour before midnight :
it was hoped that this would draw off the Germans' attention and so enable the Seventh to effect a surprise.   The
German lines here formed a salient, and while the 20th
Brigade, on the left, faced about S.E. astride Prince's Road,
the 22nd, attacking on either side of the Rue de Cailloux,
faced nearly East.   After storming the front trenches the
troops were to push ahead as rapidly as possible, the 22nd
Brigade's left and the 20th's right being directed on a house
in an orchard [1] just about S.E. of the road junction at La
Quinque Rue ; from this the 20th Brigade would extend
North nearly to Ferme Cour d'Avoué, where they should

---

[1] Marked as M 9 on the map.

12

get touch with the Second Division, the 22nd's line facing about South towards Rue d'Ouvert along a German communication trench.[1] This brigade's bombers were to work to the right and clear the German front line, opposite the London Division.

In the attack the 20th Brigade had the Borders on the left, supported by the Grenadiers, and the Scots Guards on the right, with the 2nd Gordons behind them and the 6th Gordons back in Brigade Reserve. A gap of about 200 yards separated the Scots Guards from the Welch Fusiliers, the left battalion of the 22nd Brigade, who had the Queen's beyond them on the outer flank. The Warwickshires and South Staffords were in support trenches 150 yards in rear, the Royal Scots in reserve. Of the 21st Brigade the Yorkshires and Bedfords were holding the trenches, which they cleared to some extent to allow the assaulting battalions to form up : the Scots Fusiliers were 200 yards behind, the Camerons and Wiltshires being back along the Rue de l'Epinette in reserve.

All troops were in position before midnight and listening intently to the noise of the heavy fighting which had begun on the Rue du Bois front. At 2.45 a.m. their own guns, hitherto silent, chimed in and for thirty minutes plastered the German lines with shell. Then the guns lifted to the second line and the infantry poured over the top of the trenches. On the left both battalions crossed No Man's Land without much loss, carried the German front line with a rush, and began pushing forward. The Borders, however, had not got far beyond the first line before enfilade fire from two strong points on their left[2] caught them, inflicting heavy losses, including the C.O., Colonel Wood, though on the right they reached a communication trench running South to a small orchard.[3] They made various efforts to work down the German front trench to the left, but after clearing about 200 yards were

---

[1] Called North Breastwork for purposes of this account.
[2] Marked P 7 and P 8 on the plan.   [3] Marked P 4 on the map.

driven back by the accurate fire of a trench-mortar which
had escaped the bombardment. The Scots Guards, more
fortunate, pressed on ahead, their leading companies
penetrating over half a mile into the German lines, while
the supports stopped level with the Borders and began
consolidating a line from the small orchard Southward.
On their right the Welch Fusiliers were also pushing ahead
with the greatest impetuosity. The 22nd Brigade had
met an even greater volume of fire than the 20th, but the
Fusiliers, though staggered and for a moment checked,
went right in and carried the trenches opposite them.
Colonel Gabbett was killed and there were many casualties,
but once into the German lines the Fusiliers forged ahead
rapidly, the two supporting companies backing up the
leading lines and carrying them forward over the support
trenches. Advancing farther the leading lines came under
fire from the left and some men swung to that flank to face
it, joining the leading party of the Scots Guards, while
others pushed on more S.E. towards La Quinque Rue.
On the outer flank of the brigade the Queen's had suffered
terribly, being caught by enfilade fire from the right which
the Welch Fusiliers had escaped.[1] As they crossed the
parapet they were promptly mown down, but they went
forward line after line till, seeing that his men were being
sacrificed to no purpose, Major Bottomley stopped the
second wave of " C " Company and telephoned to the
supporting artillery for another fifteen minutes' bombardment. At the end of this " C " Company went over,
closely followed by " D " and with the leading company
of the South Staffords coming up in support. As they
pressed across No Man's Land the survivors of the leading
waves sprang up and joined in, and advancing with great

---

[1] Among the lessons of this attack it is specially noted in the C.R.A.'s
Diary that it is essential to maintain a continuous fire on the trenches on the
flanks of the line attacked during the assault and for some time after it.
There was hardly enough artillery available and another 18-pounder
brigade to bombard the German trenches from M·1 South would have been of
the utmost value.

dash they reached and carried the German lines, though
Major Bottomley was mortally wounded, and the casualties, even in the second attack, were heavy. But losses
notwithstanding the Queen's were not to be stopped and
pushed on, driving the Germans before them. The South
Staffords promptly began to work forward along the
German front line to the right, clearing it with the help of
some of the Brigade Grenade company. It was daylight
now and the Royal Warwickshires also were coming
forward, one company pushing on after the Welch Fusiliers,
a second, followed later by another half-company, supporting the Queen's who were making for La Quinque Rue
and the North Breastwork beyond. Progress was slow,
for the German resistance was stubborn and the ground
intricate. The Welch Fusiliers indeed in their advance
towards the orchard had to swim to cross one deep ditch
that barred their path.

Nowhere was such good progress made as by the parties
working South along the German front line. Splendid
work was done by Lieut. Hassell and the battalion bombers
of the South Staffords, while C.-S.-M. Barter [1] of the Welch
Fusiliers called for volunteers to help him bomb down the
trenches and, aided by 8 bombers, cleared nearly 500 yards
and took 3 officers and nearly 100 men. Meanwhile two
companies of the South Staffords working forward on the
left rear of the bombing party secured the line of the road
between the German second and third lines before 7 a.m.,
some time before which the Queen's had crossed La
Quinque Rue and reached the North Breastwork about
due N.W. of the road-bend at Rue d'Ouvert. Reinforcements of the Royal Warwickshires came up to assist them,
and shortly after the Queen's gained their objective the
Welch Fusiliers under Captain Stockwell [2] reached and

---

[1] He was subsequently awarded the V.C.

[2] This party represented the right half of the battalion, of the left a large
number were missing, having pushed on ahead and become isolated, a few
survivors falling back upon the Scots Guards.

occupied the orchard farther to the left, taking a machine-gun. With them was another party of the Royal Warwickshires as well as some 30 of the Scots Guards.

These Scots Guardsmen, however, had lost touch with their battalion, and as reports reached Divisional Head-quarters it became clear that there was a gap between the two brigades. At 8 a.m. the Borders were still held up ; repeated attempts on the two strong points had failed, though German counter-attacks had been repulsed. Some of the 2nd Gordons had come up between the Borders and the Scots Guards and were helping to consolidate the German third-line trench, the Scots Guards continuing the line South of the small orchard, though under machine-gun fire from strong points in front. Of " F " Company, however, on the right of their leading line nothing had been heard ; it had vanished into the German trenches. Not for some days was its fate cleared up, and then when the last British advance carried the line forward considerably nearer to Ferme Cour d'Avoué a large number of dead Scots Guardsmen were found in a rough circle,[1] surrounded by German corpses, having evidently been counter-attacked in force and overwhelmed.[2]

To carry on the 20th Brigade's advance General Hey-worth about 9 a.m. ordered the Grenadiers forward. Colonel Corkran, seeing that to follow the Borders would bring his men under heavy machine-gun fire, moved to the right and went over from the Scots Guards' trenches. Two companies were left to help consolidate the German front line while the other two reached the German third line and joined the Scots Guards, who had just repulsed a German counter-attack, driving their assailants back with

[1] About the point marked P 11 on the map.

[2] The evidence of the few survivors who were taken prisoners confirmed this story ; the party while consolidating its final objective was attacked by superior numbers in front and flank. This counter-attack seems to have been delivered by a half-battalion of the 57th Infantry Regiment, the local reserve, which was moving up the communication trench from Rue du Marais to reinforce the front line.

loss.[1] From here the intention was that the Grenadiers should swing round to their left and attack the strong points which were holding the Borders up, but when No. 4 Company tried to advance over the open, heavy machine-gun fire checked it, two officers being hit, and although No. 3 and the battalion bombers cleared a stretch of a communication trench and took several prisoners, the obstructing strong points defied all attacks. These were bombarded afresh, but there was some misunderstanding between the 20th Brigade and the Division about the time for the new attack, and the bombardment stopped before the men were ready to go forward. The advanced detachments of the 22nd Brigade remained therefore unsupported and in danger of being cut off by a German advance along La Quinque Rue behind their exposed left flank and rear.

Vigorous efforts were being made meanwhile to secure the ground gained. The Bedfords and Yorkshires were now digging communication trenches across to the captured line. The Scots Fusiliers were brought up to the assembly trenches and in the afternoon " B " Company of the Wiltshires assisted the Brigade bombers to clear the German front line, as far as a point[2] level with the Southern end of Rue d'Ouvert, bringing the bag of prisoners up to nearly 200 and the total advance Southward to 700 yards. But though the Grenadiers and the 8th Royal Scots, who had come up on their right, had another try at the troublesome strong points they made little headway, and about 7 p.m. orders were issued to consolidate the line gained. Unluckily, about this time, or rather earlier, the weak and unsupported advanced detachments of the 22nd Brigade had been forced to relinquish their hardly-won positions at the orchard and along the North Breastwork. The day thus ended with the Division consolidating a line far short of the advanced points reached, but con-

---

[1] This counter-attack was apparently delivered by the 57th I.R. after it had overwhelmed " F " Company of the Scots Guards.

[2] L 2 on the map.

tinuous and defensible. On the right the South Staffords held a line just South of La Quinque Rue astride the German second and third lines and connecting up with the 7th London, who had taken over the German front trench as far as the strong point known as L 2. Their left was flung back almost at right angles to face East and was continued Northward by the Royal Scots and the Grenadiers, the latter having the 6th Gordons on their left facing P 7 and P 8. The Borders meanwhile had withdrawn to the old British front line, where were also half the 2nd Gordons and the remnants of the Royal Welch Fusiliers. The old German front trench had been consolidated as a second line of defence and was held by the Warwickshires, the Scots Guards, and the rest of the 2nd Gordons. The Queen's, reduced to under 300 of all ranks, had been taken right back to reserve.

Elsewhere the attack had fallen short of the Seventh Division's measure of success. The Indian Corps and the Second Division's left had been checked and the Second's right brigade had not managed to take either of the two main German strongholds on their front, Ferme du Bois and Ferme Cour d'Avoué, or to obtain touch with the Seventh Division, but enough progress had been made to warrant the issue of orders that the 21st Brigade should press the attack next day, advancing from the West against Ferme Cour d'Avoué and the trenches thence to La Quinque Rue, while the Second Division attacked them from the North.

During the night consolidation was pressed on, the three Field Companies giving great help in the wiring, in constructing strong points, and in pushing on with the communication trenches, the 54th Company working with the 22nd Brigade, the 55th with the 20th, the Highland Field Company with the 21st. Slow fire was maintained during the night and all the guns were ready to open fire if a counter-attack should be attempted, but the two German regiments holding the front attacked, the 55th and 57th, had both suffered too heavily to contemplate another attack and apparently the reserves as yet at hand were insufficient for the purpose, so that by daybreak the captured lines had been put into quite a defensible state.

After several postponements 10.30 a.m. on May 17th was fixed upon for the renewal of the attack, but before that time the Second Division reported that about 700 Germans had suddenly moved forward from Ferme du Bois, apparently intending to surrender, for their own guns had opened upon them and between their fire and that of the British artillery the party had been mostly wiped out, though about 200 gave themselves up to the 6th Gordons. That battalion had been working forward to close in on the left flank of the Germans in the sector between the two British attacks, and had suddenly seen this mass of enemy advancing : it had promptly opened an effective fire but ceased when it became evident what the real intention of the enemy was. This incident was thought to indicate a weakening of the German resistance, so the attack was put forward to 9.30, at which hour the Scots Fusiliers advanced through the 6th Gordons against the strong points on the left, the Wiltshires simultaneously passing through the Royal Scots, making for the La Quinque Rue orchard.

The Scots Fusiliers' attack went very well, although while waiting for orders to advance they had been subjected to a heavy shelling [1] and had had many casualties, including two officers killed. As the two leading companies dashed over the parapet the Grenadiers on the right opened heavy covering fire. This time the defenders of the strong points could offer little resistance : they had been shelled with great accuracy and effect and the Scots Fusiliers' rush swept clean over them. The left company, " D," pushed ahead well, overcoming considerable resistance, while " C " Company stormed an orchard [2] which had been strongly organized for defence, and a platoon specially detailed to

---

[1] Apparently our obsolete and inaccurate 4·7's were again responsible.
[2] P 9 on map.

bomb down the German front trench to the N.E. made splendid progress, clearing several hundred yards and taking several prisoners, including a company commander.[1] Unluckily, just as the other companies came forward in support, British guns started shelling[2] the points which had just been captured, and instead of pressing on towards Ferme Cour d'Avoué the Scots Fusiliers had to recoil half-way back towards the starting-point. A company of the Yorkshires reinforced them, and Major Pollard (R.S.F.) soon reorganized his men for a fresh advance, but the great opportunity was lost.

This unfortunate check to the Scots Fusiliers when in full cry was mainly responsible for the Wiltshires' inability to retain the positions they had reached. That battalion's leading company, " B," followed the North Breastwork[3] almost to the house in the La Quinque Rue orchard, but a German barrage checked the advance of supports and the company[4] found itself isolated. It hung on some time, but its left flank and rear were completely open, and early in the afternoon the survivors fell back on their second company, which was digging in on the Royal Scots' right. The latter had been unable to carry out their orders to swing their left forward and secure the line of La Quinque Rue, as this move was to depend on the left getting forward and covering them. This the left had not accomplished, for though about this time the Scots

[1] The artillery had been able to register their targets carefully, and the batteries employed, three 18-pounder and five howitzer, of the Second and Seventh Divisions aided by three 9·2-inch howitzers, had fairly demolished the defences and had pinned to the ground many Germans who would otherwise have managed to escape. Specially good work as a forward observing officer was done by Major Allardice of the 106th Battery, who pushed forward to P 8 and sent back most valuable reports.

[2] It seems that this was a barrage put down by the Second Division to assist a fresh attack on Ferme Cour d'Avoué.

[3] About as far as the point marked M 5 on the map it was held by the South Staffords.

[4] Apparently it was almost up to the point reached on the previous day by the Welch Fusiliers.

Fusiliers had again tried to advance they had once again been checked by our own guns.[1] However, further efforts to advance N.E. along the German front trench were successful, and about 4 p.m. it was reported that 2nd Lieut. Cleaver's platoon of the Scots Fusiliers had obtained touch with the 1st King's of the Second Division.[2]

It was now decided to utilize the reserve of the Second Division, the 4th (Guards) Brigade, to attack Cour d'Avoué from the Westward, as it had defied all attempts against it from the North. Orders were accordingly issued for the Seventh Division's line to be consolidated prior to the 4th Brigade's advancing through it. At the same time the two battalions of the 21st Brigade still in hand, the Bedfords and 4th Camerons, were to pass through the 7th London, who were still holding the extreme right of the line, and to advance S.E. making for Rue d'Ouvert and a German trench running thence about S.W. Both moves were to be preceded by a bombardment, lasting till 6.30 p.m. However, at that hour neither Bedfords nor Camerons had reached their "jumping-off line," and the 4th Brigade was only just beginning to cross the old British line, so the bombardment of the 21st Brigade's objectives had to be continued for another half-hour, while the 4th Brigade's attack was postponed till next morning, to allow of more adequate preparations and reconnaissance.

The 4th Brigade therefore merely took over most of the Seventh Division's frontage, allowing the 20th Brigade to be withdrawn, though the Grenadiers remained in the German second line, now the support trenches of the British position. They had had the curious experience of

---

[1] These guns were apparently some of the Second Division's, who were preparing for a fresh attack by the 6th Brigade and were unaware of the Seventh Division's exact position. The difficulties of co-ordinating the action of infantry and artillery, which this and similar incidents brought out, were in the end overcome by allotting a special staff to that purpose, but in May 1915 much that afterwards became almost routine was still in the stage of experiment.

[2] This was at Q 2, about 600 yards N.W. of Ferme Cour d'Avoué.

having their own 2nd Battalion, the right unit of the 4th Brigade, come suddenly up alongside of them and pass through them. Of the 21st Brigade the Scots Fusiliers and the two companies of the Yorkshires who had been supporting them were sent back into reserve, the rest of the Yorkshires moving over to the right and being placed on the flank of the Wiltshires, now somewhat mixed up with the South Staffords.

Meanwhile after many delays the Bedfords and Camerons had started their attack about 7.35 p.m., Bedfords on the right, Camerons on the left. It was a dark evening and both battalions were soon lost to sight of the troops holding the old German front line, but heavy rifle and machine-gun fire from away to the right told that the Germans had seen them coming, and before long news came back that the Bedfords had come across some deep ditches [1] which had much disorganized them while machine-guns which enfiladed them from the right had inflicted heavy casualties, Major Mackenzie being killed as he left the jumping-off trench. Finally their advance was checked by a ditch 12 feet broad and 5 feet deep and full of water. On the right their bombers led by Lieuts. Stonier and Brewer gained some ground and cleared two strong points, but on approaching a third [2] they found that the communication trench had been destroyed 50 yards short of it and all their efforts to cross the open were stopped by machine-gun fire. The survivors of the leading companies, too few to achieve anything even if they could cross the big ditch, [3] had there-fore to come back. The Camerons, though more fortunate

---

[1] The attack unfortunately had had to be made without previous recon-naissance, and looking at the ground from the British front line it seemed to be plain going over grass which was about a foot high, so that no sign of the ditches could be seen. Had the attack been postponed so as to allow of reconnaissance the ditches would have been discovered and planks taken by which to cross them, in which case a big success might well have been achieved, so splendidly did the two battalions struggle against their disadvantages.

[2] Marked respectively K 3, K 4, and K 5 on the map.

[3] This ditch would seem to have been between K 5 and L 6 on the map.

as regards the enfilade fire, also met a succession of deep and wide ditches. However, they pushed steadily on, showing great courage and steadiness in their first attack, wading and even swimming the ditches, and despite losses established themselves in a German trench about S.W. of Rue d'Ouvert [1] road-bend with Germans on both flanks. It was about midnight that news of this success reached Brigade Headquarters. Orders were promptly issued for the two nearest companies of the Yorkshires to push forward on the Camerons' left and link up with them, and the artillery were informed of their position and ordered to shell the Germans on either side of them, while the Bedfords were to renew their attack on the strong point at K 5 and then press forward towards the Southern end of Rue d'Ouvert. These movements, however, were to be subsidiary to the main attack, in which a Canadian brigade which had been placed under General Gough's orders was to attack the La Quinque Rue orchard, the troops of the Seventh Division still in line swinging forward their left as the Canadians advanced and the 4th Brigade tackling Cour d'Avoué.

However, long before the main attack could get going or even before the Yorkshires could get forward to their help, the Camerons had been forced to relinquish their precarious and isolated position. They were little over 200 strong, most of their bombs had been lost or rendered useless in crossing the ditches, and counter-attacks on both flanks before long dislodged them. They had the greatest difficulty in extricating themselves owing to the maze of ditches and trenches, mostly water-logged, behind them— many of them so deep that they had to be swum—and they lost heavily in retiring. The Bedfords' bombers meanwhile found K 5 extremely difficult to approach. The communication trench being at right angles to the strong point, it was almost impossible to get effective covering fire, and the machine-guns [2] swept the open ground around it.

---

[1] About L 8 on the map.

[2] When finally taken K 5 was found to contain six of them.

The rest of the Seventh Division spent May 18th in hanging grimly on and enduring punishment. " It was the worst day for shelling " is the Royal Scots' verdict, and other units agree. The Germans had brought up many more guns and were not stinted for ammunition, so the troops holding the captured lines had a bad time. Luckily they had worked hard to put their trenches into a good state of defence and they were now repaid for their exertions. In the main attack, delivered about 3.30 p.m., the Seventh Division itself had little part. The Canadians passed through instead of wide of the Royal Scots, and that battalion, its front thus masked, could not join in on the right as ordered. The Canadians pushed on, however, and reached La Quinque Rue, while the Guards, though checked by fire from Cour d'Avoué and from a strong point [1] to the South, gained enough ground to link up with the Canadians' left. This advance was followed by the withdrawal from the fighting area of most of the infantry of the Seventh Division, though some of the 21st Brigade with the 7th Londons attached were left to hold the right of the captured line. Thus the Wiltshires and a company of the Yorkshires took over from the South Staffords and Royal Scots, and another company of Yorkshires replaced the Bedfords at the far end of the line. The 22nd Brigade now moved back into billets in the Béthune area, the 20th already having proceeded to Hinges, en route to Robecq and Busnes. On the evening of May 20th the Canadians relieved the Yorkshires and Wiltshires, and those battalions moved off to the area round Gonnehem and Lillers to which the rest of their brigade had preceded them that morning. The R.E. came out of the line with the infantry, exhausted by their incessant labours, though they had been fairly fortunate as regards casualties. The artillery, however, were left behind to support the continuation of the offensive by the Canadians and the Forty-Seventh Division. They remained in action under General Alderson, the G.O.C. Canadian

---

[1] Marked P 14 on map.

Division, until May 23rd, and did most effective work, though the scarcity of ammunition restricted their expenditure very considerably.   The XXXVth Brigade R.F.A., for example, only fired 200 rounds on the 19th and about 700 on the 20th as against over 1,800 on the first day of the attack.   But their accurate and judicious support contributed materially to the Canadians' success in capturing the La Quinque Rue orchard and gaining ground to the South along the German front line.

" Festubert," though far from the complete failure of the May 9th attack, cannot be pronounced a great success. In comparison with the casualties and the ammunition expended—a question of paramount importance at that time and only second in seriousness to losses in men—the gain in ground was insignificant and the enemy's losses an inadequate set-off.   The Germans had not, as at Neuve Chapelle, counter-attacked across the open in mass, and the increased strength of their defences had enabled them to endure the heavier bombardment with less loss than the lighter bombardment of two months earlier had inflicted.   Still they had been well punished ; the Seventh Division had had the satisfaction of finding the captured trenches full of German dead besides taking some hundreds of prisoners.   Once again it had shown itself capable of storming the enemy's positions, formidable though these had now become, and of such success as British arms had had in the recent fighting it could claim its full share.   The unlucky accident of the British barrages which had twice stopped its advance, the water-logged country in which every ditch between fields was a serious obstacle, the difficulty of maintaining communication with the artillery and indicating to it the precise position of the advanced infantry and the exact location of the points they wanted shelled, the advantage which the Germans enjoyed both in the quantity and quality of their bombs—these were the main reasons for the failure to achieve a greater success, not any lack of dash and devotion on the part of officers

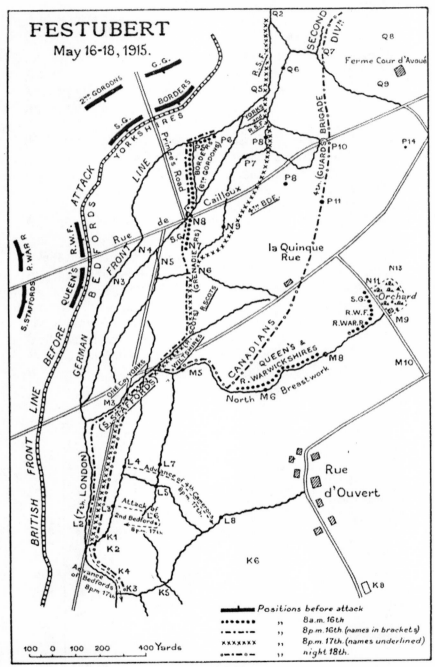

FESTUBERT
May 16-18, 1915.

2ND GORDONS

S.G.

G.G.

BORDERS

YORKSHIRES

R.W.F.

ATTACK

QUEEN'S

R.WAR.R

S. STAFFORDS

BEDFORDS

BEFORE

Prince's Road

Rue de Caillou

GERMAN

FRONT

Q2

R.S.F.

SECOND DIV.

Q8

Q7

Ferme Cour d'Avoué

Q6

Q5

YORKS 2ND R.S.F.

4TH (GUARDS BRIGADE

Q9

P6

BORDERS (6TH GORDONS)

P8

P10

P14

P7

P8

P11

4TH BDE.

N8

la Quinque Rue

N9

S.G.

N7

(GRENADIERS)

N4

N5

N6

N3

R.SCOTS

N13

N11

S.G.

Orchard

R.W.F.

R.WAR.R

M9

CANADIANS

QUEEN'S & R. WARWICKSHIRES

M8

M10

ONE Co.YORKS

WILTSHIRES

M5

North M6 Breastwork

M3

(S. STAFFORDS)

L2 (7TH LONDON)

L4 Advance of 4th Cameron
8 p.m. 17th.

L7

L5

L3

Attack of
2nd Bedfords
8 p.m. 17th

L8

BRITISH

FRONT

LINE

K1

K2

K4

K3

K5

K6

K8

Advance
2nd Bedfords
8 p.m. 17th

Positions before attack

● ● ● ●   ,,   8 a.m. 16th.

— ·· — ··   ,,   8 p.m. 16th (names in brackets)

×××××××   ,,   8 p.m. 17th. (names underlined)

— ○ — ○   ,,   night 18th.

100   0   100   200   400 Yards

MAP 14.

and men.   Of those qualities ample proof had been given ;
the impetuous and determined advance of the Scots Guards
and Welch Fusiliers in the first assault was specially praised
by the Divisional Commander, though it was far from
standing alone.

But the Division's losses had been terribly heavy, 50
per cent. higher than those of Neuve Chapelle, amounting
in all to 170 officers and 3,833 men.[1] No less than five
battalions, the Borders, Queen's, Welch Fusiliers, Yorkshires, and Royal Scots, had lost their C.O.s, all valuable
officers who could ill be spared, the first four of whom had
all been wounded at Ypres and had since rejoined.   The
Queen's and Welch Fusiliers had been particularly unlucky
in officer casualties, both having 11 killed and missing, and
their total casualties were 472 and 581 respectively.   In
the 21st Brigade the Bedfords were the heaviest sufferers,
but the Camerons, who had come splendidly through the
trials of their first big fight, had lost nearly a third
of those in action.   In the 20th Brigade the Scots Guards
and Borders had been the hardest hit, but the 2nd

[1] The figures were 59 officers and 647 men killed, 11 officers and 615 men
missing, 100 officers and 2,633 men wounded.

By units the details were :

	Killed.		Missing.		Wounded.	
	Officers.	Men.	Officers.	Men.	Officers.	Men.
Staff	—	—	—	—	2	1
R.A. . . .	3	7	—	—	9	20
R.E. and Signals . . .	—	—	—	1	1	13
Grenadiers	1	15	—	3	3	111
Scots Guards	1	48	6	171	3	181
Borders	11	110	—	35	5	240
2nd Gordons	3	53	—	10	10	204
6th Gordons	—	4	—	—	2	27
Bedfords	2	40	—	67	9	276
Yorkshires	6	23	—	9	2	135
Scots Fusiliers	4	29	—	15	2	137
Camerons	2	24	3	66	8	125
Wiltshires	1	14	—	—	2	115
Royal Scots	1	36	—	1	10	141
Queen's	10	154	1	47	8	252
Warwickshires	2	25	—	21	3	158
R.W.F.	10	119	1	165	9	277
S. Staffords	2	41	—	4	6	197
R.A.M.C.	—	5	—	—	6	13

Gordons had suffered very heavily seeing that they had been mainly occupied in consolidating the positions gained. The Royal Scots also had had more casualties from the persistent bombardment than had some battalions who had had a more active part to play. As at Neuve Chapelle the artillery in the absence of much German counter-battery work had escaped lightly, as had also the R.E. despite the bombardment of the positions they were consolidating.

For about a week after the withdrawal of the infantry of the Seventh Division the operations were continued, though without any substantial additional gains. The fighting, which was heavy and involved serious losses, only emphasized how formidable were the defences which the Seventh Division had tackled and what difficult obstacles it had encountered. The main purpose of the operations was to prevent the Germans on the First Army's front from thinning their line to find reinforcements to oppose General Foch nearer Arras, but by May 26th shortage of ammunition compelled Sir John French to abandon further attacks and content himself with consolidating the line gained. At the same time orders were issued to the First Corps to relieve a French Division South of the La Bassée Canal, and for the reconstitution of the Fourth Corps, which was now to include the Seventh, Fifty-First (Highland Territorial), and Canadian Divisions; it was to take over the line from the Canal Northward, having the Canadians in the Givenchy sector and the Seventh on their left, holding the trenches taken in the recent fighting.

CHAPTER VIII

FROM FESTUBERT TO LOOS [1]

THE interval between the relief of the Seventh Division's infantry on May 20th and their return to the line on the 31st had been all too brief to give the shattered battalions the rest they required and the chance to assimilate their drafts. These had appeared with satisfactory promptitude, but many battalions had lost so heavily that they were quite disorganized; the command of companies had devolved on subalterns of little experience or training, while to find N.-C.-O.s was in many units a most serious problem. It would be idle to pretend that all the units which took over the frontage East of Festubert on the last day of May were worth as much as they had been a fortnight earlier. The reconstruction which they now had to go through for a third, in some cases a fourth, time became increasingly difficult as each successive offensive swept away more of the few really trained officers and N.-C.-O.s who survived. The new material which filled the gaps was often excellent, but the difficulties which handicapped the British forces in the field, the lack of appliances of every kind, were equally felt by the training and draft-finding units at home; and though trench warfare provided a severe enough test of soldierlike qualities, of discipline, of endurance, of spirit, it afforded little time and few facilities for training. Even officers and men who had endured several months of trench warfare and had become thorough adepts at the tricks of that trade knew little of any other kind of warfare. Reinforcements both of officers and of men had to be pushed out from home before their training was anything like complete; and not until the " New Army " Divisions began to reach France in large numbers was there any

[1] Cf. Map 15.

opportunity to take Divisions out of the line for periods
long enough to allow of systematic training and of starting
Corps and Divisional schools of instruction.   But in the
middle of 1915 very few " New Army " Divisions had as
yet found their way to France, and the first arrivals were
utilized rather to take over more line from the French—
whose need for such relief was urgent enough—than to
give the older Divisions a chance of either rest or training.
It was hard on the Seventh Division that it should so soon
have been called back to the trenches, harder still on some
of its units that they should have been required to undertake yet another attack before June was out.   But while
the strategical situation forbade a complete relaxation of
pressure the tactical situation on the Fourth Corps' front
made an improvement in the line highly desirable, especially
in the low-lying ground just North of Givenchy.

Here the last offensive had left the line in an unsatisfactory state.   The Forty-Seventh Division had pushed
forward at the foot of the Givenchy bluff, but the trenches
and redoubts it had captured were overlooked from the
top of the bluff and were liable to be bombed from the
enemy's positions on the higher ground which more or less
enfiladed our advanced line.   On the bluff itself the situation was most unsatisfactory ; it was hard to make out
the exact line in the maze of old trenches, shell-holes, and
craters formed by mine explosions, and its irregularities
gave chances to German snipers and led to many casualties.

The 20th Brigade, the first to take over the new
frontage, had the 6th Gordons on the right on the bluff
itself, the Grenadiers in the low ground opposite the
Southern end of Rue d'Ouvert, the 2nd Gordons on the
left facing the Northern end.   It was decided to begin by
attempting to improve the position on the bluff, and on
the night of June 3rd two companies of the 6th Gordons,
supported by 20 bombers from the Borders and four
machine-guns from the Scots Guards, endeavoured to
capture a strong point known as I 4 at the apex of a pro-

jection from the German lines [1] just North of what had once been an orchard. The assault was preceded by a mine explosion which produced a big crater and did great damage both to the German trenches and to their garrison, so that the assaulting columns secured their objectives with little difficulty, capturing some fifty prisoners of the 56th Infantry Regiment. The right company pushed Southward along the German trenches and began to erect a barricade fifty yards beyond a point known as I 2; the left company reached another strong point at I 3, East of the point of entry, and established connexion with the right attack by occupying a communication trench leading towards I 2. Assistance was promptly given by a detachment of the 55th Field Company, who helped to wire the position, besides making communication trenches back to the British lines. By 2.30 next morning (June 4th) the R.E. withdrew, the captured position having been successfully wired and seeming quite secure; six more platoons of the 6th Gordons had reinforced the garrison and the Borders had taken their places in the original front trenches.

However, about 3 a.m. the Germans began counterattacking in force, backed up by trench-mortars against which it was difficult to make any effective reply, while their bombers were down in deep trenches which sheltered them from the British rifles. For a time the Gordons kept the attackers at bay, but before long their supply of bombs ran out and they were gradually forced back from the captured trenches. Some bombers from the Borders tried in vain to stop the retirement, but they too were out-bombed, and by 7.30 a.m. the Germans had recovered all their lost ground and occupied the crater, beating off two efforts by the Borders to retake it. Plans were started for a fresh effort, but General Gough decided to postpone it to allow of further preparation, especially a larger supply of bombs: so that night (June 4th/5th) the

[1] This was at the Northern end of the spur, the German trenches being just on the crest line and the ground sloping gently up to them.

22nd Brigade took over. The 20th Brigade had had a rather costly turn in the trenches; the 6th Gordons alone suffered nearly 150 casualties, their 2nd Battalion—which had been very busy in clearing up the line, retrieving equipment, burying the numerous dead, and getting the trenches into a more sanitary condition—lost 40 men and the Borders rather more.

The 22nd Brigade had a disturbed ten days in the line, especially on the right where the Queen's relieved the Borders on the evening of June 5th. There was constant shelling, intermittent bombing and sniping, and with the weather very hot and so many unburied corpses lying about clearing up the area was a particularly trying task, besides more than usually dangerous owing to the enemy being so much on the alert. The Royal Warwickshires in the centre did very good work in patrolling, bringing in valuable information ; and their snipers were very successful, two men in particular who lay out 200 yards in front of the line getting ten Germans on one day. The Queen's tried to improve the position at I 4, but ran into thick wire and were heavily fired upon and had therefore to come back ; the Royal Scots who relieved them on the night of June 9th/10th made two efforts without any better success, having several casualties. On one occasion they were checked by finding the trench completely blocked by coils of wire in front of our barricade,[1] and when our bombers tried to drive the Germans back so as to let our men get in and clear away the wire they found themselves out-bombed, the German bombs out-ranging ours and bursting far more regularly. On the morning of June 11th it was noticed that Lieut. Martin, who had been missing after the previous night's attack, was lying out wounded in No Man's Land. Corporal Angus (8th H.L.I., attached to 8th Royal Scots) went out in broad daylight to his officer's help, crawled out to him despite a heavy fire and succeeded in rescuing him, though in doing

---

[1] These were thrown over the parapet in thick loose coils and proved difficult to deal with, only heavy H.E. shell having much effect on them.

so he was himself badly wounded by bombs.   His gallantry
was rewarded with a V.C.

It had been decided, however, to try yet another attack,
strong as the German lines in front of Givenchy and Festubert had proved themselves to be, and to employ once more
the much-tried Seventh Division, despite the inexperience
of so many of its officers and men.   Its objective was a line
running from due East of Givenchy [1] to the Southern
end of Rue d'Ouvert, the 21st Brigade being detailed for
the task and employing the Yorkshires on the right and
the Wiltshires on the left.[2]   On the Division's right the
Canadians were to attack a strong point called by them
" Dorchester " and to form a defensive flank covering the
further advance of the Yorkshires towards Chapelle St.
Roch.   On the left the Fifty-First Division was attacking
Rue d'Ouvert from the North, connexion between them
and the 21st Brigade being maintained by the Grenadiers,
who were to push forward across the flats in front of Rue
d'Ouvert.

After several postponements the attack was finally fixed
for the evening of June 15th.   For some days previously
the artillery had been trying to destroy the German wire
but with indifferent success, bad light and long grass
helping to impede accurate observation of results.
Throughout the 15th a slow but steady bombardment was
maintained until 5.30 p.m., when it became intense, being
continued for 30 minutes, at the end of which the attackers
went over.   Unluckily the German defences were extremely
formidable : the trenches were nine to ten feet deep and
very narrow with deep dug-outs admirably protected ; and,
accurate as our fire was, only direct hits from our heavier
howitzers could produce much effect on such positions.
The Germans could thus man their lines with practically
unshaken troops in great numbers, and even before our

---

[1] The right flank was a strong point marked as H 3 on the map.

[2] The Yorkshires' frontage extended from opposite H 3 to opposite I 4, the
Wiltshires continuing the line along the British front trench as far as J 7.

guns lifted off the front trenches the Germans were swarming up from their dug-outs to open fire directly our advance started.

In such circumstances it was enormously to the York-shires' credit that their assaulting companies went forward unflinchingly and with great dash. Some of "A" Company headed by 2nd Lieut. Belcher actually got into the German trenches and spread out to right and left, killing several Germans and starting to push forward along a communica-tion trench leading to the second line. But all the other officers and most of the men had been hit in crossing No Man's Land and the little party was soon stopped and then driven back. "B" Company fared even worse. Captain Raley and two subalterns were hit as they crossed the parapet, and machine-guns, rifles, and shrapnel brought down three-quarters of the company without its even effecting a lodgment in the enemy's trenches. On the left a bombing party under 2nd Lieut. Lloyd Jones pushed down a sunken road to the edge of the mine crater and carried on a vigorous contest till all their bombs were exploded and every man had been hit.[1] Meanwhile the Wiltshires also had been hotly received and had lost heavily, especially to enfilade machine-gun fire from a communica-tion trench running Eastward from the mine crater.[2] The leading companies, "C" and "D," pushed forward neverthe-less, but came under more enfilade fire from the foot of the hill,[3] while from their left machine-guns concealed in long grass did much damage. Some few men seem to have got within 50 yards of the German trenches in front of Chapelle St. Roch,[4] but failed to get in; and when the supporting

---

[1] Of "A" Company who went over the top 5 officers and 170 other ranks only 40 men were unhit; "B," with 1 officer and 31 men unhit out of 5 officers and 180 men, lost even more heavily, the battalion's total losses coming to 6 officers and 158 men killed and missing, 5 officers and 250 men wounded.

[2] Marked I 4–I 9 on the map.

[3] About I 12 on the map.

[4] J 14 on the map.

companies tried to get forward they were checked only a little distance beyond the original front line, mainly by enfilade machine-gun fire from the right. Before long the survivors of " C " and " D " crawled back to the starting-point.

Orders were issued for the two battalions to reorganize prior to another attack and for the Bedfords to be put in between their inner flanks; but they had been too hard hit to be fit for a second attempt and the orders were cancelled, the Scots Fusiliers relieving the Yorkshires and the Bedfords replacing the Wiltshires. This was done, but rather slowly, the congested state of the trenches causing much delay; and the attack, originally ordered for 1.30 a.m., was postponed first to 5.30 a.m. and then to the afternoon to allow of a careful bombardment of the objective.

The 21st Brigade had not been alone in their lack of success. The Canadians had also made a lodgment but failed to retain it, and though the Fifty-First Division had begun by establishing themselves in the German lines they had had the greatest difficulty in holding their ground against persistent counter-attacks, and were eventually driven out. Meanwhile the Grenadiers had gone forward as ordered to link up the attacks of the Fifty-First Division and 21st Brigade. The ground to be covered was the same water-logged flats over which the Bedfords and Camerons had struggled forward a month earlier. It was slightly drier now, but though the Grenadiers established themselves on a line parallel to Rue d'Ouvert,[1] without encountering much opposition, by the time they had got there the 21st Brigade's attack had failed and the Grenadiers' patrols could not find any of the Wiltshires. The battalion hung on, however, though isolated and without support on its flanks, till, on the news of the Fifty-First Division's enforced retirement, it was decided to withdraw it also. Shortly before daybreak on June 16th the Grenadiers were back in

---

[1] About J 10–K 6 on the map.

their trenches. To have remained out in front in daylight must have led to disaster and the battalion was lucky to have escaped with some 60 casualties, including Lieut.-Colonel Corkran who was slightly wounded.

Despite the evidence as to the formidable character of the task before the Division which the ill-success of the attack had afforded, the attempt was renewed next day East and N.E. of Givenchy. The Canadians were to try " Dorchester " again ; the Scots Fusiliers were to attack from the right and centre of the frontage formerly assigned to the Yorkshires, the Bedfords on their left attacking the crater, while machine-guns from selected points farther back, such as Windy Corner and Le Plantin, gave covering fire.[1]

The hour for the assault was earlier than on the previous day, 4.45 p.m. as against 6 p.m. The objective had been steadily bombarded during the morning and early afternoon and this was intensified for three-quarters of an hour before the assault, but nevertheless two minutes before it stopped the Germans manned their parapet in strength and opened fire, catching the Scots Fusiliers in the act of leaving their trenches. More than half the stormers were down before they could pass the British wire ; in one section five men out of thirteen were hit in their own trenches, and very few managed to get more than fifty yards. Two subalterns pushed ahead and were shot on the German wire, but the two leading companies were almost wiped out and the C.O. promptly prohibited any further advance, the uselessness of which was only too apparent. The Canadians also had failed, and though the Bedfords got into the crater and made a most gallant fight they were ultimately bombed out. They had the satisfaction, however, of inflicting heavy losses on the Germans, particularly in their retirement, very skilfully conducted by 2nd Lieut. Gibson, the only

---

[1] This had been quite effective on the previous day's attack, very good practice being made by the Borders' machine-guns, which enfiladed German communication trenches with great accuracy.

officer who remained unhit. Two machine-guns on the left got good targets in covering the retirement, but it was clear that the difficulties of attacking the position were hard to exaggerate and that its capture, even if it could be accomplished, was not worth the loss of life involved. After dark the survivors of the attack crawled back; some who had worked forward through the long grass nearly to the German wire reported that the enemy had been lining the parapet two and even three deep, those in rear acting as loaders. The deep dug-outs which the Germans had excavated on the bluff had provided shelter which was proof against anything but a direct hit from a 9·2 : and the authorities had at length to recognize that Givenchy was not a suitable place for a local offensive without a far heavier weight of guns and ammunition behind it than was available. Orders were now issued for the 22nd Brigade to relieve the 21st, and on the night of June 17th/18th this was completed and the 21st Brigade was concentrated round Robecq, over a thousand weaker than on June 15th. It had been a disastrous experience ; and though no little gallantry and devotion had been displayed in the attacks, such losses with nothing to show for them were calculated to have a depressing effect.[1] It was the third time within four months the 21st Brigade had had to " go over the top," and of the three this third task had been the hardest. On battalions which had suffered as heavily as those of the 21st Brigade the strain was very great ; and to convert collections of drafts, many of whom had but little training, into effective

[1] The casualties were :

					Killed and Missing.		Wounded.	
					Officers.	Men.	Officers.	Men.
Bedfords	.	.	.	.	5	45	2	72
Yorkshires	.	.	.	.	6	158	5	250
Scots Fusiliers	.	.	.	.	4	73	2	127
Camerons	.	.	.	.	—	20	3	35
Wiltshires	.	.	.	.	4	72	5	128
Total	.	.			19	368	17	612

battalions needed a respite of some duration from active operations. But the brigade only got ten days' respite from the trenches. Before the end of June it was back in the line, taking over from the Fifty-First Division the front-age opposite the Northern end of Rue d'Ouvert. The Wiltshires, however, who had been particularly handicapped in reconstruction by having relatively so few Ypres wounded to return to them, were sent down to G.H.Q. for a month's training, Majors Leathem and Forsyth of the Yorkshires being transferred to them as C.O. and Adjutant.

The second attack by the 21st Brigade had not been quite the last episode in this abortive offensive. On the evening of the 17th two companies of the 2nd Gordons tried to occupy a German trench on either side of a strong point West of Rue d'Ouvert [1] and to connect up with the Fifty-First Division. There seems to have been some misunderstanding with that Division, and though the Gordons advanced and some men actually got into the German trench, the greater part of it proved to be strongly held and protected by uncut wire ; and after lying out for some time in front of the wire, enfiladed and much exposed, the Gordons were withdrawn, after suffering 150 casualties [2] without having been able to gain ground or inflict appreciable punishment on the enemy. The Division was not a little relieved at the abandonment of an offensive so little likely to be successful, which may perhaps have indirectly contributed to help the French nearer Arras, but for which little other justification could be urged.

The three months which followed the abandonment of the attacks at Givenchy were perhaps more devoid of incident than any period of equal length in the Division's experience in France. Offensive action against the enemy was reduced to a minimum—it was before the days when vigorous raiding was the order of the day even in the " quieter " parts of the line ; artillery ammunition was

---

[1] Marked as K 6 on map.
[2] Three officers and 52 men killed and missing, 2 officers and 90 men wounded.

exceedingly scarce and was being carefully husbanded;
there was much less rifle fire, though snipers were alert
enough and took their chances when they got them;
and neither machine-gunners nor the Trench-Mortar
Batteries developed any special activity. The long hours
of daylight did not allow of much work in the open or
of much sapping forward, even where the ground was
dry enough to permit it; and the shortness of the nights
restricted the activities of patrols and wiring parties.
Still our patrols succeeded in discovering that the enemy
made a practice of working whenever we had working-
parties out who masked our fire. One night therefore
after our parties had started working they were quietly
withdrawn, fire being then opened by rifles and machine-
guns, apparently with excellent results. There were many
changes in the frontage held : the Division relieved the
Canadians as far as the Canal on June 24th, then was
out of the line for a few days early in July, being in Corps
Reserve, but went back into the line between Neuve
Chapelle and La Quinque Rue in the middle of the month.
Battalions were gradually brought up to strength after
their Givenchy losses and the diminution in the activities
of both sides allowed of a little more rest and relaxation,
while the formation in July of a Divisional Band was a
welcome innovation and increased the amenities of periods
out of the line.

The chief incident of July was General Gough's promotion to command the First Corps, now vacant as Sir Charles
Monro had been appointed G.O.C. of the newly formed
Third Army. The Division, however, did not part company with General Gough; it had been definitely transferred to the First Corps at the end of June, and had
received very handsome compliments on quitting the
Fourth Corps from Sir Henry Rawlinson, who spoke
of his " appreciation for its very gallant services " and his
" gratitude for the admirable spirit displayed at all times
by the Division, sometimes under the most trying cir-

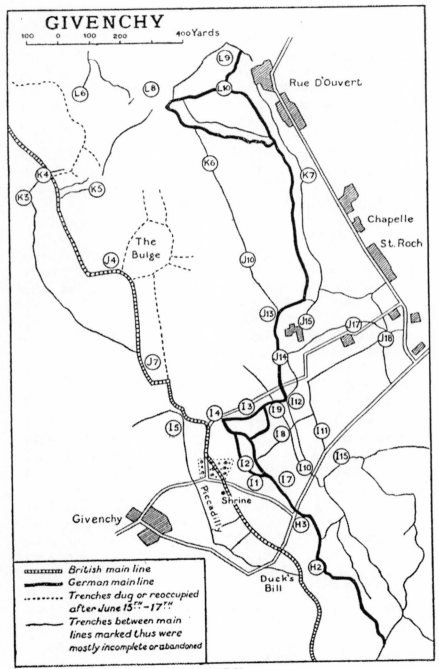

MAP 15.

cumstances." It was to fight under Sir Henry Rawlinson
again and to win his high approval once more ; but for
the moment its transfer from the Fourth Corps to the
First meant that it was serving under both its G.O.C.s,
as General Capper had fortunately recovered just in
time to return and resume command of the Division. He
rejoined on July 24th, shortly after which the Division
was taken out of the line again, only to relieve the Ninth
Division in the middle of August on the familiar frontage
between Festubert and Neuve Chapelle.

By this time an important change had taken place.
A complete Guards Division was being formed, and this
involved the departure from the 20th Brigade of its two
Guards battalions.[1] The Division was naturally sorry
to lose two battalions with such records, which had been
to the fore in all its battles, and speculation was rife,
once it was known the Guards were going, as to how they
would be replaced. The troops were not a little interested
to learn that the vacancies were to be filled by two " New
Army " units, the 8th and 9th Devons, Army Troops
respectively of the " First " and " Second New Armies,"
more familiarly known as " K 1 " and " K 2."

There were not a few spectators about to see the new
arrivals march into the Divisional area and take over
their new billets, the 8th arriving at Calonne on August
4th, the first anniversary of the declaration of war, and
the 9th following four days later. The new-comers
created a very favourable impression by their good turn
out, their steadiness, and their soldierly bearing ; and
this impression they speedily confirmed on being attached
by companies to the 21st and 22nd Brigades for instruction
in trenches. By August 26th, when the 20th Brigade
relieved the 21st in the right section of the Divisional
frontage opposite Rue d'Ouvert, the 8th and 9th Devons
were entrusted with the front line.

---

[1] General Heyworth also went to the Guards Division, being succeeded by
B. General J. H. S. F. Trefusis.

Several other changes had also taken place ; the Division lost the last of its original Brigadiers in August when General Lawford went home on promotion to command the newly organized Forty-First Division ; he was replaced in the 22nd Brigade by Colonel Steele of the Coldstream Guards, who then began his long association with the Seventh Division ; General Birch had left in July, General Rotton arriving on July 26th to replace him as C.R.A. Major Stewart had been transferred to the Highland Division in June as G.S.O. I and was succeeded as G.S.O. II by Major Needham of the Gloucesters. Major Darell left to become A.A. and Q.M.G. of the Third Division and his place as D.A.Q.M.G. was taken by Major Tompson, R.F.A., Major Hobbs went to the Fifth Division as D.A.Q.M.G. (July), Captain Riddell Webster of the Scottish Rifles replacing him as D.A.A. and Q.M.G. The Division lost the 8th Royal Scots, who had been selected for duty as the Divisional Pioneer battalion,[1] but were transferred to the Highland Division on August 20th, but it had gained two batteries of the XXXVIIth (How-itzer) Brigade R.F.A. in July, while in the first week of September the 55th Field Company was transferred to the Guards Division, being replaced by the 95th.

August had been uneventful, though towards the end of the month the Yorkshires had some exciting times on the Givenchy front, which the 21st Brigade had just taken over from the Second Division. Minenwerfer were greatly in evidence, there was much bombing from saps, and rifle-grenades were so freely used that our guns had to be turned on to suppress them. The Germans exploded a mine near the Duck's Bill, but failed to damage the British parapet or to prevent the Yorkshires from denying them the use of the crater. But things were fairly brisk, and in two short tours in the trenches the Scots Fusiliers had over 20 casualties, and the other battalions lost more than they had lost since Givenchy.

[1] A Pioneer battalion had been made part of the establishment of a Division.

With September the Division shifted to ground quite new to it—the frontage South of the La Bassée Canal and East of Vermelles, which the British had recently taken over from the French. The Division's new line ran Northwards from the Vermelles–Hulluch road on the right almost to the famous Hohenzollern Redoubt. Some of its battalions, the Queen's, the Borders, and the 2nd Gordons, had been attached to the First Division to hold these trenches before General Capper took over the line on September 4th. It was a comparatively narrow frontage and only one brigade was in trenches at a time, but any amount of work was in hand, mainly the digging of new lines in No Man's Land, here of ample extent, Germans and French having remained at a respectful distance from each other since the line had been taken up in October 1914. This digging entailed constant working-parties, but the troops worked with a will; they were not slow to realize what these labours pointed to—the long period of inactivity was nearing an end, the British were about to deliver a fresh blow at the German lines.

CHAPTER IX

LOOS [1]

The country South of the La Bassée Canal was very different both from the marshy flats round Festubert and at the foot of the Aubers Ridge and from the woods and more sandy soil in the Ypres Salient, in which the Seventh Division had hitherto served. The Division now found itself on drier and stiffer ground where the chalk ridges North of Arras sloped down towards the Canal in long spurs separated by shallow valleys. It was to find that in rain chalk had its own peculiar disadvantages ; but the weather was fairly dry when it first crossed the Canal, and for the extensive trench-digging which the coming offensive made necessary the stiffer soil was really an advantage : less revetting was needed and the sides of the trenches could be cut much steeper.

Of digging the Division was to have its fill. No Man's Land was, as already explained, much too wide ; so to secure a satisfactory " jumping-off line " for the attack the British front line had to be brought within 500 yards of the German trenches and two new support trenches dug between the new and the old fronts. Much of this had been done before the Seventh took over its new frontage, the support lines were well in hand and the front line half completed ; however, it needed deepening, while any number of communication trenches had to be dug and dug-outs were required for advanced dressing stations, bomb and ammunition stores, ration and water dumps, and similar purposes. There were therefore tasks and to spare and the Division set about its work with a will, the two newly arrived battalions distinguishing

[1] Cf. Maps 16, 17, 18, and 19.

themselves by their prowess as diggers.[1] As the front was held by one brigade only plenty of labour was available from the brigades not in the line, so the troops in front were not unduly pressed. They were active in patrolling and in foiling the enemy's attempts to inquire into the preparations in progress. This led to several sharp encounters, in one of which, on September 7th, a fighting patrol of the 8th Devons drove in a German covering party after a brisk " scrap." The British guns were registering but without drawing much of a reply from the enemy, whose inactivity was quite noticeable, casualties being satisfactorily low.

The decision to undertake another substantial offensive on the Western Front, despite the scanty success which had attended the Allied efforts of the early summer, had been arrived at mainly in the hopes of assisting the hard-pressed Russians, with whom things were going none too well, while the prospects that the Gallipoli expedition might help them, at one time promising, were rapidly fading away. The ammunition and artillery situation of the British forces was still far from satisfactory, while although nearly a dozen " New Army " Divisions were now in France they were as yet inexperienced and untried. It might therefore have been well to postpone any substantial British participation in the offensive till these new units had been acclimatized and tested and more guns and shells were available. However, the French Higher Command was set upon another attempt at breaking through the German lines and full of confidence that the lessons learnt from the earlier attacks had shown the high road to success ; if the French were going to attack in force the British could hardly remain inactive. Moreover, after their use of poison-gas at Ypres it had been decided to pay the Germans back in their own coin, and great results were anticipated from what the

[1] The 9th Devons contained a substantial contingent of Welch miners to whom the work was mere child's play.

operation orders for the attack euphemistically described
as the "accessory." As it was, though the British were
employing more than double the force engaged on May
9th, their attack was only subsidiary to an attack of
General Foch's group of Armies between Arras and Lens,
which in its turn was subsidiary to the main French
offensive in Champagne.

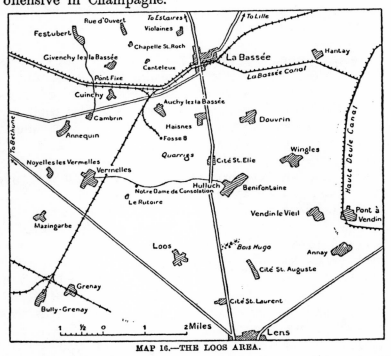

MAP 16.—THE LOOS AREA.

The British, besides making two large and three small
diversions elsewhere, were putting in three Army Corps
in their principal attack. The Fourth Corps was attacking
on a frontage from just South-West of Loos to the Vermelles–Hulluch road, the First on its left carried on to
the Vermelles–Auchy lez La Bassée railway with two
Divisions and had a third attacking astride the La Bassée
Canal; the newly formed Eleventh Corps was held in
reserve along with masses of cavalry, ready to exploit

the advantage should the first attack succeed in breaking through the German defences. It was hoped to push on between Lens and the La Bassée Canal, to reach the Haute Deule Canal, crossing it at Pont à Vendin and establishing touch well East of Lens with Foch's attack. If this could be achieved Lens would be pinched out and the necessity for attacking it direct avoided, while the successful passage of the Haute Deule Canal would almost certainly lead to the rolling up of the German front North of La Bassée.

In this project the First Corps's objective ran from the La Bassée Canal by Pont à Vendin to Bauvin, and its first aim was to secure the line Hulluch–Cité St. Elie–Haisnes–Canal. The Seventh Division on its right and the Ninth on the Seventh's left would attack in a roughly North-Easterly direction, while the Second with its left and centre astride the Canal faced more nearly East. Its function, after capturing Auchy, was to form a defensive flank from Haisnes to the Canal and so cover the further advance Eastward of the Ninth and Seventh Divisions.

The Seventh, whose right rested on the Vermelles-Hulluch road, had before it two clearly defined trench systems, the second of which, running just behind a gentle rise about 1,500 yards in rear of the front, covered Hulluch, Cité St. Elie, and Haisnes. Both systems were formidable : the wire was thick and strong, the trenches were well sited and constructed. There were numerous well-placed " strong points," machine-guns had been skilfully distributed so as to give enfilade fire, " switches " and communication trenches connected the two systems and provided intermediate obstacles to an advance ; while if the defences were not very strongly held a well-placed and adequate artillery was in support. Behind the frontage which faced the Division's left brigade a group of quarries formed a tactical feature of importance ; and the villages just in rear of the second system had been turned into virtual fortresses.

Against these defences a considerable weight of artillery had been concentrated and enough ammunition collected for a systematic bombardment to be begun on September 21st and continued until the evening of the 24th. The Divisional Artillery had taken up their positions between August 30th and September 2nd, and for three weeks before the bombardment began had been systematically carrying out registration, corrected by ground and air observation and by air photographs, which were now being issued. One of their chief tasks was to enfilade the North and South faces of the great Hohenzollern Redoubt, which lay outside their own Division's frontage, being among the Ninth's objectives, but from their positions enfilade fire could more easily be brought to bear. They had also to enfilade the line of the Hulluch–Vermelles road as well as cutting the wire in front of their own infantry and shelling the trenches they were to assault.[1] Special attention was paid on the third and fourth days to the bombardment of Breslau and Goeben Alleys and the other communication trenches, and observation officers and patrols were active in trying to observe the results of the fire, to report if and where additional bombardment was needed, if wire was not properly cut or if any particular strong point needed more attention. On the second day, for example, uncut wire was reported for 150 yards opposite a " White Mound " on the right brigade's front and for 100 yards South of the " Pope's Nose," a strong point some way farther North, while after the first day's firing this same " Pope's Nose " was reported to require much further bombardment.

The ammunition at the disposal of the bombarding artillery exceeded the meagre supplies available for Neuve Chapelle and the other earlier attacks, but the frontage to be bombarded was also very much larger

---

[1] As the long forward slope East of Vermelles was exposed to view from Fosse 8 and the Dump the guns had to be right back behind the Vermelles–Cuinchy ridge, which rather handicapped them in cutting wire.

and quite out of proportion to the ammunition available.
A thorough destruction of the German defences was out
of the question, but it was hoped to inflict upon them
an amount of damage which, coupled with the use of gas,
would offer good prospects of a successful assault. Unfortunately the German wire was extremely thick and in
places concealed by the long rough grass which had
covered most of No Man's Land ; indeed when General
Trefusis investigated the wire on the 20th Brigade's
frontage on the evening of September 24th he found
patches of it still uncut. The 8th Devons turned their
machine-guns on to one bit with satisfactory result and
after dark parties were sent out to cut the wire by hand,
which was done without much interruption by the enemy.
On the 22nd Brigade's front observation was more difficult : the long grass effectually concealed the wire and
prevented discovery of the fact that much of it was not
properly cut : where Spurn Head Sap joined the German
front line in particular the failure to cut it was to prove
only too costly next day. But over much of the frontage
it was no longer an effective obstacle ; and the trenches
bore ample testimony to the accuracy of the bombardment, though the German trench garrisons had escaped
with fewer losses than might have been expected, owing
to the deep dug-outs which gave them such effective
shelter.

The 20th Brigade was taking the right half of the
Division's frontage and the 22nd the left. Each brigade
had two battalions in its front line and provided its own
supports and reserves, the 21st Brigade forming the
Divisional reserve. The assaulting battalions were the
2nd Gordons, 8th Devons, South Staffords, and Royal
Warwickshires, the dividing line between the brigades
being a British communication trench called the Fosse Way
and in the German trenches a strong point called the
" Slit." The Quarries with Cité St. Elie behind them were
thus on the 22nd Brigade's front, while that of the 20th

extended from just South of Cité St. Elie to the Northern
end of Hulluch. The total frontage was about 1,200
yards, and the distance between the lines about 500
yards for the 22nd Brigade and slightly more for the 20th.
In that brigade the Border Regiment were in the Old
Support Trench and Curly Crescent, for not only the new
front line but the two support trenches and the old front
line were occupied by the four waves of the assaulting
battalions. Behind them were the 6th Gordons in the
Chapel Bays, the fifth battalion of the brigade, the 9th
Devons, being still farther back in reserve. The 22nd
Brigade, only four battalions strong, owing to the recent
departure of the Royal Scots, had the Welch Fusiliers
in support and the Queen's in reserve. Of the Divisional
Artillery the XIVth Brigade R.H.A. and the XXXVth
Brigade R.F.A. were attached respectively to the 20th
and 22nd Brigades, to be ready to move forward if a real
break-through was achieved.

The concentration of the assaulting brigades began
soon after nightfall on September 24th. It was well that
ample time had been allowed, for, largely owing to the
torrential rain, it was not completed until 3.30 a.m.,
about two hours before the guns opened the intense stage
of the final bombardment. It was just sunrise when this
began, at 5.50 ; then with a tremendous roar the guns
simultaneously gave tongue all along the frontage to be
attacked, smoke candles were ignited and gas poured out
from the cylinders which the Division had been so
laboriously lugging along the communication trenches
for the last week. What wind there was blew from the
desired quarter, the S.W., but it was too light to carry
the gas along properly. It hung about, in places it blew
along the front and, despite gas-masks and all precautions,
put out of action many of the assailants. Better results
were achieved by the smoke, but on the whole the carefully
concealed " accessory " was far from the conspicuous
success on which so much depended.

For forty minutes the guns rained shells on the German trenches and wire and then at 6.30 the infantry climbed out of their trenches and pushed steadily across No Man's Land. Some battalions had begun moving a few minutes earlier, so as to be nearer the German trenches when the guns lifted, and some of the rear companies had closed up to the front line before it started. With so wide a No Man's Land to have advanced at a run would have merely exhausted the assailants before they could reach their objective, so the lines went forward at a walk. The 20th Brigade took just twelve minutes to reach the opposing trenches and in that time both Gordons and Devons had suffered severely, for, as the guns lifted, the enemy's trenches were manned and rifles and machine-guns opened a heavy fire ; while German guns, well back for the most part behind the second line, shelled No Man's Land vigorously. On the right the Gordons were heavily punished by machine-guns in Hussey Redoubt ; Colonel Stansfeld was mortally wounded before the German lines were reached, a company commander was killed, two more were wounded, and losses among the men were heavy. The Devons too suffered severely ; on their front the wire was only partially cut and there was much crowding at the gaps, which gave good targets to the rifles and machine-guns of the defence. Colonel Grant was killed together with Major Carden, the second in command, Captain Kekewich, the Adjutant, and several fine subalterns, while three company commanders were wounded. But both battalions pushed on un-flinchingly, the new hands of the Service battalion carrying themselves splendidly through this devastating baptism of fire, and the German front line was stormed in fine style. It was not very strongly held and the survivors of the leading companies pushed straight on to the support trench, 150 yards farther on. Here there were more Germans, and resistance, especially to the Gordons, was more stubborn. Their rear companies, however, were

up now, and by 7.25 a.m. not only had the support trench
been taken, but the two battalions, now sadly reduced in
numbers, were pressing ahead towards the German second
line, here nearly a mile away. The Gordons had taken
50 prisoners in the support trench and the Devons had
also captured a fair number. Directly the leading battalions had gone over the top the Borders and 6th Gordons
had started moving, and General Trefusis lost no time
in sending them ahead, the 6th Gordons in the wake of
their Regular battalion keeping their right on the Hulluch
road, the Borders advancing on their left. By 8 a.m.
both battalions had passed the German front trenches
and were pressing forward. The 9th Devons also had
reached the British front line, while two batteries of the
XXIInd Brigade [1] R.F.A. were moving forward along
with a section of " T " Battery R.H.A. which Colonel
Tudor sent forward on his own initiative. The latter
crossed No Man's Land and took up its position near the
Slit ; the field batteries were placed South of the Vermelles–Hulluch road about 700 yards behind the old
British front line, and ordered to enfilade the German
trenches opposite the 22nd Brigade, where matters had unfortunately gone nothing like so well as on the 20th's front.

On this part of the line the gas seems to have hung
about the British trenches, and many men, particularly
in the Royal Warwickshires, were incapacitated by it,
while, as already mentioned, the wire had been hidden
by long grass, and when the South Staffords and Royal
Warwickshires reached it they found great stretches
uncut. Determined efforts were made to get through
the obstacle and to cut the wire by hand, but from the
trenches behind a deadly fire was poured in, machine-
guns in the Pope's Nose being specially effective, and
casualties were numerous. Both the leading companies
of the South Staffords had their commanders, Lieut.

---

[1] The 105th and 106th Batteries : orders for their advance were issued at
7.3 a.m.

Cooper of " C " and Captain de Trafford of " A," killed on the German wire, and Lieut. Burke was hit in bringing " B " Company across No Man's Land to reinforce. The Royal Warwickshires had their C.O., Colonel Lefroy, killed, several other officers fell with him, and the Adjutant, Captain Duke, was wounded. Here and there a few men contrived to push through the gaps and to gain entrance into the German trenches, but the wire was still a most formidable obstacle, especially where Spurn Head Sap joined the German front line, and the attack was hopelessly held up.

However, the Welch Fusiliers soon reached the front line, and with their support a fresh attack was organized, Captains Cartwright and O'Connor of the brigade staff doing splendid work, while Private Vickers of the Royal Warwickshires distinguished himself by the conspicuous courage and devotion with which he cut a lane through the wire.[1] This time the attackers' gallantry was attended with better results, though many of the Welch Fusiliers were shot down by machine-gun fire from the left. The front line was stormed, though at the German support line there was more resistance. The attacking battalions had now got inextricably mixed and casualties had been so heavy that the further advance lacked weight, especially as the South Staffords on the right were still being delayed by the Pope's Nose and by the Slit in the support line also. These continued to hold out for some time longer, their defenders firing into the backs of the attackers as they pressed forward towards the Quarries. Not till over an hour after the support trench had been carried[2] was their resistance eventually overcome, and then only by the assistance of some of the Borders. That battalion's bombers under Captain Sutcliffe, backed by two platoons of " D " Company under Captain Ostle, attacked the Pope's Nose from the flank and after a stubborn fight

[1] He was awarded the V.C.
[2] It would appear that this happened about 7.30 a.m.

took it with 70 prisoners, while the South Staffords eventually captured the Slit with another 120 Germans.

Meanwhile the Queen's, the reserve battalion of the 22nd Brigade, had reached the front, moving over the open, and were available to support the attack on the Quarries. Machine-guns in the German front line were still sweeping No Man's Land as the battalion entered it, but its leading company, "C," pushed forward towards the Quarries without meeting much opposition ; the other companies, however, who seem to have crossed more to the left nearer Fosse 8, had quite a hard fight to capture the German first line. Captain Brocklehurst, the commander of the second company, "B," was wounded, and the Germans were not overcome till the battalion bombers under Lieut. Taylor-Jones bombed down the line and outflanked them, on which these companies pressed on towards Cité St. Elie, eventually establishing themselves in Cité Trench about 200 yards from the village about 11 a.m.[1] Farther to their right but not actually in touch with them were other detachments of the 22nd Brigade, who had pushed on towards Cité St. Elie after the capture of the Quarries. This had been accomplished somewhere about 9.30 after some hard fighting, for the Germans resisted stoutly and were not overpowered till many had been bayoneted or shot, the decisive factor being apparently the attack of "C" Company of the Queen's who came in from the N.W., taking about 50 prisoners.

The Quarries once taken, Colonel Ovens of the South Staffords started to organize an advance on Cité St. Elie.[2] He himself with some of his own battalion pushed

---

[1] The details of the move are very hard to establish with any accuracy, but the main body of the Queen's would seem to have passed to the left of the Quarries and approached Cité St. Elie from the North-West.

[2] Support was given by the 12th Battery R.F.A., which took position near the Pope's Nose rather after midday, having its forward observing officer in the Quarries, whence good observation could be obtained : a section of the 35th (Howitzer) Battery also came forward.

on up a communication trench leading to Cité Trench, while other parties went forward over the open. The party taking the communication trench was before long held up by bombers, and Cité Trench proved to be protected in front by thick and uncut wire, so the few men who had penetrated thus far found their advanced position untenable. They were under heavy fire from Haisnes and were altogether too weak to achieve anything against Cité St. Elie, from which plenty of machine-guns were firing, so Colonel Ovens had before long to fall back towards the Quarries and assist in their consolidation. About 2 p.m. Captains Heath and Philpot of the Queen's organized an attack from Cité Trench on Cité St. Elie and actually entered the village, but were driven out by shell fire, and after that most of the main body of the Queen's seem to have retired also to the Quarries and taken post on Colonel Ovens' left rear. Even then some of the Queen's remained in Cité Trench till after nightfall, although Captain Heath had been killed. About 6 p.m. they beat off an attack, but they were a mere handful and were mixed up with the right of the Ninth Division, who had established themselves in Pekin Trench and Fosse Alley on their left. But it was not by the dispersed and disorganized survivors of the captors of the front system that strong posts like Cité St. Elie were to be taken. If the German second system was to be captured, it must be the work of fresher troops from reserve.

With the 20th Brigade the situation was by this time very much the same. After storming the front trenches the survivors of the two assaulting battalions had not stopped to consolidate, but had pushed ahead up the slight slope leading to the second system of defences. There were not many of them, the 8th Devons had only two officers left unhit, and these were leading a mere handful of men, 100 to 150; the 2nd Gordons, though in slightly better case, had also lost heavily.

As they pushed forward both battalions disposed of

several small parties of Germans, many of whom seemed
to have lost their way in the fog of smoke and dust.
Somewhere ahead of them guns were firing and both
Devons and Gordons were drawn towards them as if
to a magnet. Suddenly a line of smoking muzzles appeared

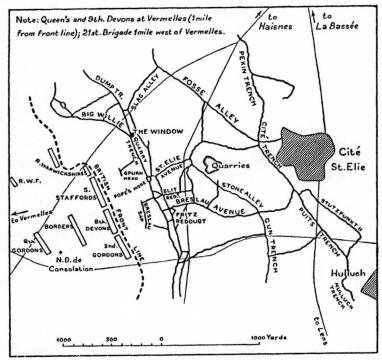

MAP 17.—LOOS: THE DISPOSITIONS FOR ATTACK.

out of the fog and was promptly rushed, the survivors
of the German artillerymen bolting after a sharp scuffle.
There were eight guns, four falling to the Devons, four
to the Gordons, and their emplacements were about 800
yards from the German front line.[1]

---

[1] These guns were subsequently removed by " A " Squadron, Northumberland Hussars, who manhandled them away, though the Germans were quite
close to Gun Trench at the time, getting them back to a point where teams
from " F " Battery R.H.A. were awaiting them.

Elated by this capture, Devons and Gordons pressed on
farther still, and not until they reached the point where
the Lens–La Bassée road crosses that from Vermelles
N.W. of Hulluch was their progress arrested.   To their
right front was Hulluch, to the left Cité St. Elie, both still
in German hands, and from Cité St. Elie in particular
machine-guns were in action.   Here therefore the much-re-
duced battalions halted, the Gordons taking post South of
the road, the Devons, the smaller of the two parties, being
to their left North of it.   They had reached the limit of
their tether and could gain no more ground, though after
the arrival about 10 a.m. of two companies of their 6th
Battalion the Gordons twice tried to advance.   In the first
effort about 50 men under Captain Finlay advanced nearly
300 yards towards Hulluch, but were then stopped by
frontal fire from a well-wired trench just outside Hulluch
and by enfilade fire from their left : Captain Finlay was
killed and the few survivors came back to the cross-roads,
on which 2nd Lieut. McPherson organized a bombing
attack on the trench from which the enfilade fire had come,[1]
only to be beaten back, he himself being killed.   Major
Ross, now in command, then sent back for reinforcements,
ammunition, and tools ; and pending their arrival the
men set to work with their " grubbers " to improve their
position.

The two companies of the 6th Gordons, who had joined
the remnants of their 2nd Battalion, had lost heavily during
their advance, mainly from shell fire in crossing No Man's
Land, and the other half-battalion had remained behind
to consolidate Gun Trench, as the line of gun emplacements
came to be called.   Here also most of the Borders had
halted : as already mentioned, the attack on the Pope's
Nose had drawn off part of that battalion and reduced the
number available for pushing home the advantage gained
by the leading battalions, and Colonel Thorpe felt that
the best course was to secure the line of Gun Trench.   Thus

_____
[1] Probably Puits Trench.

hardly any reinforcements reached the remnant of the 8th Devons North of the cross-roads, who remained dangerously isolated with their left completely " in the air." [1]   The only chance of a speedy advance against Cité St. Elie or Hulluch was that the 9th Devons, who had left the British front trenches about 8.30 a.m., would reach the new front in sufficient numbers to pierce the German second system before German reinforcements could arrive. Reinforcements were coming up : about 9 a.m. a column nearly 600 strong was seen marching into Cité St. Elie from the N.E. [2]   The 2nd Gordons promptly opened fire with good effect, but other reinforcements arrived and until the British guns could get on to and silence the German machine-guns the chances were none too promising.   It seems too that it was from these machine-guns that the 9th Devons suffered so severely.   Their advance was carried out with admirable steadiness, but the battalion was scourged by machine-gun fire, some of which from the Quarries took it in flank, and was heavily shelled by guns right back behind the German second line.   Colonel Storey was badly wounded, Major Anderson, the second in command, was also hit with two of the company commanders, and the battalion reached Gun Trench with a dozen officers down and its numbers sadly reduced.   A small party, 3 officers and 100 men, pushed on to reinforce the 8th, the remainder with a few leaderless men of the 8th stayed at Gun Trench helping to consolidate.

By noon then the two attacking brigades had shot their bolt.   They had achieved much in the face of considerable

[1] In an action like this times are notoriously very hard to establish with any degree of accuracy, but if one may put the capture of the Pope's Nose as somewhere after 8.30 and that of the Quarries as an hour or so later, it seems that the leading units of the 20th Brigade must have reached their advanced position no later than the capture of the Pope's Nose, even if not a trifle earlier.

[2] This was a battalion of the 11th Reserve Infantry Regiment, the other battalions of which were holding the front lines from the Hulluch road to the Hohenzollern Redoubt and finding the supports also for this sector.

difficulties and stubborn opposition, their capture of the formidable lines they had assaulted, despite the disappointing results of the gas, was a notable, if costly, triumph ; it was hardly wonderful if for the moment they could go no farther. All depended on whether the 21st Brigade could break through the German second system of defences, and its chances of doing so turned largely on the ability of the artillery to locate and silence the machine-guns in Hulluch and Cité St. Elie and to effect the necessary breaches in the German wire and other defences. It was a good deal to ask of the gunners, for the German second line was nearly as strong as the front system and very well wired, while there had been no opportunities for its registration. " T " Battery R.H.A., however, had pushed a forward observing officer up to Gun Trench who was able to bring its fire to bear effectively on German reinforcements entering Cité St. Elie. By this time the rest of the battery had joined the advanced section, coming forward at a good pace down the Hulluch road despite artillery fire and reaching its position with little loss. The sight of these guns advancing at the gallop was a great encouragement to the troops : it had not been seen since the Aisne and was greeted with cheers.

The 21st Brigade had taken up its assembly positions by 3.30 a.m., the Yorkshires and Wiltshires in the Noyelles lines, the Scots Fusiliers in Noyelles itself, the Bedfords and Camerons a mile farther back in the Labourse lines. Brigade Headquarters were at Vermelles with an advanced observation post, to which General Watts moved on the opening of the intense bombardment, in a " keep " 300 yards East of the railway. As the assaulting brigades went forward the 21st began making its way to the front, the Wiltshires on the right using Chapel Alley and the Bedfords following them, while the Yorkshires and Camerons filed up Gordon Alley on the left. The communication trenches were already somewhat congested, so orders were sent back for the men to get out and move over the open. The orders took some time to reach the battalions, which were strung out in the trenches ; but by 9.30 the whole brigade was collected in the old British front line, except for the Scots Fusiliers who were still West of the railway. It was reported that though the 22nd Brigade had been checked the 20th was getting on well, and the 21st was therefore ordered to push forward and exploit the 20th's success. However, before a move could be made the orders were changed : news had come in that the 22nd Brigade had secured its first objective, and the Yorkshires and Camerons were diverted to support it. Thus the brigade was split up from the first, General Watts being left with only two battalions to carry out the advance originally ordered.

This advance began about 11.30, the Wiltshires being on the left, while the Bedfords' right was on the Hulluch road. Each battalion covered a front of 250 yards, having two companies in front, in column of platoons 50 yards apart. At first the advance encountered little fire, but as the battalions pushed on over absolutely open ground devoid of all cover the German fire increased in volume and accuracy and both suffered heavily. The Bedfords' C.O., Colonel Onslow, was hit together with the Adjutant and 4 other officers ; and before they reached Gun Trench nearly 250 men were down, while the Wiltshires had suffered almost as heavily. Two platoons of the Bedfords gallantly but fruitlessly attempted to push on down the forward slope beyond Gun Trench ; the machine-guns bowled the majority over and the few survivors fell back to Gun Trench. Unless the artillery could deal effectively with Cité St. Elie any further advance would merely be throwing away lives, so the two battalions settled down to help consolidate the line of Gun Trench and Stone Alley,[1] the Bedfords on the right reaching to Point 54, the Wiltshires carrying the line into Breslau Avenue on as far as Point 22 about South of the Quarries.

[1] Stone Alley ran roughly from N.W. to S.E., passing South of the Quarries.

15

Meanwhile the Yorkshires also had advanced, their objective being to clear Puits Trench. "C" and "D" Companies led, passing through the Southern portion of the Quarries, which they cleared ; but on advancing farther they encountered heavy rifle and machine-gun fire from the direction of Puits 13 and were soon held up. The long grass in front concealed Puits Trench, and although an artillery observing officer who had come up to the Pope's Nose did his best to get the guns on to it the trench was almost impossible to locate. There were big gaps between the battalion and the troops on its flanks ; the parties of the 22nd Brigade who had pushed on against Cité St. Elie were far away to the left, and on the right none of the 20th Brigade could be discovered ; so there was nothing for it but to dig in and get some cover from the machine-guns and the increasing shelling. A little later, about 1.30 p.m., the Camerons came up on the left and established touch with the 22nd Brigade, while two platoons pushed out to the right and found the Wiltshires in Stone Alley.

Thus the 21st Brigade also had come to a standstill : had it been possible for the guns to deal even as effectively with Cité St. Elie as they had already done with the German front system, there were enough infantry up in front for an assault to have had a fair chance ; but although a bombardment was carried out in the early afternoon it lacked weight and hardly damaged the wire. Colonel Leathem therefore reported that an attack could only result in disaster and, the Brigadier concurring, the assault was put off. In the meantime General Watts had got forward almost to Gun Trench, and he and General Trefusis reported after careful reconnaissance that an attack South of the Hulluch road offered more prospect of success than a direct advance against Cité St. Elie. After various conferences and consultations General Capper decided to concentrate the 21st Brigade on that flank and to use three battalions from the reserves of the Second Division, described as Carter's Force, which had been put under his orders, for a fresh attack on the left.   After dark therefore steps were taken to get the 21st Brigade concentrated behind the right of the line ; the Scots Fusiliers crossed from the old British front line, which they had reached about 1 p.m., and took position in the old German front trench, the Camerons being shifted across into Breslau Avenue from their position in front of the Quarries.[1]   The relief of the Yorkshires was then begun, about 80 South Staffords moving up to replace " C " Company of the Yorkshires East of the Quarries.   Just as this party reached the front line Germans were seen approaching and were at once fired on, their advance being effectually stopped, but simultaneously very heavy fire burst out farther to the left to the N.E. and North of the Quarries. Here the line was held partly by the 22nd Brigade but also by the right of the Ninth Division.[2]   Casualties had been very heavy ; the men were exhausted with the long day's fighting following a night under arms and on the move, while the ground was so slippery with rain that any movement was fatiguing.   Indeed the position at the Quarries was much less satisfactory than it may sound when one talks of them as held by a brigade.   The 54th Field Company had succeeded in putting up wire in front of them, but even so the position was none too secure.

Exact accuracy as to the confused fighting which followed in the Quarries is quite beyond attainment.   The Quarries were very extensive, a maze of trenches and dug-outs in which it was hard to find one's way in the dark.   Apparently about 11 p.m. the Germans broke in near the point of junction between the Ninth Division and the 22nd Brigade.

[1] It does not seem to have been known that part of this battalion was actually in the front line, as it was believed that the whole battalion was in support to the Yorkshires.   Actually their move was misunderstood by some of the small parties of leaderless men holding the Quarries who took it as the signal to retire.

[2] This Division had carried the German front line as far North as the Hohenzollern Redoubt, and advanced detachments had pushed well forward towards Haisnes, but had been in insufficient force to maintain their ground ; they had had therefore to fall back.

This exposed the left flank of the Queen's, on the North and N.E. sides of the Quarries, and at the same time the Queen's were attacked in front and by bombers on the right. They made a valiant effort to drive the Germans off, Colonel Heath and Captains Philpot and Longbourne being specially prominent. But they found themselves nearly surrounded and only with difficulty did they ultimately cut their way out and get back to the old German support lines, Colonel Heath being missing in the process. Details of what happened to the parties of the Royal Warwickshires and Royal Welch Fusiliers farther to the right are lacking,[1] but they also were driven back to the German support line, where they rallied. At the Southern end of the Quarries the Yorkshires and South Staffords had barely beaten off the Germans in their front before they discovered more enemy actually in the Quarries behind them. The Yorkshires' bombers supported by a platoon were promptly sent to clear this party out, but found it in considerable force and were driven back.[2] " D " Company was thereupon ordered to clear the Quarries and " B " to support it ; but " D's " commander was hit at once, as was also Captain Chauncey, the Adjutant, and a confused struggle resulted in these two companies being ousted from the Quarries and pushed back to Breslau Avenue, where they rallied and linked up with the Wiltshires. This left " C " Company, with whom was the C.O., Colonel Young, as well as Colonel Ovens and his South Staffords, still holding out in the front line but dangerously isolated. Their case was not improved when the British heavy artillery, to whom the loss of the Quarries had been

---

[1] Both these battalions had suffered terribly, especially in officers, and had had many men gassed.

[2] At this time the Germans had a great advantage in the bomb they were using, their pattern being more reliable and easier to throw than any of those in use by the British, who constantly found themselves outranged and outthrown by the enemy's bombers. It was not till the more handy and efficient Mills bomb came into general use some time later that the advantage was wrested from the Germans.

duly reported, opened fire on that position and shelled it very accurately. Colonel Young therefore decided to get away to the South, and eventually found his way to Breslau Avenue after several encounters in the dark with various parties of Germans. Here he regained touch with " B " and " D " Companies, subsequently establishing communication also with " A " Company and battalion headquarters, now back in the old British front line.[1]

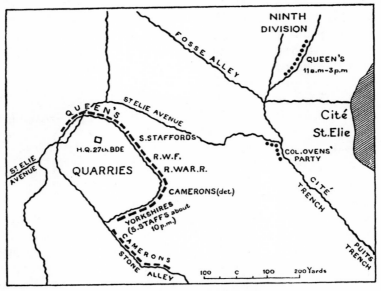

MAP 18.—LOOS: THE QUARRIES.

But the night's tale of mishap was not complete. The advanced position at the Hulluch cross-roads had been maintained all through the afternoon with little difficulty. Without anything in the way of tools beyond their " grubbers " the men could not do much to consolidate their position, but they did some effective sniping and felt secure enough to send parties back after dusk to fetch rations and water and ammunition. However, somewhere

[1] This counter-attack seems to have been carried out by the 2nd Guard Reserve Division, which had arrived during the afternoon and evening.

about 10 p.m. as these parties were returning to the cross-roads they were attacked in flank, while simultaneously a strong force advanced against the cross-roads. There was a sharp fight, but the party of the 20th Brigade was out-flanked and after a stubborn resistance forced back towards Gun Trench, the Germans pressing hard on its heels. As the men neared Gun Trench they were fired upon by the garrison, who mistook them for Germans, and for a time there was considerable confusion. The Germans profited by this to push forward to Gun Trench. One company of the Bedfords just North of the road was driven back but rallied at the support trench, from which it counter-attacked with complete success. Their left company, " D," was never dislodged, and farther to the right the Borders, responding to Colonel Thorpe's exhortations, met the Germans on the parapet with the bayonet and drove them back, the 6th Gordons being equally successful in keeping their line intact. Meanwhile the Brigade Major, Captain Foss, and other officers had rallied the survivors of the party from the cross-roads and brought them back. It was a fierce struggle, but it ended with Gun Trench in British hands and the complete repulse of the Germans, many of their number being left behind dead and wounded. But the advanced position was lost, and this with the loss of the Quarries completely upset the plans for the next day's attack. Among other things the artillery observation gained during the day was lost, and the batteries which had come forward had to fall back to their old positions, as they were exposed to rifle fire at quite short range. The 12th Battery indeed seemed to have no one between it and the Germans until an infantry officer, whose name was not ascertained, collected a small party of men and took post to cover its retirement, while a section of howitzers which had come forward had a dozen horses hit in getting away.

By the morning of September 26th the Division's situation was therefore nothing like as satisfactory as it had promised to be. On the right were the Borders and Bedfords in Gun

Trench, mixed up with detachments of the Gordons and
Devons, and in touch on their right with the left of the
First Division South of the Hulluch–Vermelles road. The
Scots Fusiliers were in support,[1] their front company about
300 yards behind Gun Trench, and with them were some
of the 2nd Gordons. From the 20th Brigade's left the
Wiltshires continued the line along Stone Alley to Breslau
Avenue, which the Yorkshires were holding, being reinforced
later on by " A " and " D " Companies of the Scots Fusiliers. The 4th Camerons were in support North of the
Hulluch road, and a detachment of the Yorkshires was in
reserve in the old British front line. From the junction
of Breslau Avenue with the German support trench, here
called Quarry Trench, the 22nd Brigade continued the line
Northward to the junction with the Ninth Division not far
from the " Window," the Queen's being on the outer flank
while the remnants of the Welch Fusiliers provided a scanty
reserve. There was not a battalion in the Division but
had lost heavily, nine had lost their C.O., and it was clear
that if the Quarries were to be recovered—still more if
Cité St. Elie was to be taken—fresh troops must be found
to do the work; the Seventh Division's infantry had done
splendid work, but were terribly reduced and in no condition
for another big effort.

But the Seventh Division was not to be required to
attack again on September 26th. The fresh battalions
which had been placed at General Capper's disposal were
available to recover the Quarries, and the infantry of the
Division had merely to hold on, consolidate the ground
gained, and assist the attack as best they could with covering fire from rifles and machine-guns.

The first effort to retake the Quarries was made about
6 a.m. by the 9th Norfolks, a battalion of the newly arrived
Twenty-Fourth Division, rather inexperienced troops for
so difficult a task. The 4th Camerons were just about to

---

[1] This battalion had moved forward on hearing the noise of the attack on
Gun Trench, but had resumed its former positions on its repulse.

attack when the Norfolks arrived, and the latter battalion, having been specially detailed for the task, went through the Camerons, though after their long and exhausting march up they were probably the less fresh of the two. They were unsuccessful and fell back to Quarry Trench just to the right of the South Staffords, where they were reorganized, being placed under General Steele's orders. After this there was a long pause till the arrival, about 1 p.m., of two battalions [1] of Carter's Force, the 2nd Worcestershire and the 1st K.R.R.C. The headquarters of this force were established at General Steele's headquarters and it was arranged that the Quarries should be bombarded from 4 p.m. till 5.30 p.m., and that bombers from the 20th Brigade should co-operate by bombing down a communication trench leading to the Quarries, the Scots Fusiliers in Breslau Avenue covering the advance with machine-guns and rifle fire. But the attack, which started from the line held by the 22nd Brigade, encountered strong opposition. It was gallantly pushed and the leading lines established themselves along a half-dug trench about 200 yards from the Quarries, and here proceeded to build up a firing-line and engage in a contest for fire superiority with the defenders of the Quarries, while the 20th Brigade's bombers worked their way towards the N.W. corner of the Quarries. The rear lines followed and reinforced the leading platoons, but losses had been heavy and beyond the line already gained it proved impossible to advance, and before long orders were issued to abandon the fruitless attempt and consolidate the ground gained. Among those who had fallen was General Capper himself. He was right up in the front, actually directing this advance, and was dangerously wounded by the side of a platoon commander of the Worcestershire, falling, as he would himself have chosen, practically in the firing-line and close up to his enemy. He was taken back to a Casualty Clearing Station, but from the first

[1] The third battalion, the 1st Royal Berkshires, had been diverted towards the Hohenzollern Redoubt.

it was recognized that his condition was most serious, and his death, which followed next morning, was not unexpected. " All those who knew him," writes the Divisional Diary, " will mourn the loss of a gallant soldier who, by his courage and devotion to duty, set a splendid example to every officer, N.-C.-O., and man in the Seventh Division." With that Division and its gallant and devoted struggle for Ypres his name will always be associated. A fighting man, who courted danger and was ready to face every risk himself that he asked his men to encounter, he had set his stamp on the Division ; his energy, his vigour, and his talents as a trainer of troops had contributed their share to its making and frequent remaking no less than his personal bravery and readiness to assume responsibility.

With the suspension of the second counter-attack on the Quarries matters became somewhat quieter on the Seventh Division's frontage. It was round the Hohenzollern Redoubt on its left and far away on the extreme right nearer Loos that the next few days were to see the heaviest fighting, the most determined German effort to win back lost ground and the chief British attempts to improve their position. Not that the Seventh Division, command of which had passed to General Watts as senior Brigadier, was either quiet or inactive. There was intermittent shelling, snipers were active, and at several points bombing fights went on without much definite result beyond adding to the casualty list. Thus early on the 27th German bombers gained over 100 yards of St. Elie Avenue, only to be driven back by the South Staffords ; and the Queen's were able to give some help to the troops on their left, where fighting was almost continuous. During the night of September 26th/27th some readjustment was effected, what was left of the 20th Brigade being relieved by the 21st, who held Gun Trench from the junction with the First Division, just South of the Hulluch road, and continued along Stone Alley to Point 54 just South of the Quarries. The Scots Fusiliers were on the right, the Camerons on the left in

Stone Alley and Breslau Avenue, the Yorkshires behind them with the Wiltshires in local reserve and the Bedfords back in the old German front line. Of the 20th Brigade only the Borders were left on the German side of what had been No Man's Land, the remnants of the other battalions being back in the old British lines, reorganizing as far as was possible. The officers who had been left out of action had rejoined, some drafts had arrived, scattered parties who, in the inevitable turmoil and confusion of the battle, had got detached from their own units and tacked to some other battalion, were sorted out and redistributed.

On the whole the 21st Brigade was more actively engaged than the 22nd. Its line formed a pronounced salient ; and though to some extent this allowed of enfilade fire at the Quarries and their communications with Cité St. Elie, the Germans could return the compliment. Something was done to improve the position by getting up wire and digging new support and communication trenches, blocking those leading back to the German lines and repairing damages. But this work was carried on under great handicaps, owing to the wet and slippery state of the ground, the exhaustion of the men, the scanty supply of tools [1] and the difficulty of getting them up to the front. The German shell fire added to the difficulties and swelled the casualty list ; on the 26th the Wiltshires lost Colonel Leathem, a very able officer who had done great things in rebuilding the battalion after its heavy losses earlier in the year, while two days later the Scots Fusiliers had their acting C.O., Captain Connell, and two other officers killed and a company commander wounded, with 50 casualties among the men, though they in turn got effective fire at Germans moving from Hulluch to Cité St. Elie. Early on the 27th the Germans developed very heavy shell fire against the Camerons in Stone Alley and Breslau Avenue, supported by a great volume of rifle fire from the Quarries. The Camerons had many casualties,

[1] The C.R.E. had fortunately arranged before the battle for forward R.E. dumps to be formed and these proved extremely useful.

and when an attack in some force began to develop from the Quarries the situation looked threatening, for the line was but thinly held.   However, Major Forsyth—now C.O. of the Wiltshires—was quick to grasp the situation and sent two of his companies dashing across the 300 yards of open between their reserve trench and Breslau Avenue.   They had to swing to the left to reach the Camerons' trenches and they came under heavy fire as they rushed across, both company commanders, Captains Geddes and Mudge, being killed in heading the rush ; but the bulk of them reached Breslau Avenue all right and dropping into the trench opened fire on the advancing Germans.   Their spirited conduct and timely arrival saved the situation : with their aid the Camerons brought the Germans to a standstill and forced them back to the Quarries, leaving many of their number behind.

After this things were quieter : on the 28th and again on the 29th the Germans tried to bomb their way up communication trenches leading into the Camerons' line from Cité St. Elie and from the Quarries, but all these attacks were repulsed, the Camerons having the satisfaction of inflicting heavy casualties on their assailants.   By this time too the artillery had been able to register on Cité St. Elie and other points in the German defences, and could retaliate effectively whenever, as was the case particularly on the 29th, the Germans bombarded our front line ; they were kept busy also in assisting the Twenty-Eighth Division in its efforts to regain ground round the Hohenzollern Redoubt. Various readjustments and changes of position were made, with the result that on September 30th " A " Company of the Yorkshires was on the right of the 21st Brigade's line South of the Hulluch Road, the Scots Fusiliers were in Gun Trench, with the rest of the Yorkshires in a support trench behind them, the Bedfords were on the Scots Fusiliers' left from where the communication trench from Cité St. Elie entered Gun Trench, the Borders being in Breslau Avenue beyond them.   The line was continued Northward by the 83rd Brigade, whose Division, the Twenty-Eighth, had now replaced the Ninth also, the relief of the 22nd Brigade and of Carter's Force having been completed by 4 a.m. on September 30th. The 22nd had had a lively last two days in the trenches, being repeatedly attacked by German bombers, who profited greatly by the marked superiority of their bombs, but nevertheless failed to make much impression on the Queen's and South Staffords, who kept them at bay, being splendidly helped by the Brigade Grenade Company. Lieuts. Brunt of the Royal Welch Fusiliers and Dibben of the Royal Warwickshires were particularly to the fore in this work, and Colonel Ovens, the one C.O. who had survived, superintended the defence with vigour and determination. One great difficulty was that of keeping the units in the front line supplied with bombs. The calls on the Brigade Grenade Company exceeded all expectations ; at one time it was meeting demands from 20 different units, and from first to last it sent up over 15,000 bombs of one pattern and another.

One particularly serious attack, early on September 29th, for a time drove the K.R.R.C. back down St. Elie Avenue almost to the old German front line, but the South Staffords' bombers counter-attacked with marked success, thrusting the Germans back nearly to the Quarries and inflicting many casualties. The Queen's also beat off a determined attack by the 5th Infantry Regiment farther to the left, and the brigade's machine-guns were able to take no light toll of Germans who were endeavouring to consolidate Slag Alley, the communication trench just South of Fosse 8, or advancing across the low ground to counter-attack the Hohenzollern Redoubt.

All was now in train for the completion of the relief of the Division, but the Seventh had still to see heavy fighting in the battle of Loos. During the morning of the 30th there was a fair amount of more or less desultory shelling, and German reinforcements were seen to be being dribbled in small parties into Hulluch, but otherwise there was little to merit special notice. About 4.30 p.m., however, the German artillery suddenly roused themselves into activity and in a few minutes an intense bombardment was beating down on the British trenches, Gun Trench coming in for particular attention. Practically all the telephone wires were cut in a minute, making it very hard to get the British guns on to the right targets. For two hours the storm of shells raged, doing great damage and inflicting heavy casualties. Then about 6 p.m. the bombardment lifted and the German infantry pressed forward. Some pushed up the communication trench from Cité St. Elie to Gun Trench, others passed forward over the open. The brunt of the attack came about the junction between the Bedfords and the Scots Fusiliers. Great havoc had been wrought here by the bombardment, among other things nearly all the bombs of the Fusiliers' left company had been buried, and it was no wonder that they found themselves at a disadvantage.[1] For a time they held the enemy off, their machine-guns bowling over numbers of those who tried to cross the open ; but in the end the German bombers forced their way up the communication trench, got into Gun Trench, and forced the Fusiliers back Southward for over 100 yards. Here, however, a stand was made, reinforcements having come up from the right while other platoons occupied a new communication trench which joined the front line just South of where the Germans had got in. The Yorkshires also sent up a weak company to secure the support trench, followed a little later by two more. On the left the Bedfords had been forced back about 30 yards, their " ball bombs " being quite outclassed by the German " stick bombs " ; and two machine-guns which had been getting good targets in Germans who tried

---

[1] A transport driver of the Scots Fusiliers who had come up with a load of bombs to the old German front line, hearing that bombs were badly needed, drove forward along the Hulluch road under heavy fire, and though his brakesman and one of the horses were hit delivered his precious load almost to the firing-line.

to cross the open were only extricated and brought into position farther up Stone Alley with difficulty ; from here, however, they assisted most effectively to cover the erection of a block, preventing German attempts to work across the open round its ends.

However, if on both flanks the Germans had been checked they had secured a substantial portion of Gun Trench and it was essential to recover it. Bombing parties were therefore organized to attack the lodgment from both ends, and Colonel Berners of the Welch Fusiliers, who had been acting as Brigadier since General Watts took over the Division, ordered the Yorkshires to advance from the support trench at the same time. Unluckily their move was stopped by the wire which had been put up in front of the support trench. Several gallant efforts were made to crawl through this wire, but the accuracy of the enemy's fire made it necessary to suspend these attempts, and the bombing attacks made little headway. It was nearly 10 o'clock by now and for the moment the supply of bombs was nearly exhausted. It was decided therefore to wait for a few hours until additional bombs could be fetched up and a fresh attack organized.

This was delivered about 1.15 a.m. (October 1st), bombers from the 4th Camerons having come up to help the Scots Fusiliers. The Yorkshires opened covering fire from the support trench and at first the attack made more progress. But the Germans had the handier and more accurate bomb, less liable to be made unserviceable by wet ; they could throw five to our three and throw them farther. Neither Bedfords nor Scots Fusiliers could make any real progress ; Major Monteith, who had been commanding the Bedfords since Colonel Onslow was wounded, was killed, and as daylight drew near it was decided to block the trench at both ends of the lost portion and to defer further attempts till fresh units could relieve the utterly exhausted men of the Seventh Division. They had been in action for five days continuously, in miserably

cold and wet weather, rations had been irregular in arrival,
fighting heavy, casualties heavier, hardly a battalion had
enough officers left to go round the companies, and all
ranks were absolutely worn out.   Accordingly the blocks
were made and the line maintained without further mishap
until after nightfall the 5th Brigade arrived to replace the
weary 21st, who crawled away to the welcome shelter of

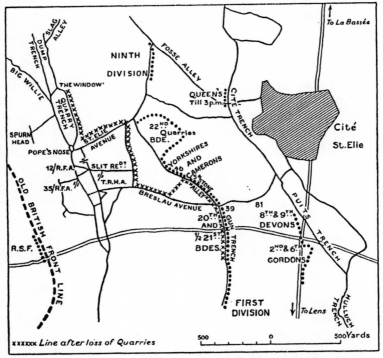

MAP 19.—LOOS: THE POSITION HELD AFTER LOSS OF THE QUARRIES.

billets in Le Quesnoy and Le Preol.   Here they found
themselves reserve brigade to the Division, which, far from
getting the rest to which its exertions and losses had
entitled it, had been detailed to relieve the Second Division
in front of Cuinchy and just South of the La Bassée Canal.
This line had been included in the frontage attacked on
September 25th, but the attack had failed altogether here

and had not been renewed. But while the infantry of the Seventh Division, though on the edge of the still disturbed area were no longer within it, the Divisional artillery continued to support the Second Division for nearly three weeks more until the battle had completely worn itself out.

In war, perhaps more than in other forms of human activity, wisdom after the event is specially easy and specially misleading. It is easy enough now to point out all that went wrong at Loos, the many reasons why instead of the grand results that had been pictured in the orders for September 25th only such very modest gains had been achieved, so modest indeed that in relation to the efforts put forth and the losses the result may seem more like defeat than victory. It is easy to see now that a great success was perhaps never very likely, even if some special causes of mishap and delay could have been avoided, such as the uncut wire in front of the 22nd Brigade or the crowding of the communication trenches which delayed the advance of the reinforcements. But Loos will only be fairly judged as one of a series of experiments, from which valuable lessons were learnt, not less about things to do again but to do better next time than about what to avoid. That the Seventh Division would have fared better had its objectives been limited to the line of Gun Trench and the Quarries, and the capture of Cité St. Elie entrusted to fresh troops, may be admitted ; that the best methods of assisting the later stages of an infantry advance by artillery had yet to be devised is a mere platitude ; that the whole plan was rather ambitious for the force available and depended too much on a big success with the gas, that the Seventh Division was asked to undertake more than the available artillery and ammunition warranted, are matters of argument by the compiler not of a Divisional history but of a critical discussion of the whole battle. Looking at Loos from the Seventh Division's standpoint it may be said that the Division did its work well and achieved about as much as any other ; others may have penetrated farther and gained more at the outset—did any other retain so large a proportion of its original gains ?　Its losses [1] were very heavy, over 2,100 in the 20th Brigade, nearly 1,500 in the 21st, nearly 1,700 in the 22nd,[2] with another 130 for the artillery, R.E., and other Divisional troops, not far short of 5,500 in all.　In quality too it had lost very heavily. The Divisional Commander's death was a severe blow, in Colonels Leathem and Stansfeld the Division had lost battalion commanders of great distinction and long service with it, and if Colonels Grant (8th Devons), Heath (Queen's), MacQueen (6th Gordons), Lefroy (Royal Warwickshires), and Captain Connell (R.S.F.) were comparative new-comers to it they were all men whom their battalions and the Division could ill afford to spare.　Many others had fallen who had served long with the Division or had returned to it after recovery from wounds received at Ypres or elsewhere ; not a battalion but had been fairly

[1] The figures are as follows :

	Killed.		Wounded.		Missing.		Total.	
	Officers.	Men.	Officers.	Men.	Officers.	Men.	Officers.	Men.
R.A. . . .	1	7	6	43	1	4	8	54
R.E. and Signals .	1	5	1	30	—	6	2	41
Divn. Mtd. Troops	1	—	1	9	—	1	2	10
8th Devons	8	149	10	343	1	128	19	620
9th Devons	3	59	12	326	—	76	15	461
Borders . .	3	25	6	175	—	47	9	247
2nd Gordons	8	73	8	310	1	116	17	499
6th Gordons	3	37	7	172	5	34	15	243
Bedfords . .	5	43	11	303	—	16	16	362
Yorkshires . .	7	37	3	204	7	83	17	324
R.S.F. . .	5	43	2	176	—	27	7	246
Wiltshires .	10	58	4	247	—	20	14	325
Camerons . .	2	22	9	113	—	22	11	157
Queen's . .	5	24	6	102	1	130	12	256
R. Warwickshires	8	56	10	143	1	318	19	517
R.W.F. . .	3	41	13	244	—	137	16	422
S. Staffords .	6	78	22	253	—	84	28	415
Total . .	79	757	131	3,193	17	1,249	227	5,199

[2] This brigade had only four battalions and proportionately lost as heavily as the 20th.

16

hard hit; only one, the Camerons, had under 200 casualties, and the 8th Devons, the 2nd Gordons, and the Royal Warwickshires all exceeded 500. The infantry therefore once again needed a period of comparative quiet for rebuilding the shattered battalions, and if the artillery and R.E. were in happier case they could not do the whole work of the Division without enough infantry to man the trenches. The artillery owed their comparative immunity from casualties largely to the fact that the Germans had not yet developed counter-battery into an almost scientific process, but partly to the fact that the advance had not gone far enough to allow most batteries the chance of limbering up and galloping forward to speed up the pursuit; though it was noted that the batteries which had had the chance to advance had done so in a fashion which showed that the long period of stationary warfare had not impaired their morale or their mobility. The R.E., who had been constantly up in the firing-line, helping to consolidate, may be reckoned exceptionally fortunate in their low casualties; it was not for want of gallantly exposing themselves in the dangerous places to which their duties took them, and many officers have drawn attention to the unflagging exertions and devotion to duty of the Signal Company, which was indefatigable in its efforts to maintain the constantly interrupted communications. Among the infantry the performances of the two new battalions had been watched with special interest. They had been long enough with the Division for the expectations formed of them to be highly favourable, but they had fully come up to those anticipations. They had borne themselves well, had taken their heavy punishment unflinchingly, and had established themselves as worthy of a place in a Division second to none in the B.E.F. in reputation, which had added notably to its laurels in their real baptism of fire.

CHAPTER X

IT was fortunate for the Seventh Division that the line it took over on October 1st actually proved quiet. It was in no state for further heavy fighting till the gaps in its ranks could be filled up and till officers and men could recover from the strain and exertions of the recent strenuous struggle. But, as already mentioned, its new frontage lay outside the area which saw the last phases of the battle of Loos. A few of the eddies set in motion in those last phases just extended to it. When the Germans delivered their great counter-attack on October 8th they bombarded the Seventh Division's line very heavily, causing orders to be issued to battalions in reserve to stand to and for all " keeps " and defended posts to be occupied by their garrisons. At the time the 21st Brigade was holding the right sub-sector, having replaced the 22nd on October 4th and enabled that brigade to relieve the 58th Brigade just South of the Canal three day later. The 20th were still in the centre of the Division's front, astride the La Bassée road. Each brigade had two battalions in front line, providing its own supports and reserves. But supports and reserves were not required on this occasion, the German infantry attacks did not extend beyond the Hohenzollern Redoubt, and by judicious distribution of the trench garrisons heavy casualties were successfully avoided. Five days later (October 13th) the British made their last attempt to improve the position on the Hohenzollern–Hulluch front and the Division co-operated by releasing gas and smoke and bombarding the German lines. If the

[1] Cf. Maps 9 and 16.

gas proved really effective the 21st and 22nd Brigades [1] were to have advanced and occupied the sector immediately opposite them, pushing out patrols and bombing-parties to cover its consolidation. Unfortunately the wind proved far from satisfactory and very little gas could be let off, while the hostile retaliation for our bombardment caused over thirty casualties.

Shortly after this the whole Division was relieved, but its spell out of the line was of the briefest. Its relief by the Second and Twenty-Eighth Divisions had only been completed on the morning of October 17th; by the evening of the 19th the 20th Brigade had begun relieving the Ninth in the Givenchy area. It was to hold this section of the line with various modifications of boundary for the next six weeks, a period not without minor activities and excitements, besides constant hard work and a steady drain of casualties, but not marked by any outstanding incident. Mining was the chief activity practised by both sides; and though this was out of the question in the water-logged low ground just North of Givenchy with which the Division was already only too painfully familiar, on the drier Givenchy bluff mines were constantly being exploded, usually followed by sharp contests for the possession of the craters thus formed. As the result No Man's Land here soon became a maze of craters, more or less consolidated and wired, presenting almost as serious an obstacle to movement as did the ditches and swamps farther to the British left. This was one reason for the abstention from raids which were to form so marked a feature of other periods of that form of strategical inactivity usually described as "normal trench warfare." In the winter of 1915–1916 raiding had not become a regular policy, much less systematized and standardized. Shortage of ammunition also helped to make raids infrequent.

[1] The 20th had been taken out of the line three days earlier; the 21st, which had been relieved by the 5th Brigade, having side-stepped to the left to relieve the 20th.

Loos had seen nearly all the carefully accumulated ammunition-reserve expended and there was hardly any to play with, indeed the Diaries of this period refer frequently to the way in which the artillery found themselves handicapped when retaliation was called for. Patrol activities were less restricted, though here again the ground North of Givenchy was a serious impediment, especially when November rains filled ditches to overflowing, reduced communication trenches to waterways, and gave all hands all they could possibly do in keeping the fire trenches even approximately dry.

Apart from the rains the trenches needed constant care.[1] Partly owing to the preparations for the offensive the defensive needs of the line had been not a little overlooked ; the older trenches especially had been allowed to fall into disrepair, and when in November the Division extended to its left up to La Quinque Rue it found this bit of the line particularly bad owing to the wet. Parapets were falling in, the trenches were in places waist-deep in mud, in the worst parts the line had to be held by "islands," and in November the R.E. had to start constructing a completely new breastwork line from La Quinque Rue to Givenchy. There was no lack of work therefore,[1] and the Germans had also acquired a distinct superiority in sniping before the Seventh Division took over the line. This the Division could not allow and special measures were taken to suppress the hostile snipers, who took only too heavy a toll before they were mastered. Their most notable victim was General Trefusis, killed on October 24th when going round his trenches with General Berners just before the 21st Brigade relieved the 20th at Givenchy. A vigorous and capable commander, he was a great loss to his brigade and was much regretted. The mining activity led to several sharp encounters and afforded no small opportu-

---

[1] The figures of the R.E. stores issued to two infantry brigades in one month are instructive : they included 5,500 cubic feet of timber, 472 sheets of corrugated iron, and 106,000 sandbags.

nities for officers and men to distinguish themselves. It reached its height towards the end of November, two large mines being exploded at the Duck's Bill on the 25th after a smaller mine had been exploded in the hope of inducing the Germans to man their trenches in anticipation of an attack. To increase this impression our men started throwing bombs and opened rapid fire for ten minutes before the big mines, each loaded with 3,000 lb. of explosives, went up. The explosion was completely successful, though the Wiltshires had a company commander and several men killed by falling debris ; this, however, did not prevent their dashing out and successfully consolidating the crater. Four days later another small mine was blown at the Warren, just North of the Duck's Bill ; but it was too small to damage the German mine-galleries appreciably, so the work had to be resumed and a new mine prepared. In the middle of it two German deserters came over, announcing that the Germans were going to blow up big mines at the Warren and the Duck's Bill next day. To anticipate them, two mines, one containing 2,000 lb., the other 1,500, were fired at 4 a.m. on the 30th, and the Yorkshires hastened to occupy and consolidate the craters. They were hard at work at this when at 7.30 a.m. the German mines went off, doing much damage and burying over twenty men, but without preventing the Yorkshires and the R.E. from consolidating the new crater as well as those formed by our mines and from digging out most of the entombed men. But this mining left its mark on the casualty list, and of over 130 casualties suffered by the 21st Brigade in November over two-thirds occurred in the last fortnight.

These two deserters were not the only specimens who surrendered to the Division while in this area, and though their total was not high their appearance corroborated the impression that the Germans were not finding the Givenchy and Festubert sectors any more attractive than the Seventh Division did. The Intelligence Summary for

November 2nd, for example, records a German attempt
to enter into conversation with our men. One of them
having shouted out " Want some coffee, Tommy ? " without
getting the invitation accepted, went on to call out " Well,
you can have our bloody trenches on the 28th." This
was answered by shouts of " Why ? " giving the Germans
a chance of the effective repartee, " Wait and see." But
frequent cries of " Damn the Kaiser ! " and similar
remarks left the impression that the Germans were somewhat dissatisfied with life, and certainly they proved far
from aggressive or enterprising. All the same the Division
was not sorry to learn that it was shortly to be relieved by
the Thirty-Third Division, to some of whose units it had
been imparting instruction in trench warfare, and that it
would this time really have a rest of some duration. This
came with the beginning of December, command of the
line being handed over to the Thirty-Third Division on
December 2nd and the Division withdrawn to a rest-area
round Busnes, whence three days later it started entraining for the South on transfer to the Third Army, which
had been formed in July to take over the line East of
Albert in the Somme valley. The move was soon completed and December 7th saw Divisional Headquarters
established at Cavillon, the 20th Brigade being at
Picquigny, the 21st at Saleux, twelve miles N.W. of Amiens,
the 22nd near Molliens. It was to have a real rest this
time : February came before it had to return to the line.

This period was the more valuable because until then
there had been no chance of really assimilating the large
drafts which had been poured in after Loos. Changes also
had been numerous, nine battalions had required new
commanding officers and there had been many alterations
in the Staff. In the first place General Watts had, to the
general satisfaction, been confirmed in the command of the
Division, Colonel Berners of the R.W.F. getting the 21st
Brigade but relinquishing command early in December,
when Brigadier-General the Hon. C. J. Sackville West

succeeded him.　To the vacancy in the 20th Brigade there had succeeded an officer of marked personality, destined to leave a very strong impression on his brigade and to lead it in two of its most conspicuous successes, Brigadier-General C. J. Deverell of the West Yorkshires.　Colonel the Hon. M. Wingfield of the Rifle Brigade had joined as A.A. and Q.M.G. just before Loos, while in December the Division got a new G.S.O.I in Colonel Bonham Carter of the Royal West Kent, Colonel Gathorne Hardy having been promoted B.G.G.S.　The 22nd Brigade lost Major Thurlow in October, his successor as Brigade Major being Captain Chads, the Staff Captain of the 21st Brigade.　In the 20th Brigade the vacant battalion commands were filled by Colonel Ingles and Major Milne of the Devons, who took over the 8th and 9th Battalions respectively, the 2nd Gordons also getting one of their own Regular officers in Major B. G. R. Gordon, who had been wounded at Ypres in 1914.　In the 21st Brigade Major Bidder of the Royal Sussex, the Brigade Machine-Gun Officer, took command of the Bedfords on October 1st, but was relieved by Major Poyntz on November 10th.　The Scots Fusiliers got one of their own officers in Major R. K. Walsh, and the Wiltshires an ex-Regular officer of their Regiment in Major Martin, who held command till November 23rd when Major Gillson rejoined on recovery from his Loos wounds.　All four battalions in the 22nd Brigade got new C.O.s, Colonel H. W. Smith joining the Queen's on October 9th, Major Minshull-Ford reappearing on October 5th to command the Royal Welch Fusiliers, and Major A. G. Pritchard, an Indian Cavalry officer, taking command of the Royal Warwickshires.　Colonel Ovens, the only C.O. of the Brigade not in the Loos casualty list, was invalided shortly after the battle, Major H. E. Walshe replacing him.

Changes in the junior ranks were even more numerous. The 2nd Gordons, for example, got 3 captains, all pre-war Regulars, 2 lieutenants, and 11 2nd-lieutenants in October, November, December, together with drafts amounting to over 450. The Yorkshires got 15 officers and 294 men in October and mustered 31 officers and 872 men by December 1st, while before the end of the year all the battalions of the 20th Brigade were over 900 strong. But though the drafts included a proportion of experienced men, recovered sick and wounded, the majority were only partially trained and required much instruction. This was the harder to impart because of the inexperience and want of training of so many of the subalterns and N.-C.-O.s ; and to make things worse many of the more experienced and competent officers were taken away from their battalions for the new posts which were constantly being created. Thus one C.O. is found complaining in November that although he had twenty-three officers on his strength he had hardly two officers to each company, nothing like enough for the adequate supervision of the men in the trenches, which were long and difficult to patrol. On paper he had with him five other pre-war Regular officers, but two had been taken away as Brigade Machine-Gun officer and to command the Brigade Grenade Company, and in the battalion a second Machine-Gun officer was needed as well as a Bombing Officer and the Signal and Transport Officers of pre-war days, so that the subalterns available for company work were very few.[1] Many of the newly arrived officers were now drawn from units of the so-called " Fourth New Army," or " K 4," battalions originally created in the autumn of 1914 out of the Special Reserve, but since then allotted to draft-finding purposes. Posting of officers and men to battalions not belonging to their own regiment was rather less general at this period than it was to be in 1916 and later, and this partly accounted for the difficulty of keeping the three Territorial battalions [2] of the Division up to establish-

---

[1] It may be worth mentioning that at this period two battalions in the 22nd Brigade had respectively six and five pre-war Regular officers, seven and six Regular officers commissioned since the outbreak of war, five and eight Special Reserve officers, also commissioned since August 4th, 1914, and three officers each holding temporary commissions.

[2] The 7th King's had joined the 22nd Brigade in November.

ment : their " Second Lines," originally intended for draft-finding purposes, had accepted liability to service overseas, and drafts were in consequence very hard to find.

An even bigger change was, however, in store for the Division. It had been decided to transfer to the older Divisions whole brigades from some of the later-formed " New Army " Divisions which were now arriving in the country. By this means these new Divisions would include a proportion of experienced infantry and the Service battalions transferred to old Divisions would gain by serving alongside troops already inured to active service and well up to all the tricks of the trade in trench warfare. That the transfers were much to the advantage of the Army was obvious ; but it was equally obvious that the brigade selected for transfer from an old to a new Division should greatly regret parting from its old associates and commander. In the Seventh Division the lot fell upon the 21st Brigade, which was transferred on December 20th to the Thirtieth Division, exchanging with the 91st Brigade, composed of four battalions of the Manchester Regiment, the 20th, 21st, 22nd, and 24th, the first three raised by the City of Manchester, the last by the town of Oldham. The Brigadier was General F. J. Kempster, D.S.O., an officer on retired pay ; he had Major A. K. Grant of the Royal West Kent Regiment as Brigade Major and Captain L. J. Kentish as Staff Captain. To further equalize the brigades throughout the Division the 20th and 24th Manchesters were posted to the 22nd Brigade, the Queen's and South Staffords replacing them in the 91st, so that all three brigades now consisted of two Regular, one Territorial, and two Service battalions.

The departure of the 21st Brigade, which left the 4th Camerons behind it, was naturally much regretted both by the brigade itself and by the Division. The 21st Brigade had taken its full share in the hard fighting and hard work that had fallen to the Division. At Ypres it had shown itself steadfast and determined in defence, at Neuve Chapelle it had attacked with vigour and spirit, if circum-

stances beyond its control had robbed it of a full measure
of success. It had done well again at Festubert despite
great difficulties, and the failure at Givenchy had been a
failure to accomplish what was without any exaggeration
practically impossible in the conditions then prevailing.
At Loos again it had been confronted with a most difficult
task, in which success could only have been achieved had
far more artillery support been available with adequate
facilities for its observation and direction ; the brigade had
shown real tenacity and resolution in maintaining its
position for so long in such adverse conditions. For its
part the 21st Brigade was reluctant to go. " I could have
cried when I heard we had to leave the Division," is what
one of its officers has said. " It was such a splendid Division, it worked so well together and it had such a good
commander."

Another six weeks elapsed after the 91st Brigade joined
before the Division went into action again. The interval
was devoted to training, though recreation was not overlooked and leave was now open on a scale far more generous
than had hitherto been possible. A Divisional School was
established under Colonel Minshull-Ford, three fortnightly
courses being got through for the instruction of young
platoon commanders and N.-C.-O.s. This proved of great
benefit, and the long rest was of enormous value in enabling
units to get really shaken down, to work off all kinds of
accumulated arrears and put their organization and interior
economy in good working order. Much re-equipping was
necessary, and the men's physical condition improved
almost as much as their training and turn-out. Trench
warfare, especially in the damp and mud of a Flanders
winter, was anything but conducive to smartness in appearance and in carriage ; and units which contained so many
only partially trained officers and men could not be brought
to any high pitch of efficiency without some such opportunity as that now presented to the Seventh Division. How
well that chance was turned to account, more particularly

by those specially responsible for its training and instruction, the Division's record in 1916 was to show.

Before it returned to the line, however, another important change had taken place in its composition. It had been decided to reduce all brigades to a uniform strength of four battalions, and this involved the withdrawal from the ten Regular Divisions of the Territorial battalions which had been added to their brigades in the winter of 1914–1915.[1] For the Seventh Division this involved the departure early in January of the 6th Gordons and 4th Camerons to join the Fifty-First (Highland) Division to replace Lancashire battalions now transferred to the Fifty-Fifth, to which Division the 7th King's proceeded at the same time. The Highland Field Company also left the Division to join the Fifty-First, being replaced by the 3rd Durham Field Company, which arrived on January 29th. Major Hamilton also left the 20th Brigade to become Brigade Major to the new 166th Brigade, Captain Carr of the Gordons becoming Staff Captain. The 6th Cheshires arrived on January 8th to replace in the 20th Brigade the 9th Devons, who had been selected for conversion into Pioneers, but the order was cancelled before the end of January [2] and until May the Division remained without a Pioneer battalion of its own, having to borrow one from Divisions which were out of the line. Ultimately the 24th Manchesters were detailed to become Pioneers.

[1] This allowed of the reconstitution of the First London and the West Lancashire Territorial Divisions, now numbered Fifty-Sixth and Fifty-Fifth respectively.

[2] The 9th Devons accordingly remained in the 20th Brigade, the 6th Cheshires after a short stay in the Division leaving to join the Thirty-Ninth Division.

CHAPTER XI

WHEN early in February the Division returned to the line it was on the frontage opposite Mametz and Fricourt that it relieved the Eighteenth Division. The British line in this quarter followed the lower slopes of the high ground which runs roughly N.W. from Péronne and separates the basin of the Middle Somme from those of the various small rivers which drain away E. and N.E. towards the Upper Scheldt. This ridge, not sufficiently prominent as a geographical feature to have any special name, sloped gradually up from the right bank of the Somme, reaching in places a height of 500 feet above sea-level, the British trenches being approximately 200 feet lower on the Mametz and Fricourt line, so that the Germans enjoyed considerable tactical advantages, not the least being their much better facilities for observation. Opposite Fricourt the lines which had been running East and West for a distance of nearly 7,000 yards turned abruptly to the North, Fricourt village thus marking the point of a sharp salient so that the Seventh Division's new line formed a re-entrant. There had been heavy fighting in this quarter during the "Race to the Sea," but since the autumn of 1914 a virtual stalemate had prevailed, both sides having abandoned the effort to push their opponents back. The substitution of British troops for French in the summer of 1915 had not been followed by any change in policy : there had been no ammunition to spare for serious attempts to gain ground, and if the British had been more active in patrolling, less inclined to " live and let live " and more disposed to worry the enemy whenever chances presented themselves, they had been unable to prevent the Germans from adding systematically to their defences. By the time the Seventh

[1] Cf. Map 20.

Division confronted Mametz and Fricourt the German lines had been developed into a veritable fortress, bristling with redoubts and strong points, a most formidable front system containing several lines of trenches being backed by an almost equally strong second system a mile or so in rear and higher up the slope. If so strong a position were ever to be stormed far more extensive preparations than those which had preceded the " push " of September 1915 would be needed, the output of the munition factories would have to be multiplied many times ; without a far greater weight of artillery and an infinitely larger supply of shells no attack could possibly succeed, and in February 1916 the artillery and ammunition situation was such as to postpone almost indefinitely any serious offensive. Shells were not quite the scarce article they had been a twelvemonth earlier, but they still had to be doled out with a rigid parsimony and the daily allowance could only be exceeded in urgent emergencies.

There was no prospect therefore of any major operation in the near future for the Division, but that was not allowed to preclude doing all that was possible to harass the enemy. The chalky ground allowed more activity in mining than had been possible in any sector as yet held by the Division, and Tunnelling Companies were extremely busy, making great demands on the infantry for working-parties. These were generally taken from the battalions in support or reserve, so that a turn out of the line might involve more work and even more casualties than a period in the line. Not that the battalions in the line ever lacked work. Chalk country was all very well in dry weather, trench-walls stood up then without requiring much revetment ; but dry weather was no clue to the performances of chalk under the influence of wet, especially when a sudden thaw followed a hard frost. Even without the Germans the Division would have found plenty of occupation in keeping its lines in repair in the early months of 1916, when frost and thaw alternated rapidly enough to produce the maximum of

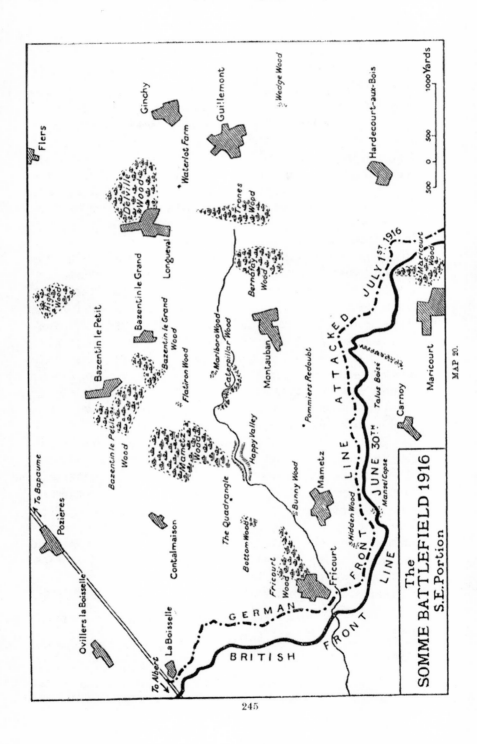

The
SOMME BATTLEFIELD 1916
S.E. Portion

MAP 20.

difficulties for those responsible for maintaining the trench-line.   But the Germans were far from inactive, retaliating vigorously with artillery and trench-mortars to the bombardments in which the British guns were occasionally able to indulge, and using their numerous and well-placed machine-guns to good effect.   Their retaliation was often only too effective, and it was disheartening after building up a really nice bit of parapet to have it battered down by a bombardment next day, as always seemed to be happening.   However, all three brigades had energetic commanders who were determined to see their brigade's bit of the line kept up to a high level, and they were well supported by the regimental officers and men.   These were times too when the R.E. were kept specially busy, for though much more skill in the construction of fortifications was now expected from the infantry than had been contemplated in pre-war days, the more elaborate tasks—and they were plentiful—required trained sappers to carry them out or at any rate to supervise them.   The entry in one Field Company's Diary for February 16th may serve as a specimen of the day's work required of the R.E. :

" M.G. emplacement at junction of 101 Street and Shuttle Lane continued : poor progress owing to wet.   Revetment of front line and work of clearing Tambour continued. Trench boarding King's Avenue continued.   Dug-outs at Tangier continued.   Excavation for Indian pattern dug-outs in Surrey Street begun.   Tunnelling under railway embankment for M.G. emplacement at Fricourt Station continued.   Dug-outs at Bonté almost completed.   Work on timbering for above continued in carpenter's shop."

When the Division first went into the line [1] it had all

___

[1] It was now in the Thirteenth Corps (Lieut.-General Sir W. N. Congreve), which included also the Eighteenth and Thirtieth Divisions, so that it was not very far away from its lost 21st Brigade.   From March 1st onward the Thirteenth Corps formed part of the newly organized Fourth Army under the Division's original Corps Commander, General Sir H. Rawlinson.   On April 29th the Division was transferred to the Fifteenth Corps (Lieut.-General Sir H. S. Horne), in which were also the Seventeenth and Twenty-First Divisions.

three brigades in the trenches, the 91st on the right opposite
Mametz, then the 22nd in the centre, with the 20th on the
left facing Fricourt, the Brigade Headquarters being
respectively Bray sur Somme, Morlancourt, and Méaulte,
with Divisional Headquarters back at Treux. At first
the 20th and 91st Brigades had two battalions each in the
line, one in support, one in reserve, the 22nd, with a
shorter section to hold, only putting in one battalion and
having a much larger reserve. But these arrangements
were frequently altered. At the end of February, for
example, the Division took over some trenches to its right
from the Thirtieth, actually relieving its old friends of the
21st Brigade, but gave up a corresponding bit of its left
sector to the Fifty-First. In April again the line was reorganized, the trenches renumbered and the distribution
into sections altered, while the Twenty-First Division took
over the left sector. In May the Eighteenth Division took
over some of the right trenches, and early in June the 22nd
Brigade, which had continued to hold the middle section,
finding its own reliefs, was relieved by the Seventeenth
Division.

The activities and incidents of such a prolonged period
of trench warfare can hardly be described at any length
even in a Divisional history. February and the early
part of March were rather more disturbed than the period
from the middle of March to the middle of April, when
there was another outburst of activity, followed by a
relapse into comparative quiet in May. As the opening
of the British offensive drew nearer things became more
active again, more patrols went out and several raids were
attempted, mainly in hopes of gaining more accurate
information as to the German defences. At first the
Germans were on the whole the more active, their chief
effort being an attack on a salient in the left section known
as the Tambour. Here the opposing lines were fairly
close together and constant mining and counter-mining
had left No Man's Land composed largely of craters. On

17

February 21st the Germans shelled the Tambour fairly steadily all day, doing great damage, though considering the violence of the bombardment casualties were wonderfully low, amounting to less than a dozen. Next day soon after 5 p.m. the shelling started again, extending also to the support trenches of the next section, known as D 2. The 8th Devons were holding D 2 with the Borders on the left in the Tambour. It was soon evident that a raid was coming, and the " S.O.S." was sent up, to which the artillery responded by shelling Fricourt vigorously and barraging the trenches opposite the Tambour ; the support and reserve battalions also were turned out and moved up, the 9th Devons to Queen's Redoubt and Bécordel, the Gordons to near Carcaillot Farm. For an hour the bombardment raged, knocking the trenches about frightfully and inflicting many casualties.[1] Then the guns lifted on to the support line, and as the Borders hastened to man the battered parapet the enemy were seen climbing out of their trenches and advancing across the open. The Borders' rifles and machine-guns promptly opened fire, and the artillery behind, taking the lifting of the bombardment as a signal, quickened their fire with most effective results. The infantry too found themselves in a safe position, with the shells of both sides passing well over their heads and with nothing to do but to shoot down the attackers, which they did most effectually. Accounts vary as to the force in which the Germans attacked, one version speaking of eight or nine parties, others of three only. That three got into or close up to the Borders' trenches seems clear, but if any advance was attempted against the 8th Devons it was effectually prevented from developing and the battalion brought cross-fire to bear against the Borders' assailants. Of these the right party, which tried to get round the Northern end of the craters, was held up by the wire, failed to get through, and edged away

---

[1] " F " Battery R.H.A., which was covering this part of the front, had one gun put out of action.

into the craters under heavy fire, eventually retiring in confusion. A second, threading its way between the craters, got in between two saps, but was promptly bombed out again. The third, which worked round the Southern end of the craters, was more successful, entering a point known as the Poste de Bussy. Here the bombardment had done great damage, knocking out a Lewis gun and its team and forcing the platoon sergeant to shift the surviving men to the right to avoid the worst of the shelling. When the barrage lifted he moved back to the evacuated trench, but the enemy had effected an entrance, and bombed a mine shaft, suffocating several men, and when at last they were ejected several more of the defenders proved to be missing. However, a wounded German who was taken prisoner admitted that the raid had aimed at destroying our mine-shafts, for which purpose the raiders had carried explosives. This object they certainly had failed to effect, and though the 20th Brigade had nearly 70 casualties, two-thirds of them falling on the Borders, the enemy had certainly lost heavily; quite 20 Germans could be seen lying dead in front of the Tambour, and the men were much encouraged by the chance of shooting down Germans in the open. The conduct of the Mining Company was conspicuously good and won high praise from General Deverell, by no means an easy man to satisfy, while the 95th Field Company who came up directly the fight was over worked to such good purpose that the whole position had been cleared up and most of the damage made good by 6 a.m. next day.

After this nothing of much note happened for some weeks. One reads in the different Diaries of dispersing German working-parties by rifle and Lewis gun fire; of our guns cutting stretches of wire or damaging parapets and of Lewis guns and riflemen keeping the damaged portions under fire and impeding the work of repair; of patrol encounters; of effective retaliation by our guns and trench-mortars; of the 8th Devons frustrating an attempted raid near the Tambour on March 1st by effective rifle fire; of the 22nd Brigade successfully exploding four mines near the Matterhorn. But not till April does one come across references to any really outstanding incident, this time a German raid near Mansel Copse, just South of Mametz. As luck would have it it was again the Borders who had to face this raid : the 20th Brigade was actually out of the line but had lent a battalion to help the 91st Brigade to hold the right sector immediately opposite Mametz. A deepish valley here ran up the hill into the German lines, providing a path for a light railway and for the Fricourt–Carnoy road ; and Mansel Copse was a prominent landmark on the Western bank of this valley, the British front line running just through it. The German guns had been specially busy for the last few days, having possibly been stung into activity by an effective bombardment on April 17th of Kiel and Kiel Support Trenches, with Bois Français Trench and Orchard and Shrine Alleys. About 7 p.m. on April 19th they suddenly developed an intense bombardment of Mansel Copse and the adjacent trenches. Communication with the front line was completely severed and it was hard to find out exactly what was happening, but the artillery put down a barrage on the German trenches and the reserve battalions stood to. "B" Company of the Borders which was holding Mansel Copse suffered heavily, many men being buried under the ruins of their trench, but when the Germans advanced they were warmly received by the surviving defenders. They attacked at two points, at Mansel Copse itself and at the head of a communication trench farther to the left. The platoon just to the right of Mansel Copse beat off its assailants, the Queen's on their right fired to their flank across the frontage attacked, and a party near the head of the communication trench also fired· with great effect. But in between the points attacked most of the garrison seemed to have become casualties, though when the barrage lifted the company commander, Captain Kerr, who had closed his left platoon to the flank

to avoid a specially bad bit of line, promptly pushed along
with a bombing-party and reoccupied this bit without
meeting any Germans. A working-party, which lost no
time in repairing the damages, soon made the line defensible
again, while a fresh German effort about 8 p.m. next day,
although preceded by a violent shelling, was successfully
repulsed, many casualties being inflicted. The Borders
had suffered considerably, having 3 officers and nearly 80
men hit, but their steadiness was warmly praised and they
had the satisfaction of having punished their assailants
severely, many corpses being left out in No Man's Land.
Moreover, the British artillery retaliated most effectively,
smashing some big gaps in the German trenches, of which
our snipers took advantage next day.

After this it was rather from the British that the offensive
movements came. On May 20th the scouts of the 24th
Manchesters found Germans out in front of Sunken Road
Trench, covering a big working-party behind, whereupon
a fighting patrol of an officer and 30 men went out and
engaged the covering-party and drove both it and the
working-party in, Lewis guns and the artillery co-operating
most successfully. A raid on Kiel Trench by the Welch
Fusiliers a few days later found thick wire on the edge of
the craters and the craters themselves strongly held, while
on June 3rd the 22nd Manchesters got well into the German
trenches at Bulgar Point, bombing dug-outs, taking some
prisoners and disposing of several others with the bayonet.
Unluckily they ran into uncut wire when withdrawing, so
that German bombers could attack them at an advantage,
over 30 out of the 60 raiders being casualties.

Casualties on the whole were not high during this period.
Not all units obey the injunctions to record them accurately
and it is only possible to give a few representative figures.
Thus the five months cost the 20th Brigade 6 officers and
115 men killed, 20 men missing, 30 officers and 494 men
wounded, with 24 officers and 1,771 men admitted to
hospital. The 91st Brigade came off much better with only

404 battle-casualties to the 20th's 665, and one of its battalions—the Queen's—records 16 men killed, 58 wounded, and 122 with 4 officers admitted to hospital as against 9 officers and 314 men received as reinforcements.

Such moderate losses meant that units had an opportunity of getting together, officers had time to know each other and their men, battalion commanders and brigadiers got a chance of estimating, training, and improving their commands. The battalions which went over the top on July 1st, 1916, were naturally very different from the rather scratch collections of drafts which had held the Givenchy and Festubert sectors immediately after Loos. However good the quality of its drafts and however good the nucleus of survivors, a battalion which has lost 50 per cent. or more naturally finds it far harder to assimilate the big drafts needed than one whose reinforcements do not outnumber its old hands. But by June 1916 even the units most heavily shattered at Loos were themselves again and ready for anything.

That a British offensive could not be long delayed had for some time been clear. Shortly after the Seventh Division took over the Mametz–Fricourt sector the Germans had begun that attack on Verdun which was to strain the resources and endurance of France so severely. It had early become apparent that the British Armies must afford some relief to their hard-pressed allies, who had already borne the brunt of the strain over-long. But the British Armies had as yet neither the artillery nor the ammunition required for a sustained effort of any magnitude, and while the arrival of half the forces employed in the Gallipoli expedition and of another dozen " New Army " Divisions had expanded the force at Sir Douglas Haig's disposal, the latest additions from Home required much training in the face of the enemy before they could take part in an offensive. At first therefore the assistance could only take the form of relieving the French Tenth Army on the front between Arras and Lens, thereby providing a substantial reinforcement for the much-

enduring defenders of Verdun. Moreover, even when the
passing of the Military Service Act at last provided for the
systematic replenishment and reinforcement of the Armies
in France, the recruits whom the Act brought to the colours
had to be trained and would not be beyond the barest
rudiments for some months. As far therefore as the British
Armies were concerned a big offensive in the middle of 1916
might be reckoned premature, but Sir Douglas Haig had
to consider the general situation on the Western Front and
to subordinate to the common good the special needs of his
own command. Could the British offensive have been
postponed even until the beginning of September its
prospects of substantial success would have been much
improved ; the tasks which the Seventh Division was called
upon to tackle in July 1916 were the harder because the
British Armies had to undertake a gigantic offensive before
they could be tuned quite up to the pitch of preparedness
to be desired.

Preparations for the coming offensive, digging new
assembly and communication trenches, improving roads,
developing the water supplies, preparing places for dumps of
ammunition and other stores, constructing dug-outs for use
as dressing-stations, battle headquarters and other purposes, had taken up an increasing share in the Division's
labours as the spring gave place to summer. Units were
almost busier out of the line than in. To be in reserve
meant an almost continuous working-party with occasional
interludes of training. The fighting man in 1916 had not
yet been relieved of " coolie work " as he was afterwards
by the development of the Labour Corps and by recruiting
efficient labour from China and South Africa. However,
the Division managed nevertheless to work itself up to a
high standard of training for the offensive, even though
never entirely relieved of a section of the line. Several
changes in its composition had taken place since the
beginning of February. In the Staff the most important
was that Brigadier-General Minshull-Ford took over the

91st Brigade from General Kempster on February 3rd.   In April Colonel Way, the A.D.M.S., left to take up an appointment in the East and was replaced by Colonel Hooper. Colonel Ingles left the 8th Devons in May to command a brigade in the Thirty-First Division, being replaced by Major James, while Colonel Storey rejoined the 9th Devons on recovery from wounds received at Loos.   Colonel H. W. Smith of the Queen's was invalided home in February, Major Longbourne succeeding him.   All three Infantry Brigades saw their Staff Captains transferred to other Divisions as Brigade Majors, Captain Burmann of the Borders, Captain Furze of the Queen's, and Captain D. R. Turnbull of the Gordons getting the vacancies thus caused.

In units the first change was the departure of the 6th Cheshires to the Base on February 25th after little more than six weeks with the Division, which remained a battalion short until on May 22nd the 2nd Royal Irish arrived and were posted to the 22nd Brigade in place of the 24th Manchesters, on whom the lot of conversion into Pioneers had finally fallen.   In May the Cyclist Company and the squadron of the Northumberland Hussars left the Division on the formation of Corps Cavalry regiments and Cyclist battalions, while Brigade Ammunition Columns were abolished and the Divisional Column reorganized in four sections. Brigade Machine-Gun Companies had been added to the Division rather earlier, those of the 20th and 22nd Brigades being formed by transferring to the Machine-Gun Corps the officers and men who manned the battalion Vickers guns, Lewis guns being now issued to battalions in their stead.   The 91st Brigade's company came out straight from the Machine-Gun Corps centre at Grantham, arriving on March 24th.   Trench-mortar Batteries were also now definitely allotted to the establishment of each brigade. A change of some importance which occurred on May 17th was the reorganization of the Divisional Artillery, all R.F.A. brigades now being made up of four batteries, three armed with 18-pounders, the fourth with 4·5-inch howitzers. This involved the breaking up of the XXXVIIth Brigade R.F.A., its two batteries being added to the other brigades, the 31st joining the XXXVth Brigade and the 35th the XXIInd, while a battery formed from one section of each of the 31st and 35th Batteries and known as D/XIVth R.H.A. was added to the R.H.A. brigade.

CHAPTER XII

THOUGH the Somme offensive is by convention dated as beginning on July 1st when the often postponed infantry attack was finally launched, it might with equal justice be reckoned from the start of the great bombardment a week earlier. The 18-pounders had opened the ball on June 24th when they started wire-cutting, the heavy guns registering prior to joining in next day. For days before this ammunition had been systematically dumped round the gun positions to the tune of 1,100 rounds per 18-pounder, 1,010 per 4·5-inch howitzer, 500 per 2-inch trench-mortar, and 300 per Stokes mortar. The accumulation of these dumps was a most laborious process, especially as the Decauville railways proved a disappointment, their use involving more labour and risk without any saving of time. Accordingly the plan was changed and the ammunition transported by lorries direct from rail-head to the gun positions.

All through the 26th the heavy howitzers were at it, with a special concentration of fire between 9 and 10.30 a.m. Then at 11.30 gas was released and at 12.54 the guns lifted on to the German support line, in the hope that the enemy would man their front trenches in anticipation of our attack and would be caught there by the guns shifting back after two minutes. Similar tactics were pursued next day, the concentration of fire being from 4.30 to 5 a.m. Good progress had been made with the wire-cutting, though the "knife-rests" defied attack by shrapnel and could only be destroyed by using high explosive. At night patrols were pushed out to investigate the wire and

[1] Cf. Maps 20 and 21.

German trenches.   Thus on the night of June 26th/27th a patrol of the Gordons got into the enemy's trenches, bringing back useful information, and the Borders examined Danube Trench and reported it much damaged.   The Seventeenth Division, which was in reserve to the Corps, had lent two battalions to hold the Seventh's line during the bombardment and so allow the assaulting troops to go into the fight as fresh as possible ; but the attack, originally intended for June 29th, had to be postponed 48 hours, partly because of the rain, partly to allow of completing the wire-cutting where it had been unsuccessful.   Accordingly these two battalions had to be relieved on the 28th as intended and the attacking Brigades, the 20th and 91st, took over the portions of line allotted to them each with one battalion.

During these days the Germans had been far from inactive : their guns had replied most vigorously to the bombardment and had rendered the British front and support lines quite useless as jumping-off places.   This had been provided against, however, by digging special assembly trenches 250 yards farther back ; and though this gave the assaulting battalions that extra distance to cover as well as No Man's Land they escaped almost without any casualties before " Zero," as the starting time was now known, whereas had they assembled in the old front line they must have lost heavily long before it came.

The objective of the Fifteenth Corps on July 1st was a line running South and S.W. of Mametz Wood.   The Seventh Division on its right was attacking Mametz village, advancing due North, while the Twenty-First was to strike Eastward on the other side of Fricourt, which village was not to be attacked direct but to be " pinched out " by the inner flanks of the attack uniting in rear of it in Willow Avenue.   From this point the Seventh Division's line was to run Eastward to a track leading N.E. from Mametz to Caterpillar Wood.

The 91st Brigade on the right had first to capture

Bucket Trench and Bulgar Alley, then to reach Dantzig
Alley and secure that trench as far Westward as Mametz.
Its second objective was formed by Fritz Trench, Valley
Trench, and Bunny Alley, its third the line assigned as the
Division's final objective.   In the later stages this advance
would find its left protected by the 20th Brigade, whose
duty it was, after capturing the German trenches immedi-
ately in its front, South and S.W. of Mametz, to form a
defensive flank facing N.W. and running along Bunny
Alley, Orchard Alley, and Apple Alley.   After the final
objective had been secured two battalions of the 22nd
Brigade would make a subsidiary attack on the 20th's left,
aimed at clearing the trenches North of Bois Français.
Their first objective was Rose Alley from its junction with
Orchard Alley, which would involve capturing Sunken
Road Trench, Bois Français Trench and its support trench,
and an area known as the Rectangle ; its second objective
was a line from Willow Avenue to Bunny Wood.

The 91st Brigade was employing two battalions to attack
its first and second objectives, the 22nd Manchesters on
the right with Bucket Trench and Dantzig Alley as first
objective, the South Staffords on the left making for the
N.E. part of Mametz.   These units were to keep reserves in
hand for the capture of the second objective, and two hours
after " Zero " the Queen's were to go through and take the
third objective.   The 21st Manchesters less one company
detailed for " mopping up " formed the Brigade reserve.
The 20th Brigade was using three battalions in the first
attack, the Gordons on the right with Mametz as objective,
the 9th Devons in the centre, the Borders on the left with
Hidden Wood as the chief landmark on their frontage.
This left General Deverell with the 8th Devons as his
reserve.   The 22nd Brigade was entrusting its attack to
the 20th Manchesters with the Welch Fusiliers in support,
the Royal Warwickshires and Royal Irish forming the
Divisional Reserve along with six platoons of the 24th
Manchesters and the 54th Field Company.   The R.H.A.

brigade and two batteries of the LXXIst Brigade R.F.A. from the Seventeenth Division were detailed to support the 20th Brigade, the XXIInd Brigade R.F.A. and another battery of the LXXIst were covering the 91st, the XXXVth Brigade R.F.A. was helping the 22nd Brigade, and the LXXXth R.F.A. from the Twenty-First Division was in reserve, there being thus seventy-four 18-pounders and sixteen howitzers under General Watts. The Durham Field Company and a company of Pioneers were to establish strong points along the final objective, in Fritz Trench and at Bunny Wood. The 95th Field Company and another company of Pioneers were to place Mametz in a state of defence, while half a company of Pioneers opened up communication tunnels across No Man's Land to Bulgar Point and Mametz Trench. Shallow galleries had already been driven out at five points and mines placed ready to be exploded 15 minutes before " Zero."

The administrative arrangements for a set-piece of this magnitude had been elaborate and complicated and the orders filled many pages. Careful provision had been made for replenishing ammunition, especially bombs, for forwarding water and rations, for the wounded, for the reception of prisoners, for traffic control, for transmitting messages and reports. The orders were the product of weeks of careful work and had been constantly revised, indeed as far as was humanly possible nothing had been left to chance. But everything really depended on the success of the bombardment in breaking down the elaborate and carefully constructed German defences ; and heavy as had been the weight of metal concentrated against them, their formidable nature left that success an open question.

On the evening of June 30th all battalions had taken up their allotted positions. A steady fire was kept up all night, and then at 6.25 a.m. (July 1st), an hour and five minutes before " Zero," the final intense bombardment began. The din was tremendous, the heavy guns pounding away at the trenches at an incredible rate, the

lighter pieces trying to put the final touches to the destruction of the wire. To add to the noise the Germans
answered the bombardment by a furious rain of shell upon
the evacuated British front and support lines, but they were
wasting their fury on empty trenches and the assaulting
battalions could watch this bombardment with impunity.
Three minutes before " Zero " the Stokes mortars opened
a rapid fire, and on that the leading lines of infantry
started forward. Four minutes later they had reached
the British front line and almost without a check they
poured across No Man's Land, though not without casualties ; despite all the bombardment many machine-guns
opened on the attackers and some rifle fire spluttered out
from the German front line.

The 91st Brigade had the simpler task inasmuch as No
Man's Land was not complicated on its frontage as it was
on that of the 20th by the valley up which ran the light
railway. It was obvious that the German machine-guns
would be able to sweep this valley, and a bank on its West
side was known to be full of dug-outs ; so it had been
decided to leave a gap between the Gordons and the 9th
Devons and to trust to cutting off these dug-outs by an
advance on either flank. The 91st Brigade had formidable
enough defences to tackle, however, but despite machine-
guns and rifle fire the leading battalions made short work
of the German front line and its surviving defenders and
pushed on against the support line, a company of the 21st
Manchesters following hard on their heels and mopping up
the captured trenches. Within 15 minutes of " Zero " the
22nd Manchesters had reached Black Trench, and the South
Staffords were close to the S.E. corner of Mametz. Here,
however, sterner resistance was encountered ; machine-gun
fire checked the South Staffords, and though before 8 a.m.
the 22nd Manchesters had reached Bucket Trench their
casualties had been appreciable, and when they attempted
to push on into Dantzig Alley resistance stiffened. About
9 a.m the forward observing officer of the XXIInd Brigade

R.F.A. reported that a German counter-attack had reoccupied part of Dantzig Alley just East of Mametz, and though
the brigade promptly got its guns on this advance with good
effect, stopping its further progress, the Manchesters were
pushed back and reported themselves as consolidating
Bucket Trench, while the South Staffords were holding on
along the hedges just South of Mametz.   The artillery were
therefore asked to bombard Dantzig Alley again preparatory
to a fresh attack, the 106th Battery helping the South
Staffords considerably by shelling Bunny Wood, while the
104th fired on some German guns which were retiring from
Mametz Wood and knocked one out, killing the whole team.
The attacking battalions had already thrown their reserves
into the fight and two companies of the 21st Manchesters
had gone forward before 10 a.m. to reinforce the South
Staffords, leaving only one company of the support
battalion in hand; it was necessary therefore to call upon
the Queen's, who, directly the attack started, had occupied
the assembly trenches vacated by the 22nd Manchesters.

The 20th Brigade, like the 91st, had begun moving forward just before " Zero " and was well into No Man's Land
before the barrage lifted.   On its right the Gordons,
advancing on a front of 400 yards, rushed the front and
support trenches, Mametz Trench and Mametz Support,
in rapid succession, overpowering all opposition.   They
were so quickly on top of the Germans indeed that many defenders threw their bombs with the pins in for want of time
to draw them out.   The Gordons then pushed on towards
Mametz, though the left companies, " C " and " D," ran
into uncut wire at a point which had been specially hard to
observe and were held up, losing heavily.   By 8 o'clock the
leading waves of " A " and " B " on the right were on the
Southern outskirts of Mametz, holding on to a sunken road
North of the Cemetery and getting ready to rush the village.
In the centre the 9th Devons came under heavy machine-
gun fire, and " A " Company in particular had many
casualties in moving past Mansel Copse.   It had been

anticipated that this would be a danger spot, the lie of the
land made that clear ; and well-concealed and protected
machine-guns in Shrine Alley took a heavy toll, the company
commander being killed and most of his men falling with
him.   But the left company, shielded by the ground from
these deadly machine-guns, fared better ; it reached and
carried Danube Trench and Danube Support and forged
ahead, disappearing over the sky-line and out of sight of the
watchers at Brigade Headquarters.   The Borders on the
outer flank were so close on the barrage, thanks largely to
the splendid way in which the R.H.A. had cut the wire, that
they had to halt to escape running into it ; within 10
minutes of " Zero " they had not only cleared the front and
support lines, the Western part of Danube Trench and
Danube Support, but had wheeled half left and were ready
to push on towards Hidden Wood, while by 8 a.m. prisoners
were already reaching Brigade Headquarters.   After reaching Shrine Alley their first line was checked for a time by
machine-gun fire from Fricourt and from Mametz, but
reinforcements arriving took it on towards Hidden Lane.
They were attacked in flank by parties from Kiel Support
and Bois Français Support, who were disposed of, and then
a dash across the open carried the Borders into Hidden
Wood.   But they had got split up, and though they continued to fight their way forward in small groups, having
sharp struggles with parties of the enemy in shell-holes
and communication trenches, they made ground but
slowly ; eventually a detachment got into Apple Alley on
the left near the junction with Pear Trench, though some
hours elapsed before they could clear the whole trench.   But
the checks to the 9th Devons' right and to the Gordons'
left meant that there was a gap in the line.   The left
companies of the Gordons had lost heavily, and though
they tried to work round the obstructing barbed wire they
could not regain touch with their right companies.   These
held on to their sunken road and there defied all German
counter-attacks, but without reinforcements and support on

their left they could not take Mametz, though behind them
specially detailed parties were "mopping up" and more and
more prisoners were being passed down to the wire enclo-
sures prepared for them.   East of Hidden Wood the 9th
Devons had made lodgments in Shrine Alley and in Tirpitz
Trench, but though their reserve companies were pushed
forward they too were caught by the machine-guns : " D "
in particular lost heavily, all its officers were hit in crossing
No Man's Land and the men got much scattered in the
complicated tangle of trenches, the more puzzling owing
to the damage wrought by the bombardment.   Not enough
men reached the front line to give it the weight needed to
take it on, though the area in rear was gradually being
cleared.

Thus by 10 o'clock the 20th Brigade had also been brought
to a standstill and had to call on its reserve battalion, the
8th Devons.   Its leading company went forward about
10.30 to try to fill the gap between the Gordons and 9th
Devons, but it also could not escape the Shrine Alley
machine-guns and was checked.   A similar fate attended
the second company's attempt to run the gauntlet of the
Mansel Copse danger spot, but the third was more
successful ; moving across No Man's Land farther to the left,
it reached Hidden Wood almost without loss and pushed
on towards Orchard Alley, before long getting in touch
with the Borders.   This company was soon all mixed up
with the survivors of the 9th Devons, who had been clearing
up the trenches behind them, capturing many prisoners,
bombing dug-outs and generally making good their gains.
About the same time Lieut. Duff of the 8th Devons, who
had been sent forward by his commanding officer to see
what had happened to the two leading companies of that
battalion, found and reorganized their survivors and with
the aid of two C.-S.-M.s, Holwill and Melhuish, advanced to
Dantzig Trench and cleared up the dug-outs in the bank
West of the railway, making a fine haul of prisoners.   It
was now possible to work to the right along Shrine Alley

18

and to reach and take the machine-guns which had done so much damage : a vast pile of empty cartridges around them told their tale hardly less plainly than the lines of dead and wounded lying out in No Man's Land near Mansel Copse.

Meanwhile help had reached the right of the Gordons, who had been severely pressed. The first reinforcement was half the last company of the 8th Devons, who did some useful "mopping up" on their way forward ; the last two platoons followed a little later ; and about 1.30 p.m. two companies of the Royal Warwickshires from reserve were placed at Colonel Gordon's disposal and ordered up to Mametz. By the middle of the afternoon therefore the 20th Brigade, though its units were somewhat mixed up and disorganized, was in a position to press home its attack. Many prisoners had already been taken, at one point nearly 100 surrendered to one officer and two men of the 8th Devons, and resistance was tending to weaken. Orders were sent therefore to the Borders to secure Apple Alley and co-operate with the 22nd Brigade whose attack was just starting, to the Gordons to press the attack on Mametz, and to the Devons to push forward between the other two battalions.

In the meantime the 91st Brigade's situation had been much improved by the intervention of the reserves and by the capture of Pommiers Redoubt on their right flank, which position fell to the 54th Brigade about 10.15 a.m. The South Staffords had renewed the attack, and though still stoutly opposed reached the N.E. corner of Mametz soon after midday. Pushing on beyond they found their position insecure until Fritz Trench could be taken, so about 3 p.m. they had to fall back into Mametz, where they occupied Dantzig Alley and held on. Meanwhile the 22nd Manchesters also renewed their attack upon Dantzig Alley and made some progress, but the decisive element was the arrival of the Queen's on the scene. Two of their companies, " A " and " C," had moved forward to

Bucket Trench and Bulgar Alley rather earlier and had helped to build up a firing-line before, about 1 o'clock, they started to advance to the final objective on the right. The other two companies, quitting the old British trenches about the same time, made for the junction of Fritz Trench and Dantzig Alley. One party worked along by Ferdinand Alley towards the Mametz end of Dantzig Alley with great success, taking about 50 prisoners with two machine-guns and two automatic rifles. Farther to the right Dantzig Alley was reached and taken, and " B " Company started to work forward down Fritz Trench, making more captures. A considerable stretch of Dantzig Alley West of the junction with Fritz Trench proved to be still held by the enemy in strength ; bombing-parties were formed therefore and their attack resulted in the surrender of another big batch of prisoners. Meanwhile " A " Company had done good work in Fritz Trench, which was cleared about 4.30 p.m., Corporal Shaw turning a captured automatic rifle on to the Germans as they bolted from the trench. Bright Alley was then attacked and cleared by the 22nd Man-chesters, and about the same time Major Morris of the South Staffords organized an advance of that battalion and detachments of the Royal Warwickshires and 21st Manchesters to Bunny Trench and Bunny Alley, the Queen's opening fire to assist this attack, which reached its objective in Bunny Alley about 7.40 p.m.

By 8 p.m. the 91st Brigade, though sadly diminished [1] and greatly exhausted, had secured the line Fritz Trench–Valley Trench–Bunny Alley–Bunny Trench. Engineers and Pioneers had come forward and were assisting to consolidate the line, erecting strong points and making machine-gun emplacements, the Durham Field Company giving useful help, though it was not till dusk that the fighting was all over and that they could get to work. They then found some German dumps containing R.E.

---

[1] The approximate casualties were: Queen's, 300; South Staffords, 350; 21st Manchesters, 250; 22nd Manchesters, 500.

material which came in most usefully. Touch had been secured on the right with the Eighteenth Division, and on the left the 20th Brigade had also achieved its errand. The renewed attack of the Gordons supported by the Royal Warwickshires and some Devons on the Western portion of Mametz had succeeded completely, some 600 defenders surrendering almost en masse; and about 5 p.m. the brigade was on the line of its objective. The Borders profited by the 22nd Brigade's advance to clear the rest of Apple Alley, and pushing on to Orchard Alley established themselves there; the Devons were filling the gap between them and the Gordons, and Major Dobson now brought up the 95th Company R.E. and a company of Pioneers to assist in securing the gains.[1] Here also, however, success had cost the assailants dear : the 9th Devons had lost 480 all told, the Gordons 460, the Borders 340, and even the 8th Devons had just over 200 casualties.

As the other brigades had not secured their objectives at the scheduled time the 22nd Brigade had had to postpone its attack from 10.30 a.m. to 2.30, until when the 20th Manchesters had to remain in readiness watching the progress of the fight as best they could. At 2 p.m. the supporting group of artillery began to belabour the trenches opposite, dealing with them so effectually that when the 20th went over the top they swept over Sunken Road Trench almost without casualties; within ten minutes they had reached Bois Français Support and were struggling hard to secure it. Unluckily direction was to some extent lost, the two leading companies, " A " and "B," swung too much to their right and when their supports went forward they were enfiladed by machine-guns from Wing Corner just S.W. of Fricourt with disastrous results : the C.O., Colonel Lewis, was killed, two platoons of " D " Company were badly cut up, and the parties who should have bombed down the trenches leading to Fricourt were shot down almost to a man. A third company, " C,"

[1] They arrived just before 7 p.m.

had been detailed to clear the craters on the right of the main attack, which task it accomplished after some sharp fighting, but pushing on into Bois Français Support it was soon held up. Thus the battalion found itself checked, the Germans being in force in the Rectangle, in Rectangle Support Trench, in Zinc Trench, and in Orchard Alley. Some confused fighting followed : part of the left company got into the Rectangle, were bombed out and driven away to their right, rallied on " C " Company in Bois Français Support, organized a fresh attack which worked North along Orchard Alley, but were then fired into from the left rear by machine-guns and finally forced back into Bois Français Support by lack of bombs. Battalion headquarters meanwhile had reached Sunken Road Trench only to find themselves isolated and vigorously assailed by Germans, whom they kept at bay and finally drove off by the aid of " A " Company of the Welch Fusiliers, who crossed over by the craters so as to avoid the machine-gun fire from Wing Corner and lent the Manchesters valuable help, ultimately getting level with the 20th Brigade on the right. More of this battalion, however, had to be put in, and about 5.30 p.m. it was ordered to send up bombing-parties, tackle the Rectangle and push down the trenches leading towards Fricourt. This they accomplished, not without severe fighting ; by 8 p.m. they had cleared the Rectangle with parts of Kitchen, Copper, and Sunken Road Trenches, having taken 100 prisoners in the process, and forced the obnoxious machine-guns to withdraw from Wing Corner to avoid capture. It gave the Welch Fusiliers particular satisfaction to put out of action one trench-mortar which for months past had made itself a special nuisance to the troops opposite. By this time the 20th Manchesters, now only about 150 strong, were in Bois Français Support from Zinc Alley to Apple Alley, where they got touch with the Borders. If the 22nd Brigade had not accomplished quite all that had been set it enough had been done to secure the flank of the Division, and orders were accordingly issued to consolidate the line gained, which was continued along Orchard Alley by the 20th Brigade, two companies of Royal Warwickshires connecting up the 20th Brigade with the 91st about the N.W. corner of Mametz.

The Seventh Division had had to fight hard for its gains [1] and to pay no light price, but its success had been undeniable and coupled with that of the Eighteenth and Thirtieth Divisions on its right had gone some way to compensate for the failure of the left and left centre to retain the initial gains which they had made. Just North of Fricourt the Twenty-First Division had gained enough ground for it to be practicable during the next few days to complete the original programme for " pinching out " Fricourt and linking up the inner flanks of the two Divisions.

Orders for the continuation of the attack were received from the Corps in the small hours of July 2nd and promptly passed on to the brigades. The main share was allotted to the 22nd Brigade, which was to move against Fricourt from the South, while the Seventeenth Division, who had come in on the right of the Twenty-First, attacked from the North. The Divisional Artillery, besides covering the front held by its own infantry, was able to enfilade from the South the positions which the Seventeenth Division was attacking and rendered effective help in this way. To the 22nd Brigade's right the 8th Devons were to support the advance with covering fire, and as soon as Fricourt Wood had been cleared they were to seize the Northern portion of Orchard Trench and establish a strong point at the Orchard, the 91st Brigade meanwhile pushing forward to the final objective of the previous day, a line on the high ground South of Mametz Wood, and overlooking the valley running up past Caterpillar Wood.

In the early hours of the morning the Welch Fusiliers

---

[1] The amount of work the Divisional Artillery had got through may be realized from the fact that one brigade alone fired nearly 7,000 rounds from 18-pounders and 900 from howitzers in the course of the day.

MAMETZ VILLAGE DURING THE BATTLE OF THE SOMME, JULY 1916

had worked forward along Sunken Road Trench, but
between 6 and 7 a.m. their advanced parties were withdrawn to allow of a fresh bombardment of Fricourt. However, it soon appeared that the enemy were no longer in
strength at Fricourt and the bombardment was stopped
to allow patrols to investigate. The Welch Fusiliers and
20th Manchesters accordingly pushed parties forward
both to the N.E. and N.W., and before long all the trenches
behind Sunken Road Trench up to and including Rose
Alley had been cleared, and patrols advanced into Fricourt,
entering it just as the Seventeenth Division came in from
the other side. Little opposition was encountered, though
a fair haul of prisoners was made. This allowed the 8th
Devons, who had already disposed of a half-hearted
counter-attack, to reach the Orchard, establish a strong
point there, and eventually gain touch with the Seventeenth
Division in Willow Trench, capturing many prisoners in
the process without much resistance. This advance
crossed and covered the front of the 22nd Brigade and
allowed it to be drawn back into reserve between Mansel
Copse and Carnoy.[1] In the same way the 91st Brigade's
advance crossed the 20th Brigade's front and brought it
into second line, so that next day (July 3rd) it also could be
withdrawn, leaving only the 8th Devons and the 20th
Machine-Gun Company to continue consolidating the line.
With the infantry thus established on their final objectives
the guns were rather too far back to give them full support,
and about midday on the 2nd they began to move forward,
the 25th Battery being the first to advance. The move
was a good deal delayed by the difficulty of crossing the
German trenches and large working-parties of gunners had
to be detailed to help, by laying bridges across them and
clearing away obstructions.

---

[1] The Royal Irish had sent two companies up to the front on the previous
evening, one to help consolidate Mametz, one to support the 22nd Manchesters
in Bunny Alley ; both rejoined battalion headquarters in Divisional Reserve
by dawn on July 2nd.

The 91st Brigade had not had much opposition to overcome. Early in the morning (July 2nd) Germans moving about in Bottom Wood had given the Queen's good targets for machine-guns, and about 11 o'clock that battalion moved forward to Cliff Trench, taking a machine-gun and several prisoners; by 2 p.m. it had established itself in White Trench on the high ground South of Mametz Wood, which was found to be only half dug. Patrols were pushed out to the front; these came across two abandoned 77-mm. field-guns 150 yards farther North, one of which was successfully brought in next day, the other being too much damaged to be moved. Touch was gained with the 54th Brigade farther to the right, and later in the day the 21st Manchesters came up on the left and helped to consolidate White Trench. This being so incomplete real hard digging was needed, and the Germans shelled the position persistently; but by the aid of the Durham Field Company the line was made good, special attention being paid to the left flank, against which a small counter-attack was delivered about 10.30 p.m., only to be repulsed by the rifles of the 21st Manchesters aided by an effective artillery barrage.

Meanwhile good progress had been made North of Fricourt towards Contalmaison, and Sir Douglas Haig was anxious to push on with the reduction of this and other intermediate positions between the German front system and their second line of defence higher up the slope. In this the Seventh Division was to take a share, using the 22nd Brigade, of whom only the 20th Manchesters had so far been much punished. On the evening of July 3rd it received orders to occupy and consolidate a line from the Southern end of Mametz Wood along Strip Trench and Wood Trench to Quadrangle Trench.[1] This would enable them to help the Seventeenth Division, which was approaching Mametz Wood from the West. Earlier in the day the 91st Brigade had extended its left to Bottom Wood, which

---

[1] The XIVth Brigade R.H.A. was covering the left of the line, the XXIInd Brigade R.F.A. covering the right.

had been heavily barraged in the morning, after which patrols of the 21st Manchesters entered it and found it empty, securing three derelict guns. This barrage had driven a good many Germans into the open, providing targets for the Lewis guns of the Queen's, which did some effective shooting at ranges of 1,100 to 1,500 yards, one party of about 50 Germans being brought down as they bolted from Bottom Wood towards Quadrangle Copse. Meanwhile the troops on the left had made good progress, capturing Fricourt Farm about 3 p.m. and gaining touch with the 21st Manchesters.[1]

Two battalions, the Royal Welch Fusiliers and the Royal Irish, were detailed by General Steele to carry out the attack. They left the Halte, South of Mametz, soon after midnight July 3rd/4th, but the Welch Fusiliers' guide lost his way, so the battalion did not reach the deploying position till day was breaking and it was too late to attack. Accordingly the Royal Irish had to act alone. Colonel Dugan began by pushing scouts into the wood, and on their reporting that it was held in strength [2] he organized a bombing attack up Strip Trench on the S.W. side of the wood, with one company in support and two others forming a defensive flank on the left facing towards Quadrangle Trench, which contrary to all reports proved to be still in German hands. The attack started well, bombing up Strip Trench to its junction with Wood Trench; but the supports came under heavy fire from Quadrangle Trench, and gradually the bombers were forced back by counter-attacks to the Southern edge of the wood, where a stand was made, in touch with the support company who had lined a bank running from Mametz Wood towards Bottom Wood. Other companies reinforced and protected the right flank which was being threatened from the N.E., but

[1] The Divisional Artillery did some very effective shooting to help this advance, " T " Battery R.H.A. stopping a German counter-attack from Shelter Wood.

[2] It appeared later that all three battalions of the 16th Bavarians had just arrived.

the position was untenable, and after a sharp fight the
Royal Irish had to withdraw.[1]   They did so, however, in
good order, bringing with them the breech-blocks of two
guns which had been found just South of the bank between
the woods.   Their casualties amounted to 80, but they
had the satisfaction of inflicting a good number on the
Germans.

It was clear now that the Germans were in force in and
round Mametz Wood and that a really serious operation
would be needed to dislodge them.   In the afternoon of
the 4th the guns were turned on to cut the wire opposite
the 22nd Brigade, but this proved difficult owing to bad
light and was only satisfactorily accomplished when in
the evening the XXXVth Brigade R.F.A. took on the
task.   Orders had meanwhile been issued for the 22nd
Brigade to attack again at 12.45 a.m. on July 5th, using
the same two battalions, as the Royal Warwickshires had
already relieved the 91st Brigade and the 20th Manchesters
were too weak to be used.   The Seventeenth Division was
attacking on the left, and farther North the Twenty-Third
was tackling Contalmaison.

Directly the barrage lifted the two battalions advanced ;
the night was dark and the ground heavy and slippery
after recent rain, but the men went forward well.   The
Welch Fusiliers got well into the left of Quadrangle Trench,
obtained touch with the 9th Northumberland Fusiliers of
the Seventeenth Division, and promptly started bombing
to their right, where " B " Company had lost direction and
got held up.   Half " A " Company from reserve was put in
to fill the gap and by its aid " B " also secured its objective.
Bombers then started to bomb along the trench to its
Eastern end, a little distance short of the light railway,
and a party under an officer dashed across the 70-yards
gap which separated Quadrangle Trench from Wood
Trench and made a lodgment.   But they could not effect

---

[1] The orders had been definite that the battalion was not to let itself get
committed to really serious fighting.

a junction with the Royal Irish, for that battalion having a larger stretch of open to cross had been caught by enfilade fire from the right and lost heavily, while on reaching Wood Trench uncut wire confronted it,[1] and though a bombing-party cleared 150 yards of Strip Trench counter-attacks from the wood finally forced it back. This failure did not deter the Royal Irish from twice renewing the attempt, but without any better success, two officers being shot down in trying to force their way through the wire. It was now nearly daylight, and as the Welch Fusiliers had got a secure hold on Quadrangle Trench, the Royal Irish were withdrawn, covered by effective fire from the XXIInd Brigade R.F.A., which put down a smoke barrage. The little party of the Welch Fusiliers who had reached Wood Trench had to make the best of their way back to Quadrangle Trench, after which the artillery shelled Wood Trench and the Southern portion of the wood system-atically. On the other flank, however, more success was achieved, for while the Seventeenth Division got on well, the Welch Fusiliers' bombers pushed along Quadrangle Alley till nearly half-way to Quadrangle Support. Here they made a block and though twice counter-attacked by enemy working down Quadrangle Alley from Quadrangle Support maintained their position successfully,[2] not a little helped by the shallowness of Quadrangle Alley, which forced the attackers to expose themselves so that Lewis guns enfiladed them and nearly wiped them out.[3]

The Welch Fusiliers had thus wound up the first of the

---

[1] As before a bombing-party tried to work up Strip Trench while two com-panies attacked Wood Trench and a third formed a defensive flank on the right.

[2] Useful help in consolidating the position was afforded by the 54th Field Company.

[3] The Welch Fusiliers were fortunate in achieving this success at the low cost of 60 casualties. The Royal Irish, less lucky, had more than double that number hit, including three company commanders, their total losses since July 1st coming to nearly 230, those of the Royal Warwickshires being 120, of the Welch Fusiliers 130, and of the 20th Manchesters 330, a total for the brigade of about 800.

Division's "battles of the Somme" with a substantial success. That evening units of the Thirty-Eighth Division arrived to relieve the 22nd Brigade, and during the next twenty-four hours it was taken back to Heilly for a brief rest, the 20th Brigade being already established at Treux and Ribemont, the 91st round Buire and Divisional Head-quarters at Treux. With the infantry the R.E. and Pioneers were also withdrawn; not so the artillery, who remained in position to support the Thirty-Eighth Division and was still in line when its own Division came back for its second turn in the fight.

The capture of Mametz is one of the outstanding successes to the Seventh Division's credit. The defences which faced it were most formidable and were held by a well-trained, well-equipped, and resolute garrison ; and only by skilful planning, careful preparation, good leading, and great determination, devotion, and daring was success achieved. The cost had been heavy, 65 officers and 814 men killed, 1 officer and 471 men missing, 85 officers and 2,388 men wounded, a total of 151 officers and 3,673 men. Still, relatively to the results achieved, the loss, grievous as it was, may be pronounced lighter than at Loos or Festubert or Neuve Chapelle, and the large haul of prisoners —23 officers and 1,333 men were recorded on July 1st alone—was something substantial to set against them. What further losses the Germans had suffered could only be guessed, but quite apart from those caused by the bombardment, which had been much reduced by the deep dug-outs in which the bulk of the trench garrison had found effective shelter, many must have been inflicted on July 1st. The Division had taken toll of their enemies with bomb and bayonet in the close-quarter fighting in the trenches and there had been many chances for effective use of rifles and machine-guns, though if the old 1914 standard of musketry had been maintained the rifle would have claimed many more victims.

All ranks and all arms had contributed of their best to

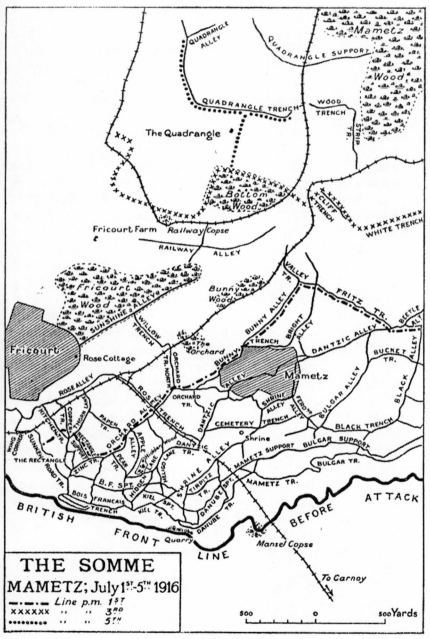

QUADRANGLE ALLEY

QUADRANGLE SUPPORT

Mametz

Wood

QUADRANGLE TRENCH

WOOD TRENCH

STRIP TR.

The Quadrangle

XXX

Bottom Wood

×CLIFF TRENCH

WHITE TRENCH

Fricourt Farm   *Railway Copse*

RAILWAY   ALLEY

Fricourt Wood

Bunny Wood

VALLEY TR.

FRITZ TR.

BEETLE ALLEY

SUNSHINE ALLEY

WILLOW TR.

BUNNY ALLEY

BRIGHT ALLEY

DANTZIC ALLEY

BUCKET TR.

Fricourt

• Rose Cottage

The Orchard

BUNNY TRENCH

BUNNY ALLEY

Mametz

BULGAR ALLEY

BLACK ALLEY

ROSE ALLEY

ROSE TRENCH

ORCHARD ALLEY

ORCHARD TR.

DANTZIC ALLEY

SHRINE ALLEY

FEROS ALLEY

BLACK TRENCH

PAPEN TR.

APPLE ALLEY

CEMETERY TRENCH

○ Shrine

BLACK SUPPORT

THORN TR.

COPPER TR.

RECTANGLE SUPPORT

ROSE TRENCH NORTH

HIDDEN LANE

COTTAM LANE

DANTZIC TR.

Shrine

MAMETZ SUPPORT

BULGAR SUPPORT

BULGAR TR.

WING CORNER

HITCHEN TR.

ZINC TR.

DEER ALLEY

B.F. SPT.

TIRPITZ TR.

SHRINE ALLEY

MAMETZ TR.

THE RECTANGLE

SUNKEN ROAD TR.

BOIS FRANCAIS TRENCH

KIEL TR.

KIEL SPT.

DANUBE SPT.

DANUBE TR.

MAMETZ TR.

BRITISH

FRONT

Quarry

LINE

Mansel Copse

BEFORE   ATTACK

To Carnoy

THE SOMME
MAMETZ; July 1st–5th 1916

— · — · —   Line p.m. 1st
×××××× ,, ,, 3rd
•••••••• ,, ,, 5th

500   0   500 Yards

MAP 21.

this substantial success and to differentiate would be idle and invidious. It may be mentioned, however, that when General Watts addressed the 8th and 9th Devons shortly after the battle he reminded them that when, nearly twelve months earlier, their two battalions had been posted to the Division, General Capper had said he wondered what sort of substitutes for the Guards the new-comers would prove. " I do not think," the Divisional Commander went on, " he is wondering now." The same might well have been said of the Manchester battalions who had replaced the 21st Brigade. Mametz had been their first trial in battle and they had acquitted themselves splendidly, while the old Regular battalions had shown that though hardly any of those who landed in Belgium in 1914 were still in their ranks, and not too many who had fought at Neuve Chapelle or Festubert, the mantle of the original Seventh Division had fallen on worthy shoulders.

Of the R.E. and Pioneers all the infantry brigadiers spoke in the highest terms ; they had been prompt to push forward and get to work the moment an opportunity offered and their work had been admirably and expeditiously done. Medical and Supply arrangements had, in the words of a brigadier who was notoriously not easy to satisfy, " worked throughout without a hitch according to the prescribed programme " ; and the maintenance of telephone communication had been astonishingly good, enabling General Watts and his brigadiers to keep well in touch with the progress of the fight. A very substantial share of the credit was due to the artillery. The guns under Divisional control had not had to do the work of battering down the actual German defences—1915 had shown that only the heavier pieces could produce any effect on them ; but the 18-pounders had done their wire-cutting excellently, especially considering the difficulties of observation, and their barrages had been both accurate and effective. The co-operation of all ranks and all arms in the actual attack itself was in large measure responsible for the success achieved, and this can be largely traced to the careful and systematic training for which the long pause in active hostilities since Loos had given chances, and to the lessons which the Divisional Commander and his staff had been careful to inculcate.

CHAPTER XIII

IT was only a brief rest which the Seventh Division enjoyed after Mametz. There was barely time to incorporate the large drafts which were poured into the shattered battalions, most of them from any regiment but their own. The 9th Devons, for example, got only 50 men from their own reserve units out of a total draft of nearly 500, and the Gordons were the only unit to be reinforced mainly by their own men ; the 20th Manchesters actually got 160 Irishmen, at a time when it was proving very hard to provide Irish units with recruits from Ireland ; this draft, however, was subsequently transferred to the Royal Irish. Luckily the practice had now been adopted of leaving out of action not only a fair proportion of officers but a nucleus of N.-C.-O.s and " specialists " to serve as the basis for reconstruction in case of heavy losses ; it was therefore less difficult to re-form companies and platoons. Even so a bare week out of the line gave all too little time to bring battalions up to the level of July 1st. The Divisional Commander and his senior Staff officers did not even get that amount of rest. The Thirty-Eighth Division's first efforts to capture Mametz Wood had not been too successful, matters had got into a tangle, and General Watts was called on to take charge. He went up, therefore, taking Colonels Bonham Carter and Wingfield with him, besides Captain O'Connor and the Divisional Signal Company, and succeeded in straightening things out and in clearing up Mametz Wood, an important success and essential as a preliminary to the launching of the next big attack.

The Divisional Artillery also had little or no rest during

---

[1] Cf. Map 22.

this time. It had remained in action when the infantry were relieved and played a big part in the hard
fighting of the next week, supporting first the attacks of
the Seventeenth and Thirty-Fourth Divisions on Contalmaison and then those of the Thirty-Eighth on Mametz
Wood. Guns and men were both worked to the verge of
exhaustion, but, thanks largely to the splendid work of
the forward observing officers, their efforts were most
effective and by the evening of July 11th Mametz Wood
had been cleared and the guns could begin to cut the wire
in front of the second system of defences to which the
Germans had now been pushed back. This ran from the
Albert–Bapaume road on the West to Longueval and
Delville Wood opposite the junction of the British and
French. This second system it was Sir Douglas Haig's
intention to pierce, using the Thirteenth Corps on his right
against Delville Wood and Longueval, the Fifteenth
against Bazentin le Petit and the adjacent woods, and the
Third to cover the Fifteenth's left flank.

Orders for this attack were issued on July 11th, and
Divisional orders were sent out next day. The Division
was to be on the right of the Fifteenth Corps, having the
Third Division on its immediate right and the Twenty-
First on its left. Its immediate objective was the trench-
line running South of Bazentin le Grand Wood, here
known as Flatiron Trench, its final objective the establishment of a line from the N.E. corner of that wood to the
Northern edge of Bazentin le Petit. The 20th Brigade
was to lead the attack and to secure the wood, after which
the 22nd Brigade would go through it and attack Bazentin
le Petit village, that wood on its left being on the Twenty-
First Division's frontage. The 91st Brigade was to remain
in reserve South of Mametz.

The German retirement to the Southern crest of the
main ridge had left about 1,000 yards between the position
to be attacked and the new British front line. This line
on the Seventh Division's frontage ran along the bottom
19

of the valley which separates the Montauban–Mametz
spur from the main ridge, passing between Caterpillar and
Marlborough Woods on the right and along the Eastern
edge of Mametz Wood on the left.   In front the ground
sloped steadily up towards Bazentin le Grand Wood, but
a small subsidiary valley running N.E. from the main
depression separated that wood from the wood and village
of Bazentin le Petit.   The highest point in Bazentin le
Grand Wood was about half-way through from South to
North, and beyond it the ground dipped fairly sharply.
Bazentin le Petit village stood on slightly higher ground
on the Northern slope up from the subsidiary valley,
which at its N.E. end widened into a broad but shallow
depression with High Wood on the far side and to the
N.E. of Bazentin le Petit.   The general trend of the line
to be attacked was from S.E. to N.W., and 200 to 300
yards behind Flatiron Trench a second line, known as
Circus Trench in Bazentin le Grand Wood and as Forest
Trench farther to the British left, ran roughly in the
same direction.

This second system, though formidable enough, was
hardly as strong as the lines which the Division had carried
a fortnight earlier.   The real difficulty was to get the troops
into assaulting distance of their objectives, and the problem
of crossing the wide No Man's Land was extremely awkward.   To attempt it by day was to invite destruction ; it
was therefore decided to make a night advance, trusting to
darkness to conceal the approach until the attackers could
get close enough to the German lines to have a real chance
of success.   But such an advance could only hope to escape
detection through extraordinarily careful arrangement and
timing, and great dexterity and care in execution.   Above
all the troops must keep as silent as possible, and to preserve formations and distances during so long an advance
would tax their discipline and training almost as severely
as the keeping of silence.   Had this task been set to the
battalions who had mustered for the attack on June 30th

the Seventh Division would have had little doubt in its
ability to do what was asked of it, but with its battalions
full of fresh men, whom their officers had hardly begun to
get to know, there may well have been misgivings in some
minds.

One means of maintaining secrecy was to omit entirely
any preliminary bombardment ; guns had registered
on the new line, but were to hold their fire until five minutes
before the hour of the assault.   There was of course the
risk that German patrols might be out in No Man's Land
and detect what was coming, but German patrolling had
not been conspicuously active of late and it was not
unreasonable to hope that they would fail to detect the
advance if it did not give itself away.

On the evening of July 11th the 9th Devons took over
the new front from the Thirty-Eighth Division.   It ran
from the East of Mametz Wood in front of Caterpillar
Wood with outposts in Marlborough Wood.   Caterpillar
Wood was itself untenable owing to shell fire, so a line was
taken up at the foot of the rise towards the next ridge
where good cover could be obtained, and though the enemy
fired away steadily during the next two days casualties
were remarkably low.   On the 13th the Divisional Artillery,[1]
still at it without having had a day off since the preliminary
bombardment had begun, maintained a steady bombardment, which proved to have been most effective, especially
in cutting the wire ; and at 10 p.m. the assaulting
battalions of the 20th Brigade, the Borders and 8th Devons,
moved up to the deployment position, which was reached
in time, although they had to cross broken and intricate
ground, traversed in all directions by wire and trenches.
The Gordons were in support, the 9th Devons were to
withdraw into reserve after the attacking battalions had

---

[1] Several R.F.A. brigades belonging to other Divisions were under General
Rotton's orders to support this attack.   Most batteries had moved forward
to new positions on the night of July 11th/12th, though several of them were
heavily shelled while doing so.

gone through. Of the 22nd Brigade the Royal Warwickshires and Royal Irish led, the other two battalions being
in support.

About 2.30 a.m. the 8th Devons and Borders, on the
right and left respectively, began to move forward. The
night was cloudy, and covered by scouts in front the
battalions got level with the Southern edge of Flatiron
Copse undetected. Here they halted for a few minutes
and then started off again crawling up the slope. They
moved steadily and with an incredible silence, gradually
getting nearer the German line without any indication
that their advance had been detected. An occasional
shell from the German guns burst over them, but it was
nothing more than the usual intermittent firing, and as
the lines crawled forward yard by yard hope rose high that
they would effect the desired surprise. From the British
guns a few rounds were fired, while every now and then
a machine-gun let off a burst of fire to keep up the impression that nothing unusual was afoot.

The last moments of this stealthy crawl were tense with
excitement. Every minute that passed without detection
saw the silent lines of crawling men steadily nearing their
objective, every second meant a foot gained. At last
the silent British guns suddenly roared off together, and
as the barrage came hurtling down on the German trenches
Borders and Devons sprang to their feet with the leading
lines only 100 yards away and rushed forward, entering
the enemy's position just as the barrage lifted on to the
second line and almost before the Germans knew they
were coming. The surprise had come off completely and
the wire had been so admirably cut that it presented no
obstacle, while the German trenches were full of dead,
victims of the bombardment. The Devons' right company,
" A," met very little resistance and pushed quickly on to
the second objective, the Eastern portion of Circus Trench,
which also was quickly secured, many Germans being
killed and about 100 taken. " D " Company on the left

had more difficulty with the first objective, as the Germans
had managed to man their trenches and put up a stout
fight. Both companies seem to have diverged to the
flanks, so that for the moment a projecting piece of line
called the Snout was left unattacked : however, the support
company," C," was led straight at this point, cleared it
after a hard fight and then, pressing on into the wood,
linked up " A " Company with " D," which by 4 a.m. had
reached its second objective on the Northern edge of the
wood. A short pause followed and then the 8th Devons
pushed on to complete their task, establishing themselves
with one company on the right overlooking Bazentin le
Grand village, one at the Northern end of the wood, the
third on the left facing N.W. towards Bazentin le Petit.
A couple of companies of Germans who had been
encountered in this last advance were driven off up the
slopes opposite, giving the rifles and Lewis guns a chance
by which they were quick to profit, the two companies
being pretty well wiped out. Thus the 8th Devons had
achieved a substantial success, capturing an 8-inch
howitzer and more prisoners than they had suffered
casualties. The Borders also had carried all before them.
Their objectives had been in the Western portion of the
Bazentin le Grand Wood and in the valley beyond and had
been captured with great promptitude ; indeed they were
so far forward that they had to wait for some minutes
before the barrage lifted off the wood. Their casualties
were quite light and they found a good position to consolidate in a bank parallel to the edge of the wood and about
30 to 50 yards outside it.

Thus by five o'clock the 20th Brigade had secured its
objectives without having had to call on the Gordons, and
the way was clear for the 22nd Brigade to go through.
The Royal Warwickshires who led were detailed to secure
the Western end of Circus Trench, and cover the advance of
the Royal Irish. They had started forward at 4.45 a.m.,
passed through the Borders and made good Circus Trench

practically unopposed. The Royal Irish then moved upon Bazentin le Petit, " C " Company making for the village, " A " for the cemetery to the East of it, " B " acting as left flank guard, " D " being in reserve. Their advance was rapidly successful. They kept so close to a splendidly accurate barrage that they were into the village almost before it lifted and " C " Company caught the defenders in their shelters, capturing about 150, among them one regimental Colonel. " A " secured the cemetery with more prisoners and pushed a patrol with a Lewis gun out to a windmill 300 yards to the Eastward. " B " meanwhile had found some of the Twenty-First Division on the Northern edge of Bazentin le Petit Wood and was establishing its defensive flank. Before 7 o'clock the battalion was con-solidating its farthest objective and the Division had still two-thirds of its infantry in hand, while orders had been issued to the LXXXIst Brigade R.F.A. to advance to new positions near Marlborough Wood—it had sent for its teams as early as 6 a.m., though it took them some time to get up through the throng of traffic—and officers had gone forward to obtain observation from the new front line.

Before long, however, the situation on the left changed for the worse. Exactly what had happened there was uncertain, but a certain amount of fire began coming from Bazentin le Petit Wood. Accordingly the reserve company of the Royal Irish was put in to clear the wood. After moving for some distance in extended order it gained touch with the Twenty-First Division and so withdrew to rejoin its own battalion. Apparently the Twenty-First Division had been forced back from the edge of the wood by heavy shelling and had now come forward again but only to be forced back once more, as a little later on " B's " patrols failed to find any British troops in the North end of the wood. The 95th Field Company and a company of the 24th Manchesters had come up to help consolidate,[1] but

---

[1] The Field Company reached the front about 10 a.m.

the German guns had begun to shell the village, their fire soon increasing greatly in intensity.

Meanwhile on the other flank the Royal Warwickshires were busy consolidating and had sent half " B " Company along a narrow ravine leading East to investigate affairs in Bazentin le Grand. This party came on Germans on the North and N.E. edges of the village and engaged them, at the same time gaining touch with some Northumberland Fusiliers of the Third Division, with whose help it soon cleared the village. Shortly afterwards the Germans began moving forward from High Wood to counter-attack, but the artillery were warned and got their guns on in good time, while part of " A " Company reinforced " B," lining the road running North to the cemetery, and the Germans were thrown back in some disorder.

It was now nearly 11 o'clock, the German artillery fire had increased considerably and under its cover strong counter-attacks were developing. The Royal Irish were soon in trouble ; their right from the cemetery Northward faced N.E. but their left flank had had to be flung back to face N.W., so that the Northern end of Bazentin le Petit formed the apex of a sharp salient. The battalion therefore was exposed to converging attacks ; Germans advanced in force from High Wood against " A " Company at the cemetery, capturing its advanced post at the windmill, and simultaneously the Northern end of the village was attacked. They were also pressing hard against Bazentin le Petit Wood, so two platoons of " B " Company, supported by two of " D," were sent forward about 11.45 to counter-attack, but meeting Germans advancing in force out of the wood they were pushed back into the village, just as a strong attack in four lines forced its way into its Northern end. This attack came mainly from the N.E. and was kept at bay for a long time by the R.E. and Royal Irish, though some officerless men of the Twenty-First Division farther to the left fell back almost at once. Before long shortage of ammunition compelled the rest of the defenders to retire, some of the R.E. holding on to the N.W. corner till nearly surrounded.[1] But though the village was lost the Royal Irish managed by steady shooting to bring the main attack from the N.E. to a standstill 150 yards away from " A " Company's line, being very greatly assisted by the Divisional Artillery, whose shooting was extraordinarily accurate and effective. Meanwhile a mixed crowd of all regiments, who had been driven back out of Bazentin le Petit Wood, was rallied at the Southern end of the village by Captain Lowe, the Adjutant of the Royal Irish. Here a " keep " which the 24th Manchesters had constructed and helped to defend proved of great use, and about 1.30 Captain Lowe actually counter-attacked a party which tried to push forward from the windmill. Appeals for reinforcements and ammunition had already been passed back, and detachments of the 20th Manchesters had arrived with ammunition, " D " Company of the Royal Warwick-shires came up to counter-attack, and the Gordons and Welch Fusiliers were both ordered up, the former to clear Bazentin le Petit Wood, the latter to retake the ground between the cemetery and the windmill.

Farther to the right the German counter-attack made no ground whatever, either against the Royal Warwick-shires or against the 8th Devons in Bazentin le Grand Wood, though for a time the 95th Field Company had to abandon work on the strong points it was constructing[2] to assist in repulsing it. By 2 p.m. all was over, the work of con-solidation had been renewed and the 8th Devons[3] could spare reinforcements to help the Royal Irish at the cemetery. The Devons had many casualties from the German shell fire, in fact it cost them more to hold the position than to take it, but even so they came off fairly well.

---

[1] The 95th Field Company had nearly 30 casualties and the Pioneers over 50.

[2] Marked A, A, A on map.

[3] They were the only part of the 20th Brigade now in front line, the Borders, though they suffered severely from shell fire, being in second line behind the Royal Warwickshires.

The arrival of reinforcements soon enabled Colonel Dugan and the Royal Irish to restore the position at Bazentin le Petit. The company of the Royal Warwickshires pressed forward up the village, pushing the Germans back. The fighting was severe, but luckily the Germans had run out of bombs ; by 2 o'clock they had been ousted from the village and had lost heavily under Lewis-gun fire which caught them as they fled. Captain Lowe and his mixed party moved across into Bazentin le Petit Wood and working from South to North cleared it and established themselves on the Northern edge, the position here being secured by the arrival of the Gordons later in the afternoon. That battalion had reached the road junction S.E. of Bazentin le Petit Wood [1] and from there pushed a company forward to take up a line from the N.E. corner of the wood to the North end of the village. This company, " D," advanced most successfully, capturing over 20 prisoners, pushing the Germans back and establishing itself on the prescribed line, which was later on continued to the right by two companies of the 21st Manchesters who had been sent up earlier. Meanwhile the Welch Fusiliers, though heavily shelled while .advancing, deployed East of Bazentin le Petit Wood, and covered by four guns of the 22nd Brigade Machine-Gun Company carried out their counter-attack with complete success, the line being retaken before 3 p.m. with little trouble or loss. It was promptly consolidated without much difficulty, a feeble counter-attack being easily repulsed. This success made it possible for the Division to attempt in the late afternoon a move which General Watts had been urging on the higher authorities ever since the success of his first attack on Bazentin le Petit.

The Seventh Division's rapid success had certainly opened up possibilities which, if promptly turned to account, might have been of the utmost importance. Hardly any point on the whole Somme battlefield witnessed more

---

[1] Marked B on map.

bitter fighting or cost more to take than High Wood.
Not till the middle of September was its capture finally
achieved, and in the two months before that not a few
Divisions had tried in vain to secure it. Yet about 9 a.m.
on July 14th a rapid advance, either of a fresh Division or
of all the reserves of the Seventh, might have led to the
capture of High Wood. Only four battalions had been
employed to secure the Division's objectives, and General
Watts with two-thirds of his infantry in hand had been
most anxious to be allowed to exploit the opening which his
leading battalions had so brilliantly made. The artillery,
as already mentioned, had pushed forward and taken up
new positions in Flatiron Valley and Caterpillar Valley
and could have supported a further advance. Two hours
passed before the Germans ventured on a counter-attack,
and though later in the morning they, as already described,
had counter-attacked with vigour and persistence, these
efforts apparently exhausted all their immediately available
reserves, and when the 91st Brigade eventually advanced
the resistance that it encountered at first was neither well
organized nor determined. An advance at 9 a.m. therefore might not have met more opposition than the Division
could deal with successfully. It might of course have been
difficult to get the reserves forward or to move up the guns
in time for an advance as early as 9 a.m., but if the whole
91st Brigade had gone forward after the recovery of
Bazentin le Petit, instead of being kept back by orders to
let the cavalry advance, there would still have been a
chance of a considerable success. General Watts had had
the 91st Brigade ready soon after 11 a.m., and had it
advanced about 3 p.m. the cavalry might have achieved
more by following it up than was actually done.

It is one of the drawbacks of attacks with strictly limited
objectives that complete and rapid success may sometimes
not be fully exploited just because it has exceeded expectations. The Seventh Division had done its task so quickly
and so cheaply that the limitation of its objectives was for

once a handicap. It is easy to be wise after the event, but had General Watts had a freer hand it does look as if High Wood might have been secured ; and High Wood, as after-events showed only too clearly, was the key to much. Its capture would have, for example, outflanked Switch Trench and the other defences between it and Longueval, doubtless with very salutary results on the struggle for Delville Wood. The opening was not fully improved, but the Seventh Division deserve all the credit for having made it.

The belated effort to utilize the chance of capturing High Wood was made by the South Staffords and the Queen's, who were to be supported on their right by the advance of the Secunderabad Cavalry Brigade of the Second Indian Cavalry Division, and on their left by the leading brigade of the Thirty-Third Division, who were to come through the Twenty-First. The Queen's and South Staffords had moved up earlier in the morning to a position East of Mametz Wood, where they dug in under heavy shell fire, disposed in artillery formation. Here they remained for over six hours, enduring the German bombardment with but slight casualties and waiting for their chance.

It was well after 5 o'clock when at last the orders reached them : the South Staffords were to lead and to deploy with their left on the Bazentin le Petit cemetery ; the Queen's were to form on the South Staffords' right, their right flank being approximately North of Bazentin le Grand village. The 21st Manchesters behind were to provide a reserve and a right flank guard of one company. The barrage was to lift at 6.15 p.m., when the Thirty-Third Division was to advance against Switch Trench N.W. of High Wood. There was no chance of reaching the position of deployment before the barrage lifted, but the two battalions pushed ahead and about 6.45 p.m. deployed behind the Welch Fusiliers with about a mile to cover to reach the wood. The country ahead was a refreshing sight, green pasture land unscarred by shell-holes and broken by an occasional hedge, while High Wood itself was in full leaf, not a tree as yet damaged by shell fire. Nothing was to be seen of the Thirty-Third Division, so there was some delay while the South Staffords arranged for the protection of their flank by a Lewis-gun detachment and part of a company. By 7 p.m., however, all was ready and the advance started. At once it came under machine-gun fire from the high ground just West of High Wood, which enfiladed it [1] and caused the South Staffords several casualties, while there was some fire from Germans in shell-holes straight ahead. However, orders were issued to the Queen's to push on hard for High Wood, hoping that they would be able to get into the wood and outflank the troublesome machine-guns. Advancing in four lines 150 yards apart on a front of 350 yards they made splendid progress. As they came on they dislodged the Germans in the shell-holes, a few of whom stopped to surrender or be bayoneted ; the majority bolted, giving good targets to the Queen's, who shot them down from the standing position, knocking many over. About 700 yards from the starting-point—they had covered the distance in 10 minutes—the Queen's took three field-guns at a hedge, and half an hour later the leading lines reached the edge of the wood.

Meanwhile the South Staffords also had been pushing on, disposing of not a few Germans in shell-holes and hollows, though hampered and delayed by the persistent machine-guns on their flanks. They were therefore a little behind the Queen's, whose advance they had to some extent shielded, but before long their leading lines were up level with the Queen's and the two battalions plunged into the wood together. It was thick with dense undergrowth, in which it was hard to see twenty yards ahead, so direction was difficult to keep, but there were not many Germans in

---

[1] This was to some extent kept down by the Welch Fusiliers, whose covering fire was very useful, Lewis guns at the windmill knocking out several machine-guns.

the wood, not enough to prevent the Queen's from pushing through to its Eastern edge, which was reached before 9 p.m. There they proceeded to dig in, having three companies along the S.E. and part of the N.E. edges, with "B" in reserve. The South Staffords came up on their left and established themselves on a line through the wood, though they could not clear the whole of the Northern angle, in which the enemy continued to resist, despite some gallant efforts in which Lieuts. Potter and Seckington were conspicuous. However, consolidation was started, while a little later the Durham Field Company came up and assisted to prepare the position for defence,[1] making strong points at the Southern and Eastern angles of the wood but having frequently to stop work to pick up their rifles and help to repulse counter-attacks.

The night indeed was not destined to be quiet, least of all for the South Staffords. Some useful work was done in clearing up the interior of the wood, bombing dug-outs and making a haul of prisoners, but about midnight the Germans from the Northern corner of the wood counterattacked. The left company of the Queen's, "D," was hard pressed in front and in flank, but used rifles and Lewis guns effectively and held its own. But the South Staffords' right was pushed back and the Queen's had to throw "D's" left platoon back and utilize "B" Company from reserve to form a defensive flank facing N.W. through the wood.

Morning therefore found the 91st Brigade established in the Eastern and Southern parts of the wood, but with the Germans holding the Northern and Western portions in strength. The Thirty-Third Division had come up under cover of night, and during the day it made various ineffectual attempts to dislodge the Germans. The South Staffords had been reinforced by the 22nd Manchesters, who had sent one company forward on the previous

[1] The 21st Manchesters remained in position outside the wood and S.E. of it, covering the right flank.

evening, followed about 11 a.m. on the 15th by two more, the fourth going up later again. But even with this help [1] the position was hard to maintain against the German counter-attacks, backed up by well-handled and placed machine-guns.

About 6 o'clock there was a sudden retirement on the left, but the troops rallied in the open and re-entered the wood. Meanwhile the Queen's had been holding on to their original line along the N.E. edge despite heavy artillery fire from which they suffered severely ; they now put in two companies, " A " and " B," to assist in this counter-attack. These companies, however, met stubborn opposition and after gaining a little ground were compelled to retire to the Eastern side of the wood. Here they were rallied and eventually came forward again and established themselves along a track running N.E. from about the middle of the S.W. edge, to form a defensive flank. With them were mixed up many Manchesters and South Staffords. The position was far from satisfactory. The Thirty-Third Division's efforts to capture the trench line running N.W. from High Wood had met with no better success than those of the 91st Brigade to clear the wood. It was very difficult to arrange for artillery support or maintain communication with the Division, for despite the devotion of those responsible for them the telephone wires were cut by the shell fire almost as quickly as they were laid, while runners suffered severely in crossing the exposed slopes behind the wood. The artillery therefore were severely handicapped and found it extremely difficult to maintain an effective barrage or to stop the development of counter-attacks. Gallant and resourceful work on the part of the Quartermasters and transport detachments had brought up rations, water, and ammunition to the wood during the night, the Queen's Quartermaster, Lieut. Belchem,

---

[1] About 3 p.m. the 21st Manchesters also were moved across from the right flank and gradually absorbed into the struggle, but even then the wood could not be cleared.

doing conspicuously fine work in keeping his battalion
supplied with cartridges : but the position was so far in
advance of the general line and so pronounced a salient
that to maintain a hold on it would be very difficult and
even to some extent invited disaster.

The decision was accordingly taken to evacuate High
Wood, and at 11.15 p.m. on the 15th orders for this were
forwarded to the 91st Brigade. It was well after 2 a.m.
before they reached the advanced battalions, and as they
had to be out of High Wood by 3.30 there was no time to
spare. But it was managed; and despite the Germans
constantly sending up flares and rockets and opening
bursts of machine-gun fire, which compelled the last
detachments to lie down to avoid being caught by the
stream of bullets, the defenders of High Wood got clear
away, bringing with them most of their wounded.

During the struggle for High Wood the consolidation of
the objectives of July 14th had been steadily continued.
That evening the troops had been redistributed. The 20th
Brigade withdrew to Mametz, though " D " Company of
the Gordons was left in front line ; the Royal Irish were
drawn back into reserve, being relieved by the Royal
Warwickshires, who held from Bazentin le Petit to the
cemetery with the Welch Fusiliers thence to Bazentin le
Grand Wood ; this line the 22nd Brigade handed over on
the night of July 15th/16th to the Thirty-Third Division,
but reoccupied the right of it from the windmill South-
Eastward next night, for there was still work required of
the Seventh Division. A fresh attempt on High Wood
was in contemplation, and it was proposed that the 20th
Brigade should attack it again on the 18th. Actually the
attack was postponed to July 20th, before which some
readjustments were carried out, the 22nd Brigade extending
to the right, relieving the left of the Third Division, and the
Thirty-Third taking over the frontage immediately opposite High Wood. The 20th Brigade remained in its
bivouacs, while the 91st, much the hardest hit of the three

brigades in their last battle,[1] was sent farther back to
Mansel Copse and its neighbourhood. The interval between
the Seventh Division's two attempts on the High Wood
position was decidedly lively. The German artillery were
very much on the alert, blazing away freely, at times
shelling our front line, at others barraging the approaches
with high explosive and generally making things uncomfortable. On the British side the guns were active,
consolidation was vigorously carried on, the 54th Field
Company constructing three strong points East of Bazentin
le Petit about 400 yards beyond the cemetery, and patrols
were pushed out, who brought in plenty of information
about the German defences, while by Corps orders a line
of outposts well dug in and wired was established some
way in front of the main line.

In the new attack the Seventh Division had a much
more limited frontage and much less elaborate task than
on July 1st or 14th. The Thirty-Third Division was
attacking High Wood itself ; the Seventh was advancing
clear of its Eastern edge with two roads, later known as
the Black Road and Wood Lane, running S.E. from the
wood to Longueval, as its objectives. The Gordons were
on the left, the 8th Devons on the right, with the Borders
and one company of the 9th Devons in support in Caterpillar Wood, and the Royal Warwickshires as Brigade
reserve. They had been lent by the 22nd Brigade, as the
rest of the 9th Devons had been sent back to rest.

Wood Lane and the Black Road ran parallel along the
ridge connecting High Wood with Longueval and Delville
Wood. Behind them some distance back lay Switch
Trench, which ran East and West through the Northern

---

[1] The approximate figures for July 10th to 17th were : 20th Brigade, 23
officers and 754 men ; 22nd Brigade, 29 officers and 754 men ; 91st Brigade,
30 officers and 1,167 men ; Pioneers, 7 officers and 62 men ; R.E., 11 officers
and 76 men ; R.A., 11 officers and 82 men. The heaviest sufferers were the
Royal Irish, Queen's, and South Staffords, with over 300 casualties apiece, the
21st Manchesters being only a few short of that figure, and the Borders, Royal
Warwickshires, and 22nd Manchesters all well over 200.

part of High Wood and was full of machine-guns. The ground was littered with the dead horses of the Secundera-bad Cavalry Brigade, not exactly a very promising augury for the attack. From the assembly position N.E. of Bazentin le Grand the ground rose fairly steeply, covered with coarse grass or standing corn and giving some cover in the first stage of the advance. On the Devons' right the Fifth Division was also attacking.

The two battalions detailed for the attack began moving up into their positions at 10 p.m. on July 19th. By this time the Germans had developed the habit of shelling the valley South of Mametz Wood,[1] where some of the support-ing artillery were in position, with systematic frequency ; and they also barraged the depression North of Bazentin le Grand Wood persistently, and to reduce casualties the supports had to be scattered about and well dug in. The attacking battalions, however, reached their positions with but little loss, and about 3.15 a.m., 20 minutes before " Zero," they began crawling forward up the slope.

As on the 14th this plan worked well. The leading lines were quite close to the Black Road when the barrage opened, and rushed it without meeting any serious resist-ance. Beyond it the ground rose to a crest, Wood Lane lying just over the far side, and the advance to the second objective came under very heavy fire, especially as the men crossed the top of the rise. Ahead of them were riflemen and machine-guns scattered about in the standing corn, well hidden and therefore hard to locate and impossible to indicate to the guns,[2] even when communications were not cut. From Switch Trench more machine-guns were in action, and from HighWood others enfiladed the advance.

---

[1] This came to be known as the " Happy Valley."

[2] Observation of fire either by forward observing officers or by aeroplanes had been very difficult and for once the wire was not thoroughly cut, while the same difficulties hampered the artillery's efforts to prevent the advance of hostile reinforcements. But, as the official report says, it was no fault of the artillery personnel that, for the first time, their operations were not entirely successful.

20

Gordons and Devons both struggled gallantly forward, the former in particular suffering severely from the enfilade fire from High Wood.   One platoon of their right company reached Wood Lane but was wiped out, only the officer and five men getting back, and though many Devons got within about 50 yards anyone who pushed on farther was shot down.   Eventually, after hanging on for an hour, the survivors of the leading companies had to crawl back to the Black Road which the supports were consolidating. In covering this retirement specially fine work was done by two Lewis-gun teams of the Devons, who remained out in front and effectually prevented any counter-attack. One team on the left got some splendid targets in German reinforcements advancing from Switch Trench, the other farther to the right fired with good effect at Germans nearer Delville Wood.[1]

Reinforcements came up to assist in consolidating the Black Road, the company of the 9th Devons which was supporting the Gordons having its commander killed and many other casualties, but with High Wood untaken farther progress was hopeless.   The Thirty-Third Division gained some ground, though it could not capture a redoubt at the Eastern angle of the wood which contained the machine-guns that enfiladed the 20th Brigade.   Eventually these gains were wrested from them by German counter-attacks, and before long the British hold on the wood was reduced to the very fringe, a line being maintained just inside the S.W. edge, from which it was continued to the right by the Gordons and Devons, who though sadly reduced retained their first objective and had consolidated it satisfactorily before in the evening two battalions of the Fifth Division relieved them.

This relief was made doubly difficult because the

---

[1] The V.C. was awarded to Pte. T. Veale of the 8th Devons for conspicuous gallantry in repeated attempts to bring in a badly wounded officer who was lying out close to Wood Lane, a task which was eventually accomplished successfully.

Germans, having detected that it was in progress, put down a heavy barrage which added considerably to the already high toll of casualties.[1] Among the killed was Colonel

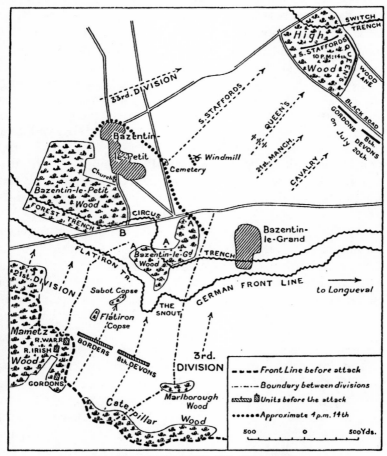

MAP. 22—THE BAZENTINS AND HIGH WOOD.

B. G. R. Gordon of the Gordons; he had been slightly

[1] The total casualties for July 20th were nearly 400, about half being incurred by the Gordons, who had 2 officers and 52 men killed or missing, 5 officers and 140 men wounded; of the rest the 8th Devons had 160 casualties, while to these must be added another 160 incurred by the 22nd Brigade in holding the line before the attack.

wounded on the 14th but had remained at duty. The
third C.O. of the Gordons killed in action since the war
began, he had taken command of his battalion just after
Loos and had been most successful in building it up to a high
standard of efficiency after its heavy losses in that battle.

With the 20th Brigade's withdrawal, followed that
night by the relief of the 22nd Brigade by the Thirty-
Third Division, the first stage in the Seventh Division's
experience of the Somme came to an end, even the long-
enduring Divisional Artillery being actually taken out of the
line. Since July 1st its guns had fired nearly a quarter
of a million rounds of 18-pounder ammunition, and over
40,000 from the 4·5-inch howitzers,[1] figures which do give
some slight idea of their almost continuous work, the
fearful strain on the personnel, and the wear and tear
of the material. In the preliminary bombardment eight
18-pounders had been put out of action, one being destroyed by a premature, and two jamming, the others
having their inner tubes worn out. There was hardly a gun
which did not need thorough overhauling ; and in the
advanced positions they had taken up on July 14th the
batteries had been subjected to an almost incessant bombardment, in which lacrymatory and gas shells had been
freely used. Certainly if any branch of the Division had
deserved a rest it was the artillery.

But there was not a unit in the Division which was not
in sore need of rest. Several other Divisions which had
taken part in the attack of July 1st had been engaged again
in that of the 14th, the Seventh had remained in longer
than any of the others, and on the 20th the 20th Brigade
had actually had to make its third attack within three
weeks. The total casualties suffered in the fighting for
the Bazentins and High Wood amounted to within a few
hundreds of those incurred round Mametz, coming to 125
officers and 3,443 men, with the grand total since July 1st

---

[1] The R.H.A. Brigade had fired over 4,200 rounds per gun and nearly 2,800
per howitzer in the four weeks ending July 20th.

of over 7,500 of all ranks. Two battalions, the Gordons and the 22nd Manchesters, had actually lost over 700 apiece ; the Queen's and South Staffords both exceeded 600 casualties ; both Devon battalions, the Royal Irish, the Borders, and the 20th and 21st Manchesters had lost upwards of 500 ; and the losses of the Royal Warwickshires and the Welch Fusiliers, 350 and nearly 400 respectively, were only light in proportion to the enormous casualties of the other battalions. In the second phase of the operations both Artillery and Engineers had suffered much more than in the earlier fighting : the R.A. losses mounted up from the 3 officers and 21 men of July 1st–5th to 15 officers and 82 men, several of the officers being forward observing officers, but many of the casualties were due to the increasing counter-battery work of the Germans and their constant shelling of back areas, which frequently caught the drivers and their teams as they brought up ammunition by tracks on which the Germans were only too accurately ranged. The R.E. and Pioneers in the same way, who had got through the earlier fight with under 30 casualties, had 165 between July 13th and 20th, figures which pointed clearly to the splendid work they had done in assisting the consolidation of the positions gained, in opening up communication trenches, and helping the infantry in every conceivable way.

The Seventh Division came out from its first share in " the Somme " exhausted and sadly reduced but with every reason for pride and confidence. Hardly any other Division had been asked to do so much or had succeeded in accomplishing so much. Soon after the Division had settled down into its rest billets it was visited by the Army Commander, General Rawlinson, who congratulated it warmly on its achievements. " Confidence," he said, " had always been placed in the Division, a confidence which had never on any occasion been found to be misplaced. The gallantry and behaviour of the Division had become a byword not only in the Army, but at home."

CHAPTER XIV

THE SOMME—GINCHY [1]

THE billets to which the Division now moved lay in a real " rest area," well to the N.W. of Amiens and quite out of the zone of hostilities. It was a great relief to get away from the neighbourhood of the fighting into country untouched by war and out of contact with things which suggested war. Conditions had been almost as unpleasant and uncomfortable in the bivouacs and camps in which battalions had found themselves when in reserve, as in the fighting-line itself. The noise, the smells and sights, the filth and squalor, were almost as bad there as up in front, and the heavy " fatigues " that fell upon battalions in reserve entailed considerable danger as well as very severe exertions. The zone through which the carrying-parties had to make their way with rations, ammunition, R.E. stores, and wire had been constantly barraged by the Germans, and casualties among these parties had added appreciably to the Division's long list.

Divisional Headquarters were at Belloy, the artillery were established round Heilly, the 20th Brigade's centre was Picquigny, that of the 22nd Yseux, of the 91st Vaux. Leave was opened on a generous scale, there were ample opportunities for recreation ; horse-shows and gymkhanas were held and proved great successes ; and though it was the hottest part of the year the men indulged extensively in football. Training was not neglected and several ceremonial parades were held ; the Army Commander inspected the 20th Brigade on August 25th, for example, and presented decorations, when considering the scanty time that had been available for ceremonial the drill and bearing of the troops were most creditable.

[1] Cf. Map 23.

There was not quite the same difficulty over the rebuilding of the Division as there had been after Loos, because
the system of leaving out a nucleus on which to reconstruct
units provided a guarantee against that wholesale sweeping
away of competent administrators and instructors which
had made reconstruction so difficult after earlier battles.
Moreover, the Division had been fortunate in not losing
so many C.O.s; Colonel Gordon and Colonel Lewis were
the only battalion commanders who had been killed,
while Major Miller of the 91st Machine-Gun Company had
been wounded. Reconstruction therefore went on apace,
though there was some dissatisfaction over the physique
and general quality of some of the drafts which were
poured in. One battalion received about 25 men who
were physically and generally quite useless, another had
40 men too undersized to march in full marching order,
and the musketry and marching capacities of the new
hands provoked some severe criticisms. But though in
most cases the drafts exceeded the old hands in numbers—
the 20th Brigade received drafts amounting to over 2,000
men in July—there was no battalion which had not got
a substantial leaven of experienced hands and plenty of
competent instructors ; and by the middle of August
when the Division left the Belloy area for Ribemont and
its neighbourhood it had gone far to assimilate its reinforcements. In the interval the Division had lost General
Deverell on his promotion to command the Third Division.
An officer of marked character and personality, he had won
the confidence of his whole brigade and had shown himself
a remarkably competent commander with the highest
standards of discipline and efficiency, a ruthless critic if
things ever fell below those standards, but one who never
spared himself in the least and was always ready to recognize good work. In his place came Brigadier-General H. R.
Green from the K.R.R.C., an officer who soon established
himself in the confidence of his brigade.

The Division was now in Corps Reserve, but there was

apparently no immediate idea of employing its infantry
again and they settled down in its new quarters, the 20th
Brigade round Buire sur Ancre, the 22nd and 91st round
Dernancourt. The billets here were most unsatisfactory,
absolutely filthy, swarming with refuse and flies : no unit
had apparently been in them for more than a couple of days
since July 1st, and no one had bothered to clean them up
till the 22nd Brigade undertook the task. In a few days it
left its mark on Dernancourt, it cleaned the streets, burnt
mountains of refuse, and transformed the sanitary (or
rather insanitary) arrangements into a model. The
Divisional Artillery, however, went back into the fighting
without waiting for the infantry and on August 21st relieved the artillery of the Fifth Division, which artillery
were assisting to cover the frontage held by the Fourteenth
Division in Delville Wood. It was now under Brigadier-
General Seligman, who had just joined on General Rotton's
promotion to be C.R.A. XIth Corps.

Since the Division had left the fighting area on July 21st
desperate struggles had been going on, round Guillemont,
Ginchy, and Delville Wood on the right, round High Wood
in the centre, and round Pozières on the left. It had been
an unsatisfactory and disappointing time. Division after
Division had been put in and had lost heavily without
apparently achieving anything appreciable or in any way
commensurate with the casualties. Some progress had
been made ; but every yard gained had had to be fought
for with desperation and represented a long casualty list.
The Germans too had suffered severely, especially in their
repeated counter-attacks, and they had only retained a
grip on the points of contention by tremendous exertions
and desperate endeavours. It had been a contest of
attrition, and if the British had used up a terrible amount
of man-power the strain on their opponents' resources had
been not less great, and in the aggregate these weeks had
yielded gains. But the last week of August came without
the British obtaining complete control of Delville Wood

and without the barrier represented by the line Ginchy–
Guillemont–Falfemont Farm being broken through.   But
it was essential that this should be accomplished before
Sir Douglas Haig could start his next really big attack in
which he proposed to employ the new weapon, whose preparation had been enshrouded in such careful secrecy, the
Tanks.   Had things gone better the Seventh Division was
to have been kept back to be fresh for this attack, but
·they were going none too well round Delville Wood and
Ginchy, and the Division was called upon therefore to take
a share in the preliminary work of securing a good starting-
line for the big effort.

On August 18th the 22nd Brigade had been placed under
two hours' notice, so the summons to the front which it
received on the 26th was not altogether unexpected, and
that evening it relieved portions of the Fourteenth
Division on the Eastern edge of Delville Wood and of the
Twentieth Division facing Ginchy.[1]   At the moment the
Germans, though dislodged from all but a small corner of
Delville Wood, were holding several trenches running into
the wood and had prevented the British from establishing
more than a slight hold on them.   But these trenches
ran across the top of the ridge leading from Delville Wood
Eastward and flanked the approaches to Ginchy from the
West.   Their capture was therefore essential ; and early
on the morning of August 27th bombers of the Royal
Welch Fusiliers began fighting for the possession of Ale
Alley, which entered Delville Wood at its N.E. corner.[2]   A
bitter struggle followed ; after two hours the Fusiliers had
gained about 30 yards but were held up by machine-gun

---

[1] The Royal Welch Fusiliers took over the left of the line, the 20th Manchesters being on their right, the Royal Warwickshires in support, and the
Royal Irish in reserve.

[2] The Welch Fusiliers' line formed a sharp salient ; their left company, " B,"
lined Hop Alley, a trench which entered Delville Wood just South of its N.E.
corner, " D " in Beer Trench, which faced Eastwards, was at right angles to
" B," " C " on the right faced S.E. towards Ginchy, forming a more or less
" refused " flank.

fire from farther along the Alley ; from Hop Alley they
had also pushed North along Beer Trench for about 90
yards and for a rather less distance East along Vat Alley,
while about 50 prisoners had been taken.   Further efforts
to gain ground in Ale Alley, however, were unsuccessful,
even when assisted by a battalion of the Fourteenth
Division farther to the left, though they tried rushing it
after a barrage of rifle-grenades.   On the right fair progress
had been made with a new trench, Stout Trench, some little
distance up the slope in front of ZZ Alley, till then the
advanced line, though the work was greatly impeded by
German shelling, which inflicted many casualties, among
them Major Greig, commanding the 54th Field Company,
who had brought his men up to assist in consolidation.
The shelling indeed was so heavy that the old trenches,
already bad, became almost unrecognizable, and it was
simpler to dig new ones than to try to repair the old ones.
On the night of the 28th/29th, working-parties of the
Royal Warwickshires did fine work in pushing forward
over 100 yards from Stout Trench and beginning a new
trench to which the name Porter Trench was given.   These
trench-names became distinctly unpopular later on—those
condemned to hold them in sultry weather, with only a
very limited supply of water to drink, complained bitterly
that the trench-names excited rather than assuaged thirst.
    For three more days the 22nd Brigade stuck to its line,
despite constant shelling and sniping ; the Welch Fusiliers
indeed gained some ground in Ale Alley by bombing,[1]
while on the right the new trenches were getting on well.
On the night of the 29th/30th, the South Staffords and
21st Manchesters relieved the front-line battalions [2] and
next day the relief was completed, the Queen's taking their
place as support battalion, the 22nd Manchesters being

    [1] In all they made about 170 yards and nearly reached the junction of Ale
Alley and Beer Trench.
    [2] The Welch Fusiliers' casualties testified to the severity of the fighting,
coming to over 200 in four days, while the 20th Manchesters had nearly 150,
practically all due to the bombardment.

farther back in reserve. The 22nd Brigade had found
things lively enough at this much-contested corner : the
91st was to be even more severely tried. It had found the
trenches little better than a line of shell-holes linked up
together hastily, waist-deep in liquid mud ; communication between battalion headquarters and the front line
was with difficulty maintained by runners who took at
least an hour to make the journey, the communication
trenches being often three feet deep in mud, while torrential
rains on the night of the 29th/30th had made bad worse.
The 30th passed off fairly quietly, save for barrages on
Delville Wood ; but about 10 a.m. on August 31st the
Germans started a heavy bombardment, using a large
proportion of gas shell. This was not confined to the
front line, but was distributed over back areas also, the
Divisional Artillery mostly just North of Montauban
coming in for a very heavy shelling and having four guns
put out of action, the 31st and 58th Batteries being the
worst sufferers. Casualties were heavy, especially among
the South Staffords, who got the worst of the bombardment.[1] However, when, about 1.30 p.m., German infantry
began attacking the South Staffords beat them back, their
snipers being very successful in picking off German bombers
who tried to work forward along the communication
trenches. After two repulses the Germans stopped
attacking but resumed the bombardment with increased
intensity ; a third company of the South Staffords had
to reinforce the front line, and General Minshull-Ford
called up three companies of the Queen's. Somewhere
about 5 p.m. the Germans came on again ; a fold in the
ground 300 yards away gave them a chance to assemble
under cover and they now swarmed forward in strength,
being apparently fresh troops.

The South Staffords put up a good fight, the platoon in

[1] The South Staffords had two companies in their front line, which ran
along Hop Alley to Beer Trench and then followed Beer Trench to Pilsen
Lane ; one platoon also held the Western portion of Ale Alley.

Ale Alley under Lieut. Henderson making a particularly stubborn resistance ; but the Germans outnumbered them, and eventually, all their bombers being casualties and all their bombs used up, for the barrage had prevented fresh supplies from reaching the front line, they began to give way. About 7 p.m. a sudden German rush got into Hop Alley near the junction with Bitter Trench and overwhelmed " B " Company's right, and shortly afterwards the survivors of the front companies were pushed back into Delville Wood. Here Captain Burt and Lieut. Jones-Mitton managed to rally some 50 men and checked the Germans along the line of shell-holes which had once been Diagonal Trench. Before long they were reinforced by two companies of the Queen's, who took over from them, holding part of Devil's Trench on the left, the part of Diagonal Trench inside the wood, and a short length of the edge near the S.E. corner.[1] The rest of that battalion came up a little later and occupied part of ZZ Alley with reserves farther back. The attack had not extended to the front held by the 21st Manchesters, but the bombardment had, both Diagonal Trench and ZZ Alley being heavily shelled, notwithstanding which work on Stout and Porter Trenches had been steadily pushed on, so that they were now ready for occupation by day. In this the 24th Manchesters did splendid work, toiling away devotedly despite the intensity of the shelling.[2]

Early in the morning the 22nd Manchesters relieved their 21st Battalion, who withdrew to Pommiers Trench to rest, the South Staffords, who had lost very heavily,[3] being collected in Montauban Alley, while the Welch Fusiliers

---

[1] The frontage lost was rather over 200 yards and included much of the ground gained in the attack of August 24th when the Divisional Artillery had been supporting the Fourteenth Division.

[2] Five M.M.s were awarded to N.-C.-O.s and men of this battalion who distinguished themselves specially by their coolness under fire and devotion to duty.

[3] Out of a trench strength of 18 officers and 700 men 9 officers and 264 men were casualties.

were placed at General Minshull-Ford's disposal.   The
great tactical importance of the Eastern corner of the
wood, and of the ridge along which Ale Alley ran, made
it imperative to recover the lost ground before the next
advance against Ginchy or Guillemont.   Orders were
accordingly issued to the Queen's to bomb up the edge of
the wood [1] as far as the Eastern corner, and at 5 a.m.
(September 1st) two platoons essayed the task.   It was
not easy, the trench along the edge was too shallow and
too much damaged to protect the bombers from machine-
guns in trenches outside the wood ; and though the Queen's
bombed their way as far as the junction with Hop Alley
and even worked along Hop Alley almost to the
junction with Bitter Trench, they could not retain all
they had gained, but established a bombing block in
Edge Trench and dug a new length of line behind it at
right angles, which prevented the Germans from regaining
any more ground.   They were heavily shelled, too, nearly
all day, and the left flank of the company in Devil's Trench [2]
was a source of danger, being quite in the air, while communication between the front companies and battalion
headquarters was maintained with the greatest difficulty ;
all the telephone wires were constantly cut by the bombardment and orderlies had most perilous journeys, but the
position was maintained and on the right the 22nd Manchesters were digging away most energetically extending
Porter Trench North towards Pilsen Lane.

Orders had by now been issued for the Ginchy–Guillemont–Falfemont Farm line to be attacked in force on
September 3rd.   This increased the urgency of securing
the key position at the Eastern corner of Delville Wood,
and about noon on the 2nd the Queen's resumed their

---

[1] The B.G.O. 91st Brigade reported that a small stretch of the Eastern edge
was still held but that North of Pilsen Lane we retained nothing outside the
wood.

[2] The next unit on the left belonged to another Division and its position
was hard to ascertain, the wood being a tangle of debris and shell-holes in
which movement was very difficult.

attempt, and though too stoutly opposed to win the actual corner gained about 100 yards of Edge Trench. When the 22nd Brigade arrived to relieve the 91st at 8.30 p.m. on September 2nd the position had been therefore somewhat improved, while Porter Trench had been joined up with Pilsen Lane.[1]

The 22nd Brigade had only had a bare two days' rest, and its men were hardly fresh after making their way to the front line over ground torn by shell fire and slippery from rain. The Welch Fusiliers went in on the left, relieving the Queen's in the Southern portion of Edge Trench and along Devil's Trench, the 20th Manchesters took over Stout and Porter Trenches, the Royal Warwickshires were in Montauban Alley, and the Royal Irish back in Pommiers Trench. Before the attack, however, the Royal Warwickshires moved up to Folly Trench in close support to the assaulting battalions. Of these the Welch Fusiliers were to attack the trenches outside Delville Wood with their left companies, whose final objective was Pint Trench, their right companies were aiming at the Northern end of Ginchy, the 20th Manchesters were attacking the rest of that village and were to get touch South of it with the Sixteenth Division which was attacking Guillemont.

" Zero " had been fixed for midday ; punctually at that hour the 22nd Brigade went " over the top," the bombers of the 91st Brigade and a party of the Queen's specially detailed for the purpose simultaneously making a bombing attack on the old bone of contention, the East corner of Delville Wood. At first things seemed to be going well ; soon after 12.30 p.m. between 30 and 40 German prisoners were brought into brigade headquarters [2] and before 1 p.m. several reports came in that our troops had reached Ginchy and were consolidating. From both flanks successes were reported : Guillemont had at last been taken and the Twenty-Fourth Division on the Seventh's left had reached

---

[1] The Queen's casualties came to 6 officers and 113 men.
[2] In all 200 prisoners were taken.

its objective. However, before long it became clear that
all was not quite so satisfactory as it had at first seemed.
The Welch Fusiliers reported that the bombing attack
on the Eastern corner had failed and that their left companies which had attacked Hop Alley and Beer Trench
had lost very heavily from machine-gun fire and had not
reached Hop Alley, being held up some way South of it,
where the survivors had dug in among the shell-holes. One
party, however, not only got into Beer Trench, killing a
large number of Germans, but actually maintained its
position there till the night of September 5th/6th. The
right company seems to have got into Ginchy,[1] but its
supports came under heavy machine-gun fire when just
short of the orchards at the Northern end of the village and
were brought to a standstill; they dug in, however, and
held on, being joined by some Royal Warwickshires. Three
companies of this battalion had moved forward in support
of the attack with orders to consolidate a " Blue Line "
on the Western edge of Ginchy as a second line, the fourth,
" D," being detailed to form a defensive line on the left
facing North. They came under heavy fire and casualties
were numerous, but parts of the right and right centre
companies reached their objectives and began digging in.

On the right better success had attended the 20th Manchesters, who reached Ginchy with but little loss and pushed
into the village, overcoming such resistance as was offered.
But on crossing the main street and entering the orchards
to the East they came under machine-gun fire from the
North and, most of the officers being hit, the men got rather
scattered. However, they established themselves on their
objective in the S.E. of the village and started to consolidate,
the left company throwing back its flank when its patrols
discovered Germans still in force in the Northern part of
the village. On the right the 20th got into touch with
the Sixteenth Division, which had taken Guillemont, a good

---

[1] All the officers of this company became casualties and accurate information
was never forthcoming.

many Germans being rounded up from shell-holes between the two villages.

To secure Ginchy and make good the ground gained it was clear that another effort must be made on the left, where the Germans were reported to be in force in Ale Alley and Hop Alley and to seem inclined to take the offensive.[1]

The Welch Fusiliers had very few men in hand and were short of bombs, and though the left company of the Royal Warwickshires had already reinforced them their situation was not satisfactory. General Steele therefore sent up " C " Company of the Royal Irish to attack Hop Alley from the South and four sections of bombers to renew the attack against the Eastern corner. The rest of the Royal Irish had already occupied Stout and Porter Trenches and were in readiness to reinforce. Indeed " B " Company had advanced towards the farm just South-West of Ginchy. Two companies of the 21st Manchesters, whom the 91st Brigade had left behind as a reserve to the 22nd, were also ordered up to Folly Trench.

However, before these plans could be carried out a report reached brigade headquarters that the 20th Manchesters were quitting Ginchy. Unfortunately it proved only too true. The 20th had been unable to prevent the Germans from dribbling men in small groups into Ginchy from the North ; for a time their thrown-back left company held off the hostile pressure, inflicting a sharp repulse on one determined party, but gradually the Germans worked round their flank and even got into their rear ; and finally about 4 p.m. a vigorous counter-attack dislodged the survivors,[2] who were shot down in numbers as they recrossed the open

---

[1] About this time strong German reinforcements were reported to be coming up from the N.E. ; the artillery were informed and did some very effective shooting, inflicting heavy casualties.

[2] Both on this occasion and on two subsequent ones when a lodgment was made in Ginchy its defence was much handicapped by the low standard of musketry of the recent drafts, many of whom had very little idea of how to use their rifles.

towards Porter Trench by the machine-guns in Ale Alley. In retiring they seem to have carried away with them some of the Royal Warwickshires and most of " B " Company of the Royal Irish, but many of the Royal Warwickshires held on to their " Blue Line " and some of " A " Company under Lieuts. Harrowing and Sulman in a sunken road South of Ginchy brought effective Lewis-gun fire to bear on the Manchesters' pursuers and effectually checked the counter-attack. Indeed this detachment maintained its position until two nights later despite several efforts to dislodge it, as did another party under Captain Williams Freeman and Lieut. Willis farther to the left.[1]

Ginchy had been lost, but in hopes of recovering it the remaining companies of the Royal Irish were sent forward about 5 p.m., simultaneously with the renewed attack on Hop Alley. Both attempts encountered bursts of fire; losses were heavy, and few of the Royal Irish got much beyond Porter Trench, nor could they reach Hop Alley. Later in the evening flares were reported from Ginchy, and with the idea that some of our men might still be clinging to the village a fresh advance was ordered. There were hardly any men to carry it out; about a couple of hundred, mainly 20th Manchesters and Royal Irish, had been collected in Stout Trench,[2] and the 21st Manchesters had come up to Folly Trench about 10 p.m., but were needed to relieve the troops in Delville Wood. To attack Ginchy was out of the question; fortunately in the small hours Colonel Seymour, who had come up to the 20th Manchesters' headquarters, managed to get through on the telephone to Divisional Headquarters; and on his report of the situation the attack was cancelled and the 9th Devons, followed by the Borders, sent up to take over from the fragments of battalions in Stout Trench.

[1] Details about the Royal Warwickshires are lacking, but the large number returned as " missing "—about 100—suggests that many of them probably got into the outskirts of Ginchy and were overwhelmed there by the counter-attack.

[2] Porter Trench had been practically obliterated by shell fire.

21

The relief of the remnants of the 22nd Brigade [1] could not be completed till too late for any further attack to get the cover of darkness. It was under a considerable handicap therefore that, at 8 a.m. on September 4th, the 9th Devons attacked, three companies going straight for Ginchy, the fourth throwing back a defensive flank on the left, and some fragments of the 22nd Brigade still in Stout Trench opening covering fire. Directly they advanced they were greeted by heavy and effective fire from guns, rifles, and machine-guns. They pressed on gallantly and at first made good progress, but the machine-guns mowed them down in scores and a mere handful penetrated into the village, only to be overpowered. A company of the Borders reinforced them but could only dig in along with the survivors of the Devons, mostly from the supporting companies, some way short of the village. But this position could not be maintained, especially as once again the German hold on the Eastern corner of Delville Wood had proved unshakable.

This time it was the 21st Manchesters who had had to tackle that awkward proposition. They had taken over from the Welch Fusiliers, and one company, " D," which held the Southern end of Edge Trench, had extended Eastward from the S.E. corner of the wood along Pilsen Lane ; this company made several efforts to advance Northward against Hop Alley but without success ; and little better fortune attended another company, " A," which advanced about 2 p.m. through the wood against the German portion of Edge Trench. Supported by sections of bombers they attacked with vigour, but found the difficulties unsurmountable : machine-guns checked " A " Company 50 yards from the edge of the wood, and even when " B " reinforced it it could not get on.

---

[1] The casualties came to 53 officers and 1,090 men all told ; the Royal Warwickshires with 11 officers and 331 men were the hardest hit, but the 20th Manchesters lost 11 officers and 264 men, the Royal Irish 13 officers and 210 men, and the Welch Fusiliers 13 officers and 255 men.

The day closed with the survivors of the 9th Devons—of 700 men who had gone into the attack well over 300 and 15 officers had been hit—back in ZZ Alley in touch on the left with the 21st Manchesters, some of whom were holding on to Diagonal Trench inside the wood. Of the Borders meanwhile two companies were moved round to the right to replace a battalion of the King's in trenches facing Ginchy, between the Southern end of Porter Trench and the Ginchy–Guillemont road, the other two being drawn back to reserve.

That night (September 4th/5th) General Green took over from General Steele, the Gordons relieved the 9th Devons, not without much difficulty owing to the non-arrival of guides and the terribly slippery state of the ground, while the 8th Devons replaced the 21st Manchesters. This relief also was much delayed by the mud and darkness, and the intended attack at 3.30 a.m. on the 5th was impossible. It was 8 o'clock before Colonel James of the 8th Devons could announce the relief complete, and in the end the attack on Ginchy had to be postponed to the next day. This did not prevent yet another attack being made on the Eastern portion of Delville Wood, for which two companies of the Queen's had been specially brought up from Bécordel, where they had been resting since the morning of the 3rd.

This attack was launched at 5.30 p.m. in a North-Easterly direction, the right company, " D," resting its flank on the S.E. corner of the Wood, " B " on the left extending nearly to Edge Trench North of the Eastern corner. Before the assault a medium trench-mortar bombarded Ale Alley for two hours, but its fire could not be observed and did not seem to have been very effective. At any rate, directly the attack started, a tremendous fire was developed from the East corner and from Hop Alley, while a barrage of 4·2 and 5·9-inch shells was promptly put down. Under this the companies swerved to their right and " B " Company's left reached the edge just North of the junction with Hop Alley and well to the right of its proper objective. However, a block was made here, the line along the edge to the S.E. corner consolidated and a substantial gain secured, two platoons of the 8th Devons coming up on the right and helping to secure the S.E. corner. During the night consolidation was pushed on, the R.E. and Pioneers coming up to help; a block was established in Hop Alley and a support trench begun parallel to the edge of the wood.

The attack of September 6th started at 5 a.m.; Ginchy itself was the objective of the Gordons, backed up by the 9th Devons, now barely 400 strong. On their left the 8th Devons were to form a defensive flank from the Northern end of Ginchy to the S.E. corner of Delville Wood. Advancing in the dark the Gordons lost direction and Major Oxley had to take them back to their starting-point for a fresh effort; this went much better, but came under a heavy fire and was brought to a standstill about 100 yards short of Ginchy. Major Oxley, their acting C.O., was killed,[1] and casualties were heavy, especially among the officers. Two companies of the 9th Devons were therefore ordered to advance from ZZ Alley, following the light railway running North of Guillemont and the sunken road connecting that village with Ginchy; this would bring them into position S.W. of the village to assist in a fresh attack.

In the meantime the 8th Devons had established themselves roughly parallel to, but North of, Pilsen Lane and were digging in, connecting up the shell-holes into a regular line. On their right one platoon was quite close to the Northern end of Ginchy, and though rather isolated was holding on stoutly. The battalion, though steadily and heavily bombarded from about 9.30 a.m., escaped with comparatively few casualties, while the German infantry made no serious attempt at a counter-attack, contenting themselves with sniping to which the Devons replied with some effect.

---

[1] This was their fourth C.O. killed in action.

By 2 p.m. the 9th Devons had gained their appointed position on the Gordons' right and yet another assault on Ginchy was launched; the Borders' Lewis guns giving covering fire from their trenches N.W. of Guillemont. Captain Turnbull, now in command of the Gordons, had managed to reorganize his battalion for a fresh effort, and at first this attack went very well; Gordons and 9th Devons swept into Ginchy, captured over 30 prisoners of the 35th Infantry Regiment, and started consolidating. But once again Ginchy proved easier to take than to retain; it was subjected to a terrific shelling and between 5 and 6 o'clock violent counter-attacks drove the remnants of the assaulting battalions out of Ginchy. Another 8 officers and over 100 men had been added to the 9th Devons' already long casualty list, and the Gordons' losses were well over 200. That evening the 22nd Manchesters took over Stout and Porter Trenches and ZZ Alley, linking up on their right with the Borders and on their left with the 8th Devons. That battalion's position had been endangered by the loss of Ginchy, but when the Germans started attacking its exposed flank the right platoon received them so successfully as to discourage further attempts; later on this platoon was withdrawn by order to a less exposed position, but the rest of the line was made good, the 8th clinging on next day (Sept. 7th) all through a long day of shelling and sniping, strengthening the line considerably and repulsing yet another counter-attack.

During the 20th Brigade's attack on Ginchy there had been the usual struggle on the edge of Delville Wood, the Queen's, now under General Green's orders, again endeavouring to dislodge the Germans from the N.E. corner. As before heavy fighting produced no very definite result, though the position at the S.E. corner and along Edge Trench was improved. But the Seventh Division had nearly seen the last now of Delville Wood and Ginchy. The Fifty-Fifth Division was coming forward and on the evening of September 7th began relieving

the 20th Brigade and attached units. Before that, however, the Queen's had made a last attempt on the N.E.
corner, attacking at 4 p.m. and trying to work forward
along the edge of the wood behind a barrage of rifle-grenades.
Once again the great superiority of the enemy's position
stood them in good stead; it was hard to approach them
without exposure to flanking fire; and though the Queen's
got within about 70 yards of their goal and well past the
junction with Hop Alley, they could go no farther and had
to quit the wood without the satisfaction of mastering
the corner that had baffled so many attacks.

By the morning of September 8th all the infantry of the
Division were on their way back to a rest area round
Hallencourt, sadly depleted and exhausted by hard work
and the struggle against disadvantages of ground and
position. The slippery ground alone had handicapped
the attacks enormously and the unending digging needed
in the middle of the fighting and shelling had added to the
strain. If the 20th and 91st Brigades had not suffered as
heavily as the 22nd their casualties came to over 800
apiece, the 9th Devons heading the list with 23 officers and
405 men while the Gordons had lost nearly 250.

The artillery and R.E., however, were denied the rest
given to the infantry, though the artillery had again
suffered much more severely than in earlier actions : the
Germans were doing more counter-battery work than ever,
being evidently convinced that barraging back areas and
the lines of approach to the front was fully as effective in
stopping attacks as bombarding front-line trenches; and
the artillery's 300 casualties were due largely to the
systematic searching by the German heavy guns of the
back areas. Their task had been peculiarly difficult, owing
to the fluctuating character of the fighting and the conflicting reports received, these being mainly due to the
uncertainty as to the exact position and the difficulty of
discovering which of the trenches marked on the map
could be found still in existence on the ground.

From first to last Ginchy was a most unsatisfactory battle for the Division. It was even worse than the unsuccessful efforts of June 1915 at Givenchy; there the British had had the scantiest artillery support and could feel that they had been attempting the impossible. At Ginchy there had been plenty of guns to back up the attacks

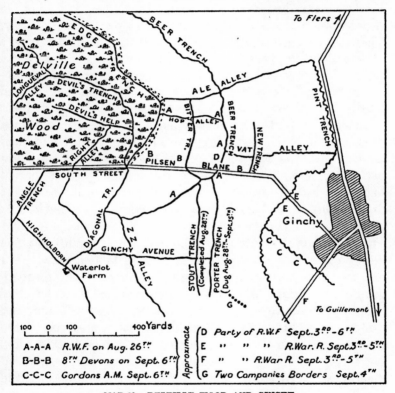

MAP 23.—DELVILLE WOOD AND GINCHY.

and no restriction on the expenditure of ammunition, but even so Ginchy had defied every attack; and such ground as had been gained was a wholly inadequate set-off against the heavy casualties. In Delville Wood too the Division had had a very difficult task and had not managed to wrest from the Germans all that their counter-stroke of August

31st had won for them.   To no small extent the attacks
on Ginchy contributed to the substantial successes secured
at Guillemont and at Falfemont Farm beyond it, by
covering their flank; certainly by attracting large German
reserves to Ginchy the Division had prevented them from
being sent to reinforce the line farther South,[1] and had
thereby contributed to the break through.   Yet even so
Ginchy remained a disappointing and distressing memory.
There had been no lack of will and spirit in the Division's
attacks, and in the almost unending bombing fights round
the N.E. corner of Delville Wood plenty of grit and determination had been shown, but the Division felt it had
hardly had a fair chance; it had been used up by driblets
in a series of partial attacks when a combined effort on a
broader front might well have fared better, and it had been
thrown into the fighting again without a really adequate
period of rest.   The failure to retain the ground gained
had been largely due to the lack of training of the recent
drafts who formed so high a proportion of its battalions
and to the inexperience of most of its officers and N.-C.-O.s.
The men had too often not known what to do and the
heavy casualties among the officers had left them with no
one to show them.   Movements by night over unknown
ground and along damaged and unrepaired trenches had
been a severe strain, leading to constant loss of touch and
direction and much straggling, which with more experienced
troops would never have occurred.   Inexperience too had
been responsible for indifferent musketry and some un-
steadiness.   Anyhow when September 15th came and
the Tanks emerged from concealment the Division, instead
of having the satisfaction of sharing in one of the chief
successes of the Somme offensive, was preparing to move
to a " quiet " section in Flanders, where it might recuperate
and rebuild its shattered units.

---

[1] There had been practically no counter-attack on Guillemont, which had
therefore been secured and consolidated without much difficulty.

CHAPTER XV

By the autumn of 1916 large stretches of the line held by
the British Armies were conventionally distinguished from
the area of active operations by being known as " quiet."
By this time the line had remained stationary so long and
had been so much strengthened with wire, redoubts, dug-
outs, machine-gun posts, support and reserve trenches,
connected up by " switches " which limited the possibilities
of a break through, that only by the collection of a really
overwhelming artillery and by a really sustained bombardment could any substantial gain be made.   Greatly as the
production of guns and shells had been increased it was
not yet equal to supplying more than one major attack at
any one time ; and though raids and occasional bombardments and gas attacks were indulged in freely as diversions
to the main operations on the Somme, it had been realized
that local offensives of a more sustained character were not
likely to produce results worth the inevitable casualties.
One or two such efforts had been tried without much success
in July, and in many sectors both sides tended to be content
with merely harassing each other with minor operations,
and abstained from anything on a large scale in view of the
proved futility of anything short of a really serious and
sustained effort.

When the Seventh Division, therefore, after ten days' of
rest round Hallencourt, received orders to start entraining
for the North on September 17th with Flêtre, Bailleul,
and Godewaersvelde as its destinations, it could feel that
no very strenuous effort was likely to be required of it in
the near future.   The infantry went first, being concentrated in the new area in time for the 20th and 91st Brigades

[1] Cf. Map 24.

to take over the Le Touquet and Ploegsteert sectors from the Nineteenth Division on September 19th, the 22nd Brigade coming into line three days later. The R.E. and Pioneers had been relieved in time to move North with the Division, but the Divisional Artillery had remained in action till after the battles of September 15th, when Tanks were first used, and of September 25th, when Morval and Lesboeufs were taken, and only came out of action on the 28th after a very hard and exhausting five weeks. All the Divisions whom it had supported were loud in its praise, its barrages had been splendidly accurate, and in spite of heavy casualties and great discomforts and hardships it had never failed the infantry. On relief it promptly proceeded North, rejoining the Division on October 1st, whose artillery support the Nineteenth Division's guns had till then provided.

The new line had been traditionally " quiet " ever since the Fourth Division had established itself at Ploegsteert in the autumn of 1914 so solidly that there seemed no shaking its grip. It ran Northward from the Lys for 3,000 yards, being about 500 yards from the Germans on its right or Southern end but sloping diagonally away till on the left it was nearly 1,000 yards off. There was a continuous trench-line, but it was held with gaps to economize men : the ground in rear of these gaps was strongly wired and the gaps were covered by the fire of well-placed strong points about half a mile behind the front, with another continuous fire-trench as a subsidiary line 1,500 yards farther back. The trenches on the whole were in good repair, but the country was very low-lying and in wet weather they required draining.

The Seventh Division undoubtedly needed an opportunity of assimilating the large drafts which nearly all its units had received before the end of September, but neither General Watts nor his Brigadiers had any intention of allowing any relaxation of such activities as were practicable ; and from the first taking over of the new line much was done to worry the Division's "opposite numbers," to harass their wiring and working-parties, as well as to improve the British line. Nearly a dozen raids were attempted during the six weeks that the Division spent in these trenches, none on a very large scale. About the most successful was one by the Welch Fusiliers on the night of September 30th/October 1st in which the German trenches were entered, the defenders being completely taken by surprise. Several were shot down and half a dozen dug-outs which seemed full of men were bombed, but, though at the lowest computation 30 casualties were inflicted on the enemy at a cost of 2 killed and 2 wounded, the raiders failed to take any prisoners or obtain any identifications of value. The Royal Warwickshires who made a raid the same night also effected an entrance and inflicted several casualties on the enemy in a bombing fight, getting away with the loss of only 9 wounded, all of whom were brought in. They also failed to take prisoners or establish any identifications, as happened also to the 9th Devons who simultaneously raided a post known as Machine-Gun House and put several Germans out of action at the cost of only 3 casualties. Another triple raid a fortnight later by one battalion from each brigade was less successful; one party was caught by machine-gun fire in No Man's Land and dispersed, too few men reaching the German line to achieve their object or get any prisoners; the second got in but failed to get any identifications; the third was checked by a wide ditch at the foot of the German parapet, half full of water and full of wire. A small raid by the South Staffords on October 14th was more satisfactory, as some prisoners were secured and useful identifications obtained.

Of other activities the most important was a discharge of gas on October 8th on the 20th Brigade's front. The wind was right in direction and strength, and as the enemy's reply seemed to indicate that he was holding his trenches in force there was reason to hope that between the gas, the bombardment which was put down simultaneously, and the heavy fire from 'rifles and Lewis guns which the Queen's and 22nd Manchesters poured in from the flank, the Germans must have suffered appreciably. On their part they were far from active, never attempting any raids and doing hardly any patrolling, while their artillery retaliation for the attentions of our guns was never heavy. At one time they developed considerable activity with trench-mortars, but this our artillery promptly repressed.

Casualties were not numerous : the 20th Brigade's for October came to 4 officers and 150 men, the 22nd and 91st faring much better, the latter only having 5 men killed, 3 officers and 14 men wounded, and 4 men missing. Sickness was more prevalent, and the drafts by no means compensated for the wastage, but thanks to the large drafts which had arrived in September [1] the Division was fairly strong when it was pulled out of the line in the first week of November and moved back to the Second Army training area, Divisional Headquarters being established at Renescure on November 9th and moving two days later to Tilques. One important change had taken place during the Division's stay in the Lys Valley, the Royal Irish leaving on October 14th to join the Sixteenth (South Irish) Division. In their place the 2nd Battalion of the Honourable Artillery Company joined the Division, which had thus included almost every variety of British Infantry, Guards, Highlanders, Fusiliers, Territorials, ordinary Service battalions, locally raised Service battalions, Scottish,

---

[1] The Borders, for example, received no less than 404 reinforcements in September ; 67 of these, just one in six, had served with the battalion before, the rest came either from the Lancashire Fusiliers, the Yorkshire Light Infantry or the Manchesters, which did not make the task of assimilating so large a proportion of new hands appreciably easier. The Gordons were rather luckier, getting back several of their own recovered wounded, as well as many who had been out with other battalions of their regiment, no less than two-thirds of the 227! men who joined them in October having already seen service.

Irish, Welch, English battalions,[1] and now added to these
various categories a unit which, though reckoned as part
of the Territorial Force, was far older than that force
or its ancestors the Volunteers, was in fact part of the
oldest military formation in the service of the King.

At the same time as the Royal Irish left Colonel Bonham
Carter departed on appointment to command the Senior
Staff School. He had been with the Division for a year
and had had no small share of responsibility for its
successes on the Somme. His place as G.S.O. I was taken
by Colonel G. W. Howard of the Essex Regiment. The
20th Brigade lost its Brigade Major, Captain Foss going
to the Second Canadian Division as G.S.O. II at the end
of October and being replaced by Captain A. N. Acland of
the D.C.L.I., who had succeeded Major Grant as Brigade
Major of the 91st Brigade six weeks earlier on the latter's
promotion.

The 91st Brigade had had a change of Staff Captain before
moving North, Captain Turnbull returning to the Gordons to
take command and Lieutenant O. F. Morshead being given
the vacancy; Brigade Major Captain R. N. O'Connor from
the Divisional Signal Company became Brigade Major in
place of Captain Acland (Oct. 28th) ; and then on November
20th Brigadier-General Minshull-Ford, who had been away
owing to ill-health most of October, had to be transferred
to a command in England and was replaced by Brigadier-
General H. R. Cumming of the Durham L.I., so that within
three months the Brigade Staff had been radically changed.

By November 20th the Division was no longer in
Flanders or in the Second Army, but was five days gone
on a march Southward, back to the Somme. It had started
on November 15th in weather which was none too bad
for the season but turned to snow and rain on the 18th,
so that next day the Division had to trudge on through the
wet, nor were things much pleasanter on the 20th and

---

[1] No Rifle or Light Infantry unit was ever represented in the Division, nor
did any Extra Reserve battalion ever figure in its ranks.

21st, which were foggy. The march brought the troops into the neighbourhood of Doullens on November 21st, and ended next day with Divisional Headquarters at Marieux, the 20th Brigade at Beaumont and Bertrancourt, the 22nd at Raincheval and Marieux, and the 91st at Lenvillers. The Divisional Artillery had not accompanied the rest of the Division, having been left in Flanders under the Second Army. So long a march—the Division had covered 82 miles in seven days of actual marching—had been an unusual experience and had given opportunities for testing march discipline—on the whole it had reached a very high level—and had got the men into quite good training. An officer who joined the Division about this time wrote of it as " a very happy Division in which everyone got on well together," and was much impressed with the efficiency of its organization and administrative services, and altogether the Division was very much the better for the quiet period it had just been through. This was a good thing, for the conditions in the quarter for which it was destined were inconceivably bad, and the months immediately ahead of it were to be the coldest and most inclement of the whole war.

The area in which the Division had now arrived lay just behind the part of the line which had witnessed the last " push " of the Somme offensive, that begun on November 13th which had seen Beaumont Hamel captured and other important gains made astride the Ancre, which here cuts through the ridge which runs N.W. from Péronne, carving quite a deep valley, from which the ground rises steeply on either side. The offensive had carried the line to the N. and N.E. of Beaumont Hamel, and though by November 22nd the heavy fighting had died down the position was far from stabilized and the section could not be reckoned " quiet." " A most irregular front line in close touch with the Germans " is one description ; " the ground has been the scene of a recent battle and is better imagined than described." At several points minor struggles were still going on, indeed when the 20th Brigade went into the trenches on November 23rd it was uncertain whether some of our men were not still holding out in the German trenches. The area was a network of trenches, some of them disused or in partial repair, others incomplete, others practically obliterated by bombardments. It was none too easy to say where the line ran, or to identify on the ground the features represented on the maps. It was really necessary to reconstruct the whole line and the ground was in a state which made this very difficult : trenches collapsed as quickly as they were dug and the Ancre mud defied all efforts. The bad weather which had been the main cause for the breaking-off of active operations, after having hampered the assailants and limited their successes, had left the ground in a fearful state ; men had to be dug out of the mud during a night relief, the communication trenches were mostly impassable, to reach the front line was an exploit, and existence in the advanced trenches—the support line was about as bad as the front—was indescribably horrible. One special difficulty was to find satisfactory places for battalion and company headquarters, for the amount of cover was limited, and though cellars were found in the ruins of Beaumont Hamel for two battalion headquarters several companies had to be content with dug-outs along the Wagon road, which had high banks on either side in which dug-outs could be made but, as it led straight towards the German lines, was liable to be directly enfiladed by their artillery. About the best battalion headquarters was found on the spur S.W. of Beaumont Hamel where a deep German dug-out was utilized, a most elaborate affair with separate dining- and sleeping-rooms and kitchen. The left brigade was badly off, as it had a dug-out in the chalk known as the White City which was always wet and most unhealthy. Later on a dug-out North of Mailly Maillet known as the Apple Trees was utilized. This, not being in chalk, was drier and better altogether.

The 20th Brigade was the first to take over the front
line in this most unattractive sector, relieving the Thirty-
Second Division, whose front line consisted of a newly dug
trench known as New Munich Trench on the spur N.E. of
Beaumont Hamel and running roughly from N.W. to S.E.
just below the crest of the spur. On the two following nights
the relief was completed, the 91st Brigade coming in on
the 20th's right and relieving the left brigade of the Thirty-
Seventh Division as well as the right of the Thirty-Second.
The British line here ran more or less East and West and
was known as Beaucourt Trench, the Germans opposite
holding a line suggestively denominated Muck Trench.
Opposite the 20th Brigade the German front line was
formed by Munich Trench, which had been reached by
more than one attack in the course of the recent fighting
but not retained. It had been greatly damaged by the
bombardment, indeed one officer has said " it was so
much easier to find on the map than on the actual ground."
With the trenches in bad condition and full of water their
garrisons had to expose themselves freely, and snipers found
the situation unusually promising. The Germans were
pretty active ; a party of about 100 attacked New Munich
Trench on the 25th but were smartly repulsed by the
South Staffords, and four nights later a fighting patrol
tried to raid a post held by the 21st Manchesters with no
better success. There were no dug-outs in this line and
by day it was held by small posts at intervals of about 30
yards. This was perfectly safe, no German attack could
have moved at any speed over the torn and muddy
ground, and there were enough Lewis guns to stop any
advance at the sort of pace the ground would dictate.
By night the line was more strongly held. The British
patrols were also active, though the ground was a great
handicap.

The wet state of the trenches was also responsible
for much sickness. Despite all precautions, such as rub-
bing the feet with whale-oil, many men had to go to

hospital as the result of exposure and wet ; the Queen's, for example, had 38 men sick after their first turn in the front line. However, the great care which was taken to cope with " trench-feet " kept the wastage from that tiresome complaint down effectively. Ration parties used to bring up dry socks along with the rations and take away the used ones, and there was a regular competition in the brigades to see which unit would have the fewest cases per week. The astonishing cheerfulness and good temper of the men was another important factor in keeping down the sick-rate. Bad as the conditions were they were faced in a splendid way and it was remarkable how well the men recovered after coming out of the trenches wet through and chilled to the bone. The excellence of the administrative arrangements helped a good deal to produce this good spirit ; the men realized that everything possible was being done to assist them and to reduce the strain on them. They were well fed and the arrangements for drying and cleaning clothes and for washing and warming the men were working excellently.

December saw little improvement on November's weather. There were some colder spells in which the ground began to dry, but whenever this happened the rain usually began again ; and when one finds the 91st Brigade reporting on December 15th " ground worse than ever " one may well feel that there is nothing more to be said. In the middle of the month the Division had the satisfaction of being again supported by its own artillery, which arrived from the North on the 12th : and from the 17th onwards one brigade only held the front line, with another at Mailly Maillet in support, the third, which was in reserve, being back at Bertrancourt.

There was much sporadic activity, many patrol encounters, a good deal of shelling, most of it coming from the British side, any amount of sniping—the 91st Brigade's snipers claimed no less than 15 hits in one day—and some

22

useful work on the trenches. The 8th Devons left their
mark on New Munich Trench, adding 200 yards to it and
closing up a gap on the left of the Division's line ; and
later in the month the two Devon battalions were mainly
responsible for another good piece of digging, an assembly
trench 250 yards long being dug farther to the right. This
was wanted to assist in an attack on Munich Trench, the
capture of which was most desirable as it was nearer the
crest of the spur than was the British front line and so
gave the Germans admirable observation over our front
line and the approaches to it. Had the weather been
drier the attack on this trench would have presented no
special difficulties : but with the ground for the last 50
yards in front of it a mass of shell craters, terribly cut up
and in a semi-liquid condition, it was almost impregnable.
Despite this it was decided to make the attempt, and as
a preliminary Leave Avenue and Muck Trench, to the
South of Munich Trench, were to be attacked by the 20th
Brigade, after which the 91st would tackle the major
problem.

Towards the end of December a new feature became
noticeable in the daily routine, the capture by our patrols
of an increasingly large number of prisoners. Rather
more than the average had been taken ever since the
Division came into the sector—the Gordons, for example,
had taken 8 from one dug-out not 50 yards from their
front line on November 27th—but in the last ten days of
December prisoners were collected with a surprising facility.
The enemy seemed new to the sector and did not know
their way about it ; on one occasion about 50 Germans
blundered into Muck Trench, into which some posts had
been pushed forward by the Welch Fusiliers, and were
dispersed, leaving 10 prisoners behind ; they had been
trying to carry out a relief and had got lost in the fog.
Almost every patrol encounter resulted in a capture, and
between December 27th and 30th the two Devon battalions
amassed about 30 captives, most of whom showed distinct

readiness to surrender. One officer of the Borders when
out on patrol ran into two Germans : he could not lay
hands on his revolver, which had got round behind his
back, but promptly covered the Germans with his pipe,
whereon one put his hands up and the other bolted. Such
incidents suggested that the morale of the Division's
opponents was weakening and that when the weather
should permit the resumption of more active operations
the resistance to be met would not be marked by that
desperate determination the Germans had shown at
Delville Wood and Ginchy.

Casualties were decidedly heavier than in the more
stabilized quarter from which the Division had come. At
Ploegsteert the lines had varied little for a couple of years ;
here small changes were constantly taking place and the very
imperfect defences afforded little protection against snipers
though mud tended to reduce the effectiveness of shell-
bursts by smothering them. December cost the Welch
Fusiliers, for example, over 40 casualties, and the sick-rate
was high, as was only to be expected in the awful conditions.
Once, when the Gordons were relieving the Borders, the
mud was so bad and so many men got embedded in it and
quite unable to move that a special rescue party had to
be sent up to get them out, taking with it various
medical comforts, despite which a large number had to go
to hospital and one man died. The weather was about
at its worst at this time ; the torrential rains which were
the only alternative to bitter cold produced an indescribable
species of mud and the strain on all portions of the Division
was tremendous. The fighting troops when in the trenches
had the worst of it, but they did get spells of rest when
out of the line, whereas the administrative branches were
at it all the time and their daily round was one of great
toil. One incident which cheered the 91st Brigade about
this period was that an officer when groping about in the
ruins of Beaumont Hamel discovered a mysterious hole,
began enlarging it and worked away till suddenly he found

himself disappearing into space. A drop of about 20 feet
ended with his landing on something soft which he discovered by the help of his torch to be a dead German, one
of several who were lying about with their gas masks on ;
but a far more welcome and attractive discovery was that
the place was an old cellar, not yet empty, though it was
soon reduced to that condition, its contents, though chiefly
only soda-water, not lasting very long.

The New Year brought no improvement in the conditions
or in the weather, but preparations for the attack on Munich
Trench were steadily pushed on and that operation was
eventually fixed for January 11th. Before it came off,
however, there had been some sharp fighting at both ends
of the line, the Germans taking the offensive on the left,
the British on the right. On the left a German communication trench called Serre Trench ran N.E. over the top
of the ridge into the German lines, its S.W. portion being
in British hands. The most advanced British post here,
Hope Post, was situated at a junction with another trench
which branched off N.W. out of Lager Alley. On the
evening of January 1st two officers of the 9th Devons, who
were then holding the left half of the front with the Gordons
on the right,[1] were floundering along towards Hope Post
with the rum ration when they met Germans advancing
down Serre Trench in some force. They had evidently
rushed Hope Post and there was nothing for it but to fall
back to the next post, Despair Post, collect some bombers
and attempt to recover the lost position. However,
this advance was checked by machine-gun fire, one of
the officers was wounded, and no progress could be made.
It gives some idea of the difficulties which confronted the
troops at this time that it was nearly 9 p.m. before the loss
of Hope Post was reported to battalion headquarters.
All telephone wires were cut : the ground was little better
than a morass, especially in this left sector where the only

[1] The dividing line was the junction of New Munich Trench and Leave
Avenue.

approach to the front line was along a much-sniped
" duck-board " track, the trenches were knee-deep in
mud, and even the most lightly equipped runners could
make but slow progress. On learning of this mishap,
Colonel Storey at once detailed an officer and 24 men
to proceed to Despair Post in readiness for an attack
at dawn and the artillery were instructed to fire on the
approaches to Hope Post in order to isolate its garrison.
However, the attempt met with strong opposition,
especially from machine-guns, and was held up, with
several casualties. Further attempts were therefore
postponed for a few days to allow of more careful preparations and to coincide with an attack which the
Third Division was making on a strong point just to the
left, known as " 88." That evening the 91st Brigade
relieved the 20th, but the recapture of Hope Post was
entrusted to the 9th Devons, who left a special party of
two officers and 50 men behind.

When the new attempt was made, at 5.30 p.m. on
January 5th, it went very well. For 15 minutes before
" Zero " the post was subjected to a violent bombardment,
no less than 500 rounds of 9·2-inch, 200 of 8-inch, and 250
of 6-inch being precipitated on it and its defenders ; and
when the Devons advanced as fast as the mud would let
them, bombing sections going over the open on either side
of Serre Trench, the Divisional Artillery put down a most
effective barrage, under cover of which the post was
captured with only one casualty, nine prisoners being
taken. The Third Division's attack on " 88 " had been
equally successful, and the Devons promptly pushed a
party along the cross trench in that direction to consolidate it.

However, all was not over, for before long the artillery had
to reopen fire as the enemy were counter-attacking, both
against Hope Post and " 88." The German shelling was
quite severe and for a time compelled the troops to evacuate
Hope Post ; but when the shelling stopped the Queen's,

who had now relieved the 9th Devons,[1] promptly reoccupied
the post and repulsed a German advance up Serre Trench.
The Germans came again, however, and shortage of bombs
compelled the Queen's to retire towards Despair Post, but
on reinforcements arriving with more bombs they pushed
forward again and this time secured Hope Post definitely
and consolidated it, capturing several more prisoners of
the 130th Infantry Regiment, the total casualties of the
Queen's and the Devons being under 30.

The next few days were marked by substantial captures
of Germans. The 9th Devons had begun the year well by
rounding up 20 in the early hours of January 1st, but the
Gordons went one better next day by taking an officer and
29 men of the 130th, who surrendered to a patrol consisting of one sergeant and two men. The 22nd Brigade [2]
continued the good work, collecting another 50 prisoners
in less than a week. The bulk of these were taken by the
Welch Fusiliers, but it was noted that many of these
prisoners needed comparatively little taking, some indeed
were rather deserters than prisoners—on the night of the
9th/10th, for example, 18 were taken, most of whom came
over of their own accord. Conditions in the German lines
were clearly as bad as or worse than on the British side,
while the intermittent bombardments which our artillery
maintained were a distinct incentive to surrender.

The attack on Muck Trench and the Triangle was
intended to protect the right flank of the bigger operation
shortly to be undertaken. The chief difficulty lay in the
ground, which was so wet and so much cut up by shell fire
that an ordinary attack in waves behind a barrage was
impracticable ; indeed the chances were that, had it been
attempted, many men would have been smothered in the
mud in the shell-holes. It was decided therefore to attack
in three bombing-parties, one working alongside Muck

---

[1] The Queen's had been lent to the 20th Brigade to allow the Borders, who
had been detailed to attack Muck Trench, time to complete their preparations.
[2] The 22nd Brigade had relieved the 20th on the night of January 5th.

Trench from the East, one advancing by the Eastern arm of the Triangle, the third along Leave Avenue from the West. On reaching the hostile position these parties were to work inwards towards each other. Each consisted of two bombing sections and one of rifle-grenade men, a Lewis-gun team, and about 20 riflemen with 20 carriers in support, and all officers and N.-C.-O.s detailed for the attack were thoroughly familiar with the ground, having patrolled over it twice. Moreover, shallow facsimile trenches had been dug near Bertrancourt, where Divisional Headquarters were situated, and the troops detailed for the attack had rehearsed it over them, a practice which had now become fairly general and was very helpful to the attacking troops.

Assembly trenches had been prepared and all three parties were in position well before 2 a.m. when the heavy artillery, which had been shelling the objective inter-mittently, lifted and formed a barrage North and East of the objective, the field batteries at the same time barraging it for the twenty minutes which it was calculated the attackers would take to cross No Man's Land. It was moonlight when the attack started, but so effective was the barrage that the assailants reached their objectives almost without casualties and speedily overcame the far from determined resistance which the garrison, demora-lized by the bombardment, endeavoured to put up. At 3.7 a.m. the Borders' C.O. reported back to the brigade that his centre company had taken Point 93, where Leave Avenue joined the Eastern arm of the Triangle, with 30 prisoners ; ten minutes later the left company had gained touch with the centre, and five minutes afterwards all objectives were reported taken and the R.E. were pushing across No Man's Land to assist in consolidating. By 4 a.m. nearly 100 prisoners had been taken and as yet the casualties had been trifling, though they soon mounted up when the Germans started shelling the captured lines.

The bombardment and the casualties it inflicted and the

damaged and water-logged condition of the trenches notwithstanding, the work of consolidation was so vigorously
pressed that before daylight it was practically complete ;
all but 50 yards had been wired, blocks established in
Leave Avenue beyond its junction with Muck Trench and
in the Southern end of Munich Trench, the enemy's dug-
outs had been cleared or inundated—with the trench
half-full of water this was easy enough—and more prisoners
had been collected, the total coming to nearly 150.   The
enemy's casualties it was impossible to ascertain exactly,
but as the attacking troops had only had 1 officer and
8 men killed or missing with 4 men dead from exhaustion
and 2 officers and 43 men wounded, less than half the
prisoners, this success was certainly not costly.   It was
a feather in the cap of the Border Regiment ; carefully
planned and skilfully executed, and well backed up by the
artillery, it deserves to be remembered as one of the most
successful of the Division's minor enterprises.

An even more substantial success was to be recorded in
the next attack.   This was on a larger scale, the 91st
Brigade, who took over New Munich Trench on the evening
of the 10th,[1] putting in no less than three battalions—the
22nd Manchesters on the right as far as Walker Avenue,
the South Staffords in the centre, and the 21st Manchesters
on the left, from Crater Lane onwards.   To let the
attacking battalions be as strong as possible, the Queen's
provided all the carrying parties.   The right and centre
battalions used two companies each, the left employing a
third to form a defensive flank along Lager Alley.   The
attack had been carefully rehearsed, and for 48 hours
before the attack the positions to be assaulted had been
heavily bombarded, though not so heavily as to put the
enemy on the alert for an immediate attack, while a thick
mist, which covered the taking up of the assembly positions,

---

[1] The Welch Fusiliers, who had relieved the Borders at 8 p.m. on the 10th,
held the right sector, including the newly captured line, and the 20th
Manchesters held Hope and Despair Posts.

further assisted to conceal what was coming from the garrison of the trench.

Owing to the water-logged ground General Cumming had arranged with the supporting artillery for a specially slow barrage, " the slowest of the war " it was said to be, not advancing more than 10 yards a minute, but even so the troops could not reach their objective quite in time to prevent any machine-guns from coming into action ; and though these could not stop the attack they did inflict a good many casualties. But the attack was a complete success, all three battalions reaching their objectives as quickly as the ground would allow and speedily overcoming the survivors of the trench-garrison, who had been completely surprised. The guns had only opened fire three minutes before " Zero." Only on the left was there any prolonged opposition. Here a strong point at the junction of Munich Trench and Lager Alley held out stoutly, although special attention had been paid to it by the howitzers. However, the 21st Manchesters were not to be denied and, after the strong point had been bombarded again, succeeded in taking it, its capture being reported to brigade headquarters within two hours of " Zero." A great part of Munich Trench had been practically obliterated ; indeed the right company of the South Staffords failed to recognize their objective and overshot it by about 80 yards. Their left company on the other hand found the ground so impassable that they had to dig in short of the trench which they could not possibly have consolidated. On the right the 22nd Manchesters also overshot the trench and pushed some way forward down the slope towards Frankfort Trench before they recognized their mistake and came back to their proper line. It was evening, however, before they could obtain touch with the Welch Fusiliers farther to the right.

By that time considerable progress had been made with the consolidation, although the sudden lifting of the fog had prevented all the Pioneers and the Durham Field

Company from getting up to help with it. They had been ordered forward in the hope that the fog would let them get across No Man's Land in safety, but when the fog cleared away the enemy's artillery had begun a vigorous bombardment in face of which No Man's Land could not be crossed. This bombardment indeed was responsible for most of the brigade's 275 casualties.[1]

The attack is described in Sir Douglas Haig's despatch of May 31st, 1917, as "the most important" of the operations carried out for the purpose of driving the enemy from the remainder of the Beaumont Hamel spur ; these before January was out had given us possession of the whole of the high ground North and East of Beaumont Hamel, whereby " a new and extensive field of action for our artillery " was opened up, observation over the whole Beaucourt valley being obtained. Moreover, life was made much more bearable because the enemy was deprived of the good observation he had till now enjoyed over the roads leading out of Auchonvillers, which were the main routes for supplies and ammunition going up to the front-line troops. Casualties from the shelling of these roads had been numerous, though by making a " duck-board " track across country to Beaumont Hamel it had been made possible to avoid the main road, which the enemy had got " taped," shelling it spasmodically, and doing no little damage.

Before the end of the month, however, the Seventh Division was enjoying a well-deserved rest. It had remained in line for ten days after the capture of Munich Trench, the 22nd Brigade relieving the 91st on the night of January 12th/13th and being itself relieved by the 20th three days later. Nothing of special note happened : the

---

[1] The figures were : Queen's, 3 men wounded ; South Staffords, 1 officer and 17 men killed or missing, 4 officers and 81 men wounded ; 21st Manchesters, 2 officers and 20 men killed or missing, 2 officers and 66 men wounded ; 22nd Manchesters, 2 officers and 23 men killed or missing, 54 men wounded. As against that, over 200 German prisoners were taken.

enemy's artillery were active, trying to hamper the consolidation of the position captured, but his infantry was far from aggressive; so, while the British guns replied effectively to the German shelling, the British patrols had matters pretty well all their own way, and brought in much useful information together with several more prisoners. But the Division had had a hard and

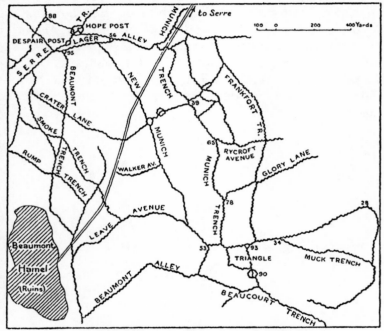

MAP 24.—BEAUMONT HAMEL AREA—MUNICH TRENCH.

unpleasant time in the Beaumont Hamel sector. As already explained, it had suffered even more from the weather and the state of the line than from the enemy, though its battle casualties for January came to 30 officers and approximately 600 men. Trench warfare in midwinter, even in relatively mild weather, and in the "quieter" parts of the line, was never an agreeable occupation. At best it was possible to make it reasonably

endurable and to keep the sick-rate within moderate
dimensions. But on the bleak and exposed uplands above
the Ancre, in the extremely inclement weather which saw
1916 out and ushered 1917 in, it was very difficult to make
conditions in the line barely endurable, and the sick-rate,
though it might well have been much higher, was a serious
drain. The 20th Brigade, which was not exceptionally
unfortunate, had over 600 admissions to hospital for the
month. It says a good deal, however, for the skill and
devotion of the R.A.M.C. and for the careful organization
of washing arrangements, precautions against " trench-
feet," and the supply of clean and warm clothing, that the
hardships and labours which the Division had had to
endure had not made even greater inroads upon its
effective strength.

CHAPTER XVI

THE rest to which the Seventh Division was withdrawn on January 20th was about the longest it had yet experienced. Divisional Headquarters were established at Marieux on the 21st and not till February 23rd did they move forward again to Bertrancourt. In the interval several important changes and incidents had taken place, the principal changes being a reorganization of the Divisional Artillery and a change in the command of the Division, and the chief incident a review by the new French Commander-in-Chief, General Nivelle, on February 17th.

The change in command was caused by the well-deserved promotion of General Watts to command a Corps. He had proved so successful as a Divisional Commander that this promotion was far from unexpected, but the Seventh Division parted from him with reluctance. He had served with the Division continuously, first as Brigadier and then as G.O.C., ever since its landing in Flanders, and there was hardly another officer and not many N.-C.-O.s and men who had such a record of uninterrupted service with it. A fine leader and a careful and considerate commander, he was liked and trusted by all ranks and had led the Division in some of its greatest achievements. His share in these successes had not been small. It has been said by one who served for some time with him : " When General Watts has passed a plan for an attack you may be pretty sure that it is a sound one." A fighting soldier himself, with a firm grasp of realities and possibilities, he was quick to detect flaws in the schemes laid before him, to see when more was being asked of troops than was

[1] Cf. Maps 25, 26, and 27.

reasonable or where probable obstacles and difficulties had been overlooked or under-estimated. On his departure for the Nineteenth Corps on February 6th he was succeeded by Major-General G. de S. Barrow, who had been commanding an Indian Cavalry Brigade since January 1915.[1]

The reorganization of the Divisional Artillery was part of a scheme which was mainly aimed at preventing that separation of a Division from its own artillery which had been so unfortunately common in 1916. The Seventh Division had more than once had to go into line without having its own guns behind it, and its Divisional Artillery had more often than not been supporting the infantry of some other Division. The disadvantages of this are obvious : it was particularly important that there should be the closest co-operation between the infantry and the guns, especially when the hostile lines were so close together and information was so hard to send back from a fluctuating front line to the guns behind. The more the same guns could support the same infantry the better the understanding and the co-operation was likely to be, and the infantry naturally preferred to have its own gunners behind it rather than strangers. By withdrawing one of the three artillery brigades from each Division a pool of field-guns was established from which brigades, now known as " Army Field Artillery Brigades," could be attached as required wherever extra guns were needed, and the other two brigades were left to work with their own Division.

In the Seventh Division it was the R.H.A. Brigade[2] which became an " Army Brigade," the XXIInd and XXXVth Brigades R.F.A. remaining with the Division. The Division was thus left with 12 howitzers and 36 field-guns instead of the 76 guns which had been the 1914 establishment of a Division, but henceforward it could

[1] At the same time the Durham Field Company R.E. was allotted a number and became the 528th Field Company.

[2] An additional 4-gun howitzer battery, the 509th, had joined this brigade in October ; it was now broken up, one section each going to the 31st and 35th Batteries, to complete them to six guns each.

LIEUT.-GENERAL SIR HERBERT WATTS, K.C.B., K.C.M.G.

fairly well count on being supported by its own gunners and the change was certainly an advantage.

The month's rest had allowed of leave to England on a more ample scale than heretofore ; it had seen the arrival of fairly substantial drafts [1]—the 91st Brigade, for example, got over 600 officers and men—but the time had not been one of complete repose, or even of uninterrupted training. There had been frequent demands for battalions to be placed at the disposal of the Corps,[2] for working purposes. The chief work required was on the roads, which the alternations of severe frost and thaw had reduced to a more than usually bad condition, so that, in view of a probable resumption of active operations in the spring, a specially large amount of labour had to be employed in getting them fit for heavy traffic.

The form which active operations would take when resumed naturally lay beyond the ken of the officers and men of the Division.   Actually while the Seventh Division was in the Beaumont Hamel sector decisions of far-reaching importance as to future operations had been taken which were destined to affect very vitally the fortunes of the Seventh Division, indeed of the whole of the British Armies in France.   Sir Douglas Haig had originally been anxious to take prompt advantage of the favourable situation existing in the region between the Ancre and the Scarpe as the result of the Somme offensive. His idea for 1917 was that the main offensive should take the shape of a big British attack from the front reached at the close of the Somme fighting, and in this General Joffre had concurred, feeling that the great strain which had already been placed upon the French infantry, particularly at Verdun, had rendered it inadvisable to ask

[1] Some battalions got some admirable drafts at this time composed of men drafted from cavalry units, but had the mortification of having them transferred back to the cavalry or to machine-gun units directly they had been properly trained for infantry duties.

[2] The Division was transferred to the Fifth Corps (Lieut.-General E. A. Fanshawe) on February 15th.

too much of it in the coming campaign. But the idea
that the leading part in the expected deliverance of France
from the intruding German should be played by the
British Armies did not commend itself to certain sections
of opinion in France, both military and political. Critics
of General Joffre's strategy were not lacking, and in
England also there were those who, estimating the results
of the Somme rather by the actual gains of ground than
by the effects produced on the enemy's morale and capacity for continued resistance, were seriously dissatisfied
with the strategy and tactics of the 1916 offensive. The
net result was a complete change of plan : the " Chantilly
plan " agreed upon by Sir Douglas Haig and General Joffre
was dropped, in its stead it was decided that the main
Allied effort should be made by the French against the
Chemin des Dames according to a scheme propounded by
General Nivelle. The British share in the offensive was
subordinated to this French attack, to facilitate which
the British were to take over a considerable frontage to
their right, stretching across the Somme towards Roye,
and all idea was abandoned of delivering the main offensive
on the Somme front. The change, however, had the
disadvantage of postponing the main offensive by some
weeks, and the Germans profited by the delay to make a
systematically planned and conducted retreat from the
awkward salient in which 1916 had left them. Retiring
more or less at their own time and " according to plan "
they escaped the difficulties and disadvantages which
would have attended upon a retreat enforced upon them
by a successful British attack delivered a couple of weeks
before their preparations were complete. Whether the
carrying out of the Chantilly plan would have materially
altered the course of events will always be a matter of
controversy, but the fortunes of the Seventh Division and
the difficulties it had to encounter in the early spring of
1917 were materially affected by the change of plan. The
pursuit of an enemy retiring according to a well-thought-

out programme was very different from the pursuit of one
who could not afford to stand upon the order of his going.
If our pursuit was marked by more than one check and
was less speedy than might have been hoped, the circumstances in which it was undertaken must not be overlooked.

The German retreat to the formidable Hindenburg Line,
the Torres Vedras of the war, was accomplished in two
sections. In the last week of February they evacuated
the pronounced salient North of the Ancre, their hold on
which the Seventh Division had done so much in January
to render precarious, and went back to the so-called Le
Transloy–Loupart Line covering Bapaume. This ran from
S.E. of Bapaume, past Achiet le Petit, to connect up with
their old second line near Bucquoy, West of which they
simultaneously evacuated Gommecourt and fell back some
distance up their old front line. Then about the middle
of March, just as the British began to develop their attack
on the Le Transloy–Loupart Line, the Germans evacuated
it also and began their main retreat to the shelter of the
Hindenburg Line.

The Seventh Division actually returned to the front
before even the first of these movements had begun. On
February 20th the 91st Brigade moved forward from
Puchevillers to Bertrancourt, coming for the moment
under the Sixty-Second Division, whose left sector it was
taking over. The line had been considerably advanced
during the Division's absence from the front, and the 21st
Manchesters, who went into the new line on February
21st, the South Staffords coming in on their right next
day, found themselves within 1,100 yards of Serre on a
line running from about S.E. to S.S.W. of that village and
separated from it by a shallow valley. The Sixty-Second
Division away to the right was on the slopes of the Serre
spur, while to the left was the Nineteenth, continuing the
line N.W. towards Gommecourt.

General Barrow had only just taken over (February
23rd) this new front, with the 91st Brigade in the line,
23

the 22nd at Beaumont, and the 20th at Bertrancourt, when things began to move. The line was a series of posts, some on the site of German dug-outs, but most in open shell-holes on a forward slope of heavy clay which a recent thaw following the prolonged frost had made even more than usually adhesive. The enemy were inactive, though on the alert to discourage inquisitiveness in British patrols. However, when early on February 24th the usual morning patrols went out under cover of a mist the 22nd Manchesters found to their astonishment that there were no enemy S.W. of Serre, and the South Staffords advanced nearly to Pendant Copse without being fired upon. It was about 10 a.m. when the news got back to Colonel Norman of the Manchesters, who at once transmitted it to the brigade and prepared to push forward to secure a line just S.W. of Serre, in readiness for an advance in force next morning. The Brigadier and Brigade Major, who were visiting the front, found a most unusual and abnormal hush : everything was so curiously and suspiciously peaceful that they did a little patrolling on their own but still found everything quiet. Indeed they were inclined to suspect a trap. The South Staffords to their great surprise had found it possible to walk about freely in the open without drawing fire, and profiting by this they were very energetic in patrolling, bringing in some excellent reports, and during the day posts were established along the 120 contour just short of Pendant Copse. On learning of the evacuation of Serre the Fifth Corps issued orders for an advance, to be started early next morning and continued to Puisieux should Serre and Pendant Copse be occupied without fighting. The 22nd Brigade was to be in readiness by 5 a.m. to support the 91st.

Starting at 6 a.m. on February 25th the advance, though somewhat delayed by fog, made good progress. Pendant Copse was soon passed, and the South Staffords secured Pendant Trench soon after. They then bore to the left,

rather losing direction in the fog, and came under machine-
gun fire from an orchard N.E. of Serre. This, however,
they captured and soon after 9 a.m. were established in
Wing Trench. A little later the 22nd Manchesters also
reached their objective, though as Serre had been practically wiped off the map it was hard to identify the point
to be reached. They had met some opposition on the
line John Alley–Maxim Trench, which they soon overcame, taking a few prisoners. Indeed the 91st Brigade

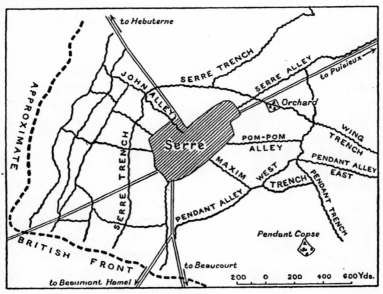

MAP 25.—SERRE.

could easily have pushed on to Puisieux, which the heavy
guns had been bombarding for some time ; casualties had
been trifling, and the troops, though tired after four very
uncomfortable days in the line, were ready to go on.
But the ground had not been reconnoitred, the brigade
was ahead of the troops on its flanks, touch could not be
obtained with either the Sixty-Second Division or the
Nineteenth till late in the afternoon, and General Cumming
had to hold back. That evening the 22nd Brigade with

the Borders attached to it in place of the 20th Manchesters
came up and relieved the 91st, who went back into reserve
distinctly elated at the change to something more like
the open warfare to which all were looking forward.   If
the occupation of Serre was achieved without much hard
fighting it was none the less a memorable incident, and the
lightness of the casualty list surprised everyone ; so much
so that the Division on receiving it rang up the brigade
headquarters to ask how many 0's had been omitted.

It was the 22nd Brigade to whose lot fell the attack on
Puisieux for which the Fifth Corps now issued orders.   It
had the Welch Fusiliers in front and two companies of
the Borders on their left, but owing to the relief the main
advance could not be started before the late afternoon.
Before that patrols had ascertained that Puisieux was held
by more than the mere rear party which had been dislodged
from Serre ;   indeed when the two battalions moved forward they encountered stubborn opposition.   Despite
this the Welch Fusiliers pushed on and by 7.30 p.m. had
reported back to the brigade that they had secured their
first objective, Kaiser Lane, after hard fighting.   From
here their right company pushed on to Sunset Trench,
while the left company worked forward into Soap Alley.
The opposition was quite stiff, but the battalion ultimately
established itself on the Southern outskirts of Puisieux, the
Borders coming up in support and taking post astride
the road from Serre.   Further progress that night was
out of the question, the enemy's shell fire was fairly heavy
and the brigade was ahead of the troops on its flanks.
Moreover it was extremely hard in the state of the roads
to get ammunition and supplies forward ; every single
round for the guns had to be brought up by pack animals,
and while the Division's horse casualties were enormous
its guns had to be careful about ammunition expenditure.

During the night the Germans launched one quite serious
counter-attack, which, however, the Welch Fusiliers
repulsed without much difficulty, their Lewis guns proving

very effective ; and then, shortly before daybreak, patrols
pushed into Puisieux and despite machine-gun fire gained
ground on both sides.   The Borders worked through the
Western half of the village and made a lodgment on its
Northern edge in City Trench, but machine-gun fire from
front and flanks prevented them getting any farther : the
Welch Fusiliers on reaching the N.E. of the village found

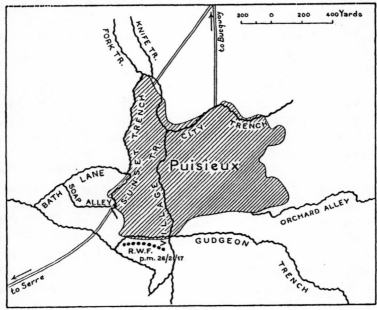

MAP 26.—PUISIEUX.

further progress barred by the church, which was strongly
held and bristled with machine-guns.   The fight continued
all day ; the Borders pushed the enemy back down Knife
and Fork Trenches towards Bucquoy, co-operating with
the Nineteenth Division who were advancing against these
trenches from the West ;   the Welch Fusiliers meanwhile
could not capture the church but had the satisfaction of
beating off a counter-attack, while touch was gained with
the Sixty-Second Division farther to the right in Gudgeon
Trench.

That evening the Royal Warwickshires relieved the Borders, but when they prepared to renew the attack next morning (Feb. 27th) they found the enemy vanished and Puisieux clear. The 20th Manchesters were ordered up to relieve the Welch Fusiliers, who had suffered severely, having over 150 casualties including 6 officers, and meanwhile the Royal Warwickshires' patrols reached the high ground overlooking the valley which runs up between Puisieux and Bucquoy. These got within rifle range of Bucquoy, but it was evident that the Germans were not intending to quit Bucquoy without a fight : they could be seen digging in vigorously just South of the village.

With the capture of Puisieux the Seventh Division's advance came for the moment to a standstill. Until the Nineteenth and Thirty-First Divisions could get forward on its left a direct advance against Bucquoy was inadvisable. Accordingly the 20th Brigade, who relieved the 22nd on the night of March 2nd, had a relatively uneventful three days in the line. Still their patrols were active enough, pushing up as close to Bucquoy as the state of the ground and the enemy's alertness would allow, and there were several brisk little encounters which did not prevent the gleaning of much useful information. However, no move forward had been made before, on the night of the 5th/6th, the Division was relieved and drawn back for a brief rest. These last days cost the Division a serious loss, Captain Lowson of the Signal Company being killed on the 5th when reconnoitring near Puisieux. He had joined the Company as a 2nd Lieut. in October 1914 and had served almost continuously with it ever since, doing admirable work all along, and had proved himself an excellent commander of his company, whose work was always up to a very high level.

The main difficulty in following up the German retreat was the lack of roads. Theoretically there was a main road from Serre through Puisieux to Bucquoy : actually even the line of the road could hardly be traced. Not only had the village of Serre been completely obliterated, but Serre hill, the scene of so many attacks, had been shot to pieces by our heavy guns and was a mass of huge shell-craters filled with water or liquid mud.   The R.E. and Pioneers, assisted by large infantry working-parties, were at once set to work to construct a road over Serre hill, but the craters swallowed up any amount of road metal and large numbers of railway sleepers had to be used before at last a practicable roadway was created. This was a costly as well as a lengthy affair ; the hill was an easy mark and was constantly shelled by the Germans, causing many casualties among the working-parties and seriously impeding the work.   But till the road was made it was extremely hard to get rations and ammunition to the front line, evacuate wounded and carry out reliefs, and the moving forward of the guns was also greatly retarded.

Divisional Headquarters during this rest were at Bertrancourt, the brigades being at that place, Mailley Maillet, Acheux and Beaussart, only a short distance back from the front.   To go farther would hardly have been worth while, for after a bare week out of the line the Division was ordered on March 13th to relieve the Thirty-First opposite Bucquoy and to prepare to attack that village two days later and to employ five battalions. However, the very day that the 91st Brigade went into the line indications of a general retreat of the Germans were reported to the Corps, and about midday urgent orders were received from the Fifth Corps to push patrols into Bucquoy and, if it should prove to be still held, to attack it that evening. The line was held at the moment by the Queen's and a company of the 22nd Manchesters.[1] The patrols, which were at once pushed forward, came back

---

[1] Six batteries had been got forward to support the attack, the 12th and 31st had been in action for over a week and the 105th, 106th, 25th, and 58th had recently managed to reach a position South of Puisieux.   Every round of ammunition, however, had to be brought forward by pack animals and only a limited amount of wire-cutting had been possible.

to report that Bucquoy, which was known to be protected
by thick belts of quite uncut wire, was still strongly held.
General Cumming accordingly protested against attacking,
and his protest was backed up by the Divisional Commander, but the Corps reported that Army Headquarters
insisted that the attack should be made and all that could
be obtained was a postponement till 1 a.m. on the 14th,
an extension altogether too short to allow of adequate
wire-cutting, especially as the visibility was poor, and
even then the heavy bombardment was to take place at
the previously arranged hour of 10 p.m. After dark
patrols attempted to cut the wire by hand, but machine-
gun fire prevented their accomplishing anything.

It was hardly surprising therefore that when the Queen's
and 22nd Manchesters, the latter on the right, advanced
against Bucquoy, the attempt proved a costly failure.
The night was dark, it was pouring with rain, the troops
could not see where they were going, did not know the
ground, which was extraordinarily heavy, some men
having to flounder through knee-deep mud, and could not
keep up with the barrage or find such gaps as existed in
the wire. They came under heavy artillery and machine-
gun fire, for the 10 p.m. bombardment seemed to have
mainly served to put the enemy on the alert ; but some
of the right company of the 22nd Manchesters managed to
find a gap and establish themselves in the German trenches,
taking half a dozen prisoners. But they could not maintain their hold and when their bombs ran out were dislodged by counter-attacks, most of the rifles having been
clogged with mud through the men slipping and stumbling
into shell-holes. An officer and 70 men were missing and
the battalion's total casualties came to nearly 150. Of
the Queen's Captain Foster and a few men got through
the wire, but Captain Foster was wounded and taken and
most of the attacking companies were held up by the wire,
and with their rifles useless owing to mud they could do
nothing but crawl back, having had over 120 casual-

ties.[1] Simultaneously an equally hurried and premature attack on Bucquoy from the West by the Forty-Sixth Division had met the same fate. Altogether it was a most unsatisfactory incident and tended to create a feeling that the higher authorities in rear hardly appreciated the practical difficulties to be encountered by those in front and were in consequence asking officers and men to attempt the impossible.

For the next three days the position remained unchanged: the 22nd Brigade, who relieved the 91st on the evening of March 14th, pushed patrols forward, only to find Bucquoy strongly held and the hostile sniping and machine-gun fire, if anything, increased. However, wire-cutting was systematically carried on and the evening of March 15th saw a heavy bombardment of Bucquoy. But before a properly prepared attack could be delivered news came in, on the morning of March 17th, that Bapaume and Achiet le Petit had been evacuated and that the Division was to push on at once. Thereupon the Welch Fusiliers thrust patrols forward into and through Bucquoy, finding the village clear. Thence they worked forward towards Ablainzeville, where the enemy held them up though not for long. Before 5 p.m. the leading troops were into Ablainzeville and pushing on beyond, though somewhat delayed by the debris of the burning village. The Germans going back " according to plan " were able to do enormous damage as they retired : obstructing roads in every conceivable way, filling up wells, cutting down trees, burning and blowing up houses, so that the pursuers should be put to every kind of hardship and inconvenience. That their measures were successful in hampering the pursuit cannot be denied : but it was the existence of the shell-shattered

---

[1] One wounded officer got back after having had his clothes literally stripped off him from the waist downward by the wire, though their absence was not at first noticed owing to the thick coating of tenacious mud in which he was encased : it took his rescuers quite a long time to scrape the mud off him. In such conditions it was hardly surprising that the attack did not succeed.

area in which the old front-line trenches had been which was the main obstacle. Once roads could be constructed across this zone it was a much simpler matter to clear away the obstructions and debris the Germans had left behind. Felled trees were soon removed and even where mines had been exploded at road junctions it did not take very long to make a way round. The " booby traps " which had been skilfully prepared were a great nuisance : helmets left temptingly about to attract collectors of " souvenirs " caused bombs and mines to explode when picked up and caught a good many unwary people. Delayed-action mines, worked by time-fuses, kept on going off long after the pursuers had settled down. It was a great relief to get out of the filth and mud of the shelled area on to the green fields and solid ground which awaited the troops behind the German lines, but in the coming months the troops were to find the destruction wrought all over the area through which the Germans had retired a serious handicap. There were no good billets, and in a late and cold spring, marked by blizzards and snowstorms in mid-April, the lack of shelter within easy reach of the front greatly complicated administrative problems and helped to swell the sick-list, while the difficulty of getting guns and wagons, to say nothing of motor-lorries, forward over the damaged roads and destroyed bridges was enough to delay the advance considerably. That the pursuit was not very rapid and failed to take a satisfactory toll of the Germans cannot be denied, and it is also true that the vast majority of the officers and men of the Division were quite without experience of open warfare and quite untrained for anything beyond the trench warfare which had been going on without a break for two years and a half ; but the leisure the Germans had had for perfecting their arrangements for the retreat, for devastating the country, and for delaying the hostile advance was the primary cause of any failure to grip and punish the retreating enemy. Moreover, he had had plenty of time to select positions for his rear-guards, especially for the machine-guns which played so prominent a part in the resistance which the Division encountered, and that resistance had been skilful and effective. The choice before the British had been to push on rapidly, trying to brush opposition aside, which would have merely meant running into carefully prepared traps and ambushes and incurring heavy casualties, or to proceed circumspectly, keeping careful look out against such pitfalls. This was a slower process, no doubt, and sacrificed speed to safety, besides allowing the enemy to get off without much loss of men or material, but it had at least the merit of not being costly in lives, and it may be doubted whether, once the Germans had been given the choice of the time of their retreat, it was any less speedy in the end than the other method, of the unwisdom of which Bucquoy had been an object-lesson for the Seventh Division.

CHAPTER XVII

NIGHTFALL on March 17th had left the Seventh Division's leading troops on the approximate line Logeast Wood (right)–East of Ablainzeville–the Bucquoy-Ayette road. During the night orders were received for an advance at daybreak to Courcelles le Comte and the dismantled railway S.E. of that village, and with the Welch Fusiliers and Royal Warwickshires leading and a section of the 104th Battery accompanying the advanced-guard, the 22nd Brigade started on its task at 6 a.m. It met little opposition, although much delayed by the numerous obstacles with which the enemy had strewn its path, and by 7.30 a.m. it had secured its objective, a few German cavalry clearing off to the Eastward as the leading line reached the railway. During the morning the Corps cavalry reported both Ervillers and Hamelincourt clear, and the Royal Warwickshires sent a patrol into Moyenneville which also was found unoccupied. On this information the Corps ordered the Division to occupy an outpost line stretching from Ervillers, which the Sixty-Second Division was holding, to Moyenneville and Hamelincourt, which last the 20th Manchesters took over from the Lucknow Cavalry Brigade. Behind this outpost line, held by the 22nd Brigade, the main body was to consolidate a line from East of Logeast Wood to Ablainzeville, as the contingency of a German counter-attack could not be left out of account.

Nothing of the sort, however, marked the night of March 18th/19th, and early next morning the cavalry pushed forward to reconnoitre the Hindenburg Line

_____
[1] Cf. Maps 27 and 28.

between Lagnicourt and Henin sur Cojeul, the Division's
advanced-guards moving forward in support of them,
though the main body did not stir. It soon appeared
that the enemy were holding a line from St. Leger to
Boyelles, but they did not offer much resistance and were
soon cleared out of Boyelles, while patrols of the 20th
Manchesters entered Boiry St. Martin and Boisleux.
However, though the Eighteenth Division, which was now
on the Seventh's right, occupied St. Leger, the cavalry's
efforts to reach Croisilles proved quite ineffectual ; and
the day (March 19th) closed with the 20th Manchesters
holding an outpost line, the Welch Fusiliers at Courcelles
and the Royal Warwickshires and H.A.C. at Ablainzeville,
little progress having been made.

This was largely due to the difficulties of getting guns
and transport forward over the ruined roads, and the
energies of the battalions not in the front line were almost
more absorbed in road repairs than in preparing a line of
resistance. The Germans had gone about their work of
destruction scientifically and there was far more work
than the Pioneers and R.E. could manage. The result
was that not only were they necessarily kept back working
on road repairs when they were needed up at the front,
but large working-parties had to be found by any infantry
battalion nominally resting or in reserve.

March 20th saw little change. The Division was up now
against the outworks of the Hindenburg Line and until
more artillery could be brought forward [1] there was little
chance of a further advance. A brigade of the Eighteenth
Division did indeed attack Croisilles but without success,
and though orders were issued to the 22nd Brigade to
repeat the attempt they were fortunately countermanded ;
instead the 20th Brigade, which had now come forward

---

[1] The XXIInd Brigade R.F.A. got into action West of St. Leger on March
21st and registered Croisilles, and the XXXVth Brigade got up into position
next day, but while field-guns found it very hard to get forward it was doubly
difficult for the heavier metal.

from reserve, relieved both the 22nd and the left of the Eighteenth Division, the 22nd retiring to Bucquoy and Puisieux for a week out of the line, though not of rest.

The 20th Brigade's new line ran from Judas Farm, N.W. of St. Leger to the cross-roads on the Mory–Ecoust road N.E. of Mory. In front of its right were the twin villages of Ecoust St. Mein and Longatte, opposite its left Croisilles, lying in the valley of the Sensée and commanded by the higher ground around. Behind this line on a rather higher ridge ran the main Hindenburg Line in a general direction from S.E. to N.W. but bending more to the North at Bullecourt. The approaches to the German defences were open and exposed, though some cover might be found in folds of the ground ; both villages were strongly entrenched and protected by broad belts of wire, so their capture did not promise to be easy, especially as there was by no means too much ammunition for the artillery up at the front. The problem before the Division was far from simple : it was urgent to push on before the Germans could consolidate their position more thoroughly, yet an immediate attack was unlikely to meet with marked success.

The 20th Brigade's immediate task was to make as much ground as could be gained without heavy fighting, so as to secure a good jumping-off place for the next attack close up to the German line. This meant pushing forward to any positions of local tactical value, a ruined building, a bank or rise in the ground, a sunken road or depression, anywhere where cover could be obtained and a small post established. This was largely done at night and was accompanied and to some extent covered by active patrolling, leading to several minor encounters with the enemy and affording junior officers and N.-C.-O.s ample opportunities for good leadership and skilful handling. The Germans repeatedly counter-attacked these posts ; on the night of March 22nd/23rd, for example, they rushed one held by the Borders, killing or taking

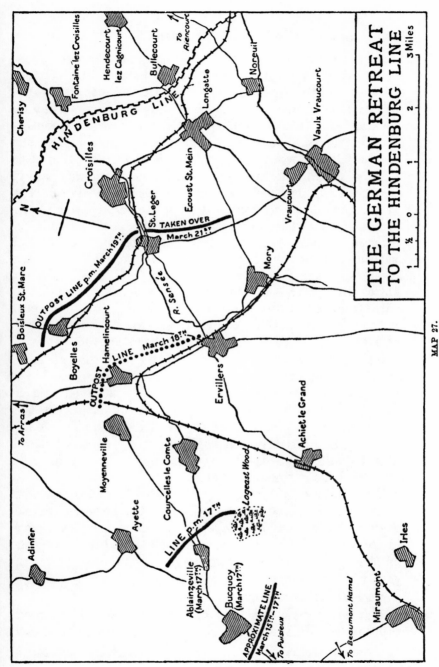

THE GERMAN RETREAT
TO THE HINDENBURG LINE

MAP 27.

nearly all its garrison, but the battalion promptly re-occupied the post and that evening both it and the 9th Devons on its right pushed forward about 200 yards nearer the Ecoust–Croisilles line, the 9th Devons having several casualties but beating off one fairly serious counter-attack. A smaller advance was made next night, but on the 25th efforts to gain ground met increased opposi-tion. The German artillery fire if intermittent was heavy, and between this and the contests for the posts and the active patrolling casualties were quite appreciable.[1] On March 24th orders were issued for the 20th Brigade to prepare to attack Ecoust and Longatte, in conjunction with an attack by the Australians, now on the Division's right, against Lagnicourt. However, on the night of March 24th/25th the 20th Brigade's patrols found the wire from 20 to 30 yards wide and not cut. General Barrow reported this to the Fifth Corps, pointing out also that his artillery had not yet been able to get into a satisfactory position for wire-cutting and that at least another 24 hours' bombardment by the heavy artillery was needed. On this the attack was postponed and it was decided that the 91st Brigade should take over the left of the line which one of its battalions, the 21st Man-chesters, had already been holding for a couple of days, and that it should attack Croisilles before the 20th made its attack on Ecoust–Longatte.

The attack on Croisilles was entrusted to two battalions, rather a small force for the frontage attacked—the South Staffordshires being on the left of the road from St. Leger to Fontaine les Croisilles, while the 22nd Manchesters on the right attacked more from the South, keeping touch with the 20th Brigade, which was to profit by the attack to push its advanced posts forward towards Ecoust.

The South Staffordshires had to reach a sunken road running from S.E. to N.W. beyond Croisilles and to throw

---

[1] For March, the 8th Devons had a total of 33 casualties, the 9th had 57, the Borders 66, and the Gordons 58.

back a defensive flank to the Westward to connect with
the Fifty-Eighth Division, and as this flank would be nearly
1,200 yards long the Queen's placed a company at their
disposal. Each battalion had two companies in its front
line, each in two waves, with a third in support, the fourth
being in reserve N.E. of St. Leger. Only two platoons
of each battalion were to enter the village, which was to
be kept under heavy fire up to the last possible moment,
the XIVth Brigade R.H.A., an Army Field Artillery
Brigade, and an Australian 18-pounder brigade coming
under General Stanley Clarke to support the attack.

At 5.15 a.m. (March 28th) the troops began advancing
from the assembly position N.E. of St. Leger Wood, so as
to be close up to the barrage by " Zero," which was at 5.45.
This approach march was carried out without mishap,
but directly the 22nd Manchesters advanced they came
under heavy machine-gun fire and were checked, having
to dig in just short of the wire, though one small party
under Captain Duguid managed to make its way through
and to hold on for 36 hours just inside the German defences.
The reserve company then tried to work forward down a
dip S.E. of the village and thereby outflank it, but the
Germans detected its movement and brought such a
heavy fire to bear that it too was checked. The South
Staffords' right company at first fared quite well and got
close up to the German wire just S.W. of the village.   Here
it was checked by a strong counter-attack ; but though rifles
and Lewis guns, most effectively handled, beat off the
counter-attack, it could go no farther.   The left company
too began well, nearly reaching the sunken road which was
its objective.   Then, however, it came under enfilade fire
and being isolated was eventually caught and nearly
destroyed by a counter-attack, only the left platoon
getting away.   The reserve company tried in vain to
help the right forward, and all that the troops could do
was to hang on to their ground till nightfall, when the 21st
Manchesters relieved the South Staffords and the Queen's

24

took over from the 22nd. Casualties had been heavy, for both battalions were well below establishment. The South Staffords had over 130, nearly 60 of them " missing," and the Manchesters over 90. The only satisfactory feature was that the 8th Devons, on the 20th Brigade's left, had pushed forward several hundred yards and its No. 2 Platoon had established itself behind a bank not far South of Croisilles Station, where it dug in, beating off a vigorous local counter-attack. The Gordons, however, were less lucky ; neither that day nor the next could they succeed in capturing some advanced posts S.W. of Ecoust which were skilfully defended by machine-gunners. One of these in particular,[1] sited in a sunken road with a good all-round field of fire, proved specially hard to capture. Then on the 30th the Borders relieved the Gordons and promptly tried to rush these posts. They failed, but at a second attempt about 10 p.m. they rushed a bombing-post on the right of the more Northerly post,[1] then, turning against the main post, they carried it with a rush. Most of the garrison escaped but left a good hot meal behind them for the benefit of the assailants, who, pressing on, cleared the second post [2] also, besides establishing a new post farther down the road leading from Vraucourt to Ecoust.[3] In the meantime the 22nd Brigade had relieved the 91st, thereby allowing the latter two days' rest before renewing their effort to take Croisilles.

This time the attack was part of a larger whole. On the left the Twenty-First Division was to co-operate against the high ground between the Sensée and the Cojeul. The Seventh Division was tackling both Croisilles, assigned to the 91st Brigade, and Ecoust-Longatte, the objective of the 20th. Beyond that brigade Australians were attacking and the frontage of the attack was nearly ten miles. A steady bombardment maintained ever since the unsuccessful effort on Croisilles had made a considerable difference to the wire, substantial lanes had been cut

---

[1] Marked on Map 28 as A.   [2] B on map.   [3] Marked C on map.

MAJOR-GENERAL T. H. SHOUBRIDGE, C.B., C.M.G., D.S.O.

in it, and all approaches to Ecoust, Longatte, and Croisilles had been well bombarded by the heavy artillery.
Before the attack could be delivered the command of the
Division had again changed hands, General Barrow being
replaced by General T. H. Shoubridge, who had recently
been commanding a brigade in the Eighteenth Division.
An energetic and vigorous officer and a splendid trainer
of troops, he was to command the Division longer than
any other of its commanders and to play a big part in its
story.

To carry out its task the 20th Brigade [1] was employing
three battalions, the Gordons on the right against Longatte,
the 8th Devons in the centre and the 9th on the left against
Ecoust and the houses along the Ecoust-Croisilles road.
Its ultimate objective was the railway line beyond the
villages. The 91st Brigade, which had the South Staffords
on the right, then the 21st Manchesters, the Queen's
being on the left, was not to attack Croisilles direct, but
to " pinch it out." Its first objective was the railway
and sunken road from the 20th Brigade's left to the factory
East of Croisilles : it was then to push patrols out across the
Sensée to get touch behind Croisilles with the Twenty-First
Division ; this, if achieved, would intercept the retreat of
the defenders of Croisilles, who were to be pinned to the
ground by continuing the bombardment of the village
until the capture of the first objective. The 91st Brigade
was then to advance to the forward slope of the spur
leading to Fontaine while a specially detailed party cleared
Croisilles.

April 2nd had been chosen for the attack and for four
days previously the German positions had been systematically bombarded, special attention being paid to wire-
cutting. Efforts were also made to gain ground in the

[1] When the 22nd Brigade took over the line the Borders had remained
opposite the frontage to be attacked by the 20th Brigade, but withdrew to
reserve when its assaulting battalions came into line on the night of April
1st/2nd.

direction of Ecoust and Croisilles, and these led to some
quite sharp fighting, of which the brunt fell on the Borders,
as already described, and on the H.A.C., who had nearly
100 casualties in three days, most of them incurred in
fights for a ruined windmill,[1] South of Ecoust. This was
taken on March 31st, lost after being heavily bombarded
in the small hours of April 1st, and then twice unsuccess-
fully counter-attacked, well-placed machine-guns proving
the chief stumbling-block. This made it necessary to
draw back the assembly position of the right of the 20th
Brigade and to detail two platoons of the Gordons as a
special attacking party for this post.

The assembly was rendered difficult by an unusually
bright moon which threatened to reveal their presence to
the enemy. The 20th Brigade had to wait till the moon
went down before it could move over the crest-line to the
forming-up tapes, while on the left one company of the
Queen's was detected as it moved down a spur and a
barrage was promptly put down, but fortunately with
such strictly defined limits that it was easily avoided. In
the end all units were in position in time, and at 5.15 they
moved forward behind a splendid barrage, which started
200 yards ahead of the assembly position and moved 100
yards every three minutes until 200 yards beyond the
first objective.

In the 91st Brigade the Queen's had the most complicated and probably the most difficult task, though the
embankment which the other two battalions were attacking was a sufficiently formidable obstacle, in places nearly
40 feet high, covered with brambles as well as being wired
and bristling with machine-guns. But as the flank
battalion the Queen's had to take special precautions to
guard their left against fire from Croisilles, and five Vickers
guns were posted behind them to bring covering fire to
bear on the village ; while instead of attacking as the
other battalions did with two companies in front, one in

---

[1] Marked as " Windmill " on Map 28.

support, and the fourth in reserve, the Queen's had only
one company in front, the second having to be detailed
to tackle a particularly nasty strong point on their left
known as the Tooth.[1] They had the misfortune, moreover, to start by suffering from our own barrage ; [2] all the
officers of the leading company were hit and the attack
was for a time disorganized. However, order was quickly
restored, and the attack resumed. This time it went
admirably, and despite enfilade fire from the Tooth and
from the railway to the East of it the Queen's secured
their first objective about 7 a.m. The 21st Manchesters
had reached the railway half an hour earlier but had
found it a formidable obstacle. They met stubborn
opposition and only after hard fighting did they storm
the embankment and establish a line on the farther side.
On their right the South Staffords had secured their
objective with quite trifling casualties, and then brought
heavy and effective fire, especially from their Lewis guns,
on to the defenders who were bolting across the open
towards the shelter of the Hindenburg Line. By 7.30 a.m.
the 91st Brigade had secured all its first objective and was
preparing to push on to the second, while the Queen's,
after repulsing one counter-attack, pushed parties across
the Sensée to establish themselves in positions to intercept
the retreat of the garrison of Croisilles towards Fontaine.
As yet, however, there was no sign of the Twenty-First
Division, and the Tooth was still holding out, although
two sections of the Queen's got within 50 yards of it and
bombarded the garrison with rifle grenades until their
supply ran out. On this the party was withdrawn so as
to allow of a fresh bombardment of the Tooth, which
proved effective, its surviving defenders retiring hastily

[1] This was where two sunken roads joined South of Croisilles and just short
of the railway line.

[2] A battery from another Division, which had been brought up to strengthen
our barrage and had not had time to register, seems to have fired short, though
the barrage as a whole was extremely accurate and effective.

into the village. It was now about 10 a.m. and the Queen's could push on to the second objective, which had already been secured by the South Staffords, followed soon after by the 21st Manchesters, the Queen's reaching it a little after 11 a.m. By this time the position of the defenders of Croisilles had become seriously compromised and already some of them had attempted to leave the village. But from their post on the left of the Senseé the Queen's could bring a fire to bear which effectually prevented any Germans from quitting Croisilles by the direct road N.E. to Fontaine, while that past the factory on the right of the Sensée was also barred. Unluckily the Twenty-First Division's failure to close the gap and get touch with the Queen's had left a way of escape open to the N.W. of which many of the defenders availed themselves. Some were seen and fired upon by the Lewis guns of the Queen's and by our artillery from farther back, and casualties were inflicted; but had the Twenty-First Division reached its objective in time not a man ought to have got away. Others made no attempt to escape but remained in Croisilles till, about 11.30, two companies of the reserve battalion, the 22nd Manchesters, were put in to clear the village.

These companies pushing into Croisilles from the S.W. soon became involved in heavy fighting, for the remaining defenders put up a stout opposition and the village, not having been reduced to mere bricks and debris like the villages on the Somme battlefield, such as Ginchy and Beaumont Hamel, afforded ample cover, one strong point on the left [1] in particular giving special trouble and holding up a bombing-party which tried to rush it. Both companies became scattered and disorganized. The reserves had to be put in, and only when the last two platoons were brought up was this strong point eventually overcome. Led by Lieut. Robinson, the Adjutant, these platoons worked round to the North-East and rushed the strong

[1] Marked " S.P." on map.

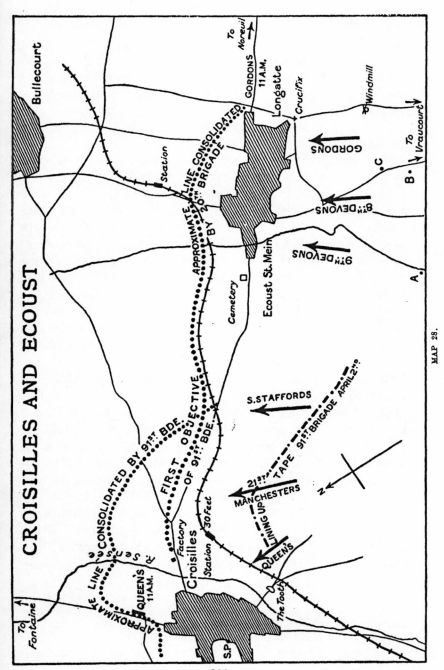

CROISILLES AND ECOUST

MAP 28.

point from the rear, killing or capturing about 30 Germans. They could do this more easily because some of the Queen's had taken a cross-roads from which a machine-gun had been covering the strong point. This completed the clearing of Croisilles and shortly afterwards, about 2.30 p.m., touch was obtained with the Twenty-First Division.[1]

The 20th Brigade meanwhile had been equally success-ful against Ecoust and Longatte, though the loss of the post near the windmill, already described, had necessi-tated the line from which it attacked being drawn back somewhat to the rear of the 91st Brigade's. The troops also, as already explained, had to wait till the moon went down and only just reached the taped line in time. More-over, though the artillery had made good use of the limited time and ammunition available—with the roads in the state in which the Germans had left them it was not easy to keep the battery wagons filled—the wire still presented a serious obstacle. There were gaps in it and it could be penetrated, but the gaps were marked down and the Germans had machine-guns trained on them, while the width of the belt made it a nuisance even where it had been fairly well cut. The 9th Devons on the left had a bad time. They suffered heavily in getting through the gaps, having two company commanders killed, one of whom, Captain Inchbald, had landed with the battalion at Havre in July 1915. However, they pushed on and though held up at the cemetery just N.W. of Ecoust by machine-guns well protected by wire, eventually captured their first objective, including the cemetery. Then, reinforced by the support and reserve companies, the survivors advanced again, making for the railway embank-

[1] The 91st Brigade had 7 officers and 62 men killed and missing, 12 officers and 159 men wounded, a total of 240 all told; the Queen's with 7 officers and 68 men and the 21st Manchesters with 6 officers and 88 men casualties were the chief sufferers, the surprising thing being that the South Staffords had only 1 officer and 26 men wounded and none killed. The clearing of Croisilles cost the 22nd Manchesters 5 officers and 39 men.

ment. Here also they encountered stiff opposition and
had many casualties, but soon after 7 a.m. it too had been
captured.

The 8th Devons also had found the wire hard to pass.
The Germans had some machine-gun posts on the British
side of it and these the 8th cleared at their first rush, but
as they crowded at the gaps they could not help giving
good targets and many were hit. However, Captain
Duff, who was commanding the attacking companies,
posted Lewis guns to bear on the machine-guns which
covered the gaps, and by this means enabled the right
company, " B," to get through and to push into Ecoust
village. Here there was hard fighting from house to
house in which the 8th, using bombs and Lewis guns to
good effect, gradually made progress. The left company,
" D," had also had difficulty in negotiating the wire and
met stubborn opposition in some trenches outside the
village, but overcame it, pushed down the main street,
disposed of a troublesome machine-gun near the church
and of two others in a strong point on the Croisilles road,
and eventually reached the railway embankment, to find
" B " Company already there on their right. Meanwhile
"A" Company had "mopped up" Ecoust effectually, though
they had some stiff fighting as a good many Germans had
emerged from cellars and houses after the first rush had
taken the Devons' leading line through the village. This
house-to-house fighting, however, gave the rank and file
plenty of chances to distinguish themselves and no little
skill and resource was shown by individuals and small
parties in the course of it.

By 7.30 a.m. resistance in Ecoust was practically over and
the 8th had secured the embankment and were establishing posts some way in advance. From the embankment
the Lewis gunners had found good targets in Germans
retiring across the open, but the enemy's artillery, at first
almost silent, now began to get active. In face of this
shelling and of heavy machine-gun fire the advance be-

yond the railway made little progress.   About midday indeed the Germans actually began counter-attacking.   However, the 8th Devons met them with a steady fire from rifles and Lewis guns and disposed of the counter-attacks even before the artillery could get the warning and bring their barrage down.

One thing which hampered the advance to the second objective was that the Gordons had found Longatte a very tough nut to crack and did not secure their first objective till some time after Ecoust had been cleared. They had met a desperate resistance ; the village was full of machine-guns and the battalion had diverged to the right, leaving a gap between itself and the 8th Devons. Fortunately the two platoons originally detailed to capture the strong point near the windmill had found their quarry evacuated, and could be put in to fill the gap.   But at 9 o'clock hard fighting was still in progress in the N.E. of Longatte, though rather earlier on the right company had secured the sunken road running towards Moreuil and had gained touch with the Australians.   Two platoons indeed pushed on beyond the limits assigned to the brigade in an endeavour to capture some field-guns, which the Germans just managed to withdraw in time, but it was 11 o'clock before Longatte could finally be reported clear. With it the Gordons had taken 3 officers and over 40 men. The two battalions of the Devons had between them collected another 60 [1] and this although the German resistance had been extremely stubborn, many men fighting on to the last and refusing to be taken.   Considering the strength of the position and the determination with which it had been defended, Ecoust and Longatte had not cost the 20th Brigade as dearly as might have been feared.   In all 7 officers and 86 men were killed or missing, 10 officers and 218 men wounded, a total of 321 : of these the 8th Devons contributed 6 officers and 112 men, the 9th, 5 and 95, the

[1] The material captured included 14 machine-guns, 2 trench-mortars, and an automatic rifle.

Gordons 6 and 92, the remainder belonging to the Brigade Machine-Gun Company, whose well-planned and effective barrages had contributed considerably to the day's success.

During the afternoon the 20th Brigade, like the 91st, consolidated its position, making the railway embankment its main line. The advanced posts which had been established beyond this line proved difficult to maintain in face of the heavy fire which the Germans developed later in the day. They did not, however, attempt any counter-attack and left the Division in possession of really substantial gains. It had good reason to be satisfied with its achievement, which was a good start for General Shoubridge's tenure of the command and was a more than adequate reply to the critics, well back behind the line for the most part, who had of late been suggesting that the Seventh Division was becoming "sticky."[1] On April 2nd the Division had shown clearly that, if it had failed at Bucquoy and in its first attempt on Croisilles, it was capable—given adequate artillery preparation and support with time for proper reconnaissance—of achieving a really considerable success in fine style. The day's fighting had been about the most important of the minor actions fought in the course of the German retreat; the capture of the " villages and well-wired trenches, forming an advance line of resistance to the Hindenburg Line,"[2] had been no mean achievement, and the Seventh Division and those which had co-operated on its flanks have legitimate reason for dissatisfaction with the ruling which has denied to the units engaged in their capture a " battle honour " for what in any other British war would have been rated as fully deserving of recognition.

[1] It is reported that when Captain Duff, who had led the attack of the 8th Devons with so much dash and skill, got back to his battalion headquarters, badly wounded but nevertheless refusing to part from a captured machine-gun which he was bringing in as a trophy, his first remark was " Who says the Seventh Division is sticky now ? "

[2] Sir Douglas Haig's dispatch of May 31st, 1917.

CHAPTER XVIII

BULLECOURT [1]

THE Seventh Division had had its full share of work in pursuing the Germans to the Hindenburg Line. In the big attack to which that pursuit had served as a prelude, that of April 9th on a 15-mile frontage astride the Scarpe with Arras roughly as centre, its infantry had no part, for on the night of April 4th/5th the 22nd Brigade was relieved by battalions of the Sixty-Second Division to which the Divisional Commander handed over early on the 5th. The 22nd Brigade had taken over Croisilles and Ecoust on the evening of their capture, having the Borders attached to it as a reserve, while the 22nd Manchesters were still completing the clearing up of Croisilles. Its orders were to consolidate its position and to push forward posts nearer to the Hindenburg Line so as to diminish the distance to be crossed when the main attack was launched. It was intended that the Fourth and Fifth Armies should combine with the main attack to be delivered by the Third and First by attacking the Hindenburg Line at Bullecourt. The guns of the Seventh Division were therefore kept busy registering the defences of Bullecourt. The Germans shelled cross-roads and other likely targets fairly severely and were on the alert to prevent patrols investigating their line too closely, so the 22nd Brigade had quite a lively time. The Division casualties for March 29th–April 5th amounted, apart from those of April 2nd,[2] to nearly 200, but the line was pushed well forward, in places as much as 500 or even 800 yards, and a quite satisfactory jumping-

---

[1] Cf. Map 29.

[2] These came to 36 officers and 525 men.

off place had been secured before the Division went out
of the line.

" Going out of the line " meant in this case the withdrawal of the infantry to Ablainzeville (20th Brigade),
Courcelles (22nd Brigade), and Bucquoy (91st Brigade) ;
it did not mean any relief for the artillery, who continued
in position, coming under the C.R.A. Sixty-Second Division from April 5th. The Pioneers and R.E. also were
little affected by the relief of the infantry, there was only
too much work for them in the devastated area, and the
infantry found its time considerably interrupted by demands for working-parties, partly to repair roads and construct light railways, partly to prepare a line of defence
as a precaution against a hostile counter-attack in force.
Drafts turned up in fair numbers, though they only about
balanced the battle casualties and did not compensate
for the wastage by sickness and the drain of officers and
men to various " employments " which was now becoming
so marked. The sick-rate was sufficiently high to keep
units down below establishment, though marvellously
low considering the weather and the hardships the troops
had had to endure. The credit for this was due partly to
the care and watchfulness of the R.A.M.C. and partly to
the excellent work of the administrative services ; even
during the pursuit there had been no failure to produce
rations and supplies. But the gap between " establishment " and " strength," particularly " trench strength,"
showed a tendency to widen, and the big demands for
working-parties interfered considerably with the programme of training. There were many valuable lessons
to be drawn from the recent fighting ; it had differed
considerably from the trench-to-trench fighting of the
Somme, and it had been only too evident that many of the
junior officers and N.-C.-O.s, who were accustomed to
trench warfare only, were not at home in a war of movement. Opportunities had been missed for this reason,
and General Shoubridge was keen to take every chance

to profit by this experience and to bring the lessons home to officers and men ; tactical exercises were held, sometimes with, sometimes without, troops and the country round Ayette and Ablainzeville afforded ideal training-ground, but the time for systematic instruction was all too short.

It was not only the demands for working-parties which cut into the time available for training. On April 11th the Division stood by all day in readiness to support the Fifth Army's attack. The Sixty-Second Division was attacking Bullecourt itself with an Australian Division on its right. Had the attack succeeded the Seventh Division would have been put in and the 20th Brigade moved forward to Courcelles, the 22nd to Ervillers, and the 91st to Ablainzeville. Unfortunately, though some measure of success attended the attack at first, the ground gained could not be held. Some of the Australians penetrated almost to Riencourt les Cagnicourt, N.E. of Bullecourt, but eventually both Divisions were thrust back to their original positions, whereon the Seventh returned to billets. The Sixty-Second Division had been badly cut up, and on April 14th the 21st Manchesters were sent up to relieve one of its battalions opposite Bullecourt. On the right the position coincided with the railway embankment South of Bullecourt, but to the left the line ran more from South to North parallel to the Hindenburg Line, which turned back at a sharp angle just West of the village. On the 17th the Queen's also were lent to the Sixty-Second Division and then next day the 91st Brigade took over that Division's frontage, holding the line till the 21st, when the 20th relieved it. The 20th Brigade held the line for a week, being under intermittent shell fire without suffering many casualties. It established some advanced posts farther to the front and accomplished a great deal of patrolling. On April 29th the 91st Brigade came in again for two nights, and even when the Sixty-Second Division took over in readiness for a fresh attack on

Bullecourt the South Staffords and 21st Manchesters were left in to support the 187th Brigade. There had been the same intermittent activity as had marked the 20th Brigade's turn in the line; our guns were firing away, the Germans replied, at times with some vigour. Patrol encounters were frequent and on one occasion the Germans succeeded in rushing two advanced posts held by the 22nd Manchesters, which were taken in flank by a strong party of bombers when the garrisons were already fully occupied with keeping off a frontal attack by riflemen. About a dozen casualties, mostly missing, resulted from this little encounter, which was more notable as the Germans were not usually inclined to try enterprises of this sort.

One serious difficulty of this period was the problem of finding suitable accommodation for Divisional Headquarters, by now a pretty big concern, what with its Intelligence Department, its pigeon-loft, a special electric-light lorry, much-enlarged Signals, and additional administrative units. Every house in the area had been systematically destroyed when the Germans went back, and even when matters had been simplified by dividing " D.H.Q. " into an Advanced H.Q. and a Rear H.Q. the C.R.E., Colonel Boileau, had to do some smart work to provide the Advanced H.Q. with huts on the Western edge of Courcelles. Subsequently a fresh Headquarters was erected for the whole of D.H.Q. at Behagnies with an Advanced H.Q. at Mory during the Bullecourt fighting.

By this time, the beginning of May, the strategical situation had changed for the worse owing to the practical failure of the great offensive on the Aisne. General Nivelle's attack had been far from fulfilling its promoter's over-optimistic expectations, and its failure had plunged the French armies into despondency and even in some cases into something not far short of mutiny. In these circumstances Sir Douglas Haig had to continue his offensive on the Arras front, mainly to distract the attention of the Germans and to compel them to employ against the

British the resources which they might otherwise have utilized in a counter-attack on the French, who were in no condition to offer a resistance comparable to the fight put up a year earlier for Verdun. The really considerable success achieved on April 9th and exploited in the next few days had given Sir Douglas Haig all he required for his own purposes, the Vimy Ridge and the German positions immediately in front of Arras as far East as Fampoux and Monchy le Preux. A heavy blow had been inflicted on the enemy, over 12;000 prisoners and 200 guns had been taken and the Germans had been forced to divert to the British Front many of their reserves, without achieving any substantial success in their counter-attacks. Sir Douglas Haig, if free to carry out his own plans without regard to the needs of his allies, would have stopped the Arras offensive in the middle of April, by which time the limits of successful exploitation had been reached, and have begun transferring his reserves of men and material to Flanders, the intended theatre of his main effort for 1917. But the consequent cessation of real pressure on the Germans would have left them free to go for the French, and to prevent this the Arras offensive had to be prolonged beyond what had been originally prepared for. Its subsequent stages were therefore largely an improvisation and were undertaken in face of considerable disadvantages ; and their comparative ill-success and costliness were in reality mainly due to the disappointing results of the great French offensive.

The practical effect on the Seventh Division was that it was called upon to deliver a series of attacks on a strong and well-defended portion of the German line under conditions which were all against success. When Bullecourt was first attacked on April 11th, it had been hoped that the Third Army's right would carry Heninel and Wancourt and reach the Sensée behind the line attacked by the Fifth Army, with whose left a junction would, if all went well, be made near Fontaine lez Croisilles. This junction had not been achieved, but the new attack, to be delivered on May 3rd, involved the same scheme. Once again the Sixty-Second Division was attacking Bullecourt, Australians tackled the Hindenburg Line to the East of that village, and the Third Army attacked Fontaine lez Croisilles with the hope of joining hands on the right of the Sensée with the Sixty-Second Division.

Of the Seventh Division the 22nd Brigade was most closely concerned in the day's doings. It had come up to Mory on May 2nd, in readiness to support the attack, and General Steele's headquarters were established in that village with two battalions, the other two, the 20th Manchesters and Royal Warwickshires, being at L'Homme Mort, South of Ecoust, and at Mory Copse respectively. General Stanley Clarke had also come up to Mory with his headquarters and had taken over command of part of the guns supporting the attack, though of these only the 25th Battery belonged to the Seventh Division. The other batteries were still under the C.R.A. Sixty-Second Division.[1] The 20th Brigade was back at Ablainzeville, the 91st, which had two battalions helping to hold the line to the left of the front attacked, being at Courcelles.

The attack of May 3rd started at 3.45 a.m.,[2] fully an hour before daybreak, and at first fared well enough, especially on the right where the 185th Brigade gained its first objective. But the frontage attacked was not so wide but that the Germans could switch on to it many guns which normally supported other parts of their line, and the heavy shelling which descended upon the 185th Brigade before it could consolidate its position, coupled with the failure of the 187th to secure its left flank, ultimately led to the 185th's expulsion from its lodgment. Before this the Sixty-Second Division had ordered the

---

[1] Most of the batteries had enjoyed a brief rest at their wagon-lines, four days or so, during April, but had otherwise been in action uninterruptedly since the capture of Ecoust and Croisilles.

[2] By " summer time."

25

20th Manchesters and the Warwickshires up to the railway embankment South of Bullecourt, the H.A.C. and Welch Fusiliers moving forward to replace them, while about 11.45 a.m. General Shoubridge also arrived on the embankment, having taken over the frontage held by the 185th Brigade.

A very obscure situation confronted General Shoubridge. The Sixty-Second Division were mostly back on the embankment, though it was believed that a few survivors were still hanging on to Bullecourt. The Australians were clinging stubbornly to about 1,000 yards of the Hindenburg Line, but unless Bullecourt could be secured it was doubtful if they could possibly maintain their hold. The Sixty-Second Division after a gallant effort had clearly shot its bolt—it had lost too heavily and its units were too much disorganized to attempt a fresh attack—so if the Australians were to be helped the Seventh Division must do it. After a hurried conference in a little tin shanty off the Ervillers–St. Leger road, at which the Army Commander (Sir H. Gough) and his Chief of Staff were present along with the Divisional Commander, orders were issued to the 22nd Brigade to attack Bullecourt, with a "Brown Line" running from S.E. to N.W. through the Northern portion of the village as its first objective and the Hindenburg Line North of the village as its final goal. This attack was to be begun by the H.A.C. and Welch Fusiliers, on the right and left respectively of the Longatte–Bullecourt road. They were to pass through the 20th Manchesters and Royal Warwickshires on the embankment, and if the attack went well and secured the Brown Line these battalions would push forward and assault the final objective. It was pointed out that the brigade did not know the ground and had no time for proper reconnaissance, but the necessity for doing something quickly overweighed these objections and the attack had to go forward, though it was postponed from 6.30 p.m. to 10.30 p.m. This just allowed the company commanders to

get their horses and ride forward as near as possible to a
point from which they could get an idea of the ground, but
even so it was a very inadequate reconnaissance.

It was still daylight when the H.A.C. and Welch Fusiliers
reached the embankment and they had to wait nearly
three hours before the attack started. Their advance had
apparently been detected by the Germans, for directly they
went forward heavy machine-gun fire opened upon them
from front and flank; they pressed forward nevertheless,
only to find that the wire, though effectively cut, still
presented a troublesome obstacle, being tangled up in
coils which were difficult to negotiate. However, both
battalions succeeded in forcing their way into Tower
Trench,[1] and cleared it after a stubborn hand-to-hand
tussle, capturing about 50 prisoners. Some of the later
waves of the H.A.C. pressed forward into the village and
were even reported to have reached the second objective,[2]
while the Welch Fusiliers tried to form a defensive flank
facing N.W. and connecting up with the Sixty-Second
Division about the cross-roads S.W. of the Crucifix. But
casualties had been heavy and Germans emerged in
numbers from dug-outs in the village to dispute it with
the assailants. There was a gap too on the right; it
appeared later that the Australian battalion which should
have co-operated had suffered so severely from a heavy
bombardment that it had had to be relieved, and in consequence Germans, making use of this gap, assailed the
H.A.C. in flank. The H.A.C. put up a good fight, but
they had Germans in front and in flank and even some
behind them, who came out of dug-outs that had escaped
the moppers-up. The Welch Fusiliers were not less
severely pressed, and in the end neither they nor the H.A.C.
could maintain their hold on Bullecourt : by 2.30 a.m. on

---

[1] The trench in front of the Southern edge of Bullecourt was subsequently
known by this name.

[2] This was doubtful—there was a second trench behind the first objective,
which was probably what the H.A.C. reached.

May 4th, it was reported that both battalions had been thrust out of the village.[1] Accordingly instead of the Warwickshires and 20th Manchesters starting the second stage of the attack at 2 a.m., they had to be put in at 3 a.m. to repeat the first phase. As they were forming up they were caught by the German barrage and lost heavily : the 20th Manchesters indeed were much scattered and disorganized, and Colonel Smalley could not collect enough of them to make much of an attack. It was 4 a.m. before the attack could be launched, and it was hardly surprising, seeing how badly both units had suffered from the barrage, that they hardly fared even as well as their predecessors. The Royal Warwickshires started quite well : like the Welch Fusiliers they got into the front trench and even penetrated into the village, only to be dislodged by counter-attacks. The majority of the survivors fell back to the embankment, but about 50 men with 3 officers managed to hold on in Tower Trench where it crossed the Longatte road and a company of the Manchesters got in farther to the right, S.E. of the village. During the day various conflicting reports came through. It was clear that some parties were still out in front of the embankment where General Steele was trying to reorganize his battalions, but not till the early afternoon was the situation more or less cleared up as the result of a recon-naissance by Captain Hunter of the Brigade staff. His report showed that about 80 Welch Fusiliers were inside the German wire near the Crucifix but had not reached the front trench : the party of the Royal Warwickshires astride the Longatte road was still holding on, but that was all. The front trench, though full of dead, both British and German, appeared to be unoccupied. The H.A.C., except for a few men still on the railway embank-

---

[1] When the 20th Brigade got into Bullecourt four days later an N.-C.-O. and 9 men of the H.A.C. were found holding out there : they had established themselves in a dug-out and, using a Lewis gun effectually, had beaten off all efforts to capture them.

ment, were back near Ecoust reorganizing, the 20th
Manchesters were doing the same near Ecoust station ;
but losses had been heavy and the 22nd Brigade was in
no condition to repeat the attack. In the evening the
Royal Warwickshires and Welch Fusiliers pushed forward
strong patrols to investigate the situation and, if possible,
occupy the road running through Bullecourt from S.E.
to N.W. and get touch with any detachments still holding
out in the village. This programme was altogether too
optimistic. The enemy held their fire long enough to
let the patrols get close up to them, but when they did
let fly the volume of their fire showed conclusively that
Bullecourt was still held in strength. Actually they had
let the patrols get so near that a few men on the left
managed to dash into Tower Trench and start bombing
down it, but these were soon overpowered, all efforts to
reinforce them being prevented by heavy machine-gun
fire.

Meanwhile the 8th Devons had been placed at General
Steele's disposal, and during the night of May 4th/5th
they took over the left of the line along the railway embankment and the only two advanced posts S.W. of the village
which it was considered practicable to retain, the other
advanced parties relinquishing the points they had so
tenaciously maintained. The Welch Fusiliers went back
to Ecoust, the 20th Manchesters and Royal Warwickshires being still behind the embankment and the H.A.C.
rather more in rear. May 5th passed quietly enough :
there was much shelling and by day it was impossible to
reach the advanced post or to do much on the far side of
the embankment. In the evening the 20th Brigade
relieved the shattered 22nd, which withdrew to Courcelles
and Gomiecourt : it had lost 16 officers and 375 men killed
and missing, 16 officers and 372 men wounded, nearly 800
in all. The Royal Warwickshires were the chief sufferers
with nearly 260 casualties, among those killed being
Lieut. Harrowing, who had done so well at Ginchy. The

H.A.C. were the next hardest hit with 11 officers and 202 men, the Welch Fusiliers having just under 200 casualties, while the 20th Manchesters escaped quite lightly with just over 100.

The 22nd Brigade's ill-success notwithstanding, there was no intention of abandoning the effort to take Bullecourt, though there was no change in scale, only two battalions being employed and no effort being made to distract attention from Bullecourt by advancing on a wider front. Originally the new attack was fixed for May 8th, but on the evening of the 5th the Corps Commander telephoned orders advancing it to the 7th, overruling a protest by General Shoubridge against hurrying things so much. The Brigadier of the 20th Brigade indeed had no chance to inspect the wire at the S.E. corner of Bullecourt and see if it was properly cut, and there was barely time to make arrangements with the Australian Division which was ordered to co-operate.

Instead of coming from the South and S.W. the 20th Brigade's attack was delivered from the S.E., more or less covered by the Australian lodgment in the Hindenburg Line, and was to sweep through the village, now fast becoming a heap of formless debris, from S.E. to N.W. The Gordons were to lead with two companies in front, followed by two of the 9th Devons who were to mop up and consolidate the first objective or " Blue Line," here the front German trench S.E. of the village.[1] The two remaining companies of the Gordons were to follow 50 yards in rear of the Devons and to push on with the survivors of the leading waves to a " Green Line " which included the S.E. corner of the village, East of the Longatte road, and ran roughly N.E. to join up with the Australians. A " Brown Line," following the road which skirts the North-Western and Northern sides of the village, formed a final goal, but all Bullecourt between the front trench and the road running through the village from S.E.

---

[1] This followed a sunken road skirting Bullecourt.

to N.W. was to be left unattacked. This area, known as the " Red Patch " from the way in which it was shown on the maps, was to be well shelled during the operation and mopped up later, if the main attack succeeded.

Shortly before the attack the 8th Devons had drawn back their advanced posts North of the railway embankment, and at 3.45 a.m. on May 7th the Gordons dashed forward. There was an excellent barrage, and the attack was delivered with real vigour and determination. The first objective was quickly taken and the Highlanders pressed on towards the second line, leaving the 9th Devons to secure their first gains. Determined opposition was offered at one strong point,[1] but it was overcome, and about 5 o'clock 50 prisoners were reported as on their way back from Bullecourt. A little later another message reported the capture of the Green Line and that bombers had worked along the German trenches towards the right and joined with the Australians. By 6 o'clock the prisoners had risen to 70, but shortly afterwards the 20th Brigade's troubles began in earnest. The German guns, at first quite inactive, now roused themselves and began to plaster Bullecourt with a steadily increasing volume of projectiles. So heavy was the fire indeed that on the left the Gordons were forced back some distance in rear of the Green Line, though on the right they maintained their hold, the 9th Devons meanwhile continuing their consolidation. The German line in Bullecourt now ran approximately just East of the Longatte road to the church, and to exploit the success already obtained General Shoubridge ordered General Green to use the 9th Devons to clear the Red Patch, giving him leave to use the 8th Devons and to bring the Borders up to the support position, replacing them in reserve by the Queen's. The 9th Devons accordingly started to work forward, pushing bombers along Tower Trench, and making the Longatte road the first objective of their main advance. By 1 p.m. they had

---

[1] Marked A on the map.

gained this and captured another 20 or 30 prisoners, and
all but reached the N.W. corner of the Red Patch before
they were brought to a standstill by increasing shell fire
and a more stubborn resistance. In this advance they
came across and relieved the handful of the H.A.C. who
had been holding out in Bullecourt since the 3rd.

By the early afternoon, then, Bullecourt seemed to have
been secured, but the Germans were not going to relinquish
their hold on it easily and about 3.30 p.m. the Divisional
Artillery received a report of a strong force of enemy
advancing upon the ruins from the N.W. The guns
were quickly turned on and shelled this party effectively,
but could not prevent most of it, well screened by the
ground, from getting into the Red Patch. Assailed by
fresh troops in superior numbers the 9th Devons had also
to face a much more effective bomb, and were gradually
pushed back through the Red Patch until about the left
of the original Green Line they at last managed to make
a successful stand.

The attack had thus not achieved all it had at one time
promised, but substantial success had been attained, and
during the night the Borders relieved the Gordons in the
Green Line, two companies of the 8th Devons replacing
two of the 9th in the Blue Line and on the left of the Green,
preparatory to a fresh attempt next day to clear the Red
Patch. The 8th had had a bad day : the embankment
was an obvious target for the German gunners and had
been persistently shelled, so that the battalion was by
no means fresh when it moved up into the front line.
However, it carried out the relief, " C " and " D "
Companies replacing the 9th on the left of the Blue Line,
though one company remained in on the right. During
the night the 95th Field Company came forward, wired
the left flank of the position, improved one " strong point "
which the infantry had made and constructed another,
while the Pioneers worked away at a communication
trench which the 528th (Durham) Field Company finished

off after daylight. It had been decided not to waste
valuable lives by pushing the R.E. and Pioneers forward
too soon, into the middle of the fight; they were held
back therefore till after nightfall, with the result that
their casualties were kept down and, on the whole, more
work was accomplished.

"Zero" for the 8th's attempt on the Red Patch was
fixed for 11 a.m., May 8th, and "C" and "D" went
forward well, in alternate sections of bombers, rifle-
grenade men, and Lewis gunners. "Got off the mark well,
full of buck, mud very bad," was the 20th Brigade's report
of the start. Some men bombed their way along Tower
Trench for nearly 300 yards, but the Germans were in
force and their resistance was stubborn. A strong point
on the Longatte road [1] held the attack up; a company
commander was killed and the German "egg" bomb
was distinctly better and handier than those of the Devons.
Eventually after clearing several dug-outs, taking some
prisoners and inflicting heavy casualties on the enemy, the
8th were forced back East of the Longatte road but consolidated a line roughly corresponding to the left of the
original Green Line. The Borders meanwhile had been
hanging on to the right of the position captured on the
7th; they were heavily shelled and much troubled by
snipers, but no counter-attack was attempted against
them, and they could consolidate their line effectually.

That night the remaining companies of the 8th Devons
relieved those of the 9th still holding part of the Blue
Line. The orders were explicit that Bullecourt must be
cleared, and accordingly at midday on May 9th the 8th
Devons renewed the attempt. As before, bombers led
the way, supported by rifle-grenade men and Lewis
gunners, and this time effective help was given by two
mortars which the 20th Trench-Mortar Battery had
established in a strong point S.E. of the village. One
platoon was told off to work down the road running

[1] Marked B on map.

diagonally through Bullecourt from S.E. to N.W., and on the embankment Lewis gunners and the Vickers guns of the Brigade Machine-Gun Company were on the alert to catch reinforcements trying to enter Bullecourt from the North.

Directly the attack started the Germans brought down a heavy barrage, but nevertheless the 8th went forward well. Once again they encountered a determined resistance, and though the platoon on the right worked forward nearly 200 yards the main attack hardly got beyond the Longatte road. Here there was hard fighting hand to hand and for some time the 8th held their own, but German reinforcements delivered a violent counter-attack which drove the Devons right back to the strong point [1] in the Blue Line. The officers with the attacking companies were all down, but C.-S.-M. Heal was conspicuous in his efforts to rally the men, and with the timely intervention of a platoon hitherto held in reserve a stand was made, which gave time for supports to be hurried up. On their arrival a fresh attack was made, and such was its vigour that the Germans were driven right back and the 8th established themselves along a bank just East of the Longatte road,[2] 100 yards in front of their starting-point. The German counter-attack had extended to the Borders' front also, but there it had met with no success whatever, and in the 8th Devons' second advance many Germans had been driven into the open South of Bullecourt where they had come under fire from the watchful machine-guns on the embankment. The British guns too had brought their barrage down most effectively, catching the Germans between it and our attack, and though few prisoners had been taken the dead with which the ground was strewn afforded ample evidence of the punishment inflicted on the Germans. Later in the afternoon a strong bombing attack developed, but was successfully repulsed by the 8th Devons. But they had been hard hit, 11 of their officers and nearly 250

[1] Marked A on map. [2] Marked C on map.

men were down and the survivors were so spent that they
had to be relieved that night, the Gordons being called
upon to replace them, though they too had lost heavily
and were far from fresh.   Luckily the Germans had had
enough for the time being, and the next two days saw a
lull in the fighting.   One or two new posts were established
and the line consolidated as far as possible, while the 91st
Brigade proceeded to relieve the tired 20th.

The 20th Brigade, with 11 officers and 157 men killed and
missing, 25 officers and 568 men wounded, had suffered
nearly as much as the 22nd, the loss falling heaviest on
the 8th Devons and the Gordons, the Borders and 9th
Devons getting off comparatively lightly with about 130
casualties apiece.   The brigade had the satisfaction of
having secured a firm hold on the South-Eastern portion
of Bullecourt and having taken a heavy toll of the Germans,
but there was something unsatisfactory and depressing
in these piecemeal attacks, repeated over the same ground
and without substantial alterations of plan to hold out
to each succeeding attack prospects of better fortune
than had attended its predecessors.   Still the Fifth Army
was insistent upon the reduction of Bullecourt, or rather
of the ruins which now represented it, for the village had
crumbled away under the repeated bombardments and
was rapidly becoming a shapeless heap of debris.

The 91st Brigade had been " out " since May 4th when
the South Staffords and 21st Manchesters, who had till
then been helping to hold the line to the left of the frontage
attacked, had been relieved.   But being " out " did not
necessarily imply a rest ; there was an unceasing demand
for carrying-parties to take wire, ammunition, and stores
up to the front and these trips often involved heavy
shelling and casualties.   The 91st Brigade therefore was
not exactly fresh when its turn in the front came.   Brigade
Headquarters had moved up to L'Homme Mort on the 10th,
on which day the Queen's and South Staffords had relieved the 20th Brigade, the Queen's being on the right,

the South Staffords on the left, with the 22nd Manchesters in support at Ecoust and on the embankment and the 21st farther back. The 11th was fairly quiet, giving the battalions who were to attack a chance of reconnoitring and studying their objective, though German shells and snipers cost the brigade nearly 50 casualties, the Queen's having one officer killed, another wounded, and nearly 20 men hit. That evening a tape line was laid by the 528th Field Company to the East of the Bullecourt–Longatte road and soon after midnight the Queen's and South Staffords formed up. Their objective was the Brown Line of the earlier attacks ; on reaching it both battalions were to construct strong points at certain selected places and to push patrols forward to reconnoitre the Hindenburg Support Line which ran some little distance to the North. Each battalion was attacking on a front of two companies, the succeeding waves having orders to follow as close as possible behind the leaders. Two companies of the 21st Manchesters were attached to each battalion for " mopping up," the 22nd Manchesters being retained in reserve. The creeping barrage was to advance 100 yards in 6 minutes, and the howitzers were to keep 50 yards ahead of the 18-pounders. The Australians were attacking on the right, while on the left the Sixty-Second Division was assailing the strong point at the Crucifix at the N.W. end of Bullecourt.

Bullecourt was being steadily bombarded while the battalions were lining up, but they got into position successfully and " at Zero," 3.40 a.m. (May 12th), both started forward together. At once the German barrage descended, but it did not stop the Queens, who were rapidly and completely successful ; at 4.15 Colonel Longbourne could report that his objective had been seized with but few casualties, and that he was consolidating a line slightly in advance of the road which defined the objective. By doing this the Queen's escaped the worst of the German barrage, which came down accurately on the road and

therefore just behind them. Work on the strong points
was promptly started and Lewis guns pushed out to the
front served to keep down the German snipers, who were
particularly troublesome on the left, and to prevent any
counter-attacks from starting. Touch was soon obtained
with the units on the flanks and before long the Queen's
were solidly established, despite persistent shell fire.
With the South Staffords things went less well. What
with the German barrage and snipers in the Red Patch
the attack South of the road towards the Crucifix was
soon held up. North of the road the advance fared better.
One platoon penetrated almost to the Crucifix and touch
was obtained with the Queen's N.W.[1] of the ruins of
Bullecourt Church. But the bulk of the battalion was
held up and formed a rough curve on the West of the
cross-roads, prevented from advancing by a strong point[2]
at the S.E. end of the Red Patch. Colonel Beaumann
vainly tried to clear the Red Patch with his reserve company, and although General Cumming sent up three
companies of the 22nd Manchesters Colonel Beaumann
could not deploy them in daylight owing to the machine-
gun fire and was only able to use one of them to fill a gap
in the right of his line. By noon the advance had come
to a standstill with the Western half of Bullecourt still
in German hands, but the position on the right materially
improved by the success of the Queen's and of the
Australians beyond them, who had taken 140 prisoners
and secured their objective.

General Cumming now proposed to make the next
attack from the East, hoping to fall on the Germans from
the rear and to do without artillery support after " Zero,"
but the Divisional Commander did not approve of this
scheme. Considering that the Brigadier was quite worn
out with the incessant fighting, and needed a rest, he
recalled him to Divisional Headquarters and eventually
sent him home on leave, Colonel Norman of the 21st

[1] Marked D on map.   [2] Marked E on map.

Manchesters taking temporary command of the brigade.
General Cumming's departure was a real loss. Officers
of his calibre were becoming increasingly difficult to find
at this period of the war. A man of strong personality
and force of character and a capable and educated soldier,
he had commanded his brigade through some arduous and
strenuous months, and had so won its affection and confidence that the brigade was ready to do anything for him.

It was now decided to renew the attack from the South
and to combine it with a fresh advance from the line
reached by the South Staffords. This was to be made
by two comparatively fresh companies of the 22nd Manchesters, while for the new attack from the South the
Royal Warwickshires were called upon. This battalion
had been placed at the 91st Brigade's disposal on May 11th
and had spent the next day in cellars at Ecoust, the usual
quarters for a battalion in reserve. These were fairly
comfortable and provided good cover, but after the losses
the Royal Warwickshires had suffered on May 3rd to put
them in again so soon was trying them pretty highly. However, they lined up on a tape from the Longatte road to that
to the Crucifix and went forward at 3.40 a.m. (May 13th)
to clear the Red Patch which the 22nd Manchesters were
attacking from the East. It was a complicated operation
and very difficult for the gunners to support, as if the
barrage which was to help the Royal Warwickshires was
the least bit too far forward it was bound to hamper the
advance of the Manchesters. From the information
gleaned by patrols it was believed that the front trench
would be found empty, but as before it proved to be held
in strength and the Royal Warwickshires were received
with a hot fire from rifles and machine-guns as well as
being vigorously shelled. On the right a few men somehow worked through the wire and reached the centre of
the village, but the bulk of the battalion got held up outside the wire and ultimately had to be withdrawn after
losing 4 officers and nearly 60 men. The 22nd Manchesters

could make little progress against the strong points : one
in particular just West of the cross-roads [1] was on rather
higher ground and overlooked the British trench just in
front of it.   During the day the South Staffords made
several efforts to bomb forward up Tower Trench, but
each time machine-guns checked them, and in the evening
a composite company of the 21st Manchesters met with
the usual fate of efforts to clear the Red Patch : attacking
from the S.W. it gained some ground but was checked by
a barrage, under cover of which the Germans counter-
attacked, driving the Manchesters back by sheer weight
of numbers.

Not even these failures could induce the higher
authorities to discontinue these costly piecemeal attacks.
The Welch Fusiliers were now sent up for yet another
effort, and the H.A.C., who could only muster about 250
men with a dozen Lewis guns, were ordered to relieve the
South Staffords.   Actually the H.A.C. were much delayed
on their way up—the communication trench was full of
Pioneers who were working on it—and the battalion only
reached Bullecourt just after midnight, so the C.O.,
Colonel Ward, after consulting with Colonel Beaumann
of the South Staffords, decided to take his men back to
Ecoust rather than risk the casualties bound to be incurred
if, as was likely, the relief had not been completed by the
hour when the Welch Fusiliers were to start.   The South
Staffords accordingly had to settle down to another day
in the line, a prospect which also awaited the Queen's, who
had got on well with their consolidation and had pushed
some posts out to the front.   On their right they had
now the 174th Brigade of the Fifty-Eighth Division, who
had relieved the Australians on the 12th and had come
under General Shoubridge next morning.   This brigade,
though twice attacked on the 13th, had beaten both
attacks off without much difficulty, and on the right of
the line the position was certainly quite satisfactory.

[1] Marked B on map.

The plan of attack for the Welch Fusiliers was that "B" and "D" Companies should attack the S.W. side of Bullecourt, starting at 2.10 a.m. (May 14th), "A" and "C" taking post meanwhile S.E. of the village. Repulsed at their first effort, "B" and "D" came again and succeeded in establishing two posts on the S.W. edge,[1] one facing the Crucifix, the other a little to the right, from which they could barrage the Crucifix and the strong point on the Mound with rifle-grenades when at 6.15 the other companies attacked from the S.E. This attack found the garrison of Tower Trench as much on the alert as ever, and after heavy fighting and many casualties the survivors of "A" and "C" were held up where the Longatte road enters the village. Here they dug in, sending back urgent messages for bombs and ammunition. These were sent up along with orders to renew the attack at 2.30 p.m. Tired as they were the Welch Fusiliers responded gallantly to this demand, and for a time looked like really clearing the Red Patch, but unluckily a big advanced dump of ammunition[2] had been blown up, and the Fusiliers found themselves short of bombs just as a strong counter-attack was developing, which wrested from the survivors all the ground the attack had gained.

Orders were now received for the relief of the battalions in Bullecourt, though Colonel Norman continued in charge of the operations and "A" and "C" Companies of the Welch Fusiliers were kept back for yet another effort. The 20th and 21st Manchesters and the H.A.C., all very weak and far from fresh, were now brought forward; the 20th Manchesters took over the line from the junction with the 174th Brigade to the church, the H.A.C. continued it to the left, holding the lodgment North of the Red Patch, the 21st Manchesters being in various posts round its Eastern and Southern edges.

The relief had not been long complete when an outburst

---

[1] F and G on map.

[2] It was near the strong point marked A.

of heavy fire heralded a vigorous German attack. It developed first against the H.A.C., coming mainly from the direction of the Crucifix. The pressure was very heavy, the Red Patch was reported to be " alive with Germans," and the much-depleted battalion could not hold its ground. The men rallied, however, and while Major Wright with some of " D " Company and a few Welch Fusiliers stopped the German advance down Tower Trench, Captain Bower of " A," after collecting his men in the N.E. of the village, advanced again and secured a line running S.W. from the church to the cross-roads, being helped by parties of the 20th and 21st Manchesters. The 20th, to whose front the attack had also extended, had beaten its assailants back without difficulty, as had the 173rd Brigade also ; it could therefore spare its reserve company to assist the troops on their left and to do good service in filling the gap which had opened between the cross-roads and the 20th Manchesters' left at the church. All units were now much mixed up and the sequence of events and the exact position of the different detachments are equally hard to establish, but it is clear that the Germans did not succeed in getting beyond the Longatte road. In delaying the German advance the remnants of " A " and " C " Companies of the Welch Fusiliers did splendid service. These were preparing to attack the Red Patch again, but the counter-stroke put this out of the question, and instead Captain Bluck and his two subalterns had to hurry forward to the cross-roads with every man they could collect and delay the enemy till a larger counter-attack could be delivered.

It was the Longatte road which constituted the left half of the line, which the 91st Brigade handed over during the night of the 15th/16th. On the right there had been no change, and though some of the enemy had got into the Australian line farther East counter-attacks had promptly ejected them. On the whole, then, if the Division had lost its rather precarious hold on the Western portion of Bullecourt, the German counter-attack could

26

hardly be reckoned a great success. Two fresh battalions
of the Guard Fusiliers had been specially brought up
for it, and prisoners admitted that the object of the
attack had been the complete recapture of Bullecourt
and the consolidation of their old front line. The
German losses had clearly been heavy, and in the next
few days the Fifty-Eighth and Sixty-Second Divisions
gradually pushed forward through the ruins of the village,
clearing up its much-contested Western portion and
ultimately completing the half-finished task which had
cost the Seventh Division so much.

The Division was certainly sadly reduced when at 10
a.m. on May 16th General Shoubridge handed over command to the G.O.C. Fifty-Eighth Division. The 20th
Brigade reported that it could produce three battalions
of about 450 men apiece and one of 250 ; the 22nd, whose
units had had another 350 casualties while in action under
the 91st, could only muster about 800 men ; and the 91st,
which had lost 700 of all ranks, was in little better plight.
The casualties of the Artillery, R.E., and Pioneers had
fortunately been low, under 80 altogether, though the
Pioneers had suffered a heavy loss in having their C.O.,
Lieut.-Colonel J. H. Chadwick, killed ; but even so Bullecourt had cost the Division 128 officers and 2,554 men,
40 officers and 879 men being killed or missing.

The tasks set to the Seventh Division at Bullecourt had
been of no mean difficulty, and it was a substantial proof
that its struggles had been fully appreciated by the authorities that the Commander-in-Chief should have paid the
Division the special compliment of calling in person
on General Shoubridge to congratulate him on the grit
and determination which the Division had displayed. Of
the reasons why it had been unable to achieve more, some
indication has already been given. Attacks on a comparatively narrow portion of an otherwise fairly " quiet "
front were never likely to be very successful unless the
enemy could be prevented from concentrating his guns

upon the frontage attacked. The German barrages and
counter-battery work had been most effective, and troops
had repeatedly been shelled out of the advanced positions
they had reached or so hampered in consolidating that they
could not withstand the counter-attacks. The unusually
great difficulties in the way of maintaining communica-

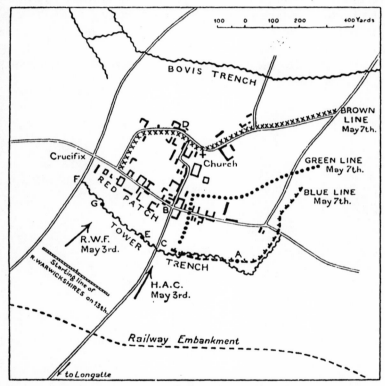

MAP 29.—BULLECOURT.

tions with the attacking troops had been one of the chief
obstacles to success, while the handy " egg " bomb had
been another important factor in the Germans' favour in
the close-quarter fighting ; but, as at Ginchy, the main
lesson to be drawn was that the narrower the front of
attack, the less the chance of success. To have to make

a series of small attacks, starting from trenches full of
unburied dead who testified to the failure of previous
efforts, was as hard a trial as the Division had ever been
put to. To have to advance again and again over the
same ground, to repeat without modification plans of
attack which had already proved unsuccessful, tested
courage and discipline highly. To be put in again, as
the battalions of the 22nd Brigade were, without any real
rest and without reinforcements, asked much of officers
and men. If Bullecourt cannot be reckoned as one of
the Seventh Division's outstanding successes it is certainly
one of the most creditable pages in its records.

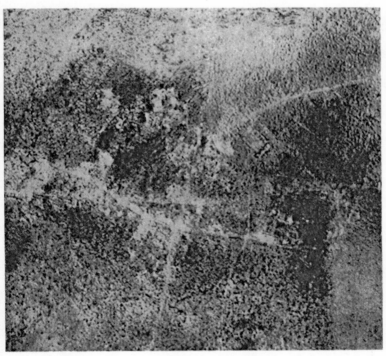

BULLECOURT: 6 APRIL (ABOVE), 9 MAY 1917 (BELOW)

CHAPTER XIX

AFTER BULLECOURT [1]

THE bitter fighting round Bullecourt was followed for the Seventh Division by a real rest, even the Divisional Artillery coming out of the line. As far as that part of the front was concerned "Bullecourt" was the last serious fighting which was to be seen for some time, although in the last fortnight of May and in the first weeks of June systematic operations were carried on between Croisilles and Bullecourt which resulted, before the Division went back to the line, in the capture of a considerable stretch of the Hindenburg Line. But the centre of interest and activity was shifting to Flanders, and after the Second Army's brilliant success at Messines on June 7th nothing of a serious nature was to be expected on the right of the British front.

As the Seventh Division was destined to remain in this quarter until nearly the middle of August, for it the summer months of 1917 were somewhat uneventful. This was just as well, its Bullecourt losses had depleted its ranks considerably and drafts were by no means plentiful. At the end of May the twelve infantry battalions could only show an average " paper strength " of 31 officers and 650 men, and " paper strength " included many officers and men not available for duty with their units : the " ration strength," a somewhat nearer approximation to the realities, averaged little over 550 of all ranks. Specialists of all sorts, signallers in particular, had to be trained to fill up vacancies, and the month's respite from front-line duties which the Division, except the much-enduring gunners, enjoyed after the 91st Brigade's relief on May 16th was equally needed and appreciated. May and June

---

[1] Cf. Maps 27 and 29.

were on the whole pleasant months ; if hardly a house in the villages in the back area still had its roof on, this mattered much less in fine weather than in the bleak and bitter closing weeks of the belated winter, and as yet German aircraft had not developed that systematic attack on back areas which was soon to become so marked.

During this period of rest, or rather of cleaning up, refitting and training, varied by working-parties for which the R.E. and the railway construction people were always calling, there were several changes in the Staff and in the command of units. The 91st Brigade got a new commander in Brigadier-General R. T. Pelly of the Loyal North Lancashires, who had been commanding Princess Patricia's Canadian Light Infantry. It had a new Brigade Major in place of Major Palairet, who left on May 22nd,[1] but his successor was no stranger, Captain Morshead being transferred from Staff Captain, in which post he was succeeded by Lieut. Colam of the Gordons from the Staff of the 20th Brigade. Colonel Norman left the 21st Manchesters on promotion to command the 89th Brigade, his successor being Lieut.-Colonel Lomax, and Colonel Pountney replaced Colonel Chadwick in command of the 24th Manchesters.

The 20th Brigade was the first to return to the line, taking over the Bullecourt sector from the 175th Brigade on June 14th and coming under the Fifty-Eighth Division. Things were fairly quiet even at Bullecourt now, though the improvement of the position afforded ample occupation. The front line consisted of small posts, held mainly by Lewis-gun teams, which were to be connected up into a strong line. A reserve line was then to be consolidated and after that a support line. Thus with the Bullecourt losses still hardly replaced—the 20th Brigade had only received 35 officers and 321 men as drafts in May and 18 officers and 486 men in June, against which sick wastage

---

[1] He had previously exchanged with Major O'Connor, who went to the Sixty-Second Division, but rejoined the Division in June to command the H.A.C.

accounted for a dozen officers and over 400 men—the troops in the line were kept busy.

The 20th had over a week in the line before coming under its own Divisional Commander again. The Seventh began relieving the Fifty-Eighth Division on June 21st and finished by the morning of the 24th, when General Shoubridge found himself in charge of a front extending from N.E. of Croisilles on the left to East of Bullecourt. This line, some 4,500 yards long, was all on the right bank of the Sensée. On the left it ran roughly from N.W. to S.E. over a broad spur which sloped gently down to the N.E. ; a little West of Bullecourt the line turned East, dipping down to cross a small valley and rising again to the slightly higher ground on which the remains of Bullecourt stood. The left half of this frontage, normally held by the 91st Brigade, while the 20th and 22nd took turns in the Bullecourt sector, consisted of part of the Hindenburg Line itself; on the right the outpost line held by the British ran North of Bullecourt and corresponded roughly on the right to the position captured by the Queen's on May 12th. In fine weather the spire of Douai Cathedral could be seen some 12 miles away to the N.E. It was possible in this part of the line to systematize things and save much trouble thereby. The artillery, for instance, were able to construct by the side of each gun-pit one tunnelled dug-out for the shelter of the gun detachment and another for the storage of 100 rounds, so that the guns always had a good supply ready for emergencies. Usually each battery had one section forward at a time, the two guns being shifted from one gun-pit to another in a position prepared for a whole battery, the other sections being in reserve some way back but ready to come forward at short notice. There was plenty of ammunition available : the daily ration was 60 rounds per 18-pounder and 50 per howitzer, and though a quarter of this was usually put aside there was enough to do plenty of wire-cutting and to engage any targets that offered. The orders were that all movement was to be engaged : " the killing of Germans is of paramount importance," and with no reason to stint ammunition much could be done. Indeed, the guns almost sniped individuals at times and could be always on the alert, with the result that they did a good deal of damage.

A new feature of the situation was the German habit of holding their line by means of concreted machine-gun emplacements, proof against anything but a direct hit from a fairly heavy gun and very difficult to tackle. These " pill-boxes," which were to figure so largely in the fighting of the late summer at Ypres, were at first known by the German name of " Mebus," formed from the initials of the German words describing them. " Mebus " was rather a puzzler to the British rank and file, in whose language the word assumed various forms, ranging from " Mebis " and " Magus " to " Mimbus," the plural varying from " Mebi " to " Mebontes " in situation reports. Several of these were included in the British line between Bulle-court and Croisilles, here a captured portion of the Hinden-burg Line, while others in No Man's Land were held as advanced posts. These occasionally changed hands ; one, for example, which the Queen's were holding was rushed by the Germans on the night of July 13th, though the garrison, who had got outside the " Mebus " to avoid the shelling, established a post a little farther back and prevented the Germans, who had several casualties, from obtaining any identifications.

Opposite the Seventh Division the enemy had relapsed into passivity, except for occasional outbursts from his artillery, and intermittent activity in the air, but it was essential to detain as many Germans as possible on the less active parts of the front. Orders had therefore been issued by the higher authorities that an active policy should be adopted, the enemy being harassed in every possible way, by bombardment, by vigorous patrolling, by raiding, and by sniping, though raiding was not to be

started until the defences had been put into a more satisfactory state than that in which the Division found them.

Raids provided the chief incidents of the Division's stay
on the Croisilles–Bullecourt front.   The first were carried
out on the night of July 14th, the South Staffords on the
left brigade's front and the Gordons on the right sector
being employed.   The South Staffords were attacking
three separate points, on the right a " Mebus " and a trench
behind it, in the centre another trench, on the left a second
" Mebus."   Each was attacked by a platoon, while two
sections took post in a sunken road as a covering party.
Unluckily the enemy were on the alert, opening fire directly
the raiders advanced and putting up a vigorous resistance.
On the left one man actually got on top of the " Mebus,"
and his effective bombing from this position let the rest
of the platoon get past the " Mebus," though sunken wire
in shell-holes in front prevented them entering the sap
behind.   In the centre one officer and one man alone got
in, but after bombing the enemy for some time had to fall
back, while the right platoon also failed to effect an
entrance, though it put a machine-gun out of action and
beat off an attempt to outflank it.   The total casualties
were over 20, but all the dead were brought back, so that
the Germans obtained no identifications, and there was
reason to think that the German losses had been high, for
apart from the bombing fights they must have suffered
severely from the accurate shooting our Stokes mortars
were observed to be making.

The Gordons, who were raiding Bovis Trench, North
of Bullecourt, with three platoons, each made up to one
officer and 29 men, were accompanied by a small party
of the 95th Field Company to carry out demolitions ; these
last being—possibly for the only time in the history of the
R.E.—attired in kilts.   Their objectives lay N.E. of
Bullecourt Church, on either side of a sunken road.
One platoon attacked on each side, the third being in
support.   The attack was most successful, though on the

left uncut wire delayed the entrance and the platoon was attacked by a party which came down the trench from the West and was only beaten off after a sharp fight. The posts were rushed, and a dug-out in which most of the garrison seemed to have taken refuge was effectively bombed by the Sappers, their kilts notwithstanding. Four charges of gun-cotton, each of 25 lb., were put down, and from the explosions and the fire which followed it was surmised that the dug-out had served as a bomb-store. After a hectic 15 minutes in the hostile trenches the party returned, bringing in one prisoner and all its wounded, of whom it had 18, without leaving anyone behind.

A week later the H.A.C. and Welch Fusiliers carried out raids. The H.A.C. on the right attempted to surprise a " Mebus " in No Man's Land just East of Bullecourt : two parties were to creep out and establish themselves on the flanks of the " Mebus," ready to intercept the garrison's retreat when a third party rushed the post. Unluckily the signal which the raiders were expecting was never given and the garrison apparently detected the flankers, and, thinking it prudent to escape, did so under cover of the long grass and thistles with which the much-broken ground was carpeted. When the attackers finally rushed the post there was nothing to be done but to blow up the " Mebus " and get back, fortunately without any casualties.

The Welch Fusiliers, whose quarry lay just West of the road leading past the Crucifix, also found the posts evacuated, so pushed on down the road towards Bovis Trench. They were just placing four Bangalore torpedoes in the wire, here 3 feet high and 20 deep, when the Germans detected them and opened fire. Simultaneously our guns opened on Bovis Trench, and after a sharp exchange of rifle fire and bombs with the trench garrison the raiders fell back, destroying the posts, which it was not considered worth while to hold, and bombing the dug-outs. Their casualties had been slight, 1 man killed, an officer and 5 men wounded ; and even if the dug-outs had not been occupied, as they were believed to be, at least equal losses had apparently been inflicted in the bombing fights.

Apart from these raids there were few incidents of note. The Germans made a few small raids; the 20th Manchesters, for example, on the left of the right sub-sector beat off a party armed with revolvers only on July 25th.   There were several patrol encounters in No Man's Land, in one of which the South Staffords inflicted several casualties and captured a prisoner, getting a useful identification.   The artillery devoted a good deal of attention to systematic " harassing fire," keeping communication trenches and other lines of approach under fire at night to catch reliefs, ration-parties, and carrying-parties bringing up materials to the front line. But they also indulged in occasional bombardments on a more extensive scale.   On July 26th, for example, the Division's guns bombarded the enemy's positions freely with gas shell and repeated the dose with good effect, to judge by many stretchers in use immediately afterwards.   But the situation is best summed up by an officer who wrote, " We are having quite a quiet time still.   I imagine the Boche has his hands full (and soon I hope up in increasing quantities) further North."   Casualties naturally were not heavy, indeed the whole Division had under 600, four-fifths of them wounded, for June, July, and August. Sickness was responsible for more wastage, though the weather was fairly fine.   Conditions in the line were as sanitary as possible considering the number of unburied and half-buried dead about, which in hot and thundery weather, of which there was plenty, made the trenches very unpleasant.   Much was done to improve matters in this respect as well as to make the line more defensible. It proved possible by using solidified paraffin to do a good deal of cooking in the front line without attracting the enemy's attention, and by this time the arrangements in the back areas for resting and refreshing the troops had been very much reduced to a system.   On one point certainly the Division was agreed, its " Q " Staff was at this period extraordinarily efficient : the arrangements for the comfort and well-being of the troops were quite a pattern to the Army and the difference which that made to the efficiency of the fighting units is hard to overstate. The men knew they were being well looked after and were happy and in good spirits in consequence. Canteens and facilities for recreation were provided, and the comparative quiet allowed of a good allotment of leave. When units were out of the line they got none too much rest, for apart from fatigues training kept them busy. A company of the Queen's, for example, had to go through special training to give a demonstration of the principles of fire and movement, run by General Pelly for the benefit of a Division which had recently arrived in France though far from new to the war, while the manifold Divisional and brigade competitions were useful in stimulating keenness and efficiency ; and the constant flow of officers to and from Army Schools helped to keep the standard up. Moreover a long spell of more or less normal work, such as the Division had now settled down to, allowed of the establishment of close and cordial co-operation between the different arms. Infantry, gunners, and R.E. got the chance to know each other well and work together in a way which was to prove most beneficial in the harder times in store for the Division.

In these periods of relative quiet the war almost seemed an established thing of quite unlimited possibilities of duration. There was no change in the situation on the Division's front, and no prospect of change. In the outlook of men and of the average regimental officer the prospects of leave were perhaps the most prominent feature, but as the summer wore on and the end of July saw the great offensive opened at Ypres it soon became apparent that the Division's inactivity would not be much prolonged, and that before long it would be finding its way to the main scene of activities in Flanders.

It was actually on August 10th that the infantry and

R.E. of the Division bade farewell to Bullecourt and
moved back to the Adinfer area for refitting and intensive
training : the artillery as usual got left in the line for
another fortnight. This was a splendid area for training ;
there was a battle-field complete with wire, trenches, No
Man's Land and everything, prepared with characteristic
German thoroughness, which the enemy had left intact
when they retired, and the care they had lavished on it
was much appreciated as it saved the troops the labour
of constructing practice trenches. The orders were that
refitting was to be finished by the end of the month, after
which there was little doubt that the Division would find
itself on its way to Flanders, an area very few of its numbers
had visited—at any rate not in its ranks. Shortly before
the Division left the line it had lost the heads of its
"Q" Staff; Colonel Wingfield went to the Second Army as
A.Q.M.G. on July 24th, while Major Riddell-Webster had
been transferred to the Forty-First Division as A.A. &
Q.M.G. a fortnight earlier. Except for Generals Steele and
Stanley Clarke, Colonel Wingfield had been longer with
the Division than any other of its senior officers and he
was much missed. The very high standard of excellence
to which the Division's administration work had attained
was in no small measure due to him : he had made things
run smoothly and efficiently and his promotion was well
deserved. His place was taken by Lieut.-Colonel Lang
of the Argyll and Sutherland Highlanders, while Major
Chichester of the Irish Guards succeeded Major Riddell-
Webster. A little before this Major Gepp had gone to
the Third Army as G.S.O. II, being replaced by Major
Boyd of the Queen's, and Captain Noble left the Division
early in August, being succeeded as G.S.O. III by Captain
Brooks of the 21st Manchesters. Captain Noble had been
with the Division from the start, having landed with it as
A.D.C. to General Capper, and his departure severed a
link with the Division's early days. He was about the
last member of the " North Pole Horse," as the original

Divisional cavalry regiment was familiarly known, still serving with the Division.[1]

There was much that was novel in the training through which the Division was now being put. Special attention was paid to musketry, an effort being made to work up to a 12 aimed rounds a minute standard, the men being taught to look upon the rifle and bayonet as their principal weapons and to regard the bomb and the rifle grenade as supplementary. Firing from the hip while advancing was also practised, more with the idea of keeping down the enemy's rifle fire during an advance than in the hope of inflicting casualties. Special importance was attached to the co-ordination of the different weapons in attacks on isolated strong points or on snipers and machine-guns in shell-holes. The progress of the offensive at Ypres was making it clear that the Germans were adopting new methods of defence. German orders had been captured which laid down the new principles, inculcating less rigid methods and in particular the abandonment of formal trench-lines in favour of nests of shell-holes linked up by tunnels and covered by wire which, though practically continuous, was to be irregular in trace so as to make the attackers change direction and come under enfilade fire. Deep dug-outs in the first and second lines were to be abandoned as having proved mere man-traps, reserves were now to be posted some little way behind, taking advantage of any facilities for concealment like woods or ravines. Indeed most of the defending infantry was to be kept out of the forward zone, the defence of which was mainly entrusted to machine-guns at irregular intervals, usually either in " pill-boxes " or in shell-holes. There would be a continuous support line, but sited a mile or so back behind the zone of fortified shell-holes.

---

[1] During this period of rest a section of the 54th Field Company was sent back to the Somme area to erect Memorial Crosses at Mametz and Bazentin le Petit : these unfortunately were destroyed in 1918 when the old Somme battle-field again became the scene of heavy fighting.

There was plenty therefore for the Division to study in the period of training, which did not end with its move to Flanders ; indeed the last day of September came before any of its infantry went into the line, though the Field Companies and Pioneers were sent up to the forward area to work on the roads some time before the infantry followed. Divisional Headquarters were first established at Reninghelst, then moved to Hazebrouck on September 3rd, shifted to Wizernes S. by W. of St. Omer on the 16th, when the Division moved to the Tilques training area, and then began to draw nearer the front. On the 28th they were established at Westoutre, and at Château Segard on the 30th. The troops had meanwhile had no lack of variety to complain of in regard to billets ; for the most part they found themselves in good quarters, being in a district untouched by war and very different from the ruined or badly damaged villages of the Somme area. There was much rain—whenever the Division was under canvas it invariably poured—but on the whole September passed pleasantly enough, and the Wizernes area provided an admirable training ground for the more open warfare which it was hoped the Division would experience in its next engagement. At last drafts began to appear in substantial numbers ; in August and September the 20th Brigade got over 40 officers and 1,200 " other ranks," the 91st had received 900 reinforcements before leaving for Flanders and got another 300 in September. These drafts were above the recent average in quality and physique, being largely drawn from " Second Lines " of Yeomanry and from Territorial Cyclist battalions which were now being broken up, and in some cases from those Second Line Territorial Divisions, the Sixty-Seventh (Home Counties) for example, which had remained in the United Kingdom. The result was that by October 1st the average of the infantry battalions had risen—on paper—to 40 officers and 960 other ranks, though the discrepancy between paper strength and effective strength showed no tendency to diminish.

The chief episode of September was a most successful
and enjoyable Divisional Horse Show, one of the rare
occasions when the whole Division met and fraternized
more or less as a unit, while on the 13th the Welch Fusiliers
and 22nd Manchesters had to be sent off hurriedly to
Etaples to quell a disturbance at the Base depot there—
a troublesome duty which detained them nearly a week
but was effectually accomplished.   There was another
change in the Divisional Staff, Major Hunter leaving for
a post in England on the 3rd, and being replaced as
D.A.Q.M.G. by Major Vyvyan of the A.S.C.   The Queen's
also lost Colonel Longbourne, promoted to command the
171st Brigade—it was the usual fate of battalions which
had specially efficient C.O.s to lose them by promotion if
they were not casualties.   About the same time Major
Burt was promoted from second in command of the South
Staffords to command the Royal Warwickshires, and
Captain Acland left for the Staff College course, Major
Carlton of the Royal Scots officiating for him as Brigade
Major of the 20th Brigade.

All this time the Division had been following as best
it could the progress of the great battle into which it was
soon to be plunged : it was as difficult for troops " out
of the line " to do this as for people at home, possibly
even more difficult, and rumour was perhaps the source
to which much of its information had to be traced.   September had brought with it some improvement in the
weather, particularly in the latter half of the month, and
with the diminution of the excessive rainfall and the
consequent drying of the ground more progress was made.
In the attack of September 20th substantial gains were
recorded on the main ridge, including the woods, or places
where there had once been woods, known as Shrewsbury
Forest and Nonne Boschen Wood, and the Western part
of Polygon Wood, with many fortified farms.   Six days
later another attack carried the line forward again, securing the rest of Polygon Wood and the ruins of Zonnebeke.

Indeed, when the Seventh Division moved up to the fighting-line, the situation looked more promising than it had at almost any moment since the great downpour which had ushered August in had robbed the Allies of most of the fruits of the success achieved in the opening stroke of the battle on July 31st.

CHAPTER XX

THE line which the 22nd Brigade took over from the Australians ran over ground already closely associated with the Seventh Division, even if few of those still with it in October 1917 had helped to make history at Polygon Wood [2] three years earlier. It was only a fraction of its 1914 line that the Division now took over, roughly the Northern portion of the Eastern edge of what in 1914 had been Polygon Wood but now in 1917 had only a few stumps sticking out from its swampy and muddy surface to suggest that it had once deserved its name. The position ran about 400 yards behind the line defended by the Wiltshires in 1914 but did not extend as far South as Reutel, while on the left the Australians were holding the frontage which the 22nd Brigade had covered in October 1914.

The Ypres Salient had changed considerably for the worse since the Seventh Division had last seen it. When the survivors of the original Division had finally withdrawn to rest the woods in the Salient had already shown the marks of shell fire, branches had been knocked off freely, here and there trunks had been split or broken off, but they were still woods. The roads even then had been badly knocked about, the Germans having already realized that by keeping them under fire they might prevent the

[1] Cf. Maps 4 and 30.

[2] Statistics are not available to show the number of those present at this time who had been serving in the Division in 1914: though they are given in the A. and Q. Diary for November 8th, on which day the Division was reviewed by the King of the Belgians (cf. p. 434).

POLDERHOEK CHÂTEAU BEFORE THE WAR.

OCTOBER 1917.

arrival of ammunition, rations, and other supplies, and
hamper the movement of troops and the evacuation of
the wounded.   But only the main roads had suffered
much in 1914 and wheeled traffic alone had found it difficult to move off the roads.   The farms and villages in the
Salient had been showing signs of damage in November
1914 ; in October 1917 there was hardly a building
between Ypres and Gheluvelt which could be recognized
as having once been a house.   The Seventh were familiar
enough with devastated areas, but there was something
peculiarly forbidding and depressing about the Salient in
the later stages of " Third Ypres."   There was a combination of the devastation of the Somme uplands with the
mud of the Lys valley that only the Ypres Salient in the
abnormally wet autumn of 1917 could achieve.   In no
place was the " high ground " more than a slight elevation.
Even from the top of the ridge near " Clapham Junction "
there was not enough fall to drain the water away with
any rapidity, so that swamps and pools even on the high
ground were not unnatural in a season of persistent and
torrential rain.   But the bombardments had .torn the
country about, had blocked up streams and ditches with
debris, causing obstructions and impeding such natural
drainage as existed.   What in ordinary times would have
been streams a few feet wide and a few inches deep had
expanded into wide morasses, partly water, partly mud
of uncertain depth.   The ground had gradually been
churned up by the bursting shells into a monotonous
expanse of oozy mud, over which even on the drier days
movement was extremely difficult.   In many places to
quit the duck-board tracks which the R.E. had laid down,[1]
and which they laboured unceasingly to keep in repair,
was to invite death by suffocation —it could hardly be
called " drowning "—in the mud ; yet to keep to these

---

[1] There had been no tracks available in this sector when the Division took
over and the work to be got through was tremendous, the plank roads having
to be doubled over bogs and other specially bad places.

tracks, most of them marked down by the German aviators and accurately recorded on their maps, was to risk being caught in the barrages which from time to time crashed down on the only routes by which troops could move. Except for the numerous "pill-boxes," for occasional rises in the ground, mounds or heaps of debris which indicated the sites of former dwellings, and for clumps of shattered tree-trunks where tall trees had stood in 1914, the ground was featureless ; and it was uncommonly difficult to identify one's position, let alone one's objective or to keep direction.

The 22nd Brigade occupied the front line with two battalions, the Welch Fusiliers on the right in Jetty Trench, the 20th Manchesters continuing the line Northward in front of Jubilee Trench ; the Royal Warwickshires were in support at Hooge, the H.A.C. back in reserve near Zillebeke, and General Steele's headquarters at Hooge Crater. The Divisional Artillery moved into position on the nights of October 1st and 2nd.

The front line represented the result of the successful attack of September 26th. This had apparently just anticipated a strong German counter-attack and had provoked a series of desperate German efforts to recover that day's losses. The fighting had been extremely stubborn, but though here and there advanced British posts had been driven in, the net result had been a severe German defeat with many thousands of casualties.

Naturally there had been little opportunity for consolidating, and the 22nd Brigade found its new line anything but good, nor had it had time to improve it before, about 5 a.m. on October 1st, a tremendous barrage was put down and maintained with great fury for over an hour.[1] Luckily the mud reduced the effect of the shell-bursts by smothering the projectiles, but casualties

---

[1] Parties of R.E. who were bringing forward stores by pack-animals to form an advanced R.E. dump at the Butte in Polygon Wood were caught by this bombardment and had many casualties.

were numerous and the strain on the defenders very great.
Then, about 6.15 thick waves of infantry began swarming
forward, pressing hardest against the Welch Fusiliers.
With such determination and vigour was the attack pressed
that, despite the Fusiliers' heavy rifle fire, some of the
leading wave actually reached the British line, only to be
wiped out without really effecting a lodgment.   The
succeeding waves achieved even less.   An accurate British
barrage crashed down on them, and the wiping out of the
first wave was followed by the turning on to them of the
rifles and machine-guns which had destroyed the leading
line.   They faltered and went back, their retreat being not
a little accelerated by a dashing counter-attack by the
Welch Fusiliers' right company, which drove the Germans
into the thickest of our barrage and captured some
prisoners.   But this repulse did not finish the Germans.
Their shells continued to pelt down and to cover repeated
efforts to advance.   But every time the British guns
brought their barrage down accurately and helped the
infantry to repulse the advance.   The infantry were kept
busy.   Between 9 and 10 an urgent request for ammunition
reached Brigade Headquarters, whereupon General Steele
sent a company of the Royal Warwickshires forward with 80
boxes of ammunition.   This company had to face the barrage which the Germans were maintaining for some depth
behind the front and support lines, but went through it
unflinchingly, though with many casualties.   Its arrival
was very welcome, for the Welch Fusiliers were beginning
to run short and had lost so heavily that Colonel Holmes
used this company to fill the gaps in his line.   All day the
struggle continued, the German guns pounding away and
their infantry repeatedly trying to advance.   Communication between the front line and the authorities in rear was
generally interrupted : all telephone lines were cut, a
power buzzer was put out of action, whilst most runners
became casualties.   But the watchful gunners never
failed to see the S.O.S. signal and answer it promptly and

accurately ; and as the day waned into afternoon the
pressure relaxed. Another company of the Royal Warwickshires brought more ammunition about 4 p.m. and
was for a time retained by Colonel Holmes, but the situation had so much improved that before midnight he could
send it back as no longer needed. There had been two
or three S.O.S. calls after dark, but, as before, directly
the barrage came down the German attacks faded away
and the 22nd Brigade triumphantly retained its line
intact. The Welch Fusiliers, who had borne the brunt
of the fight and whose stubborn defence was very specially
praised by the Divisional Commander, had 131 casualties
in all,[1] while the 20th Manchesters had 4 officers and about
100 men hit. Their casualties included Colonel Turnbull
of the Gordons, who had commanded the battalion since
Bullecourt and was sniped while going round the front
trenches just after the first attack. Great credit was also
due to the artillery, whose shooting had been extraordinarily prompt, accurate, and effective ; and, as afterwards appeared, had gone far to disorganize completely
the plans of the German commander, General von Finckenstein.[2] The attack of October 1st had been intended as
a preliminary to a much bigger stroke fixed for October
3rd ; the units engaged were so knocked about that they
had to be relieved and the big effort to be postponed till
October 4th.[3]

Largely owing, therefore, to the 22nd Brigade's fine
defence on October 1st the British attack on October 4th,
like that of September 26th, just anticipated a big German
effort, for which many troops had been massed, with the
immediate result that the barrage which preceded the
British attack caught the German lines crowded with
men and did tremendous damage. Indeed, when the

---

[1] 2 officers and 41 men killed and missing, 6 officers and 82 men
wounded.

[2] G.O.C. 4th Guard Division.

[3] This was learnt from prisoners taken on October 4th.

British advanced they found the Germans in quite unusual
force but, what was equally unusual, for the most part
so shaken and demoralized that they put up a feeble
resistance and surrendered freely.

Sir Douglas Haig's aim in this attack was to secure the
main line of the ridge East of Zonnebeke on a seven-mile
front from the Menin road to the Ypres–Staden railway.
The Seventh Division was fourth from the right of the
twelve employed in the attack and had as its objective
the ruined hamlet of Noordemdhoek on the Broodseinde–
Becelaere road, just East of which it was to establish itself.
On the Seventh's right the Twenty-First Division was
attacking Reutel, the Fifth and Thirty-Seventh beyond
it carrying on the line across the Menin road, though here
it was not intended to press the attack to the same depth
as in the centre and on the left.   Once the main ridge
was secured the chief effort was to be given a more Northerly direction ; indeed the Tenth Corps, in which the
Seventh Division was now included, was merely trying to
secure much the same line as that taken up by the Division
on October 19th, 1914, along the high ground from the
Broodseinde cross-roads Southward, from which good
observation would be obtained over the Heutebeck
valley, the Keiberg spur, and the lower ground over
which General Capper's men had made their abortive
attack on Menin.

The Seventh Division was employing two brigades in
the attack, the 91st on the right, the 20th on the left.
There were two main objectives, the first a Red Line about
a quarter of a mile short of the Broodseinde–Becelaere
road,[1] the second a Blue Line 600 yards farther on.   Each
brigade was using one battalion only to take the Red Line,
the 8th Devons and the South Staffords being those
detailed.   For the Blue Line the 20th Brigade would put

---

[1] On the right the distance was rather greater, as the road bent away
from the road junction near Noordemdhoek. This Red Line approximately
corresponded to the 1914 front line of the Division.

in the Borders on the right and the Gordons on the left, keeping the 9th Devons in Brigade reserve; the 91st Brigade[1] was using the 22nd Manchesters with the 21st Manchesters as supports and the Queen's as reserve. The forming-up line was marked by a tape 50 yards behind the existing front-line posts in Jubilee Trench; each brigade took about 500 yards of frontage and the assaulting battalions were closed up to a depth of 120 yards, with the supporting battalions 200 yards behind. The barrage was to open 150 yards beyond the front tape and cover the first 200 yards in 8 minutes, then slowing down to 100 yards in 6 minutes. After the capture of the Red Line it was to remain 200 yards in front for an hour and a half, when it would lift again, moving 100 yards in 8 minutes, till the Blue Line should be reached, three hours after "Zero."

The slow pace of the barrage represented accurately enough the difficulties of moving over such ground as confronted the Seventh Division, and it was well that more rapid progress had not been expected, as shortly before "Zero" it began to rain, making the ground extremely slippery and the going very bad. Luckily it had been dry while the troops were moving into their assembly positions, and with just enough light to move by, well-picketed tracks, and a time-table that made ample allowances for contingencies, the assembly had been carried out without a hitch. The German shelling was being mainly directed against the back areas and casualties were not numerous,[2] though several liaison officers of the 20th Brigade were hit and both the Queen's and the 21st

---

[1] On the night of October 1st/2nd the Division had extended to the right, taking over the Southern part of Jetty Trench from the Twenty-First Division.

[2] The 20th and 91st Brigades had each sent one battalion up on the night of October 2nd/3rd to relieve the 22nd Brigade in the front line. Of these the 8th Devons had about 25 casualties going up, and a few more while holding the line next day, when the South Staffords were very severely shelled and had nearly 70 men hit.

Manchesters were heavily shelled. " Zero " was fixed for 6 a.m., but about an hour earlier the Germans started a barrage just between the front line and the supports, which the rear companies of the leading battalions rendered ineffectual by closing up to the front. Then at 6 a.m. the British barrage started and 8th Devons and South Staffords moved forward together, Colonel Worrall of the Devons promptly utilizing part of his second line to fill a gap of 150 yards which had been found to exist between their inner flanks.

The British barrage gave the attacking battalions the greatest possible satisfaction : it was accurate, regular, and most effective, while its slow pace enabled the infantry to keep well up with it. Both battalions had several pill-boxes to tackle, but they were prepared for that ; and while Lewis gunners engaged the pill-boxes in front bombers and riflemen worked round to the rear and rushed them. The Germans were in unusual strength but proved strangely ready to surrender : the 8th Devons took over 200 prisoners without having half that number of casualties ; and the South Staffords, who found a lot of enemy in small pits covered over with brushwood to escape observation from the air, disposed of large numbers with the bayonet. The prisoners came from three different divisions, the 4th Guard and the 19th and 45th Reserve ; and it was elicited from them that the first and last of these had reinforced the 19th, the normal garrison of the line, for a counter-attack which the British had anticipated by ten minutes. The British barrage had therefore descended on an area packed with troops, and the tremendous casualties it had inflicted had taken the heart out of the survivors. The Red Line was thus taken well up to time and at a low cost ; and then, in accordance with the programme, the supporting battalions took up the hunt.

It was 8.10 when the advance to the Blue Line started. As before the barrage was excellent and the troops kept well up to it ; the Gordons indeed were on their objective five minutes before time. The Australians, however, had diverged slightly from their line and in keeping touch with them the Gordons also had got too far to the left, so the Borders found themselves with more than their share of the front to hold, which led to their companies getting split up; but they also had had little difficulty in securing their objective and had suffered little. Thus the 20th Brigade had fared very well—it had done all that was asked of it without calling on its reserve battalion, and could settle down to consolidating its gains with the knowledge that it had inflicted on the enemy far heavier losses than it had suffered. Up to midday the 8th Devons had only lost 120 all told, the Gordons had got off with a mere 70 casualties and the Borders had not many more.

The 91st Brigade had been less fortunate. It quickly became clear that the Twenty-First Division had not kept pace with the Seventh, and that the 91st Brigade's right was not covered. Even in advancing to the Blue Line the South Staffords had been enfiladed from the right, though an officer of the Machine-Gun Company, who was accompanying their rear wave, promptly shifted his two Vickers guns to that flank and engaged the enemy with good effect till the 3rd/4th Queen's, the Twenty-First Division's left battalion, came level and made things secure. When the 22nd Manchesters advanced towards the second objective, their left making for the In der Star Cabaret, where they expected to get touch with the Borders, they came under machine-gun fire from Joiner's Rest and were checked. The 21st Manchesters reinforced them with three companies and helped them to secure the Blue Line, but their casualties were heavier than those of the 20th Brigade, and the position was none too satisfactory as the Twenty-First Division was still behind. The 22nd Brigade, back in reserve near Zillebeke Lake, was therefore warned to hold two battalions in readiness to reinforce; and soon after noon General Shoubridge

ordered the 91st Brigade to form a defensive flank on
the right.

To assist in this the Queen's were ordered forward from
their reserve position near Hooge, but their C.O., Major
Driver, was hit and mortally wounded just as the order
reached him ; his senior company commander was
wounded a few minutes later and there was some delay
before the next senior officer could get the battalion
started. When the Queen's reached the South Staffords'
headquarters Colonel Beaumann placed two companies
along Jolting Houses Road, facing South so as to form
the defensive flank, with another in Jetty Trench and the
fourth back in reserve at the Butte in Polygon Wood.

By this means the 91st Brigade's front had been made
fairly secure before nightfall. Touch had been obtained
with the Twenty-First Division's left West of Reutel ;
strong points were constructed at positions of tactical
importance, the 528th Field Company building two on the
91st Brigade's right to strengthen that exposed point,
Vickers guns were placed to support the defensive flank
and to sweep the Eastern slopes of the ridge ; and meanwhile the South Staffords, working indefatigably, had
put a second line into a good state of defence with a good
field of fire to the Eastward. Similar work was being
done in the 20th Brigade's area by the 8th Devons, who
after " mopping up " systematically—whereby they added
considerably to the bag of prisoners—had started consolidating the Red Line.

October 4th had been among the most successful days
of " Third Ypres." Practically everywhere the objectives
had been reached, over 5,000 prisoners had been taken,
and by Ludendorff's own admission the Germans had
suffered " enormous " casualties. So hard hit indeed
had they been that only on parts of the front could they
launch those vigorous counter-attacks which were an
essential part of their defensive tactics. The Seventh
Division's frontage was not among the points counter-

attacked, though on the evening of October 4th it looked
as if the 91st Brigade's none too strongly held line was
about to be assaulted.   But the absence of counter-attacks
does not imply that the Division had an easy time.   On
the contrary it was after the attack that it suffered most
of its losses.   Its line was subjected throughout the 5th and
6th to a bombardment the intensity of which was unluckily
equalled by its accuracy.   To make matters worse consolidation was much impeded by the rain which rivalled
the bombardment in persistence.   It was impossible to
dig down more than a couple of feet : below that meant
getting into water.   The bringing up of rations, ammunition, and trench stores was greatly impeded by the rain
and mud, and the wounded endured great hardships.
Still it was "not so bad as Bullecourt," as one officer
writes, "there was not the same trouble from snipers,
even in the final positions it was possible to move about
freely without being hit."

The situation on the Division's right was, however,
far from satisfactory.   Accordingly it was arranged that
the Division should take over from the Twenty-First the
frontage opposite Reutel, and that on October 9th when
the British left was tackling Poelcappelle and Houthulst
Forest the 22nd Brigade should try its luck against Reutel.
Before that, however, various readjustments and reliefs
had to be made.   To begin with the 20th Brigade extended
to the right on the night of October 6th/7th, using the
9th Devons to relieve the 91st Brigade.   This was done
without many casualties, though just before the battalion
moved forward, its headquarters at Hooge Crater had
received a direct hit, Colonel Morris and his Adjutant
both being put out of action.   The next night the 22nd
Brigade came up and the 20th Manchesters and Welch
Fusiliers took over the front line, the latter battalion
relieving the 6th Leicesters of the Twenty-first Division
opposite Reutel, while the 7th Leicesters farther to
the right were placed under General Steele's command.

The H.A.C. and Warwickshires were in reserve along with
the 9th Devons.

October 8th passed quietly enough but damply, the
rain—which had been very heavy on the 7th, interfering
seriously with the artillery preparation for the next attack
—continued and the troops in the line had a miserable
time, not to mention the heavy shelling of the forward areas
in which the Germans indulged.   That evening General
Steele brought his headquarters up to the Butte in Polygon
Wood and issued his orders for the attack.   The H.A.C.
and Royal Warwickshires attacked, on right and left
respectively, each having two companies in front and a
third in support, the 9th Devons being available as reserve.
The objective was the Blue Line of October 4th, which if
attained would give good observation down the valleys of
the Reutel and Polygon Becks.

Wet and slippery ground made the assembly unusually
difficult, but the troops managed to get into position in
time for " Zero " at 5.20 a.m. on October 9th and started
well up to time.   Within half an hour green lights along
the line of the objective indicated that it had been taken ;
but it was some time before any accurate or detailed
information came back from the front.   Then the H.A.C.
reported that they had driven the enemy from Reutel,
shooting many down as they made off, and had secured
part of the cemetery East of Reutel but were being held
up short of Juniper Cottage by heavy fire from machine-
guns, and had lost heavily, especially in officers.   Next
it became clear that there was a gap in the Royal Warwickshires' line near Judge Copse, from which a considerable fire was being maintained.   A platoon of the reserve
company tried to clear Judge Copse, but without success.
A company of the 9th Devons was then sent forward,
which obtained touch with the left party of the Royal
Warwickshires, N.E. of the Copse ; but not till dusk was
the position finally made good by another company of the
9th Devons, who attacked Judge Copse from the S.E. and

cleared it, thereby completing the capture of the Blue Line.

During the night there was heavy shelling, but the expected counter-attack never took shape and the survivors of the attacking battalions—both had lost heavily, the H.A.C. having 16 officers hit—could begin consolidating. All through October 10th the German bombardment persisted, causing many casualties, though again no counter-attack attempted to recover their lost ground. However, relief was at hand. At 4.30 p.m. troops of the Twenty-Third Division began to appear to relieve the 22nd Brigade, and at noon on the 11th General Shoubridge handed over command and could move his headquarters back to the comparative comfort and civilization of Berthen. As usual the artillery did not share in the relief, and this time the R.E. and Pioneers, though greatly in need of rest, were also retained in the forward area,[1] where keeping roads and duck-board tracks in some approach to repair was almost the most urgent problem, not that there were not many of great perplexity.

The infantry had certainly earned a rest. If their original success had been cheaply achieved the Germans had taken a heavy toll of them since, and all twelve battalions were sadly depleted. The Queen's alone had less than 200 casualties, and their losses, 8 officers and 174 men, could hardly be called light. The 22nd Brigade with a loss of 57 officers and 1,256 men since October 1st had been hardest hit, but the repulse of the German attack on October 1st had accounted for many of these casualties, and really there was little to choose between their figures and the 56 officers and 1,039 men of the 20th Brigade and the 45 officers and 1,028 men of the 91st. The R.F.A. too had lost heavily. The German counter-battery work had now been made systematic ; and with 9 officers and 200 men in the casualty list the gunners' contribution was

---

[1] Between October 4th and October 18th the R.E. and Pioneers had another 80 casualties to add to the 131 sustained up to that date.

heavier than in almost any other of the Division's battles.
Fortunately the "missing" were below the average.
Practically all the ground covered had been retained and
nearly all the wounded had been reached and taken to
hospital. Killed and missing between them came to 51
officers and 1,032 men; the wounded were nearer thrice

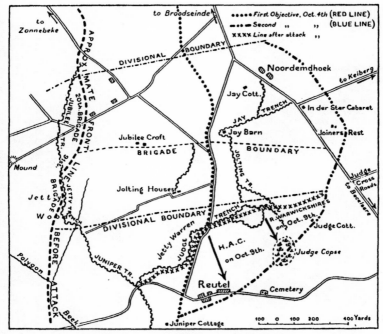

MAP 30.—THIRD YPRES: NOORDEMDHOEK.

than twice that total with 122 officers and 2,672 men. It
was satisfactory also that the Division had not lost many
senior officers : Colonel Turnbull and Majors Driver and
Kemp [1] of the 20th Manchesters were the only commanding officers killed, while Colonel Morris was among the
wounded. The Division had been well up to strength
when the battle began and had been able to leave out

[1] He had succeeded Colonel Turnbull.

a good nucleus of experienced officers and men to assist in
the reconstruction which was now begun.[1]

[1] By units the casualties were:

	Killed.		Missing.		Wounded.	
	Officers.	Men.	Officers.	Men.	Officers.	Men.
R.F.A.	2	38	1	11	6	150
R.E.	—	14	—	1	3	52
8th Devons	4	58	1	11	10	196
9th Devons	3	45	1	14	8	199
Borders	3	37	1	23	12	181
Gordons	3	47	—	25	9	203
R. Warwickshires . . .	6	63	—	84	7	230
R.W.F.	2	49	—	13	12	166
20th Manchesters . . .	3	50	1	28	5	174
H.A.C.	6	42	—	93	10	218
Queen's	1	40	—	25	7	109
S. Staffords	3	30	—	33	9	291
21st Manchesters . . .	5	38	—	11	11	162
22nd Manchesters . . .	1	44	—	28	7	211
24th Manchesters . . .	—	9	—	2	—	50
M.G.C. and Trench-Mortar .	4	21	—	5	6	80
Total .	46	625	5	407	122	2,672

CHAPTER XXI

THIRD YPRES : GHELUVELT [1]

THE infantry of the Seventh Division now entered upon ten days' out of the line and far enough back for fair comfort to be attainable. It rained most of the time, and the troops knew enough of the conditions under which the offensive was being carried on to realize that the persistent rain would make their next attack even more difficult than the last ; but they were in good billets,[2] blankets, which the increasing chilliness of the weather made welcome, had again been issued, and there were fair facilities for football and other forms of recreation, when the rain permitted. Still the prospects of another attack in the mud were not very rosy, and the fact that the drafts which appeared in this rest interval failed to fill the gaps [3] left by the recent fighting did not mend matters. Nor was it easy for regimental officers and men to understand the imperative reasons for continuing the offensive in the face of conditions so absolutely fatal to rapid progress. It was impossible at that time to announce that the French had not yet recovered sufficiently from their set-back in the spring for it to be safe for the British to relax their pressure, lest the Germans should regain the initiative and use it to fall upon the

---

[1] Cf. Maps 7 and 31.

[2] The 20th and 91st Brigades were round Westoutre, the 22nd at Meteren at first and then at Reninghelst.

[3] The Borders, for example, who had lost 14 officers and 250 men, only got 4 officers and 110 men ; the four battalions of the 91st Brigade between them received 25 officers and 580 men to set off against a loss of 39 officers and 960 men. Many of these drafts came from the R.A.M.C. and other departmental units or were Labour Corps men reclassified owing to the adoption of a less rigorous physical standard: their military training was therefore far from perfect.

French. The men in the line could see all the manifold drawbacks to continuing the offensive; they naturally wondered why it should nevertheless be necessary to go on requiring them to attempt the all-but impossible.

Those who continued to be optimistic could extract little encouragement from the conditions that faced them when on the evening of October 24th the 20th and 91st Brigades relieved portions of the Fourteenth and Thirty-Seventh Divisions astride the Menin road West of Gheluvelt.[1] Conditions had been bad enough in Polygon Wood, here they defied description. The ground was even wetter and muddier, to leave the duck-board tracks was even more likely to mean being swallowed up in some bottomless pit of a mud-filled shell-hole, and rapid movement was out of the question. However, the orders were explicit that the Division was to attack on the morning of October 26th, and it only remained to make the best of things and try to extract another success even from these highly unpromising conditions.

The immediate task before the Division was to capture Gheluvelt, or rather the knoll on which Gheluvelt had once stood, and with it to secure the Tower Hamlets ridge East of the Basseville Brook. Success would considerably improve the tactical position on the British right and the attack would, it was hoped, in any case act as an effective diversion. The main Allied attack was being delivered away to the left in a more Northerly direction. To occupy the Germans and prevent them from dispatching reserves to meet this attack was indeed the main purpose of the forlorn hope which the Seventh Division and the Fifth on its left were attempting; and in view of this major purpose the Divisional Commander could only refrain from protesting to the higher authorities that under the existing conditions success was impossible.

[1] The gun positions were about in the level of Glencorse Wood, where the XXIInd Brigade R.F.A. was in action. As usual several extra artillery brigades were under the command of the Division's C.R.A.

The attack was entrusted to the 20th and 91st Brigades : the 91st on the right was putting in three battalions, the South Staffords, 21st Manchesters, and Queen's, from right to left; the 20th on the left had the Borders South of the Menin road and the 9th Devons North of it. In the 91st Brigade the centre and left battalions after capturing the first objective or Red Line, which ran roughly from S.W. to N.E. through the Western end of Gheluvelt, were to push forward their supporting companies to a Blue Line which skirted the Southern and Eastern edges of the village and ran North towards Gheluvelt Château. To its left the capture of the Blue Line would be the work of the Gordons on the right and the 8th Devons on the left. The 22nd Brigade provided the brigade reserves, the Welch Fusiliers supporting the 20th Brigade, the 20th Manchesters being at the disposal of the 91st.

Artillery support was provided by 144 18-pounders, 48 4·5-inch howitzers, 32 medium amd 20 heavy howitzers, a weight of metal which ought to have been adequate. The barrage was to begin 150 yards ahead of the forming-up line, which was slightly in rear of the front line of posts which the Division was holding. It was to remain on this line four minutes, then do two lifts of 100 yards six minutes apart, two more at an eight-minute interval, then one after another twelve ; by which time, three-quarters of an hour after " Zero," it was hoped the infantry would have covered the 600 yards of mud which separated them from the Red Line.

A momentary break in the rain on the day after the Division had gone into the line did something to raise hopes of success, especially as it was accompanied by a strongish wind to dry the sodden ground, and a fine moonlight night seemed to promise a day without rain, though it made the withdrawal to the taped line more difficult and gave the German snipers chances. Indeed between the latter and the shelling the 91st Brigade had four company commanders hit before the attack started.

None of the ground to be traversed could be described
as dry, but parts were drier than others, while elsewhere
progress was not merely difficult, but impossible.   North of
the Menin road the going was relatively good and just South
of it there was a narrow belt of drier ground.   This unfortunately was so swept by machine-guns in some pill-boxes,
notably a group near the 7th kilometre mark, that its use
was virtually denied to the attackers.   Farther to the
right the ground sloped fairly sharp down from the Tower
Hamlets ridge into the depression S.W. of Gheluvelt
drained by the Western branch of the Kroomebeck, and
here the right of the Borders ¦and most of the 91st
Brigade had to descend into an absolute morass, practically
impassable for men equipped for fighting and retaining
a position.   The Seventh Division had met plenty of
mud in its time : those who had endured the winter of
1916–1917 on the Beaumont Hamel spur had not much
to learn about the " fifth element," but the Ypres Salient
in October 1917 opened even their eyes.   There a slimy
chalk had become something like a mixture of treacle and
glue ; here the lighter soil, if not so glutinous, became a
morass in which men sank up to their waists and might
even be swallowed completely, a fate which undoubtedly
befell some of the " wounded and missing."   But the worst
feature of the tactical situation was that the mud added so
enormously to the efficacy of the pill-box in defence.   On
ground dry enough to admit of rapid movement the pill-
box was not impregnable.   It had been shown several
times, by the Seventh Division itself on October 4th, that
if a pill-box were kept under heavy fire from rifles and
Lewis guns it might be tackled from the rear by rushing
round its flanks.   But when rapidity was out of the
question even for the most lightly equipped, the pill-box
could not be dealt with in this way ; and if the attacking
infantry fell the least bit behind the barrage the pill-boxes
would prove far tougher nuts to crack than on October 4th.

The attack started with the first faint glimmer of light.

Promptly the German barrage came down, though it mostly fell behind the attacking battalions; the 8th Devons, for example, had closed up towards the front and practically escaped the barrage. On the 91st Brigade's right the South Staffords at first fared quite well. Shielded by the ground from most of the machine-guns, their right company, " B," reached its objective—a strongly held mound S.W. of Hamp Farm. A savage fight followed, the company's two officers were killed and all the senior N.-C.-O.s, but the men stuck to their task and in the end the survivors, commanded by a corporal, found themselves in possession of the mound. They had taken a machine-gun and had inflicted heavy casualties on the Germans, but they were rather isolated; " D " Company on their left, which was attacking Hamp Farm, had been mown down wholesale by a cross-fire of machine-guns, while the left company, " C," when within 50 yards of its objective, Berry Cotts, had caught the stream of machine-gun bullets from the flank and its few survivors were sheltering in shell-holes and waiting for a chance of getting back.

The other two attacking battalions of the 91st Brigade fared even worse. The defensive flank which it was the South Staffords' task to establish ran more or less over a spur which jutted S.E. from the Tower Hamlets ridge, and the battalions had not had to descend the slope as far as the others. In this quarter the main tactical feature was the group of pill-boxes at Lewis House, from which several machine-guns maintained a heavy fire. Hampered by the worst of the mud, the Queen's soon fell behind the barrage, slow as its pace was, and they could not reach Lewis House. Some of the two battalions on their flanks converged towards Lewis House and there was crowding, loss of direction, and gaps in the line. 2nd Lieut. Howells of " A " Company and Captain Streeter of " D " headed a valiant effort to outflank the obstructing pill-boxes, but without success, and the Queen's were checked. Colonel

Birkett[1] came up to the front and eventually collected some of his men in the original front line, posting a couple of machine-guns in readiness to meet a German counter-attack ; but it was hopeless to try to push on. The 21st Manchesters also had been completely checked approximately at the original front line from which the troops had fallen back to the assembly position.

The check to the 91st Brigade was thus complete, and unfortunately it reacted adversely on the fortunes of the 20th Brigade. The Borders' right company had managed to cross the marshy ground immediately in their front, but directly they dipped down into the Kroomebeck depression they found themselves getting waist deep in the marsh. The company commander, Captain Dempster, was killed, his subaltern was wounded, and the advance came to a halt. A few men drifted across to their right on to the frontage of the Queen's, but the machine-guns at Lewis House, in the pill-boxes near the 7th kilometre mark, and in Swagger Farm behind Berry Cotts accounted for the majority.

" D " Company on the left found the ground ahead of them so impassable that they worked off to the left towards the Menin road. Machine-guns in the pill-boxes near the road knocked out many of them, and the remainder took refuge in a big crater, Captain Moore, the company commander, and his subaltern being both killed. Two platoons of " B " Company then attacked the pill-boxes with no better success, the Lewis House machine-guns helping to repulse them ; but Captain Little then brought " A " Company up and actually managed to take one pill-box though the other three defied capture. However, Captain Little, leaving " A " to deal with the pill-boxes, pushed on towards Gheluvelt with the survivors of " B " and " D " and some stray Devons. This party actually got within 100 yards of Gheluvelt Church, captured a dozen prisoners and established themselves about the

[1] He had arrived to take command on October 7th.

Western end of the village, where they hung on, hoping for reinforcements.

Reinforcements for the Borders should have come from the Gordons, but that battalion had been raked by machine-guns from Lewis House and Swagger Farm directly it passed the old front line and its attack was soon broken up. Some of its right company swerved to the right and joined the Queen's opposite Lewis House, others crossed the Menin road to avoid the machine-guns and followed the Devons into Gheluvelt, one platoon reached the big crater on the Menin road but was cut to pieces in trying to capture the pill-boxes near by. Another party was collected just to the left of the road, not far from Captain Little's party of the Borders, but the Gordons' casualties had been so heavy that they could carry the attack no farther.

North of the road the two Devon battalions had achieved a certain measure of success. The 9th, which was leading, kept up fairly well with the barrage, and though losing heavily under the machine-gun fire from South of the road it pushed on quite successfully, capturing nearly 20 prisoners. Its right came to a halt about where the light railway leaves the Menin road, but one party established itself in the railway cutting N.W. of Gheluvelt Church and others got well into the village.

Mixed up with the 9th Devons was its sister battalion. The 8th also had many casualties from the enfilade machine-gun fire across the road, but it had pressed on and, overtaking the 9th, entered Gheluvelt with it. Some of the left company strayed off outside the Division's frontage, but one party cleared several pill-boxes on the line of Johnson Trench and penetrated almost to Gheluvelt Church, and another actually got near enough to Gheluvelt Château to try to rush it. Altogether quite a number of both battalions reached the village, though in scattered parties. Indeed they might have retained their gains but that the mud which had checked the 91st Brigade had crippled them hardly less effectually. It had got into rifles and Lewis guns, and of those men who reached the village few arrived with weapons in working order. Accordingly when, about 10 o'clock, the Germans started counter-attacking, it was very hard to offer effective resistance. Captain Little's party of the Borders, for example, saw nearly 100 Germans come out of the church and move across their front to the left; had their rifles been in action they would have wiped this party out, but hardly a man had a rifle which could be fired and the Devons were in little better case.

Before long therefore those who had reached Gheluvelt found themselves compelled to fall back. Some seem to have been pushed back on to the 13th Brigade's frontage, for about 11.15 the C.O. of the 1st Royal West Kent, the right battalion of the Fifth Division, reported that stragglers of all units of the 20th Brigade were coming back towards his headquarters in Jackson Trench, where he was rallying them. Others fell back to the light railway where Captain Pridham of the 9th Devons had collected a party and was preparing to make a stand. Some rallied in the crater near the 7th kilometre mark, and Major Kerr collected about 60 of his Borders together with some Queen's and Gordons and formed a defensive flank just South of the Menin road, stretching back towards Tower Hamlets, though a big gap separated his right from the point where Colonel Birkett had collected a fairly strong detachment of the Queen's. Beyond that again the 21st Manchesters and South Staffords had reoccupied the posts which had formed the original front line, though not a single battalion could muster more than a mere fraction of its morning's numbers.[1] An even more serious cause for anxiety was the uselessness of most of the rifles and Lewis guns. Fortunately some reserve

[1] Apart from the mud there had been a certain amount of straggling and dispersion due largely to the inexperience and want of training of the last drafts.

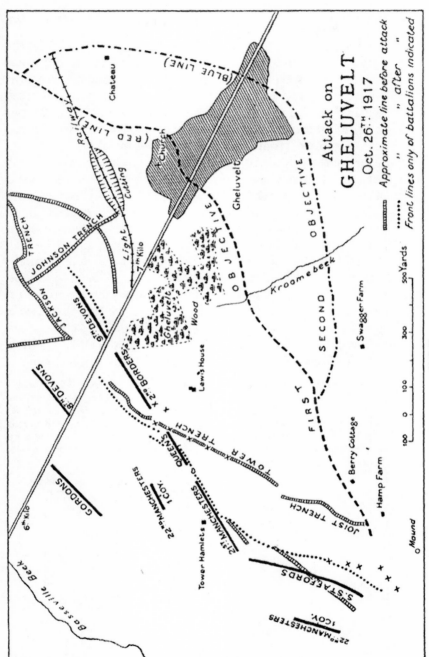

Attack on
GHELUVELT
Oct. 26TH 1917

Approximate line before attack
         "   " after   "

Front lines only of battalions indicated

MAP 31.

machine-guns had been brought up by the Machine-Gun
Companies and placed in readiness to meet the counter-
attack which everyone anticipated. Anticipations, however, were not to be fulfilled. When all units were reported
as back on the original line the artillery were told to put
down a protective barrage, which effectually discouraged
the Germans from risking a counter-attack, though
unfortunately it compelled " B " Company of the South
Staffords to evacuate their mound, which otherwise might
have been retained. Unluckily no news of its capture
had got through : all the runners who had started back
had been hit and the artillery shelled the mound in complete ignorance that it was held by our own men.[1]

Had the Germans tried to counter-attack it is unlikely
that they would have achieved much. Their approach
would not have turned the morass into solid ground and
they could not have hoped to move faster than their
opponents. It was to the mud they owed their retention
of Gheluvelt, and the Seventh Division was fully entitled
to claim that the elements and not the enemy had beaten

[1] The losses in the attack on Gheluvelt came to 110 officers and 2,614 men ;
of these the great majority fell in the 20th and 91st Brigades with 52 officers
and 1,192 men and 39 officers and 918 men respectively, but the R.F.A.
with 10 officers and 156 men came in for its share. The large number of
" missing," the majority of whom must have been killed as only a few were
ever reported prisoners, was a marked feature of the list. The figures for the
20th and 91st Brigades were :

	Killed.		Wounded.		Missing.	
	Officers.	Men.	Officers.	Men.	Officers.	Men.
8th Devons	2	19	9	134	4	105
9th Devons	1	18	5	138	8	118
Borders	5	6	3	173	1	125
Gordons	5	16	3	224	4	86
M.G. Coy.	—	3	2	24	—	3
Queen's	—	20	8	197	2	76
S. Staffords	6	38	1	140	1	92
21st Manchesters . . .	7	17	5	170	1	93
22nd Manchesters . . .	2	7	1	36	—	4
M.G. Coy. and T.M. Battery .	2	5	3	16	—	7
Total	30	149	40	1,252	21	709

it. Many had suspected before they started that what they were being asked to do was impossible : no survivor of the attempt could harbour any doubts on this point. Indeed the Divisional Commander in his letter to the troops after the battle practically admitted as much. He pointed out that the attack, though locally unsuccessful, had caused the Germans to keep back a " railway reserve " near Menin which could otherwise have been put in at the other end of the battle-field, so that the Seventh Division had not fought in vain, but had contributed definitely to the success achieved farther North. General Shoubridge was warm in his acknowledgment of the splendid behaviour of the troops. " They went forward," he wrote, " under the worst conditions of mud and fire and would not give in until they died or stuck in the mud—no soldiers can do more."

With that tribute the Seventh Division may be content. It had failed, but the causes of its failure lay outside its control. Its men had gone into the attack knowing that the chances were all against success : they had attacked as if they had believed the prospects to be all in their favour. Gheluvelt stands out in the Division's story as a day of loss and disaster, but of honourable defeat. It was to be the Division's last fight in France. General Shoubridge had written, " Yesterday's battle will be an incentive to get our own back on the next opportunity." Actually that opportunity was not to come for over a year, and then under different conditions from those under which the Division had fought at Gheluvelt. It was peculiarly appropriate that its last fight in France should have been on ground with which it was already so closely associated.

CHAPTER XXII

THE MOVE TO ITALY [1]

WITH two of its infantry brigades shattered and reduced in their struggle against insuperable disadvantages at Gheluvelt, the Seventh Division was in no condition for a prolonged spell in the front line ; and on October 29th the Thirty-Ninth Division relieved it. Since the attack the line had been held by the 22nd Brigade, which had relieved the survivors of the attacking battalions on the night of October 26th/27th, having the Welch Fusiliers on the left and the H.A.C. and 20th Manchesters on the right. They had been heavily shelled, and German snipers had been troublesome but had given plenty of opportunities for retaliation, though before relief the Welch Fusiliers had another 100 casualties and the H.A.C. over 40.

The area to which the Division now withdrew was round Blaringhem. Much refitting had to be done and many gaps in the ranks to be filled, though at first drafts came in but slowly. On November 8th when the Division was inspected by the King of the Belgians the parade state showed clearly how heavily it had suffered at Gheluvelt. In the 20th Brigade the Gordons mustered 19 officers and 627 men ; the remaining units between them did not amount to a battalion at war establishment. The 91st Brigade averaged under 400 to a battalion,[2] and even the 22nd Brigade barely reached 600. It was of special interest that there were present on parade 15 officers [3] and 948

---

[1] Cf. Map 32.

[2] Allowance must of course be made for details not on parade, " employed men " of all descriptions, and for those at courses and on leave.

[3] The officers were : Colonel Archer, A.D.M.S., Lieut.-Colonels Wright, Wells, and Brown, R.A.M.C., Major Kerr and Capt. & Q.M. Mitchell of the Borders, Major & Q.M. Mackie, Lieut. Brown, 2nd Lieut. Riddler of the Gordons, Major Strevens of the Royal Warwickshires, Major Snape of the South Staffords (2nd in command of H.A.C.), Capt. Gibson of the Queen's, Capt. Cottrill of the Welch Fusiliers, Capt. Appleyard of the Divisional Train, and Capt. Dawson, A.V.S.

other ranks who had landed in Belgium with the Division
in 1914. Of these 181 men belonged to the R.A.M.C.,
and the Divisional Train contributed 240 men, the six
original battalions [1] still present with the Division contributed 412, the R.E. 53 (only one Field Company was on
parade), and the remainder mainly came from Divisional
and Brigade Headquarters. The Divisional Artillery unfortunately were not on parade, or their contribution would
have been fairly substantial. In the infantry there were a
large proportion of returned wounded among these " old
originals," but seeing what the Division had been through,
that its total battle-casualties came to about three times [2]
the original establishment of a Division, and that some
battalions had had to be reconstructed six or seven times,
it was extraordinary that the proportion of surviving " old
originals " was as high.

Shortly after the Blaringhem review the Division received orders to move, and on November 12th Headquarters were transferred to Fauquembergues, the infantry
brigades shifting to villages close around. The wildest
rumours were current as to the Division's prospective
movements. All shrank from a return to the hopelessness
and dreariness of the Ypres Salient, where the struggle
was still dragging on. But a new factor had arisen with
the Austro-German offensive in Italy, the bewildering

---

[1] The figures were: Queen's 79, Royal Warwickshires 78, R.W.F. 47,
South Staffords 48, Borders 77, Gordons 83.

[2] The figures have been recorded and are as follows:

	Officers.	Other Ranks.
Ypres, 1914	346	9,402
Dec. 18th, 1914 . . .	34	694
Neuve Chapelle . . .	137	2,500
Festubert	160	3,933
Givenchy	52	1,402
Loos	218	5,040
The Somme	479	10,752
The Ancre	81	1,750
Arras	213	3,940
Ypres, 1917	297	6,541
Trench Warfare . . .	310	7,207
	2,327	53,161

collapse of the Italians at Caporetto and the consequent
necessity of dispatching British and French troops to stem
the hostile advance into Italy. The Twenty-Third and
Forty-Eighth Divisions were already on their way there
when rumour suddenly crystallized into fact, and on
November 14th the Seventh received orders to follow
suit. Entraining began on the 17th, the 20th Brigade at
Wavrans, the 22nd at Hesdin, the 91st at Anvin ; the
Divisional Artillery, only just that moment withdrawn
from the line, were to begin two days later.[1] The last
unit to entrain was timed for November 20th.

The situation in Italy was critical, so the movement
had to be carried out quickly, and there was no time to
transfer men from specially overcrowded trains to those
of units to which too much accommodation had been
allotted. No one knew what the detraining stations
would be and both halves of an infantry battalion hardly
ever arrived at the same point, while drafts and returning
leave parties usually got to the wrong station, thereby
augmenting the general confusion. But despite a confusion that was perhaps more apparent than real the
journey to Italy was accompanied by remarkably few
hitches. As far as the French frontier at all events, one
battalion noted, things went quite well, hot water could
always be got for washing and making tea, though after
crossing into Italy it was no longer obtainable, while the
trains then fell so much behind the time-table that the
programme as to halts, detraining to give the men exercise,
and so on, could not be adhered to. But if the Italian
railways made no very favourable impression on the
troops the warmth of the welcome they received made
full amends. Crowds flocked to the stations to see the
trains pass, cheered them to the echo, brought presents
of fruit and flowers, and displayed unbounded enthusiasm.
Most trains went by Marseilles and the Riviera, turning
Northward through the Apennines after passing Genoa

[1] The artillery took up 22 trains, the other units 39.

and crossing the plains of Lombardy to Mantua. If it was a long-drawn-out journey—most units were six or seven days on the way—its novelty helped the troops to endure with great cheerfulness the discomfort of their cramped quarters and lack of exercise; after all every mile was taking them farther away from that accursed Ypres Salient which none of them ever wanted to revisit.

The detraining area assigned to the Division was round Legnago. The first train got there on November 22nd, Divisional Headquarters detrained on the 25th, by which time most units were already there, though some belated half-battalions did not appear till after the Division had moved to the N.E. to clear the detraining area for other troops.

The first days in the new theatre of war were full of interest. One brigade, rather to its consternation, found itself issued with Italian rations—macaroni, biscuits, bread, tinned soup, and coffee—which it did not altogether appreciate. It is noted that the horses also found the crushed beans which formed the local issue unattractive and left them unfinished; it is with a sigh of relief that the Brigade Diary remarks two days later " British rations again available." The local beverage, the " Vino Rosso," won more favourable comments; though it soon appeared that it was decidedly more potent than the thin beer and light wines of France, and must be treated with respect. The local transport was another source of interest. Italian roads were not always suited to British motor transport, and while some units got hold of small three-horse wagons to carry blankets and other impediments, others had recourse to bullock carts.

If there was much in Italy for the Seventh Division to view with interest there was no question but that its smart appearance, the neatness of its turnout, the scale and excellence of its equipment, made a profound impression on the peasantry. Things like the mounting and relieving of guards, the beating of drums at Retreat, the playing of the Gordons' pipes, all contributed to surprise and encourage the inhabitants. The Italians were particularly amazed at the cheeriness of the troops, at their laughing and singing on the march ; and though the first marches were a hard trial after a week's train journey, the Division's march discipline stood the test well and stragglers were few and far between. The British troops were something quite different to anything the Italians had seen, and even before they went into the firing-line the mere arrival of the British and French troops in the country had greatly improved the situation.

When General Plumer assumed command of the British forces in Italy, on November 10th, 1917, the Italian retreat had been arrested at the Piave and there seemed some hope that this line might be maintained. As soon as the Twenty-Third and Forty-First Divisions, the first two to arrive, had completed their concentration, they were ordered forward, along with some French troops, to the hills North and South of Vicenza, which provided a good position in case the line along the Piave gave. But the Piave line held, defying the Austrian attempts to pierce it, and at the end of November the British took over a section of it, with the French on their left and the Italian Third Army lower down the river to the right. The "Montello," the actual section assigned to the British, was of special importance as it linked up the Piave line, covering Venice, with the portion of the Italian front which faced North, running from Mt. Tomba to Lake Garda, astride the valleys of the Brenta and the Adige. It stretched from Nervesa on the right to Ciano and was about eight miles in length, and its occupation by the British allowed the Italians to withdraw a substantial force to reinforce the Asiago and Grappa sectors, where the enemy were pressing hard and making constant attacks. The Seventh, the third British Division to reach Italy, did not at first have to go into the line. When the other two Divisions moved forward it was detailed as Corps reserve and followed in support of them. Originally the Seventh should have had the heads of its columns on the Brenta by November 28th, but the relief was postponed and it was November 30th before it crossed the Brenta, its leading troops reaching Loreggia that evening. December 1st saw Divisional Headquarters at S. Leonardo, next day they reached Vedelago about 10 miles West of Treviso, and the Division settled down East and N.E. of Vedelago in what was described as " the reserve Division area." It had to be in readiness to reinforce at short notice any portion of the line—and there were not a few alarms during the heavy fighting of the first half of December ; on the 13th in particular the French left in the Monte Pallone sector was reported to have broken and the 22nd Brigade at Altivola stood to all day but did not have to move. But, apart from this, constructing rear defensive positions gave ample occupation, and every opportunity had to be taken to improve the training of the large drafts which had been poured into the Division just before it left for Italy.[1] The standard of training of these drafts was very low, many had but recently been enlisted, and though the transfers from the R.A.M.C. and other Departmental Corps had been some time in the Army, they had everything to learn about musketry and the work of infantry in the field.

December passed away before the Seventh Division went into the line or before any of its members, except the few officers who went up to reconnoitre the front, came under fire. But it was a busy month and conditions were none too easy. All the elaborately organized rearward services, which by 1917 had made things reasonably comfortable for troops out of the line in France, were in their infancy in Italy. One Diary notes that it was December 13th before the second mail since the Division's arrival

---

[1] The 20th Brigade had received nearly 900 reinforcements in the first half of November, and the 91st obtained 1,400 between October 26th and December 31st, the great majority arriving before the start for Italy.

29

in Italy reached it ; another speaks of the lack of fuel
and consequent difficulty of getting enough hot water to
give the men baths. Snow, too, which the average man
was not accustomed to associate with Italy, fell in some
quantity about the middle of the month, and the weather
was decidedly cold. However, the sick-rate was kept
down to moderate dimensions, and gradually the administrative services got going properly, surprising the Italians
by the comforts and conveniences they provided for the
troops. The strategical situation also improved steadily ;
several Austrian attacks were beaten off and both Italians
and French made successful minor advances.

From a successful advance the British were precluded by
having in their front the Piave, hardly less than half a
mile wide anywhere, running as fast as twelve miles an
hour, constantly varying both in depth and speed, constantly making new channels through its broad and stony
bed, so that a patrol might find a practicable ford one
night where 24 hours earlier it had been impossible to pass.
Running in narrow and shifting channels, separated by
banks of shingle, the river was impossible to navigate, and
to lay even a pontoon bridge across it presented enormous
difficulties.[1] No Man's Land, as the Seventh Division
discovered when it relieved the Forty-First on January
19th, was a real obstacle to contact and a great hindrance
to snipers, machine-gun shoots, trench-mortar bombardments, and similar methods of annoying the enemy, while
raids were virtually impossible. Volunteers were never
wanting to attempt the passage of the Piave, but despite all
the enterprise and energy of these patrols only very occasionally could information be gathered or the enemy harassed.

The Divisional Artillery, which had gone into position
on January 15th, was not quite so handicapped as
the infantry. With the assistance of the R.F.C., who

---

[1] On the right from Nervesa Northward there was a stretch of about 1,000
yards of level ground ; beyond that the cliffs of the Montello rose up nearly
sheer from the river's edge.

were not long in establishing their ascendancy in the
air, it soon got used to the new conditions and did
some most effective shooting whenever it could find
targets.   But as a whole the Division's tenure of the Piave
line was singularly uneventful.   Apart from occasional
artillery activity and a systematic programme of harassing
fire by machine-guns it was impossible to do much damage
to the enemy.   Several attempts were made to cross the
Piave, but were nearly all defeated by the strength of the
current and the icy coldness of the water.   The brigades
did a sixteen-day turn in the line, two at a time, with eight
days in reserve.   The defences needed improvement and
this kept the men in the line busy ; those in reserve were
not less busy in bringing the local sanitary conditions up
to a passable level.   Incidents worth recording in War
Diaries were conspicuous by their absence and casualties
incredibly low : 1 man wounded in the 20th Brigade in
January, 3 killed and 13 with 1 officer wounded in February, would seem incredible if the 91st's figures were not
lower.   It was a great change after France—what had
seemed an easy and inactive time in the Bullecourt sector
in the summer of 1917 was a desperate struggle as compared
with the Piave front in the early months of 1918.

With the end of February came orders for the Division
to be relieved by the Forty-Eighth prior to returning to
France, and on the morning of March 2nd General Shoubridge handed over to General Fanshawe, only the artillery
being still in the line.   The infantry was all in the entraining areas, indeed the 20th Brigade was actually entraining,
when on March 4th came orders from G.H.Q. to stand fast.
The advance billeting parties had already gone, but the
rest of the troops were tumbled out of the train again, and
the Division moved on March 7th into the Montegalda
area S.E. of Vicenza.   Then, about the middle of the month,
it was announced that the move was finally cancelled and
that the Division before returning to the line would undergo
special training in mountain warfare.   The object of this,

though not announced at the time, was to prepare the troops for the work which the summer was to bring them on the Asiago Plateau, which the British actually took over from the Italians at the end of March. As usual the Divisional Artillery were the first to go into the new sector. Relieved from the Montello on March 17th they began relieving an Italian Division on the Asiago Plateau on March 22nd ; and on March 31st, the relief being complete, General Shoubridge took over command at noon. The new sector was the left portion of the Fourteenth Corps' front and extended from a hill 800 yards South-West of Roncalto to just East of Sculazzon.[1]

The cancellation of the move to France was full of important consequences. But for it the Seventh Division would just have been in time for the great " March push " of 1918 and must have spent the spring and summer in desperate contests with the Germans instead of carrying on a " sort of war " with the Austrians. Had it completed its move to France it could hardly have failed to have added many names to its long catalogue of battles and actions, and it was strange that a Division with the Seventh's record should have been stranded in a back-water in the greatest crisis of the war. But it had made history enough already.

[1] On April 1st the Machine-Gun Companies of the Division—a fourth, numbered 228th, had just been added—were formed into the 7th Battalion Machine-Gun Corps under the command of Lt.-Colonel Birkett, transferred from the Queen's.

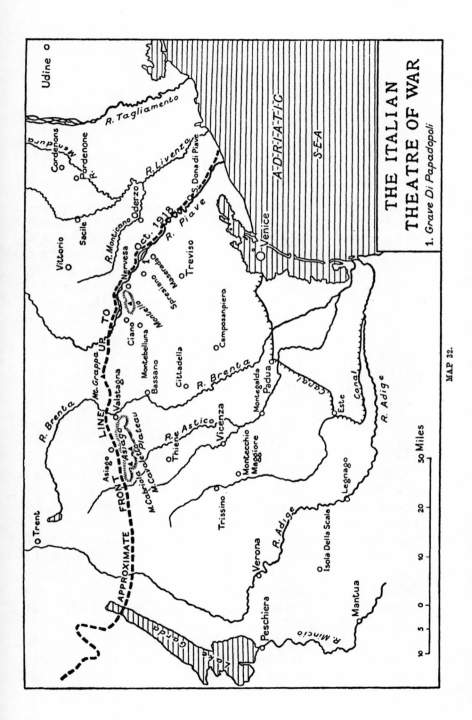

THE ITALIAN
THEATRE OF WAR

1. Grave Di Papadopoli

MAP 32.

CHAPTER XXIII

THE ASIAGO PLATEAU [1]

THE front now entrusted to the Seventh Division was the rocky plateau on the right of the Brenta N.W. of Bassano. This plateau, which here forms the Southern edge of the mountain chain, rises sharply up from the plains to about 4,000 feet above sea-level. It was a stiff climb up, and though the Division had left warm weather at the foot of the plateau, on the top it found itself back in the depth of winter. It was bitterly cold and the ground was covered with snow : sentries had to be relieved every hour. The plateau was fairly thickly wooded, so fuel was obtainable ; but the transport of ammunition, rations, and other stores was a real difficulty. Many of the tracks up the slope were only available in one direction, and where there were passing places careful arrangements were needed to avoid blocks. The R.E. and Pioneers found their hands full with work on these tracks, which were very hard to keep in decent condition. Water was another trouble ; for drinking it had to be pumped up from the plains, the pools on the plateau being only fit for washing and for horses to drink. Accommodation also was both insufficient and bad, and altogether life on the plateau was therefore strenuous and uncomfortable, both for those in front line and for those in support, while in the rocky ground satisfactory defences were hard to construct. There was little soil on the plateau and digging was so difficult that sangars of stones had to be built.

Divisional Headquarters were established at Monte Carriola, the right brigade's headquarters being at Boscon,

[1] Cf. Maps 32 and 33.

those of the left brigade at Monte Lemerle. The troops
had marched from the Montegalda area to Thiene, from
which place motor-lorries took them up to the mountains
where the reserve battalions were accommodated in huts.
The Division had Italians on its left and the Twenty-
Third Division on its right. Two brigades were in line,
the 91st being the occupants of the right sector, the
22nd on the left. From the first an aggressive policy was
pursued ; patrols reconnoitred the enemy's line to find
out spots which might be raided, and the Divisional
Artillery, which had gone into line a full week before
the infantry, was much more active than the Austrian
gunners. On April 7th the Welch Fusiliers inaugurated
the raids by which the Division was to worry the enemy
and establish over him a distinct moral ascendancy. This
started the policy well : the Austrian trenches at Casa
Ambrosini were rushed, 17 enemy killed in a sharp
encounter and a prisoner brought back, with trifling
casualties. An attempted raid on Vaister by the 22nd
Brigade a week later proved abortive, a large covering
party being encountered in No Man's Land and the garrison
thereby put on the alert. But on the 16th the Royal
Warwickshires raided Casa Ambrosini with considerable
success. The Austrians hardly waited to receive them but
fled into our barrage and suffered heavily, besides leaving
several dead in the trenches. Then on the night of April
17th/18th both the South Staffordshires and the 20th
Manchesters visited the enemy's lines. The former,
attacking Vaister, brought off a big success. " A "
Company was on the right, " B " on the left, both thrown
forward in a half-moon formation. After crawling to
within 150 yards of the objective they attacked under
cover of rifle grenades and a barrage from twelve howitzers,
and quickly forced their way in, surrounding a house and
bombing two large dug-outs which proved to be full of
Austrians, of whom they killed over 20 with the bayonet.
The flanking platoons had meanwhile got far enough round

to intercept the enemy's retreat and collect several prisoners, over 20 in all being taken, at a loss of six wounded. The 20th Manchesters, who raided Stella Trench rather later, found the enemy on the alert and had a hard fight in which, though unsuccessful in capturing prisoners, they inflicted on the enemy twice the casualties they suffered. A few days later an effort by patrols to sweep No Man's Land and secure prisoners brought the H.A.C. in for a sharp brush. The enemy were holding strong posts protected by wire out in front of their main line. These the H.A.C. attacked, and despite a stout resistance cleared their garrisons out, a dozen being killed on the spot and several others shot down as they bolted towards their main position. A little later the Austrians came out in force to recover the lost posts but were met with a heavy rifle fire and driven back in confusion, leaving the H.A.C., whose casualties were only 2 men killed, with much the best of the exchanges. Not the least satisfactory feature of these episodes was the fact that the battalions were all full of raw and inexperienced drafts, to whom the experience was of great value, steadying them and giving them confidence.

The H.A.C. were to have followed up this encounter by a raid on the night of April 24th, but a heavy fall of snow put this out of the question. However, during May the same activities were continued and with considerable success. The 20th Brigade, who had relieved the 91st before the end of April, were very active, the 8th Devons raiding Vaister with success on May 4th, capturing several prisoners, while on the 15th the Borders [1] had a turn.

The Borders' objective was some posts on Stella Spur. The night was very dark and wet, the ground heavy and

[1] The battalion was at the moment under Major Ross of the Gordons as Colonel Kerr had unfortunately been killed on May 3rd, a chance shell hitting the dug-out which served as his headquarters, wounding the Adjutant and the Signal Officer and killing the C.O. One of the veterans of the Division, having landed with it in October 1914 as Regimental Sergeant-Major, he had risen to the command of his battalion.

much pitted with shell-holes, but the raiders reached
their assembly position undetected and moved out exactly
on time as the barrage came down. Unluckily the bad
going delayed them, and although the wire was well cut
the enemy had mostly bolted before the raiders could
get in, though in their endeavours to escape they suffered
severely in the British barrage. An officer and several
men were taken, and as the Borders' casualties only came
to 2 killed and 1 missing the result was quite satisfactory.
The Gordons, however, when they raided Ambrosini were
less fortunate. Heavy rifle fire opened directly the raiders
moved off, and in trying to get through a gap in the wire
they were bombed and shot down from behind some cement
blocks. Two officers who were the first to reach the
gap were hit and several men who tried to follow them
got picked off; so the surviving raiders withdrew, bringing
several wounded with them, while the remainder were
subsequently rescued by Captain Pailthorpe, R.A.M.C.,
and three men, who searched No Man's Land, bringing in
the last man from quite close up to the enemy's wire.

These activities and much artillery fire notwithstanding, casualties were never high. In May the 20th Brigade
had exactly 40 [1] and neither of the others lost much more
heavily, though the Welch Fusiliers had nearly 30 casualties in one attack on Casa Ambrosini : they were seen
and met by heavy rifle fire, but charged home nevertheless, capturing the post and taking an officer and two
men prisoners. With the end of May came a relief by the
Forty-Eighth Division, to whom General Shoubridge
handed over on the 31st, the troops proceeding to an area
round Trissino. It was a chance for training and resting
the men, who had found two months of exile from most of
the alleviations of their lot rather long. It was a pleasant
change from the Asiago Plateau : water was plentiful,
instead of exceedingly scarce, the country was attractive,
the weather mostly warm and training mitigated by

[1] One officer and 5 men killed, 5 officers and 26 men wounded, 3 men missing.

plenty of recreation, though towards the end of May several units were visited by a mysterious epidemic, a sort of influenza, which filled their hospitals, though very few cases ended fatally. The 95th Field Company, for example, had half its number down at the same time and other units were in much the same plight. Early in June the 22nd Brigade had the honour of being inspected by the King of Italy, not the first distinguished visitor to the Division of recent times, the Prince of Wales having reconnoitred No Man's Land from the 91st Brigade's trenches in April and the Duke of Connaught having visited the Division early in March. However, the much-needed rest was to be rudely interrupted. In the small hours of June 15th sounds of tremendous firing from the direction of the Plateau disturbed the sleep of the Division, and orders were very soon received for the troops to " stand to." The Division's two artillery brigades had just returned to the Plateau and were in action, the XXXVth under the Twenty-Third Division in the right sector, the XXIInd under the Forty-Eighth on the left, while the 91st Brigade had already got the South Staffords and 21st Manchesters up on the Plateau working under the direction of the Heavy Artillery, and the rest of the brigade was promptly hurried off in motor-lorries to reinforce. The remaining troops, however, though at one hour's notice from 8 a.m. onward, were not required to move, though telephone messages and telegrams went to and fro all the morning and rumours of all sorts circulated freely. Actually, the Forty-Eighth Division's front had been penetrated, and the Austrians had pushed on to the position of the 35th Battery, which was in close support 100 yards behind the front line. Major Hartley, its C.O., emerged from a dug-out to find an Austrian planting a yellow flag at its entrance : he promptly shot him and assisted by a few men armed with rifles kept the Austrians at bay, preventing them getting into the gun-pits and allowing the breech-blocks to be removed from the guns

under the very noses of the enemy.[1] Early in the afternoon
the position was completely re-established by a counter-
attack;[2] the Twenty-Third Division meanwhile had kept the
enemy out and such gains as the Austrians had made against
the French and Italians had been short-lived, an Italian
counter-stroke actually improving the line by capturing
M. Asolone. The Montello was the point where the
Austrians were most successful, but just as the Division
had made up its mind that it would have to go down and
retake the Montello news of its recapture came in and
the Division's next move proved to be back to the Plateau
to relieve the Forty-Eighth Division. Meanwhile the
91st Brigade had come down again from the Plateau.
The men had been very uncomfortable up there ; they
had been rushed up without their blankets and as they
had just taken their khaki drill clothing into use they
were bitterly cold at nights. They had not been required
to fight, and had not got beyond M. Cavaletto, though
the South Staffords came in for some shell fire and had
about 20 casualties.

The relief of the Forty-Eighth Division began with the
move of the 91st Brigade to the Carriola area on June
22nd. Next day it took over the right half of the sector
with two battalions, and three days later (June 26th)
General Shoubridge assumed command of the frontage,
the 22nd Brigade moving into the left sub-sector on June
27th. Deserters had come in with warnings that the
Austrians would repeat their attack in the immediate
future and had brought up some German units to help
in it, so the Division, which had at first expected to attack
the Canove ridge, had to set to work putting up fresh
wire, improving the line generally and strengthening
weak spots, especially those where the enemy had got

---

[1] He was deservedly awarded the D.S.O., and four M.M.s were given to
the men who had backed him up so well.

[2] The 104th and 105th Batteries, though under enfilade fire from Austrian
infantry at short range, held their ground just East of the gap and did excellent service, shooting with great effect.

through on June 15th. The only raid of any importance in June was one by the Queen's on the 26th. This was aimed at the S.W. end of the Canove salient and was most successful, especially as the Queen's had only 3 men wounded. Three officers and 70 men lined up 250 yards from the objective with another officer and 20 men as covering-party. At 11.30 p.m. the barrage was put down, and the raiders dashing forward found the wire effectively cut and entered the trench with little difficulty, quickly disposing of the survivors of the garrison, on whom the barrage had inflicted heavy casualties, and taking several prisoners.

July saw the harassing of the enemy vigorously prosecuted. The Division's artillery were very busy, and though this occasionally provoked retaliatory bombardments the balance of advantage lay with the British gunners and the rumoured projected Austrian offensive never took shape. On the contrary the Austrians remained remarkably quiet ; they rarely ventured out into No Man's Land in any force, though several deserters came in, the number rather increasing towards the end of the month. The Division, while active in patrolling, carried out several raids, the 22nd Manchesters tackling Canove on the 3rd, the H.A.C. visiting Stella next day, the same points being again attacked a fortnight later, Canove by the 21st Manchesters, Stella by the Borders. All four were successful, the 21st Manchesters doing best as regards prisoners, of whom they brought in 20 with three machine-guns ; the H.A.C., however, would have probably beaten that total had not an unlucky and premature bringing back of the barrage by one battery on to the objective prevented the clearing of a large dug-out full of Austrians. As it was the H.A.C. captured 3 prisoners and killed about 30 enemy at a cost of 12 casualties. The 22nd Manchesters' raid almost repeated that by the Queen's a week earlier : this time the Austrians were found in shell-holes behind the main trench, from which they were quickly dislodged, and in bolting down the valley behind Gwent Trench they ran into the barrage and suffered heavily. The Borders, who attacked the salient in Gordon Trench, South of Stella, did things on the largest scale, having over 100 men in the raiding-party and 60 to cover them. They were unlucky in being checked by wire, and when they ultimately got through found the Austrians had cleared out of Gordon Trench, though it was full with victims of the British barrage, which was extremely accurate. They pushed on to and rushed Stella House, killing several enemy, but the Austrians then brought a heavy barrage down, which prevented a continuance of the advance as far as Gwent Trench.

With August came still more deserters and with them rumours that the enemy were going to withdraw to a new position some way in rear, running from Gallio by M. Catz to M. Rasta. To test the truth of this story it was decided to raid at four different points simultaneously, each attack being carried out by not less than two companies. The front at the time was held by the 91st Brigade on the left and the 22nd on the right, but while the former put in one battalion and the latter two, the 20th Brigade sent up the Borders from Divisional reserve to share in the raids by tackling Stella, with which it was already familiar. From the 91st Brigade the South Staffords were detailed to attack Canove and Bellochio, while the Welch Fusiliers and 20th Manchesters attacked on either side of them, the Welch Fusiliers on the right tackling Manchester Trench where it crosses the Vaister Spur, the Manchesters having Canove di Sotto as their goal. There was to be no artillery bombardment till "Zero," midnight on August 8th/9th, when the Divisional Artillery, reinforced by twenty 6-inch howitzers and thirty-five Italian heavy guns, would bring down the barrage with a crash that would give the infantry the signal to advance. The Divisional Machine-Gun Battalion was to cover the left flank by barraging the

Ambrosini Hill, and search-lights from Monte Lemerle and Hill 1152 would light up the areas raided.

Some wire-cutting had been done, though not on so extensive a scale as to excite the enemy's suspicions. In places, notably in front of Canove, the wire was still thick, but even here there were gaps. The enemy's suspicions had evidently not been aroused, for the forming up was carried out without drawing fire, and only at Canove, where occasional bursts of fire testified to some nervousness and apprehension, did the Austrians seem at all on the alert.

The Seventh Division's gunners had fired plenty of barrages by this time but hardly ever one so accurate or effective : not a round pitched short and the counter-battery work was equally effective, completely subduing the enemy's attempt at a barrage. Thus covered and supported the raiders were successful everywhere. On the right the Welch Fusiliers met a stout resistance, but quickly overcame it ; within 20 minutes of " Zero " the first company was on its objectives and the second was mopping up to some purpose. Despite stubborn resistance at some concreted dug-outs in the support trench no less than 120 prisoners were taken with three machine-guns, a search-light, and several mules, while two trench-mortars were destroyed. About 1.30 a.m., half an hour before the time for withdrawal, counter-attacks began to develop from Post Spur on the right and from Little Spur, but both were effectually dealt with by rifle fire. Casualties were extremely low and of all the raiders the Welch Fusiliers were perhaps the most successful. The South Staffords, on their left, were less fortunate. They had never raided Canove before and had not had time to rehearse the raid, while, as already mentioned, their opponents were nervous and on the alert. When their leading companies reached the wire in front of Guards Trench they had some difficulty in finding the gaps, and machine-guns from both flanks inflicted several casualties

on them while getting through. The enemy thus had time
to man the front trench in strength and were only dislodged after a fierce struggle. By this time the support
companies had reinforced the leaders and all now pushed
on together. The left had a sharp fight in Canove village,
took a flammenwerfer and several prisoners, but were
checked by fire from a pill-box which enfiladed the street.
On the right the advance was carried just beyond the
church, dug-outs were bombed, many enemy shot down
and several prisoners taken. But so heavy a machine-gun
fire had been opened from Bellochio and farther back
that Colonel English Murphy decided not to incur more
casualties by pushing on against the second objective but
to complete the mopping up of Canove. The South
Staffords had the highest casualties of any of the raiding
battalions, 6 officers and 53 men ; but if they had only
taken 21 prisoners they had punished their enemy severely.
The third raid, that of the 20th Manchesters against Canove
di Sotto, went very well. Little resistance was encountered in the front trench and the raiders reached their
objectives, mopped them up, taking three machine-guns
and over 50 prisoners, bombed some dug-outs and destroyed several trench-mortars. They were twice counter-
attacked, the first time from the left, the second from
Canove Cemetery, N.E. of Canove di Sotto. Both were
defeated by rifle fire, and on the withdrawal signal the
Manchesters got away easily, having only suffered 17
casualties, less than a third of the total of their prisoners.

The Borders, the leftmost of the raiding parties, had as
hard a fight as any. They knew the Stella locality already,
having raided it twice, and were employing two companies,
" B " and " D," under Captain Little. The battalion
scouts went out about 10 p.m. to lay tapes, cut wire by
hand and cover the assembly, which was successfully
accomplished, the raiders forming up in four lines, of which
" D " provided the first two. Advancing rapidly on the
guns proclaiming the " Zero " hour " D " reached Stella

House before it met serious opposition. Here a broad belt of wire covered Stella Fort, and the raiders came under heavy fire both from machine-guns and trench-mortars. However, they soon worked round the end of the wire, re-formed beyond and entered Stella Fort with a rush, taking two machine-guns. There was stubborn resistance, however, in the N.W. portion of the Fort; but gradually the defenders were forced back into the far corner by bombing them and the area cleared was mopped up. Meanwhile " B's " leading line was clearing Gwent Trench, taking several prisoners and destroying a trench-mortar, and the rear wave of the company had taken position near Stella House to deal with counter-attacks from the North. Some 20 prisoners were taken and very large losses inflicted on the Austrians; but the Borders with 14 men killed, 6 missing, and 27 and 2 officers wounded were the second heaviest sufferers among the raiders.

The total casualties, about 120, came to barely half the prisoners brought in; if the left search-light had not failed after 10 minutes it was believed many more might have been collected, and the Austrian losses in killed and wounded were by all accounts very heavy. The barrage had been most effective, knocking the defences about and inflicting many casualties, and the infantry were warm in its praise. " Nothing could have been better or more accurate," says one battalion's report, and the G.O.C. in thanking the Heavies for their good work ascribed the freedom from molestation which the withdrawal had enjoyed largely to their help in subduing the hostile artillery. Altogether, then, the raid was a great success. It was a satisfactory farewell to the Asiago Plateau. On August 14th the 70th Brigade began the relief by taking over the reserve positions from the 20th, which moved down to Centrale. Three days later the 70th Brigade moved up into the left sub-sector in relief of the 91st, and on August 19th General Shoubridge handed over command and proceeded to Trissino, round which place the Division

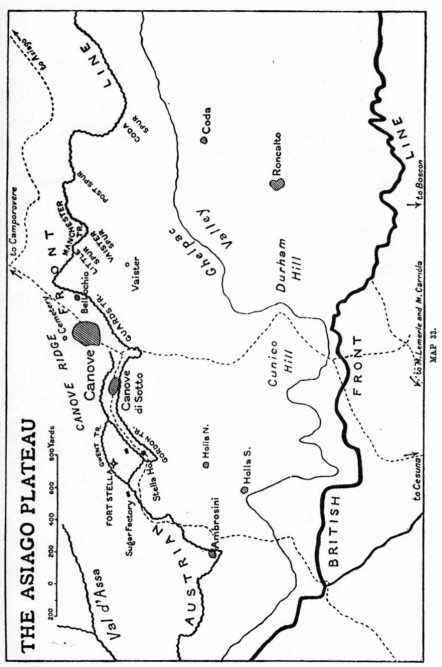

THE ASIAGO PLATEAU

MAP 33.

was now concentrated in G.H.Q. reserve, although as usual its artillery had to remain in action after the other units went out. The Division had had two hard months on the Asiago. Conditions there had been pleasanter in summer than in spring, though heavy thunderstorms with drenching rain were a marked feature ; still it was not a locality anyone was anxious to see again.

CHAPTER XXIV

THE GRAVE DI PAPADOPOLI[1]

THE Trissino country in which the Division now found itself established was indeed a pleasant change from the Asiago Plateau. The town itself was nicely situated on a hill, and Montecchio, Cornedo, and Arzignano, all within five miles of Trissino, were large enough to house a brigade each and make it comfortable. Fruit was available in profusion and reasonably cheap, and there were fair facilities for football and other forms of recreation. As a training area the district left something to be desired : even for company and battalion training suitable ground was not easy to find. To the bulk of the Division this was not a source of unmixed regret ; after two months on the Asiago Plateau they were more in a mood for relaxation than for work and there had by this time been plenty of chance of getting units together. Losses had been low in Italy ; and if sickness had caused more gaps than battle-casualties had, the drafts who had replenished the ranks after Gheluvelt were now quite old members of their respective units. The great improvement in the situation in France, which had begun with Sir Douglas Haig's victory of August 8th in front of Amiens, contributed to make the time spent round Trissino pleasant. Gone was the grinding anxiety of March and April, the doubts and despondency of May and June ; everybody was now looking forward to a not too hopelessly distant successful end to the Allies' trials and exertions, and the only question that was exercising the Seventh Division was what part it was to play in bringing that end about.

[1] Cf. Map 34.

Rumours were naturally rife ; the more imaginative contemplated the Division's transfer to Palestine or Mesopotamia, by the more practically-minded the matter was summed up " Either we go to France, or the Italians will have to put up a show here." There were no illusions as to what this meant. The Germans were still fighting stoutly, and if the tide had turned in the Allies' favour hard struggles lay ahead before the desired goal could be reached ; but it was unthinkable that a Division with the Seventh's fighting record should be left in practical inactivity. At one time it was believed that an Allied offensive in Italy would provide the Division with the necessary outlet for its energies, but the arguments against such an undertaking were weighty. The Austrian position in the mountains was extremely strong and very difficult to pierce by a frontal attack, especially as in many places, notably on the Asiago Plateau, the Allies hardly had enough depth behind their front line for organizing and developing a big offensive. Further, it outflanked any possible Italian advance in the plains, even if the Piave could be successfully crossed, and as to the practicability of that there were two opinions. As yet too the Austrians, who outnumbered the Allied forces in Italy considerably and had a distinct advantage in guns, had shown no symptoms from which their collapse could be predicted. Deserters had been fairly numerous, several had come over in the Seventh Division's last ten days on the Asiago Plateau, but in the conglomerate Austrian army, containing a high percentage of races whose hearts were not in their cause, deserters had never been uncommon nor was their appearance significant. Early in September it became known that the projected offensive in Italy had been cancelled, and from that moment all thoughts turned towards a return to France.

The first step in this direction was the reduction of the Division to the ten battalions to which Divisions in France, except the Australians and Canadians, had been cut down in February. The Division had to part with the 9th

Devons and the 20th and 21st Manchesters, who left for France on September 12th.[1]

The rest of the Division was to have followed these battalions as soon as the tired Division from France which was to replace it on the " quiet " Italian front could arrive. Just before the end of September advanced parties were detailed to proceed to France and take over the transport of the Forty-Seventh Division whom the Seventh were replacing. The reason for this was to reduce the number of trains needed, but the prospect of leaving their animals behind them was most unpopular with the transport men and officers, and there were some who were not displeased to hear that the move was off, that the advanced parties were returning from France, and that the Forty-Seventh's parties who had arrived on September 29th had started back again. The change was puzzling, the more so because it was so unexpected. Lord Cavan, now G.O.C. in Italy, had visited Divisional Headquarters to say farewell to General Shoubridge and his staff, and, even more convincing proof of the imminence of the Division's departure, its artillery, after enduring another month of the Asiago after the infantry and R.E. had come out, had at last descended to the plains and was cleaning up prior to starting for France.

The prospect of remaining inactive in Italy was not pleasing. The Division, one officer wrote, felt it " horrible to be doing nothing here while our fellows are attacking again and again in France." But the rapid change in the situation not only in France, where the driving back of the Germans into the Hindenburg Line had been followed by the piercing of that formidable and much-vaunted barrier, but in Macedonia and Palestine, was altering the

---

[1] They were formed into the 7th Brigade of the Twenty-Fifth Division, which had been reduced to cadre earlier in the year but was now being reconstituted with battalions from Italy, for the Twenty-Third and Forty-Eighth Divisions were also being cut down. Their Brigade Major was Captain Burmann of the Borders, sometime Staff Captain of the 20th Brigade, in which he had long served as a regimental officer.

situation in Italy, and the Allied offensive, inadvisable
at the beginning of September, was no longer out of the
question a month later.

The first indication of an approaching change came
when the Division shifted Eastward to an area N.W. of
Vicenza. This was completed by October 7th, Headquarters being established at Costa-bissa, and next day
battalion commanders were summoned to conferences
at their brigade headquarters and warned that they must
be prepared to attack in the near future, at a spot which
was not divulged, though it was shrewdly surmised that
it would prove to be on the Piave. The Division did not
stay long in its new area : on October 13th Headquarters
shifted to Borgofuro and the troops began moving by
rail to Treviso, some thirty miles away to the East. The
move was carried out at short notice and with every precaution to secure secrecy ; indeed the 22nd Brigade was
actually out on a route march when it received its orders
to entrain, and other units were almost equally rushed.
But despite the rush and the Italian railways the move
was completed without any serious hitch, though on
arrival in the Treviso area billeting proved a difficulty
and some units had to bivouac, which as the weather was
more than usually atrocious—it had been raining steadily
for the last few days—was far from pleasant. A more
serious result was that this wetting helped the rapid spread
of an outbreak of influenza which within the next few
days swept through the Division, prostrating hundreds,
including several " pivotal " persons like Colonel Vawdrey
of the A.S.C., Major Vyvyan, the D.A.Q.M.G., Major
Walshe, the D.A.D.M.S., and Captain Houghton, the
G.S.O. III. Several units were seriously depleted by the
epidemic, the Signal Company and 528th Field Company
being those most adversely affected, though the Welch
Fusiliers were deprived of the services of their C.O.,
Colonel Holmes, who had so frequently proved his worth
as a battalion commander.

The work of preparing for the attack was not made any easier by the re-formation at this moment of the Fourteenth British Corps, which deprived the Division of its C.R.E., Colonel Barnardiston, who went to the Corps as B.G.R.E., being replaced by Major Kerrich from the 54th Field Company, while at the same time Colonel Howard was given command of a brigade in the Forty-Eighth Division.[1] However, he did not leave the Division till he had seen it carry out the attack, in the planning of which he had had so large a share.

Orders were issued on the 17th for the relief of an Italian Division along the right bank of the Piave, N.E. of Treviso, to be begun on the night of October 18th/19th and completed two nights later.[2]   The Seventh Division was taking the right of the new British line, having Italians down-stream of it and the Twenty-Third Division on the left, while beyond the latter came the Eleventh Italian Corps, which with the two British Divisions formed the Tenth Army under Lord Cavan. It had been decided that while an attack should be made against the Austrians on the Asiago and Monte Grappa the main stroke should be delivered in a N.E. direction by the Twelfth and Eighth Italian Armies. This, if successful in securing the line Feltre–Vittorio, would sever the Austrians in the mountains from those on the Piave front and cut the line of communications on which those in the mountains mainly depended. Lord Cavan's Tenth Army was to cover the right flank of this main thrust by crossing the Piave below Nervesa and pushing forward to the Livenza, twelve miles farther East.

The main difficulty was the passage of the Piave. The Seventh Division had met the Piave already and had found it a formidable obstacle. Here it was even wider than on the Montello front, and at Salettuol, in the middle of the Division's line, it was nearly 2,500 yards from bank

---

[1] Colonel Barne, R.A., succeeded Colonel Howard as G.S.O.I.
[2] The gun positions of the Divisional Artillery were on either side of the Salettuol–Maserada road, about 500 yards back from the river bank.

to bank, though a large island, the Grave di Papadopoli, occupied part of the intervening space. This island, about three miles in length and over a mile wide at its broadest, was the largest of the many shoals and islands in the river bed, separated by channels sometimes fordable, sometimes quite deep, through which the · stream ran extremely rapidly, as fast as eight miles an hour. What doubled the hazards of the crossing was that the incessant and excessive rains had swollen the river into a high flood, submerging completely the tops of the shoals which usually gave some idea where the channels ran. All that could be seen was the tops of some trees on the Grave, which over that expanse of raging waters looked miles away. It was obvious that to ferry troops across such a stream would be far from easy, even for highly skilled boatmen ; already several units had tried their hand at rowing the quaintly shaped Italian boats on the Sile, which flows through Treviso. But even in this stream, whose pace was about half that of the Piave, control of the boats was lost and they did nothing but turn round and round. To bridge the stream with the current running so fast, the channels constantly varying and the river bed shingly and stony, was calculated to baffle even expert bridge-builders. Pontoons and trestles both seemed ill adapted to the task. It was doubtful if anchors could possibly hold and if pontoons could live in that stream. But if the Division was to attack successfully on the front assigned to it the Piave must not only be crossed but bridged, for guns and wagons must follow the infantry across. Indeed the R.E. could hardly see how the crossing was to be effected. However, General Shoubridge was insistent that some means must be devised, and eventually plans were drawn up, with a landing on the Grave di Papadopoli by the help of the Italian Pontieri as a pre-liminary measure to the laying of bridges.

The 22nd Brigade had taken over the Division's frontage on October 20th and the H.A.C. of this brigade had been

selected for the peculiarly hazardous enterprise of crossing
the Piave by boat and capturing the island ; for the latter
they were ready to answer if only they could accomplish
the passage.   Colonel O'Connor and one of his officers had
been attached to the Italians for two days to reconnoitre
the passage,[1] but it was largely labour wasted, as, at the
last moment, it was decided to attempt the crossing not
at Salettuol about the centre of the island, but to its N.W.
corner a mile and a half up-stream.   Here the smaller
island of Cosenza, separated from the mainland by a side
channel crossed by a foot-bridge, was already included
in the Allied position ; and here at 7 p.m. on October
23rd the three companies of the H.A.C. detailed for the
attack were waiting in readiness for the Italian Pontieri.

The stream was running strongly and in the faint light
of the rising moon it looked peculiarly uninviting, but the
leading party stepped into one of the gondola-like boats [2]
and pushed off.   This first trip was made by a small
reconnoitring party under Lieut. Gaud, the Intelligence
Officer of the H.A.C.   It was not long in returning with
the news that there were two deep streams to be crossed,
70 and 50 yards in width respectively, and separated by
a narrow shoal, over which the boats must be dragged.
Beyond the second stream was another shoal with a third
channel beyond it, 100 yards in width but quite fordable.

Provided with this information the two leading platoons
started off.   Two boats were swept down-stream and
failed to make the crossing ;   but the rest landed all right
on the second shoal, and their occupants waded across to
the island, promptly turned right-handed and swept
forward for about 300 yards, surprising several Austrian
posts and disposing of them with the bayonet.   But
though the strictest silence possible was preserved the

[1] To conceal the presence of British troops on this front all officers who
reconnoitred the position were fitted out in Italian uniforms and the men
were given Italian helmets and coats.

[2] There were twelve boats, each manned by two watermen and carrying
seven soldiers, so that about eighty men crossed at each trip.

Austrians could not be prevented from giving the alarm, and before the second trip could start up went the Austrian S.O.S., a rocket bursting into four red balls. Their barrage came down within a few minutes, but though it was accurate and considerably increased the difficulty of effecting the crossing, none of the boats were actually hit and neither the barrage nor the machine-guns which opened fire from farther down the island inflicted many casualties. The soft sand of the beach helped to diminish the effects of the shell-bursts, but the noise of the bombardment added to that of the river rushing over the stones and increased the general uncertainty and tension. Eventually, and with surprisingly few casualties, all three companies were ferried across, and at 11 p.m., the appointed hour, they began their advance S.E. down the island.

The Grave di Papadopoli was for the most part cultivated, being planted with vines and maize, and there was some scrub and brushwood in the uncultivated parts, while a dozen houses, mostly in ruins, were dotted about the S.E. portion. The defences consisted of two lines of trenches, one following roughly the bank of the main stream, the other some little distance in rear. This latter on its right was in front of a ditch, some ten feet wide and three deep, which ran S.E. from the N.W. corner of the island to the Isola di Inghilterra just below Salettuol. On the left the second line ran behind this ditch, joining the front trench opposite the Isola di Inghilterra. These lines contained several trench-mortar emplacements and machine-gun positions, but by attacking from the N.W. corner the trench-lines could be taken in flank. Had the passage been made from the point originally selected it would have necessitated a frontal attack on both lines.

Starting with " A " Company on the right, " D " on the left, and " C " with Battalion Headquarters following in second line, the H.A.C. swept rapidly forward. The Austrians were in force and in places fought stoutly enough,

but the H.A.C. had them at a disadvantage through taking
them in flank and within two hours " A " Company had
established itself on its objective a little below Salettuol.
" D's " left platoon, however, went too far to that flank,
mistaking a small trench for the long ditch ; and, crossing
one of the shallower streams between the Grave and the
left bank, established itself on the Isola di Francia.   This
misled " C " Company, which also went too far to the left
before discovering its error.   Two platoons worked their
way back towards the centre of the island, where firing
was still going on, and surprised an Austrian post near the
junction of the long ditch with the second line, capturing
over 60 prisoners.   Battalion Headquarters also, following
behind the leading companies, mopped up scattered
parties which those in front had missed, and the Welch
Fusiliers, who had followed the H.A.C. across, did admirable work in this way.   Fighting went on for some time,
the troops working through the scrub like hounds going
through a covert, and the haul of prisoners was steadily
increased.   By 5 a.m. all resistance was over and the
H.A.C. were consolidating a position facing S.E. across the
island, with the left company and the Welch Fusiliers
thrown back as a defensive flank to the N.E.

The day of October 24th brought no important developments.   The continual rain made things extremely uncomfortable for the troops on the island and, worse than that,
by causing the river to rise rendered their position somewhat precarious.   Not only was it impossible to establish
a bridge, but the ferrying across of rations and reinforcements was more perilous than before.   One boat indeed
capsized in mid-stream and one of its passengers was
drowned ; but the Pontieri worked indefatigably, and the
remainder of the attacking battalions got across with an
ample supply of rations.   But if the rain had made the
day miserable the rise in the river was partly responsible
for their being unmolested by counter-attacks ; the Grave
was subjected to a severe shelling and most of its Austrian

garrison [1] were still on the lower half of the island, but
they lay very low and did nothing to interfere with the
H.A.C. and Welch Fusiliers, who consolidated their position
and proceeded to mop up the captured portion systematically, adding nearly 100 prisoners to their bag. One large
party was captured by Colonel O'Connor and a few H.A.C.
who surprised it and fairly frightened it into surrender,
while another detachment at the N.W. end of the long
ditch put up a more stubborn resistance but gave in when a
section of the Machine-Gun Battalion was turned on to them.

With the morning of the 25th the rain stopped and
the soaked troops could dry themselves a little. Colonel
O'Connor was preparing to complete the capture of the
island when the Brigade Major arrived, having crossed
the river in broad daylight, getting several bullets through
his boat, though neither he nor the boatmen were touched.
He brought orders for what Colonel O'Connor had already
decided upon—the clearing of the rest of the Grave by the
H.A.C., the Welch Fusiliers covering them against the
chance of a flank attack from the left bank. This was
the main danger to be apprehended; it was only from the
British side that the Grave was hard to reach, the streams
between it and the left bank, though broad, being fordable
nearly everywhere.

Meanwhile, early in the afternoon General Shoubridge
had visited the 22nd Brigade's Headquarters and given instructions for the transfer to the island of the remainder of
that brigade. General Steele accordingly started for the
island, but his first attempt was unsuccessful: one of the
boatmen was wounded, another jumped out of the boat
and was drowned, he himself was grazed on the head and
stunned, and his boat was carried back to the right bank.
He insisted, however, on making a second attempt, this
time with success. Later on the Royal Warwickshires
crossed and took over from the Welch Fusiliers the portion
of the island already captured, thus setting all that batta-

[1] It was ascertained later that this had consisted of some fifteen companies.

BRIGADIER-GENERAL JULIAN STEELE, C.B., C.M.G., D.S.O.

lion free to support the H.A.C., who were putting three
companies into their front line, " C," " B," and " A "
from right to left with " D " in support.

Shortly before the attack the Austrians opened a heavy
fire, both from artillery and machine-guns, but the H.A.C.
pushed forward nevertheless, meeting little opposition
till they reached the houses about C. Bassetti.   Here from
a small trench running East and West across the Isola di
Inghilterra " C " Company was enfiladed and its advance
for the time held up ; but with the arrival of reinforcements
including two Lewis-gun sections the opposition was
overcome, the houses round C. Bassetti were rushed and
a platoon pushing across to Isola de Inghilterra dealt with
its defenders effectually.   Meanwhile the centre company,
" B," with some assistance from " D " and from Battalion
Headquarters, had got forward well, despite stubborn
opposition at most of the houses.   " A " Company on
the left, after at first losing direction, also reached its
objective, and aided by the Welch Fusiliers established
a defensive flank reaching to where the Austrian foot-
bridges reached the main island.

It was well that this had been done, for just as dawn was
breaking the Austrians suddenly attacked in great strength,
one detachment advancing against the Welch Fusiliers,
the other coming across the Austrian foot-bridges against
" B " Company, H.A.C., who found themselves attacked
in front and left flank and were hard pressed.   Luckily a
detachment of " D " Company which was trying to recover
touch with " C " turned back promptly and came in on
" B's " right while a platoon of " A " reinforced the left.
There was a stubborn fight.   Casualties, influenza, and
the necessity of finding escorts for prisoners had thinned
the ranks of the H.A.C., and the enemy—picked Hungarian
troops, as it afterwards appeared—were splendidly led
and fought stoutly.   Good service was done by two Lewis-
gun sections, but at one time things looked critical, for
ammunition was running short and the Austrians seemed

disinclined to give way. However, Sergeant Jenkinson of "D" Company made some Austrian prisoners who had been captured at another point march forward with their hands up as though they had just surrendered : the ruse succeeded admirably and before long the remainder followed their example and threw their weapons down or bolted, over 100 being taken and another 50 killed. Equal ill-success had attended the attack on the Welch Fusiliers, and the prisoners taken this day brought the total up to well over 600, while soon after it became light the H.A.C. pushed on to the far end of the island, clearing it completely. Touch was obtained with the Italian Division which was to be on the Seventh's right in the main attack, and during the afternoon Italian troops crossed over to the Grave and began taking up their assembly positions for the big attack which was timed for 6.45 a.m. on October 27th.

One necessary preliminary had still to be accomplished, perhaps the most difficult of all, the building of the bridge across the Piave from Salettuol. This could not be started till the capture of the island had been completed, though the Twenty-Third Division had already begun a foot-bridge across to the Lido,[1] where the first boat-loads had landed and some preparations in the way of getting out anchors to hold the pontoons in position had been made by the 54th Field Company R.E. on the night of October 23rd/24th. It had at first been thought that the work could only be done by night in order to escape observation, but the morning of October 26th was calm and foggy, and General Shoubridge, with a happy inspiration, determined to take the chance of the weather holding all day and gave orders for the work to be begun at once. He was rewarded for his enterprise. The day continued calm, the mist never cleared away, and the Austrian observers being thus blinded the work could go ahead unimpeded.[2] The first

[1] The N.W. portion of the Grave was known by this name.

[2] The bridge might have been seen but for the fog, not only from aeroplanes but from S. Daniela, a high hill North of Nervesa.

step was to get a cable across the main stream and to pass boats with the anchors across along the cable. Four volunteers from the 54th Field Company accomplished this dangerous task successfully, and then on the evening of the 25th four pontoons were placed in position by Pontieri and with much difficulty were secured. These pontoons bridged enough of the main stream for trestles, which could be set up where it shallowed, to span the gap to a shoal on the far side of the main stream. Between this and the island the remaining stream, though swift and deep, was fordable and more pontoons could be placed into position here to complete the bridge. By the evening of October 26th the bridge was ready, and the 20th and 91st Brigades, who came forward to take up their assembly positions, could cross over without a hitch. The first stage of the final stroke had been accomplished, and the 22nd Brigade and the H.A.C. in particular could feel legitimate pride in having achieved a feat of no common character. It has been impossible to go into full details of the bridge-building or to bring out the technical skill and resource as well as the courage and enterprise required for the operation. One other incident only in the war offers much of a parallel, the Norfolks' crossing of the Tigris at the Shumran Bend in February 1917; but the Tigris was neither as broad or as swift as the Piave and the physical difficulties of that operation were certainly less formidable. Once landed on the Grave the troops had had stubborn opposition to overcome, and it had needed skilful leading as well as determination and gallantry to clear the island of a garrison far outnumbering the attackers, as well as to repulse a strong and well-led counter-attack; while the battalions employed had had considerable hardships and discomforts—such as an almost constant downpour—to endure besides being vigorously bombarded. But they had done their work admirably and had paved the way to a greater if not more dramatic success.

CHAPTER XXV

VITTORIO VENETO [1]

IT had originally been hoped to deliver the main attack on October 25th, and accordingly the assaulting brigades —the 20th and 91st—had moved from Treviso to assembly positions about Maserada on the 23rd. The postponement of the attack involved their spending three most miserable days and nights in bivouac. To conceal the assembly from the Austrian aeroplanes the troops had to do without tents, and the Italian bivouac sheets which alone were available gave inadequate protection against the pelting rain, though things improved when, on the morning of the 25th, the deluge stopped and a warm sun gave the drenched troops a chance of drying their soaked clothes. It was curious how these wet nights and days in the open coincided with a remarkable decrease in the influenza epidemic ; but the weather and the necessity for keeping concealed made this waiting most tedious, and the troops welcomed the news that the bridge had been successfully completed and that the attack would take place on October 27th.

After dark on the 26th the passage began, the 20th and 91st Brigades crossing by alternate battalions. Fortunately the fog had concealed the bridge from the Austrians, and the passage, which shell fire would have made difficult and dangerous even if the bridge had not been destroyed, was accomplished without casualties. As battalions reached the Grave they moved into position to right and left, the Gordons forming the 20th Brigade's front line, and the 22nd Manchesters the 91st's. In support were the 8th Devons and the South Staffords, with the Borders and the Queen's in reserve. As these

[1] Cf. Map 35.

brigades got into their places the weary 22nd Brigade was drawn back into reserve, the troops on its extreme right being replaced by Italians.

With only one bridge the crossing naturally took some time. The Gordons were in position before 9 p.m., but the Devons not till 11, and the Borders two hours later. " Zero " was at 6.45 a.m. (Oct. 27th), so the troops had several hours to wait ; and as the rain came down heavily about 4 a.m. and little shelter was available they were most uncomfortable. Luckily, though the Austrian artillery started retaliating directly our bombardment began, their fire was not heavy, and as there was plenty of space on the island their counter-bombardment was ineffective. Not so the British fire, which was wonderfully accurate : the artillery had not done any registering from their new positions, lest they should reveal their presence on the Lower Piave, so they had to fire by the map with such assistance as a Field Survey Company could afford. Under the circumstances the accuracy and efficacy of the British shooting was extraordinarily creditable.

The preliminary bombardment, which began at 11.30 p.m., was aimed at cutting the wire in front of the high embankment or " Bund " which formed the main Austrian position. This embankment, about ten feet in height and quite broad at the top, ran about 100 to 200 yards from the river bank, the intervening ground being covered with scrub interlaced with barbed wire, in which were many trenches and machine-gun emplacements. Between the left bank and the Grave di Papadopoli was a space of about 200 yards, divided into several streams by shoals and gravel banks. The Bund itself was a ready-made fortification, affording splendid positions for riflemen and machine-gunners, while dug-outs along its far side provided good shelter against the bombardment. With thick belts of wire in front and more than 300 yards to be crossed by the attacking infantry the position might well have been reckoned impregnable, indeed the

31

Seventh Division would have backed itself to defend it against unlimited Austrians; but nevertheless it faced the prospect of attacking it without misgivings—it had seen enough of the Austrians on the Asiago to realize that they were not enemies of the same quality as the Germans, that many of them were fighting unwillingly, and that neither their discipline, training, nor morale was of the soundest. How far the news from France had reached the Austrian rank and file was uncertain, but the Seventh Division was inspired by the knowledge that the Central Powers were on their last legs and that a really determined attack would probably finish the war on this particular front.

About an hour before "Zero," while it was still dark, the attacking battalions began making their way to the far edge of the Grave, so as to get as near as possible to the Bund before "Zero." It was difficult to keep direction and intervals in the dark, but the leading lines reached the river bank at 6.25 a.m., just as the Divisional Artillery started the barrage. This was to move at 15 yards a minute, and it was calculated that the Division's final objective, the Tezze-Rai road, 5,000 yards from the starting-point, would be reached about midday. Intermediate objectives were formed by the villages about 1,000 yards from the river, S. Michele di Piave, Vendrame, and Cimadolmo, and by the road from Tezze to S. Polo di Piave about a mile beyond. But the Bund was the chief obstacle: if it could be carried the other objectives would hardly stop the advance.

The Division's frontage, which extended down-stream for 3,000 yards from Zandonadi, was a long one for only two brigades; and the 91st Brigade's supporting battalion, the South Staffords, had to come into line before the Bund was taken. The 22nd Manchesters had found the passage difficult. They came under a heavy fire directly they began crossing the river, and the speed of the current and the depth of water, in places nearly

four feet, swept some men off their feet and caused others
to bunch together in the shallower places. Sometimes
men had to link arms to help each other across, and at
their first attempt the leading companies failed to get
through the wire. Most of them took cover along the
bank which fringed the stream, though a few specially
resolute men pushed on and began cutting the wire by
hand. The check was short-lived. The C.O., Colonel
Ramsbotham, brought up the other two companies, hard
behind them came the South Staffords; and the two
battalions, pushing on together, worked through the wire.
Some men found gaps which the Austrians had left for
their patrols, others broke through places where the
bombardment had damaged the wire, others cut gaps by
hand, while covering fire from Lewis guns kept the
Austrians' heads down and prevented them from interfering. As they worked through they rushed at the Bund,
swarmed up it and went for the enemy with the bayonet.
Not many Austrians stayed to fight, the majority, surprised and dismayed by the failure of the wire to hold
up the attack, streamed back inland in disorder, almost
too fast to give riflemen and Lewis gunners much chance
to shoot them down. Those who did show fight were
soon disposed of, several prisoners being taken; and then
the two C.O.s started reorganizing their battalions for the
advance to the second objective, the " Red Dotted Line,"
the South Staffords taking the left, from Zandonadi to
Vendrame.

Meanwhile the 20th Brigade had accomplished their
first task without a check. The worst obstacle they
encountered was the last channel, which was waist-deep
and flowing rapidly. The Austrian machine-guns had
opened fire as the Gordons plunged into the water, but
Lewis guns promptly opened in reply and knocked out
the most dangerous of the hostile guns and the men
linked arms and pushed across, not letting either snipers
or machine-guns check them. The Austrian opposition

lacked determination, and the Gordons, charging up over the Bund, were quickly in possession of their first objective. Some Devons reached the Bund with them, and almost before those defenders who were sheltering in the dug-outs behind could emerge from their cover the entrances were picketed and there was no alternative but to surrender. Casualties were not numerous, and directly the barrage lifted Gordons and Devons swept forward to the second objective. To some extent order had been lost and the advance was carried out in disconnected small parties, led by a subaltern or a N.-C.-O., but there was no stopping them. The chief village on their front was Cimadolmo, and before 8 a.m. its capture had been reported at Brigade Headquarters, while twenty minutes later over 100 prisoners of the Austrian 7th Division were brought in, mostly men taken at the Bund. Cimadolmo, though teeming with enemy, was but feebly defended, and mopping-up parties gleaned a substantial haul of prisoners from the houses and dug-outs. Meanwhile, on the left a company of the Devons which was filling a gap between the two brigades had quite a sharp fight round Casa Nuova, taking four guns and many prisoners. By 8.30 the Gordons could report Cimadolmo clear and that touch had been established with the 91st Brigade, though on the right the Italians were still held up at the first objective. To remedy this Major Pepys took three platoons of the Devons off to the right: his intervention was effective; the opposition collapsed on being threatened in flank and the Italians pushed forward level with the British right. Unfortunately in their eagerness to keep up with the fugitive Austrians some of the Gordons had gone ahead too fast, and Colonel Ross, their C.O., had been hit and killed.[1] It was the fifth C.O. the Gordons had lost in action during the war.

By this time the 91st Brigade also had reached the

---

[1] There was no question in this instance of the accuracy of the barrage or of short rounds; the Gordons quite admitted they had overshot the mark.

Red Dotted Line. After reorganizing on the Bund they
had pushed on so quickly as to catch up again with the
barrage and had soon overcome the defenders of S. Michele
di Piave ; the 22nd Manchesters alone took 160 prisoners
in three houses, and nine guns, the South Staffords taking
three guns and 200 prisoners.

At 9.30 the advance to the next objective, the " Blue
Line," a few hundred yards beyond the Tezze–S. Polo di
Piave road, began. The country in between was cultivated land, dotted about with farms, the buildings of
which often covered an appreciable area and were quite
substantial ; indeed when reinforced with beams and
concrete they formed quite strong posts, especially when
they gave cover to machine-guns. As it happened, most
of these improvised fortresses were on the 20th Brigade's
frontage, and it was more delayed than was the 91st, who
had only two or three to tackle. The Gordons and Devons
who went forward more or less together had quite hard
fighting. At 10.45 a report reached Headquarters that
they were held up by machine-guns and a little later a
large farm-house at Callarge was said to be delaying them.
At 11.30 the Gordons reported that they were progressing,
but very slowly, and that nearly every house contained
machine-guns. On this General Green ordered the
Borders to cross the river to support the advance. However, before they could get into action the Gordons and
Devons had reached the Blue Line. The tactics employed
against the farm-houses had been practically those which
had proved successful at Noordemdhoek : parties worked
round their flanks under cover of Lewis guns and rifles
and attacked them from the rear. One by one these
strong points were mastered : at 11.45 the Devons reported
the capture of a very troublesome one on the brigade's
left, C. Angelina. In another the Gordons took the headquarters of an Austrian regiment, and other captures
included four howitzers which were rushed by a few Gordons under Sergeant Duncan. Just short of the road were

some specially strong farms, C. Busca, C. Marina, and two called C. Paladin, and with the attacking troops much mixed up and rather disorganized it was some time before their resistance could be overcome. The Italians were again behind the British, and the Devons had to form a defensive flank with one company along the road from C. Demioni to Camminada. Evening found the 20th Brigade established from the cross-roads South of Camminada to C. Angelina, just short of the third objective, with the Borders close behind the two attacking battalions.

The 91st Brigade, more fortunate in having fewer farms to tackle, had got on much faster ; one of the strongest of these farms, C. Paolotti, was just where the barrage had rested and had caught several shells, so that the South Staffords rushed it easily directly the advance started. Pushing ahead rapidly and meeting little determined opposition the 91st Brigade was into Tezze by 11 o'clock, the South Staffords making short work of its defenders, while the Manchesters, after clearing Borgo Zanetta, pushed on to the " Green Line," capturing five more guns before they were ordered back to the " Blue Line," which it had been decided to consolidate. The Queen's, who had come forward to S. Michele di Piave, were retained in reserve while detachments of the 7th Battalion M.G.C. took positions in the front line in readiness to meet the counter-attack which prisoners had reported to be in preparation.

If the attack had not reached the Division's final objectives it had certainly gone splendidly. Nothing could have surpassed the infantry's dash and vigour, and the artillery support had been excellent, though by 11 a.m. the infantry's advance had been carried almost beyond the range of the guns. Accordingly early in the afternoon two batteries, the 104th and 105th, had crossed to the Grave and given close support to the infantry, and were now well placed to meet the rumoured counter-attack. The gunners could not have helped the delays caused by the farms.

These buildings being scattered about the area were not as a rule on any barrage line and often were not even marked on the map ; hence the farm-houses had often escaped untouched, whereas known obstacles such as the villages had been thoroughly pounded by the guns. A battery of 2·75-inch pack howitzers would have made short work of these obstacles, but unfortunately that useful weapon was not included in the Divisional establishment. However, the success achieved had been notable. Hundreds, if not thousands, of prisoners had been captured, many of whom seemed to have no regret at being out of the war and marched quite cheerfully away under the smallest of escorts, some being utilized as stretcher-bearers, though the wounded fortunately were less numerous than had been feared. Casualties had been low, the Gordons [1] and the 22nd Manchesters being the chief sufferers ; but even these would have reckoned their losses light in any battle in France, while there was ample evidence that the Austrians' casualties, apart from prisoners, far exceeded those of the Division.

The night passed quietly : the Borders took over part of the 20th Brigade's front, allowing the Gordons to be concentrated on the right and the Devons collected in support. One company of the Queen's reinforced the 91st Brigade's front line on an alarm of a counter-attack, but whatever had been intended it quickly fizzled out, and morning (Oct. 28th) found the position well consolidated. At 7 a.m. orders were received from the Division to secure the final objective, the advance to start at 12.30 p.m. The immediate purpose was to extend the bridge-head gained by the British in order to pass over the river some of the Italian troops from the left whose attack opposite Nervesa had failed, but who, by using the British bridge-head, could outflank their opponents. This resulted in a great congestion of traffic at the Salettuol bridge, with consequent delay in forwarding rations and supplies to the advanced

---

[1] This battalion had 3 officers killed and another 3 wounded.

troops. At the height of the congestion one pontoon and three trestles were carried away and the 528th Field Company spent the remainder of the day in endeavouring to effect repairs, in which task an Italian pontooning company gave valuable help, the bridge being eventually rebuilt rather farther down-stream.

When the advance was resumed little serious opposition was encountered. The 104th and 105th Batteries had crossed to the left bank at daybreak by fords and gave excellent support, being very useful in dealing with the defended farms. On the left the South Staffordshires advancing from Tezze promptly carried Borgo Belussi, and then swinging to the right outflanked and captured C. Gregoletto just as a captured Austrian gun, manned by Colonel Oldham of the XXXVth Brigade R.F.A., his orderly officer and their batmen, was about to open fire upon it. Not only was the Green Line passed, but the troops secured the previous day's final objective, which ran just short of Vazzola. Fighting had not been heavy, though some prisoners were secured, but for the most part the Austrians did not wait to be taken.

The 20th Brigade had started well with the capture of C. Vital and the other farms which had held up the previous day's advance. There was some opposition, but not of a determined character, as was easily understood when it appeared that some Landsturm had relieved the more efficient Hungarians who had opposed the 20th Brigade on the day before. The Devons advancing in support of the Borders mopped up some pickets of enemy who offered resistance ; and soon after 3 p.m. the Borders reported the Green Line occupied and touch gained with the troops on both flanks.

The next important obstacle ahead of the Division was the Monticano river, which though shallow and only about fifteen yards across flowed in a deep bed between high banks which had been wired and turned into a formidable position. Two of its right-bank tributaries, the Piaveselle and the Favero, would have to be crossed before the Monticano could be reached; and the two bridges on the Division's front at Vazzola and Visna were believed to have been mined.

It was important to force the passage of the Monticano promptly, as a stand here might allow the extensive retirement which was now reported to be in progress to be carried out unmolested. Accordingly orders were issued on the afternoon of the 28th for an advance to the Vazzola–Rai road. These were successfully carried out by the 91st Brigade, which with the Queen's on the right and South Staffords on the left soon gained the appointed line. The enemy had apparently just been leaving Vazzola as the South Staffords came in and nearly 50 prisoners were taken in the village, some obviously making no great effort to get away. On the right the Borders' patrols advanced beyond the Rai–Vazzola road as far as Visna, and while one party came back with some 15 prisoners another went on across the Favero almost to the Monticano, only to find the bridge held and the enemy in force. The party took post at C. Grison, but in the meantime the Austrians had reoccupied Visna and the detachment, being completely cut off, was compelled to surrender after suffering several casualties. However, despite this minor success the Austrians had no intention of standing South of the Monticano, and next morning (Oct. 29th) Visna was occupied without opposition, though farther to the right the Borders had some trouble in crossing the Piaveselle ; after which, as the Italians once again were behind, they had to go outside their own frontage to clear Fontanelette, from which machine-guns were taking them in flank. Soon after midday patrols had reached the Monticano to find it strongly held, with many machineguns in action. To deal with them a section of the 104th Battery came up to Visna and did some useful work ; and all was in train for the Borders and Devons to force the passage when Major Lawrence, the G.S.O.II of the Division, arrived to announce a change of plan. The 91st

Brigade were already across the Monticano between Vazzola and Cimetta, and the Italians were about to relieve the 20th Brigade. It would then move to the left and support the 22nd, which was to relieve the 91st and continue the advance.

On the left of the Division's frontage the Queen's had advanced from Vazzola at 9 a.m. supported by an Italian mountain battery and with the Manchesters acting as right flank-guard. The road out of Vazzola was higher than the country round and troops advancing along it formed a conspicuous mark. The volume of fire which met the Queen's showed clearly that the Monticano was held in force, but they worked forward along the roadside ditches and reached the river bank. Here they were held up and engaged in a fire fight with the Austrians, while the Manchesters came forward on their right and extending on an 800 yards' frontage pressed on to the Monticano. The vineyards which covered the country gave good cover, and the Manchesters gained the near bank without heavy losses, but then had a hard fight for fire supremacy. However, their advance somewhat distracted attention from the Queen's, who succeeded in rushing the bridge, left intact by the failure of the demolition party to fire the fuse. Advancing towards Cimetta the Queen's encountered considerable opposition but made ground steadily, securing several prisoners ; while the Manchesters, having subdued the enemy's fire and driven them away from the river bank, waded across to cover their flank. Just short of Cimetta, however, the Queen's were checked by a counter-attack, and the South Staffords had to be brought forward and extended on their right. This took time, and meanwhile the 105th Battery, the Italian mountain guns, and a company of the 7th Battalion M.G.C. all came into action.[1] Austrian

---

[1] The 35th Battery had by now crossed the river and joined the XXIInd Brigade, and the XXXVth Brigade and the Divisional Ammunition Column both began crossing on the 29th.

guns were blazing away vigorously, and the fighting was
quite hot; but by 2 p.m. the South Staffords were in
position and the final advance on Cimetta could begin.
About this time the Twenty-Third Division's advance
farther to the left was making itself felt and the defence

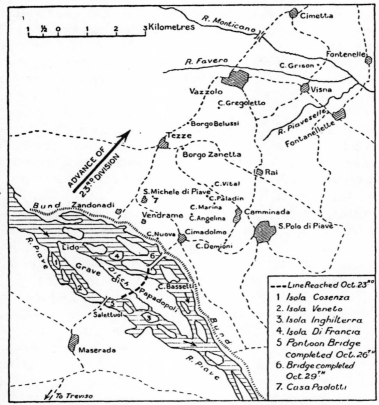

MAP 34.—THE GRAVE DI PAPADOPOLI AND VITTORIO VENETO.

of Cimetta was weakening. Still the Queen's had a hard
fight for Cimetta; and though, with the help of the South
Staffords, they eventually secured the village with a good
haul of prisoners it was no easy victory, the Queen's alone
having 100 casualties, including 23 killed and missing.
The Austrians had fought stubbornly enough, and it

speaks well for the training and discipline of the British and the judicious handling of their units by subordinate commanders that the success was achieved without much heavier casualties.

By this time the troops were much exhausted : they had been marching and fighting without any rest for three days on end. Great congestion had been caused by the Italians using the British bridges and this, coupled with the breakdown of the Salettuol bridge, had deprived them of rations since the morning of October 28th, while the expenditure of ammunition had been considerable. Communications too were only maintained with the utmost difficulty and thanks to no little enterprise and ingenuity on the part of the Signal Company, who narrowly escaped several casualties by drowning in getting their first cable across the swollen river. But the success in forcing the passage of the Monticano needed to be promptly exploited, and there could be no calling a halt. Luckily the 22nd Brigade, which had spent the day of the attack on the Grave di Papadopoli, digging in as far as possible to get shelter from the Austrian guns and bombing aeroplanes, had now reached the front. It had crossed to the left bank late on October 28th, billeting in the ruins of S. Michele di Piave that night—hardly a house had its roof left on—and had moved up next day to within two miles of Vazzola, where it bivouacked among the vineyards, the men digging holes in the ground and covering themselves with polenta stalks to get some approach to shelter and warmth. Early on the 30th it passed through the 91st Brigade and began the advance towards the Livenza, twelve miles away, behind which river the Austrians might be going to stand. The Welch Fusiliers and Royal Warwickshires were in front, in touch on the left with the Twenty-Third Division, the H.A.C. following. Progress was not rapid, the troops were far from fresh and many were footsore ; their boots had got thoroughly wetted in wading the Piave and had then dried hard, there having been no chance of getting them off or of changing socks. Moreover, as opposition was expected the leading battalions were extended in attack formation, but they met hardly any enemy: the few Austrians encountered were mostly trying to escape notice and surrendered promptly.

The advance continued through Codogne and Rover-basso to within a mile of the Livenza. Here some shell fire met the advancing troops, with a little rifle and machine-gun fire from beyond the river. All the bridges had been destroyed, and as the river was over 300 yards across and quite deep and swift in places it was impracticable to attempt to force the passage at dusk with tired troops, no chance to reconnoitre properly, and the problem of getting rations and ammunition up to the front already quite serious. This alone might well have compelled the troops to halt on October 31st, for they had almost out-marched the A.S.C.'s capacity to keep them supplied.

The supply problem was closely connected with the bridge problem. Rapidly as the Austrians had had to retreat they had left their mark on the bridges, and the R.E. and Pioneers, who worked indefatigably, had their hands full with repairs or constructing pontoon bridges where the permanent bridges were beyond repair. They had the Piave bridges to see to also, though the establishment by the Italians of several " telefericas "—baskets running on wire cables stretched across the river—enabled food and ammunition to be got across independently of the bridges.

Thanks to their labours motors could cross the Piave and ambulances reached the front by the evening of October 30th. Fortunately there were few wounded to need them East of the Monticano, as since the capture of Cimetta casualties had been trifling. Rations could now be issued again ; the troops had been eking out what they had on them with such vegetables and eggs as the inhabitants could produce, while supplies of cigarettes and dry socks were equally welcome.

During October 31st and November 1st the work of

repairing bridges and laying pontoon bridges went on steadily, while the infantry enjoyed a welcome rest. The XXXVth Brigade R.F.A. managed to get up to the front on October 31st, so that all the Division's guns were now available to cover its advance. The enemy's snipers and machine-guns were occasionally troublesome, but aeroplane observers brought back news that the roads to the Eastward were crowded with retreating columns, and on November 1st the Austrian shelling and machine-gun fire both diminished greatly. That evening the 22nd Brigade crossed the river and established an out-post line from North of Brugnera to Sacile. This meant a side-slip to the left, the 20th Brigade having now moved across to that flank, with the 22nd on the right and the 91st in support.

Early on November 2nd the advance was resumed, the 20th Brigade crossing at Sacile, while the 22nd used the pontoon and foot-bridges near Cavolano. Cyclists and Northamptonshire Yeomanry pushed on ahead, but though the roads were crowded with debris—dead horses, abandoned wagons and guns, corpses which testified to the effective bombing with which our aeroplanes had harassed the retreating columns—absolutely no opposition was encountered. Evening found the 20th Brigade at Cordenons, the 22nd at the bridge over the Meduna East of Pordenone, which place the 91st reached about dusk. The troops had been warmly welcomed by the population, whose delight at their liberation from the hated Austrians was unbounded. Everywhere were signs of rout and demoralization, the looted shops, the wanton destruction that could serve no military purpose, the abandoned stores and equipment which littered the roads. For November 3rd the orders were to push on to the Tagliamento, behind which the Austrians were standing. This involved crossing the Meduna, which, East of Cordenons, was almost dry, though a more serious obstacle where the 22nd forded it ; the road and railway bridges had both been destroyed, so wheeled traffic was delayed till the R.E. managed to construct a pontoon bridge. Once again the troops met no opposition, and the advanced guards, the H.A.C. on the right and the Gordons on the left, reached the Western bank of the Tagliamento early in the afternoon. It was a formidable position, the river bed was half a mile wide, and the main stream—there were eight in all—ran close under the far bank, which was absolutely lined with Austrians backed by long rows of guns. To have attacked with two weak and exhausted brigades (the 91st was still some way behind) and only a few field-guns with very little ammunition would have been farcical, for the Italian cavalry were not likely to be able to give much assistance in an operation like forcing the passage in face of such odds.

However, there was to be no need to attempt anything so desperate as an attack. Even before the Gordons reached the Tagliamento the Italian cavalry commander had informed General Green, that the Austrians had reported to him that an armistice had been signed, making the Tagliamento the line of demarcation, and was already in force. No confirmation of this had reached the Italians or General Shoubridge, who had now hurried up to the front. Had the Austrians liked to fight they could hardly have failed to hold the Division up ; but fighting was about the last thing in their minds, and General Shoubridge, taking a firm line, bluffed them into letting the Gordons cross the river unopposed by the partially destroyed bridge at Gradisca, and secure a bridge-head on the left bank. On the British right the H.A.C. advanced more than half-way across the bed of the Tagliamento to be told the same tale by the Austrians, who did not fire but declared they would resist any further advance. Colonel O'Connor, therefore, thinking the story quite probable and not wishing to incur casualties unnecessarily, suspended the attack till he could communicate with his brigadier. The H.A.C. remained out in this curious situation till nearly midnight, when orders from

General Steele arrived, bidding them retire to the West bank and billet at Arlamutta.

Actually an armistice had been signed that afternoon, to come into force at 3 p.m. next day, until which hour the advance might continue and any Austrians taken would become prisoners of war. This produced rather curious results next day, when the advance was resumed at 8 a.m., the Borders moving out from the 20th Brigade's bridge-head and the Welch Fusiliers and Warwickshires crossing the Tagliamento in attack formation. Some of the Austrian officers protested to General Shoubridge that they ought not to be expected to surrender pending the armistice coming into force, but nearly a whole Division laid down its arms cheerfully and submitted to be marched back in columns under infinitesimal escorts. Any amount of spoil was collected, dozens of horses and ponies, many guns, equipment of every kind, much of it quite excellent. Everyone was in high spirits, nobody minded having got wet up to the waist in wading the Tagliamento ; and the seven-miles' march which brought the Division to the line Codroipo–Coderna–Maserus lay through green fields and country lanes and was quite pleasant. But the general relief was mixed with bewilderment ; it was hard to realize that at last the Division's warfare was accomplished, that the end which only a few months ago had seemed ever so distant had indeed been reached and that each individual had come through. The Division's last success had been the least costly of all its major operations—a total of 10 officers and 146 men killed and died of wounds, 14 officers and 575 men wounded, and 3 men missing,[1] 748 in all, was remarkably light. To some extent the lightness of the casualty list reflected the

[1] Originally 3 officers and 137 men were reported missing, many of whom turned up among the wounded ; a few were drowned in crossing the rivers, and about 40 were taken prisoners but released soon after the armistice. These included a few H.A.C. and R.W.F. taken in the first attack on the Grave di Papadopoli, having lost their way and wandered into the enemy's position, and the party of the Borders captured near Visna on October 29th.

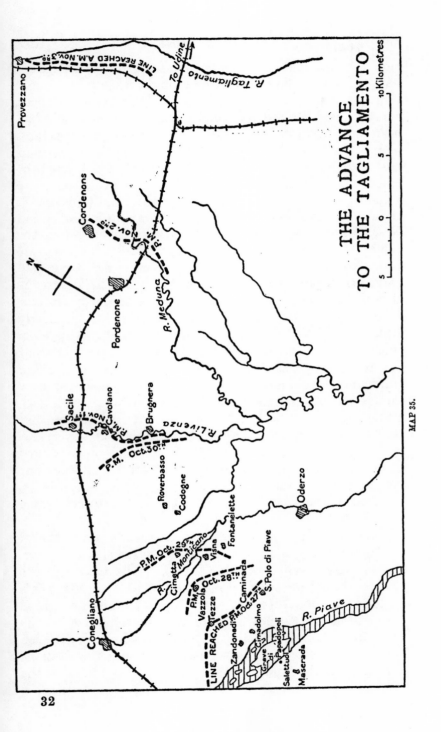

THE ADVANCE
TO THE TAGLIAMENTO

MAP 35.

32

lack of determination which had characterized the defence :
here and there the Austrians had fought resolutely enough,
some of the farms captured on October 27th had been
stoutly defended and the counter-attack on the Grave had
been quite vigorously pressed, but as a whole the Austrians
had not profited by the great strength of their positions
and had shown little of the tenacity with which the Germans had defended far weaker positions at Ginchy and
Bullecourt. Yet, even allowing for this, the lightness of
the list also reflected the skilful leadership of officers and
N.-C.-O.s, the use made of ground and of covering fire, the
combination of all weapons, and especially the accurate
and effective shooting of the artillery. All arms had
played their part well ; the work which had fallen to the
R.E. and Pioneers had been of even more than usual importance, while the R.A.M.C., who had had a peculiarly
difficult task, had risen to the emergency splendidly, even
when, as on October 27th, six miles had separated the front
line from the most advanced dressing-station and motor
ambulances could not yet cross the Piave. Of the infantry
enough has perhaps been said. Some battalions had been
luckier than others in their chances of distinction, but
all had worked well. The H.A.C. had given the operations a brilliant start, the Welch Fusiliers had backed
them up splendidly, and in the main attack all the four
attacking battalions had done well, while the Queen's,
who had a belated chance at Cimetta, had overcome some
of the stoutest opposition encountered.

The collapse of the Austrians in this last great battle of
the Italian campaigns must not obscure the special importance of the Seventh Division's work. The success of the
whole attack depended largely on the 22nd Brigade's
capture of the Grave di Papadopoli. This served as
jumping-off ground not only for the Division, but for the
units on its flanks, and the bridge-head which the British
Fourteenth Corps thus established enabled the Italians
to neutralize the failure of their own attempts to cross the

Piave. How far the news that the Piave had been crossed
and that the Allies were advancing Eastward affected the
Austrian resistance in other sections where at first they
had offered a more successful opposition it is impossible
to judge ; but in the last of its many battles the Seventh
Division had carried out admirably and accurately every
task allotted it, and it had ended the war in splendid style,
fighting as well as ever.

The collapse of Austria, followed a week later by the
armistice with the German Empire, meant that for the
Seventh Division demobilization was soon to become the
urgent problem. Most of its units being Regular—though
by this stage of the war it mattered little to the composition of a unit whether it was in name Regular, Territorial,
or " Service "—the Division was not likely to be detailed
to an Army of Occupation, as the Regular units had to be
forthwith restored to the nearest possible approach to a
normal footing. Accordingly the very day after the
armistice the withdrawal of the Division to the West
of the Tagliamento began, and on November 8th it
started on its four-days' trek back to Treviso, whence
it began entraining on November 13th for an area S.W. of
Vicenza.

November 14th saw Divisional Headquarters established
at Sossano, where they remained for nearly a month. The
troops were in comfortable billets and could at last get
a real rest, though a carefully arranged programme of
"training" in which athletics and educational facilities
figured unusually largely provided plenty of occupation.
A really impressive and memorable Divisional Thanks-
giving Service was held on November 17th ; and a picked
brigade under General Steele, consisting of the Queen's,
the Welch Fusiliers, and the Gordons, with the 12th Battery
R.F.A. and " A " Company of the 7th Battalion M.G.C.,
had the honour of representing the Division at a review
held by the King of Italy. On November 28th the H.A.C.
went off to Innsbruck, having been selected as the British

contribution to the Allied force which was occupying the
Tyrol; and in December demobilization began, the first
contingent to depart—over 500 officers and men, mainly
miners, students, and those somewhat ambiguously described as " pivotal men "—leaving on the last day of the
year.

With their departure the break-up of the Division was
in sight. Some weeks were to pass before all units had
been reduced to cadre and before those cadres had found
their way to England, the Regular units to be re-formed
with serving soldiers as quickly as possible, the Territorials
to be demobilized, the units called into existence for the
duration of the war to be disbanded. Till the last cadres
left Italy a Divisional organization was maintained, though
on January 25th General Shoubridge had relinquished
command and had taken farewell of the Division in a
special Order of the Day which summarized its achievements. He spoke with pride of his privilege in having
commanded such a Division in the field for nearly two years,
of its great deeds at Ypres, of Neuve Chapelle, of Loos,
of the Somme, of the ten nights and days' struggle for
Bullecourt, of the Broodseinde Ridge and Reutel, of its
great share in the final rout of Austria. He recalled its
68,000 casualties, reminded survivors of the sacred trust
left to them by the gallant comrades who had fallen in
the Division's ranks, and went on to speak of the qualities
on which the Division's achievements and record had been
founded—its unfailing loyalty and comradeship, its discipline, its smartness, its ready and cheerful response to
all calls.

Of the achievements General Shoubridge summarized
these pages have endeavoured to give an accurate account.
The Seventh Division was thrust at the outset into a
position of peculiar importance and prominence. In its
first battles it achieved a reputation and established a
tradition for tenacity, endurance, and hard fighting which
made great demands on those who afterwards replenished

MONUMENT DES ANGLAIS PAIVE.

its ranks. To maintain the standard set in October and November 1914 was a trying task, to add to that reputation required tremendous exertions ; and things which might have made the reputation of another Division were to some extent taken as no more than might have been expected of the Seventh. The very high level of its achievements makes its story the harder to write adequately. To do it full justice would require far more space than has been here available. Many gallant deeds have had to be omitted or too briefly sketched many of those who played important and useful parts in the Division's doings are hardly mentioned in these pages or appear less often than they should. But even the most jejune and inadequate recital of the Division's deeds and sufferings can hardly fail to show that it was one to which its members were proud indeed to belong, which Corps and Army commanders were delighted to include in their commands, which could take hard blows and return them with interest. More than one writer who has dealt with British campaigns has borne testimony to the part regimental spirit and traditions have played in building and maintaining the British Empire. It is a platitude that the war of 1914–1918 saw the rise and development of a Divisional esprit de corps and of Divisional traditions which played a similar part in the greatest of all British wars. Few Divisions can have equalled the strong Divisional spirit which inspired the Seventh Division, making it work as a team, working together towards the same end. The whole is greater than the parts, and something of the Division's peculiar strength lay in the fact that, good as its individual units were, their union in the Seventh Division added to their individual merits. It has been described as " a very happy Division," and therein lies no small part of the explanation of the wonderful record which these pages have sought to outline.

APPENDIX I

ORDER OF BATTLE OF DIVISION IN OCTOBER 1914

G.O.C. : Major-General T. Capper.

G.S.O. I : Lieut.-Colonel H. M. Montgomery.

G.S.O. II : Major I. Stewart (Scottish Rifles).

G.S.O. III : Captain W. S. Douglas (R.E.).

A.A.Q.M.G. : Lieut.-Colonel C. J. Perceval (R.A.).

D.A.A. & Q.M.G. : Captain R. F. A. Hobbs (R.E.).

D.A.Q.M.G. : Major W. H. V. Darell (Grenadier Guards).

A.D.M.S. : Colonel W. T. Swan.

D.A.D.M.S. : Lieut.-Colonel S. G. Moores.

A.D.V.S. : Major E. Brown.

D.A.D.O.S. : Major D. J. J. Hill.

Divisional Cavalry : — Northumberland Hussars. — Lieut.-Colonel P. B. Cookson.

Divisional Cyclist Company : — Captain L. Peel (Yorkshire Regt.).

Royal Artillery :

    C.R.A. : Brigadier-General H. K. Jackson.

    Brigade Major : Captain S. W. H. Rawlins.

    Staff Captain : Captain H. C. Cavendish.

    XIVth Brigade R.H.A.—Lieut.-Colonel H. D. White-Thompson.

      " C " and " F " Batteries R.H.A.

    XXIInd Brigade R.F.A.—Lieut.-Colonel D. J. M. Fasson.
    104th, 105th, and 106th Batteries R.F.A.

    XXXVth Brigade R.F.A.—Lieut.-Colonel E. P. Lambert.
    12th, 25th, and 58th Batteries R.F.A.

    IIIrd Heavy Brigade R.G.A.—Lieut.-Colonel T. A. Tancred.

      111th and 112th Heavy Batteries R.G.A.

Divisional Ammunition Column—Lieut.-Colonel H.A. Lake.

Royal Engineers :
  C.R.E. : Lieut.-Colonel A. T. Moore.
  Adjutant : Captain G. A. P. Brown.
  54th Field Company R.E.—Captain J. A. McEnery.
  55th Field Company R.E.—Captain L. St. V. Rose.
  Divisional Signal Company.—Major F. S. Garwood (R.E.).

20th Infantry Brigade :
  Brigadier-General H. Ruggles-Brise.
  Brigade Major : Major A. B. E. Cator (Scots Guards).
  Staff Captain : Captain B. N. Brooke (Grenadier
  Guards).
  1st Battalion Grenadier Guards.—Lieut.-Colonel M.
  Earle.
  2nd Battalion Scots Guards.—Lieut.-Colonel R. G. I.
  Bolton.
  2nd Battalion the Border Regiment.—Lieut.-Colonel
  L. I. Wood.
  2nd Battalion the Gordon Highlanders.—Lieut.-Colonel
  H. P. Uniacke.

21st Infantry Brigade :
  Brigadier-General H. E. Watts.
  Brigade Major : Major W. Drysdale (Royal Scots).
  Staff Captain : Captain A. L. Godman (Yorkshire Regt.).
  2nd Battalion the Bedfordshire Regiment.—Major
  J. M. Traill.
  2nd Battalion the Yorkshire Regiment.—Lieut.-Colonel
  C. A. C. King.
  2nd Battalion the Royal Scots Fusiliers.—Lieut.-Colonel
  A. G. Baird-Smith.
  2nd Battalion the Wiltshire Regiment.—Lieut.-Colonel
  J. F. Forbes.

22nd Infantry Brigade :
  Brigadier-General S. T. B. Lawford.
  Brigade Major : Captain G. M. James (the Buffs).
  Staff Captain : Captain R. V. Barker (R.W.F.).
  2nd Battalion the Queen's.—Lieut.-Colonel M. C. Coles.
  2nd Battalion the Royal Warwickshire Regiment.—Lieut.-
  Colonel W. L. Loring.

1st Battalion the Royal Welch Fusiliers.—Lieut.-Colonel H. O. S. Cadogan.

1st Battalion the South Staffordshire Regiment.—Lieut.-Colonel R. M. Ovens.

A.S.C.—7th Divisional Train.

R.A.M.C.—21st, 22nd, and 23rd Field Ambulances.

APPENDIX II

CHANGES IN COMPOSITION OF DIVISION

Divisional Cavalry :
  April 12th, 1915. " B " Squadron Northumberland
  Hussars transferred to First Division, " C " Squadron
  to Eighth : H.Q. to Base.
  May 13th, 1916. Northumberland Hussars reunited as
  XIIIth Corps Cavalry Regiment. " A " Squadron left
  Division.

Divisional Cyclist Company :
  Transferred May 10th, 1916, to XVth Corps Cyclist Battalion.

Royal Artillery :
  Oct. 19th, 1914. " C " Battery R.H.A. transferred to
  Third Cavalry Division.
  Nov. 27th, 1914. 55th (Howitzer) Battery R.F.A. joined
  Division, attached XIVth Brigade R.H.A.
  Dec. 21st, 1914. " T " Battery R.H.A. joined XIVth
  Brigade R.H.A.
  March 2nd, 1915. 55th (Howitzer) Battery R.F.A. left
  Division.
  March 9th, 1915. IIIrd Heavy Brigade R.G.A. left
  Division.
  June 24th, 1915. XXXVIIth (Howitzer) Brigade R.F.A.
  (31st, 35th, and 55th Batteries) joined Division.
  May 17th, 1916. XXXVIIth Brigade R.F.A. broken up ;
  31st Battery (4 guns) joined XXXVth Brigade R.F.A. ;
  35th Battery (4 guns) joined XXIInd Brigade R.F.A. ;
  a new 4-gun battery added to XIVth Brigade R.H.A.
  as D/XIVth Battery R.H.A. ; 55th Battery left
  Division.

Oct. 9th, 1916.   509th (Howitzer) Battery R.F.A. added to XIVth Brigade R.H.A.

Feb. 1917.   XIVth Brigade R.H.A. became an Army Brigade ; 509th Battery broken up, completing 31st and 35th Batteries to 6 guns each.

Royal Engineers :

Jan. 17th, 1915.   2nd Highland Field Company R.E. joined.

Aug. 29th, 1915.   55th Field Company transferred to Guards Division, replaced by 95th Field Company.

Jan. 29th, 1916.   2nd Highland Field Company transferred to Fifty-First Division, replaced by 3rd Durham Field Company.

Jan. 1st, 1917.   3rd Durham Field Company numbered as 528th (Durham) Field Company.

20th Infantry Brigade :

Dec. 5th, 1914.   6th Battalion Gordon Highlanders joined.

Aug. 4th and 8th, 1915.   1st Battalion Grenadier Guards and 2nd Battalion Scots Guards transferred to Guards Division, replaced by 8th (Service) Battalion and 9th (Service) Battalion the Devonshire Regiment.

Jan. 6th, 1916.   6th Gordon Highlanders transferred to Fifty-First Division, replaced by

Jan. 9th.   6th (T.F.) Battalion the Cheshire Regiment.

Feb. 24th, 1916.—20th Machine-Gun Company formed.

Feb. 25th, 1916.   6th Cheshires to Thirty-Ninth Division.

Feb. 10th, 1918.   20th Machine-Gun Company transferred to 7th Battalion Machine-Gun Corps.

Sept. 13th, 1918.   9th Devons to Twenty-Fifth Division.

21st Infantry Brigade :

April 8th, 1915.   4th (T.F.) Battalion the Cameron Highlanders joined.

Dec. 20th, 1915.   Brigade, less 4th Camerons, transferred to Thirtieth Division and replaced by 91st Brigade (q.v.).

22nd Infantry Brigade :

Nov. 11th, 1914.   8th (T.F.) Battalion the Royal Scots joined.

Aug. 20th, 1915.   8th Royal Scots transferred to Fifty-First Division.

Nov. 9th, 1915.   7th (T.F.) Battalion the King's joined.

Dec. 20th, 1915.   2nd Queen's and 1st South Staffords transferred to 91st Brigade, replaced by 20th (Service) and 24th (Service) Battalions the Manchester Regiment.

Jan. 7th, 1916.   7th King's transferred to Fifty-Fifth Division.

Feb. 24th, 1916.   22nd Machine-Gun Company formed.

May 21st, 1916.   24th Manchesters became Pioneers, replaced by

May 24th, 1916.   2nd Battalion the Royal Irish Regiment.

Oct. 14th, 1916.   2nd Royal Irish transferred to Sixteenth Division, replaced by 2/1st Battalion the Honourable Artillery Company.

April 1st, 1918.   22nd Machine-Gun Company transferred to 7th Battalion Machine-Gun Corps.

Sept. 13th, 1918.   20th Manchesters transferred to Twenty-Fifth Division.

91st Infantry Brigade (joined Dec. 20th, 1915 from Thirtieth Division)|:

   Brigadier-General F. J. Kempster.

   Brigade Major : Major A. K. Grant, the Queen's Own (Royal West Kent) Regiment.

   Staff Captain : Captain L. W. Kentish (Royal Fusiliers).

   20th (Service), 21st (Service), 22nd (Service), and 24th (Service) Battalions the Manchester Regiment.

Dec. 20th, 1915.   4th Cameron Highlanders transferred from 21st Brigade joined ; 20th and 24th Manchesters transferred to 22nd Brigade, replaced by 2nd Queen's and 1st South Staffords.

Jan. 7th, 1916.   4th Camerons to Fifty-First Division.

March 24th, 1916.   91st Machine-Gun Company joined.

April 1st, 1918.   91st Machine-Gun Company transferred to 7th Battalion Machine-Gun Corps.

Sept. 13th, 1918.   22nd Manchesters transferred to Twenty-Fifth Division.

Machine-Gun Corps :

March 25th, 1917.   228th Company Machine-Gun Corps joined.

April 1st, 1918.   7th Battalion Machine-Gun Corps formed out of 20th, 22nd, 91st, and 228th Machine-Gun Companies.

APPENDIX III

CHANGES IN COMMANDS AND STAFF [1]

G.O.C. :

Major-General T. Capper, till April 18th, 1915 (wounded).

Major-General H. de la P. Gough, till July 14th, 1915.

Major-General T. Capper, till Sept. 27th, 1915 (died of wounds).

Major-General H. E. Watts, till Jan. 6th, 1917.

Major-General G. de S. Barrow, till March 31st, 1917.

Major-General T. H. Shoubridge, till Armistice.

G.S.O. I. :

Colonel H. M. Montgomery, till Nov. 12th, 1914.

Lieut.-Colonel A. R. Hoskins (N. Staffords), till March 28th, 1915.

Lieut.-Colonel Hon. J. F. Gathorne Hardy (Grenadier Guards), till Jan. 1st, 1916.

Lieut.-Colonel C. Bonham Carter (R. W. Kent), till Oct. 15th, 1916.

Lieut.-Colonel G. W. Howard (Essex), till Oct. 27th, 1918.

Major W. B. G. Barne (R.A.), till Armistice.

G.S.O. II. :

Major I. Stewart (Scottish Rifles), till June 18th, 1915.

Major H. Needham (Gloucesters), till Aug. 12th, 1915.

Major E. FitzG. Dillon (R. Munster Fusiliers), till May 12th, 1916.

Lieut.-Colonel W. W. Seymour (R.B.), till Nov. 28th, 1916.

Major E. C. Gepp (D.C.L.I.), till July 3rd, 1917.

Major J. D. Boyd (Queen's), till March 14th, 1918.

Major E. G. L. Lawrence (Worcestershires), till Armistice.

[1] Rank given is that held on appointment.

499

G.S.O. III. :

Captain W. S. Douglas (R.E.), till Nov. 2nd, 1914 (died of wounds).

Captain L. C. Jackson (R.E.), till March 1915.

Major G. Hutchinson (Indian Army), till April 1915.

Captain R. S. Ryan (R.H.A.), till Nov. 1915.

Captain M. H. Dendy (R.A.), till Feb. 12th, 1916.

Captain L. W. Kentish (R.F.), till June 12th, 1916.

Captain P. L. Drake Brockman (Borders), till July 12th, 1916.

Captain H. Noble (Northumberland Hussars), till Aug. 9th, 1917.

Captain H. J. Brooks (Manchesters), till March 17th, 1918.

Captain G. R. Mitchison (2nd D.G.), till April 18th, 1918.

Captain F. L. Houghton (R. Warwickshires), till Armistice.

A.A. & Q.M.G. :

Lieut.-Colonel C. J. Perceval (R.A.), till Oct. 26th, 1914 (wounded).

Lieut.-Colonel C. M. Ryan (A.S.C.), till Nov. 11th, 1914.

Major A. C. Daly (West Yorks), till June 12th, 1915.

Lieut.-Colonel R. S. Gorton (R.A.), till Sept. 22nd, 1915.

Lieut.-Colonel Hon. M. A. Wingfield (R.B.), till July 24th, 1917.

Lieut.-Colonel B. J. Lang (A. & S.H.), till Armistice.

D.A.A. & Q.M.G. :

Captain R. F. A. Hobbs (R.E.), till July 27th, 1915.

Captain T. S. Riddell Webster (Scottish Rifles), till July 8th, 1917.

Major Hon. A. C. S. Chichester (Irish Guards), till Armistice.

D.A.Q.M.G. :

Major W. H. V. Darell (Grenadier Guards), till July 1st, 1915.

Major R. H. D. Tompson (R.A.), till Oct. 18th, 1916.

Major H. N. A. Hunter (Queen's), till Sept. 4th, 1917.

Major P. H. N. M. Vyvyan (A.S.C.), till Armistice.

A.D.M.S. :

Colonel W. T. Swan, till June 1915.
Colonel W. H. Starr, till July 23rd, 1915.
Lieut.-Colonel G. S. McLoughlin, till Jan. 1916.
Lieut.-Colonel L. Way, till April 7th, 1916.
Lieut.-Colonel A. W. Hooper, till Oct. 1917.
Lieut.-Colonel S. A. Archer, till Armistice.

D.A.D.M.S. :

Lieut.-Colonel S. G. Moores, till Jan. 1915.
Major G. K. Morgan, till Feb. 1915.
Major P. H. Henderson, till Oct. 1915.
Lieut.-Colonel H. S. Roch, till Nov. 1916.
Captain S. J. A. H. Walshe, till Armistice.

A.D.V.S. :

Major E. Brown, till April 1915.
Captain M. St. G. Glasse, till July 1917.
Captain T. J. Faithfull, till Armistice.

D.A.D.O.S. :

Major D. J. J. Hill, till April 1915.
Major R. O. Sheppard, till Nov. 1915.
Lieut. C. H. Deane, till Sept. 1918.
Captain E. L. Shoetensack, till Armistice.

B.G.R.A. :

Brigadier-General H. K. Jackson, till March 14th, 1915.
Brigadier-General J. F. N. Birch, till July 19th, 1915.
Brigadier-General J. F. Rotton, till Aug. 20th, 1916.
Brigadier-General H. S. Seligman, till Nov. 9th, 1916.
Brigadier-General H. C. Stanley Clarke, till Armistice.

Brigade Major, R.A. :

Captain S. W. H. Rawlins, till Sept. 1915.
Major W. G. Wynter, till July 14th, 1916.
Captain S. A. Boddam Whetham, till March 15th, 1918.
Major K. M. Agnew, till Armistice.

Staff Captain, R.A. :

Captain H. C. Cavendish, till Nov. 23rd, 1914.
Major R. G. Finlayson, till March 1915.

Captain W. G. Lindsell, till Dec. 1915.

Captain Hon. E. R. Thesiger (Surrey Yeo.), till March 10th, 1917.

Captain H. F. Barker, till June 1st, 1917.

Captain F. S. Arbuthnot (Suffolk Yeo.), till Armistice.

C.R.E. :

Lieut.-Colonel A. T. Moore, till June 1915.

Lieut.-Colonel R. P. Lee, till Sept. 18th, 1915.

Major G. H. Boileau, till Nov. 16th, 1917.

Lieut.-Colonel A. W. Reid, till Feb. 4th, 1918.

Major E. Barnardiston, till Oct. 16th, 1915.

Major W. A. F. Kerrich, till Armistice.

Adjutant, R.E. :

Captain G. A. P. Brown, till Nov. 24th, 1915.

Lieut. E. H. M. Clifford, till May 4th, 1918.

Captain C. W. F. Busk, till June 24th, 1918.

Captain A. H. Fletcher, till Armistice.

B.G.C. 20th Brigade :

Brigadier-General H. Ruggles-Brise, till Nov. 2nd, 1914 (wounded).

(Major A. B. E. Cator, Scots Guards, officiating Nov. 2nd–14th.)

Brigadier-General F. J. Heyworth, till Aug. 15th, 1915.

Brigadier-General J. F. H. F. S. Trefusis, till Oct. 24th, 1915 (killed).

Brigadier-General C. J. Deverell, till Aug. 6th, 1916.

Brigadier-General H. R. Green, till Armistice.

Brigade Major, 20th Brigade :

Major A. B. E. Cator, Scots Guards, till April 5th, 1915.

Major F. G. Alston, Scots Guards, till Aug. 1915.

Captain C. C. Foss, Bedfordshires, till Oct. 28th, 1916.

Captain A. N. Acland, D.C.L.I., till March 17th, 1918.

Captain H. J. Brooks, Manchesters, till Armistice.

Staff Captain, 20th Brigade :

Captain B. N. Brooke, Grenadier Guards, till Nov. 2nd, 1914 (wounded).

Lieut. A. E. G. Palmer, Yorkshires, till Oct. 3rd, 1915.
Major J. M. Hamilton, Gordons, till Jan. 4th, 1916.
Captain L. Carr, Gordons, till May 8th, 1916.
Captain R. M. Burmann, Borders, till April 17th, 1918.
Captain W. E. Kelly, Borders, till Armistice.

B.G.C. 21st Brigade :
Brigadier-General H. E. Watts, till Sept. 27th, 1916.
Brigadier-General R. A. Berners, till Dec. 3rd, 1915.
Brigadier-General Hon. C. J. Sackville-West, till Brigade
left Division.

Brigade Major, 21st Brigade :
Captain W. Drysdale, R. Scots, till Feb. 17th, 1915.
Captain E. R. C. Wyatt, 106th Pioneers (I.A.), till April
16th, 1915.
Captain G. L. Crossman, West Yorkshires, till Brigade
left Division.

Staff Captain, 21st Brigade :
Captain A. L. Godman, Yorkshires, till Nov. 1st, 1914
(wounded).
Captain G. L. Crossman, West Yorkshires, till April 16th,
1915.
Captain J. R. Minshull-Ford, R.W.F., till June 5th, 1915.
Captain H. F. Chads, Borders, till Oct. 24th, 1915.
Captain R. V. G. Horn, R.S.F., till Brigade left Division.

B.G.C. 22nd Brigade :
Brigadier-General S. T. B. Lawford, till Aug. 27th, 1915.
Brigadier-General J. Mc. C. Steele, till Armistice.

Brigade Major, 22nd Brigade :
Captain G. M. James, the Buffs, till Nov. 4th, 1914 (killed).
Captain E. G. L. Thurlow, Somerset L.I., till Oct. 24th,
1915.
Captain H. F. Chads, Borders, till April 2nd, 1917.
Captain A. J. Thompson, Scots Guards, till Sept. 6th, 1918.
Captain G. F. J. Cumberlege, Oxford & Bucks L.I., till
Armistice.

33

Staff Captain, 22nd Brigade ;

    Captain R. V. Barker, R.W.F., till Oct. 31st, 1914 (killed).

    Captain E. A. Parker, R.W.F., till Nov. 14th, 1914.

    Captain S. J. Lowe, R.F., till Jan. 1915.

    Captain R. T. Fellowes, R.B., till Sept. 17th, 1915.

    Captain A. B. Beaumann, S. Staffords, till May 20th, 1916.

    Captain O. W. White, Dorsets, till Oct. 23rd, 1916.

    Captain R. F. Parker, Manchesters, till Nov. 24th, 1917.

    Captain C. A. Lawford, S. Staffords, till Armistice.

B.G.C. 91st Brigade :

    Brigadier-General F. J. Kempster, till Feb. 3rd, 1916.

    Brigadier-General J. R. Minshull-Ford, till Nov. 20th, 1916.

    Brigadier-General H. R. Cumming, till May 12th, 1917.

    Brigadier-General R. T. Pelly, till Armistice.

Brigade Major, 91st Brigade :

    Major A. K. Grant, R.W. Kent, till Sept. 9th, 1916.

    Captain A. N. Acland, D.C.L.I., till Oct. 28th, 1916.

    Captain R. N. O'Connor, Scottish Rifles, till March 1st, 1917.

    Major C. A. H. Palairet, R.F., till May 22nd, 1917.

    Captain O. F. Morshead, R.E., till May 16th, 1918.

    Captain W. Ormrod, L.F., till Armistice.

Staff Captain, 91st Brigade :

    Captain L. W. Kentish, R.F., till Feb. 12th, 1916.

    Captain J. P. Duke, R. Warwickshires, till June 13th, 1916.

    Captain D. R. Turnbull, Gordons, till Sept. 14th, 1916.

    Captain O. F. Morshead, R.E., till May 22nd, 1917.

    Captain S. d' E. Colam, Gordons, till July 7th, 1918.

    Captain J. F. Bygott, R. Warwickshires, till Armistice.

APPENDIX IV

CHANGES IN COMMAND OF UNITS [1]

Northumberland Hussars :
  Lieut.-Colonel P. B. Cookson, till April 1915 (H.Q. of regiment to Base).

XIVth Brigade R.H.A. :
  Lieut.-Colonel H. D. White-Thompson, till Oct. 22nd, 1914 (wounded).
  Major J. S. Ollivant (temporarily), till Nov. 6th, 1914.
  Lieut.-Colonel W. A. Robinson, till March 1st, 1915.
  Lieut.-Colonel H. H. Tudor, till Jan. 31st, 1916.
  Major R. Preeston, till Feb. 10th, 1916.
  Lieut.-Colonel H. C. Stanley Clarke, till Nov. 9th, 1916.
  Major T. E. P. Wickham, till Brigade left Division.

XXIInd Brigade R.F.A. :
  Lieut.-Colonel D. J. M. Fasson, till Jan. 6th, 1915.
  Lieut.-Colonel E. W. Alexander, till Aug. 23rd, 1915.
  Lieut.-Colonel R. M. Johnson, till Jan. 10th, 1916.
  Lieut.-Colonel A. S. Buckle, till Aug. 18th, 1916.
  Lieut.-Colonel W. A. Short, till Sept. 13th, 1916.
  Lieut.-Colonel R. G. Maturin, till Oct. 18th, 1918.
  Major R. Abell, till Armistice.

XXXVth Brigade R.F.A. :
  Lieut.-Colonel E. P. Lambert, till Nov. 1st, 1914 (wounded).
  Lieut.-Colonel G. W. Nicholson, till July 21st, 1915.
  Lieut.-Colonel J. S. Ollivant, till Sept. 19th, 1915.
  Lieut.-Colonel H. C. Stanley Clarke, till Feb. 10th, 1916.
  Lieut.-Colonel O. C. Du Port, till Jan. 1917.

[1] A date in brackets after an officer's name is that of assuming command when an appreciable interval had elapsed since the vacancy, during which some junior officer, sometimes not mentioned in the Diary, had been in temporary command. Temporary changes due to absence on leave, etc., are not mentioned. Rank shown is that held on assuming command.

Major P. B. Dresser (temporarily), Jan.–Feb. 1917.
Lieut.-Colonel J. B. MacFarlan, till Dec. 1917.
Major G. E. A. Granet (temporarily), Jan.–Feb. 1918.
Lieut.-Colonel H. C. Oldham, till Armistice.

XXXVIIth Brigade R.F.A. :
Lieut.-Colonel E. W. Spedding, till Feb. 2nd, 1916.
Lieut.-Colonel St. G. Kirke, till May 17th, 1916 (Brigade broken up).

IIIrd Heavy Brigade R.G.A. :
Lieut.-Colonel T. A. Tancred, till March 4th, 1915 (Brigade left Division).

Divisional Ammunition Column :
Lieut.-Colonel H. A. Lake, till Feb. 20th, 1915.
Major G. J. Henderson, till March 3rd, 1915.
Lieut.-Colonel H. Montgomery Campbell, till Dec. 22nd, 1915.
Lieut.-Colonel H. H. Rogers, till Oct. 20th, 1917.
Captain A. Burrows, till Nov. 14th, 1917.
Major A. W. Lyle Kidd, till Armistice.

54th Field Company R.E. :
Captain J. A. McEnery, till Oct. 26th, 1914 (killed).
Captain G. C. Williams, till Nov. 18th, 1914.
Major D. S. McInnes, till Nov. 25th, 1914 (wounded).
Major E. Kingston, till March 28th, 1915 (killed).
Major G. F. B. Goldney, till June 20th, 1916.
Major C. J. Clark, till Aug. 2nd, 1916.
Major R. H. Greig, till Aug. 27th, 1916 (killed).
Captain W. B. T. Draper, till April 18th, 1918.
Major W. A. F. Kerrich, till Oct. 16th, 1918.
Major P. K. Boulnois, till Armistice.

55th Field Company R.E. :
Captain L. St. V. Rose, till Nov. 28th, 1914 (killed).
Captain J. O. H. Moore, till Dec. 20th, 1914 (died of wounds).
Captain A. Brough, till Aug. 1915 (Company left Division).

95th Field Company R.E. :
Major W. C. Tuck, till Nov. 18th, 1915.
Captain E. Crewdson, till Dec. 16th, 1915.

Major G. C. Dobson, till Feb. 8th, 1917.

Major E. Crewdson, till May 5th, 1918.

Major E. H. M. Clifford, till Armistice.

2nd Highland Field Company R.E. :

Major H. J. Kinghorn, till March 10th, 1915 (wounded).

Major R. Mitchell, till Jan. 1916 (Company left Division).

3rd Durham Field Company R.E. (later 528th (Durham) Field Company) :

Major H. Paterson, till Dec. 16th, 1916.

Major P. S. Watkins, till Jan. 13th, 1917 (wounded).

Captain C. P. Gibson, till Feb. 26th, 1917.

Major W. A. F. Kerrich, till Jan. 1st, 1918.

Major C. P. Gibson, till Armistice.

Divisional Signal Company :

Major F. S. Garwood, R.E., till Nov. 18th, 1914.

Captain E. A. Osborne, R.E., till Nov. 1915.

Captain R. N. O'Connor, Scottish Rifles, till Oct. 28th, 1916.

Captain F. L. Lowson, R.E., till March 5th, 1917 (killed).

Captain R. H. Keeling, R.E., till Feb. 18th, 1918.

Major J. W. Orange Bromhead, K.O.Y.L.I., till Armistice.

1st Battalion Grenadier Guards :

Lieut.-Colonel M. Earle, till Oct. 29th, 1914 (wounded and prisoner).

Captain G. E. C. Rasch, till Nov. 17th, 1914.

Major C. E. Corkran, till Nov. 29th, 1914.

Lieut.-Colonel L. R. Fisher-Rowe, till March 12th, 1915 (killed).

Major G. F. Trotter, till March 21st, 1915.

Lieut.-Colonel C. E. Corkran, till July 14th, 1915.

Major G. F. Trotter, till Aug. 4th, 1915 (Battalion left Division).

2nd Battalion Scots Guards :

Lieut.-Colonel R. G. I. Bolton, till Oct. 26th, 1914 (wounded and prisoner).

Captain G. C. B. Paynter, till March 12th, 1915 (wounded).

Captain Sir F. L. FitzWygram, till April 4th, 1915.

Major A. B. E. Cator, till Aug. 1915 (Battalion left Division).

8th Battalion the Royal Scots :
  Lieut.-Colonel A. Brook, till May 18th, 1915 (killed).
  Major W. Gemmill, till Aug. 1915 (Battalion left Division).

2nd Battalion the Queen's Regiment :
  Lieut.-Colonel M. C. Coles, till Oct. 31st, 1914 (wounded).
  Captain W. H. Alleyne, till Nov. 6th, 1914 (wounded and prisoner).
  Captain F. S. Montague Bates (E. Surreys), till Dec.20th, 1914.
  Major L. M. Crofts, till Jan. 13th, 1915.
  Major H. F. Kirkpatrick (the Buffs), till Feb. 2nd, 1915.
  Major H. R. Bottomley, till May 17th, 1915 (killed).
  Captain R. Duckworth (S. Staffords), till June 10th, 1915.
  Captain M. G. Heath, till Sept. 25th, 1915 (killed).
  Captain F. C. Longbourne, till Oct. 6th, 1915.
  Major H. W. Smith (Oct. 9th, 1915), till Feb. 16th, 1916.
  Lieut.-Colonel F. C. Longbourne, till Sept. 23rd, 1917.
  Major B. H. Driver, till October 4th, 1917 (killed).
  Lieut.-Colonel R. M. Birkett (R. Sussex), till March 28th, 1918.
  Lieut.-Colonel H. D. Carlton (R. Scots), till Armistice.

2nd Battalion the R. Warwickshire Regiment :
  Lieut.-Colonel W. L. Loring, till Oct. 24th, 1914 (killed).
  Major G. N. B. Foster, till Oct. 31st, 1914 (wounded and prisoner).
  Major R. H. W. Brewis, till Dec. 18th, 1914 (killed).
  Major A. J. Poole, till Jan. 30th, 1915.
  Major H. C. Hart, till March 19th, 1915.
  Lieut.-Colonel V. R. Pigott, till July 14th, 1915.
  Major B. R. Lefroy, till Sept. 25th, 1915 (killed).
  Major A. G. Pritchard (Indian Army), till April 14th, 1917.
  Major C. B. Hore, till Sept. 26th, 1917.
  Major C. S. Burt (S. Staffords), till Oct. 16th, 1917.
  Lieut.-Colonel H. Strevens (Nov. 3rd, 1917), till Armistice.

7th Battalion the King's Regiment :
  Lieut.-Colonel S. C. Marriott, till Jan. 1916 (Battalion left Division).

8th Battalion the Devonshire Regiment :
Lieut.-Colonel A. G. W. Grant (West India Regiment), till Sept. 25th, 1915 (killed).
Lieut.-Colonel J. D. Ingles, till May 30th, 1916.
Lieut.-Colonel B. C. James, till March 4th, 1917.
Lieut.-Colonel S. H. Worrall (Borders), till Armistice.

9th Battalion the Devonshire Regiment :
Colonel T. A. H. Davies, till Sept. 12th, 1915.
Major H. I. Storey, till Sept. 25th, 1915 (wounded).
Major R. J. Milne, till May 30th, 1916.
Lieut.-Colonel H. I. Storey, till Feb. 18th, 1917.
Lieut.-Colonel R. J. Morris (S. Staffords), till Oct. 4th, 1917 (wounded).
Lieut.-Colonel H. I. Storey, till Sept. 1918 (Battalion left Division).

2nd Battalion the Bedfordshire Regiment :
Major J. M. Traill, till Oct. 31st, 1914 (killed).
Captain C. C. Foss, till Nov. 7th, 1914.
Captain C. B. Cumberledge, till Nov. 18th, 1914.
Major W. H. Denne, till Jan. 1st, 1915.
Lieut.-Colonel C. C. Onslow, till Sept. 26th, 1915 (wounded).
Major J. C. Monteith, till Oct. 1st, 1915 (killed).
Major H. F. Bidder (R. Sussex), till Nov. 10th, 1915.
Major H. S. Poyntz, till Dec. 1915 (Battalion left Division).

2nd Battalion the R. Irish Regiment :
Lieut.-Colonel W. J. Dugan (Worcestershire), till Oct. 1915 (Battalion left Division).

2nd Battalion the Yorkshire Regiment :
Lieut.-Colonel C. A. C. King, till Oct. 30th, 1914 (killed).
Captain B. S. Moss Blundell, till Dec. 24th, 1914.
Lieut.-Colonel W. L. Alexander, till May 14th, 1915 (killed).
Major T. W. Stansfeld, till July 8th, 1915.
Lieut.-Colonel W. H. Young (E. Yorkshires), till Nov. 30th, 1915 (wounded).
Captain H. S. Kreyer, till Dec. 1915 (Battalion left Division).

2nd Battalion the Royal Scots Fusiliers :
Lieut.-Colonel A. G. Baird-Smith, till Oct. 31st, 1914 (wounded and prisoner).
Captain T. B. Traill, till Nov. 12th, 1914.
Major A. M. H. Forbes, till Jan. 19th, 1915.
Major J. H. W. Pollard, till Aug. 21st, 1915.
Captain A. H. Connell, till Sept. 28th, 1915 (killed).
Major R. K. Walshe (Oct. 9th, 1915), till Dec. 1915 (Battalion left Division).

6th Battalion the Cheshire Regiment :
Lieut.-Colonel H. Hesse, till March 1916 (Battalion left Division).

1st Battalion the Royal Welch Fusiliers :
Lieut.-Colonel H. O. S. Cadogan, till Oct. 30th, 1914 (killed).
Major R. E. P. Gabbett (Nov.10th, 1914), till Feb. 1915.
Captain J. R. Minshull-Ford, till March 24th, 1915.
Major G. F. H. Dickson, till April 15th, 1915.
Lieut.-Colonel R. E. P. Gabbett, till May 17th, 1915 (killed).
Lieut.-Colonel R. A. Berners, till Sept. 30th, 1915.
Major J. R. Minshull-Ford (Oct. 9th, 1915), till Feb. 3rd, 1916.
Major C. I. Stockwell, till Sept. 16th, 1916.
Major W. G. Holmes, till Oct. 1918.
Major L. A. Alston, till Armistice.

2nd Battalion the Border Regiment :
Lieut.-Colonel L. I. Wood, till Oct. 29th, 1914 (wounded).
Captain G. E. Warren, till Jan. 9th, 1915.
Lieut.-Colonel L. I. Wood, till May 17th, 1915 (killed).
Lieut.-Colonel E. I. de S. Thorpe (Bedfords), till Sept. 1916.
Major G. E. Beatty-Pownall, till Feb. 29th, 1916.
Lieut.-Colonel E. I. de S. Thorpe, till June 1917.
Lieut.-Colonel G. E. Beatty-Pownall, till Sept. 1917.
Major G. O. Ramsbotham (Manchesters), till Nov. 7th, 1917.

Major W. Kerr, till May 3rd, 1918 (killed).
Major H. A. Ross (Gordons), till Sept. 2nd, 1918.
Major S. Darwell, till Armistice.

1st Battalion the South Staffordshire Regiment :
Lieut.-Colonel R. M. Ovens, till Oct. 30th, 1914 (wounded).
Captain J. M. Vallentin, till Nov. 7th, 1914 (killed).
Captain R. Duckworth, till Jan. 20th, 1915.
Major A. C. Buckle, till March 7th, 1915.
Captain S. Bonner, till April 5th, 1915.
Major H. E. Walshe, till July 29th, 1915.
Colonel R. M. Ovens, till Sept. 10th, 1916.
Major A. B. Beaumann, till May 25th, 1918.
Major L. L. Hassell, till July 7th, 1918.
Major W. R. English-Murphy, till Armistice.

2nd Battalion the Wiltshire Regiment :
Lieut.-Colonel J. F. Forbes, till Oct. 24th, 1914 (prisoner).
Captain P. S. Beaver, till March 9th, 1915.
Captain R. M. T. Gillson, till March 10th, 1915 (wounded).
Captain E. L. Makins, till June 1st, 1915.
Lieut.-Colonel W. S. Brown, till June 22nd, 1915.
Major B. H. Leathem (Yorkshires), till Sept. 26th, 1915 (killed).
Major C. G. Forsyth (Yorkshires), till Sept. 27th, 1915 (wounded).
Major A. V. P. Martin (Oct. 10th, 1915), till Nov. 13th, 1915.
Major R. M. T. Gillson, till Dec. 1915 (Battalion left Division).

20th Battalion the Manchester Regiment :
Lieut.-Colonel S. Mitchell, till Jan. 1916.
Major W. D. O'Brien, till March 6th, 1916.
Lieut.-Colonel H. Lewis (Indian Army), till July 1st, 1916 (killed).
Major E. Smalley till March 1917.
Major C. E. N. Lomax (Welch Regt.), March–April 1917.
Lieut.-Colonel E. Smalley, till May 15th, 1917.
Lieut.-Colonel D. R. Turnbull (Gordons), till Oct. 1st, 1917 (killed).

Major J. A. Healing (R. Warwickshires), till Oct. 8th, 1917.

Major T. Kemp, till Oct. 9th, 1917 (killed).

Major C. S. Burt (S. Staffords) (Oct. 16th, 1917), till Sept. 1918 (Battalion left Division).

21st Battalion the Manchester Regiment :
Colonel W. W. Norman, till June 16th, 1917.
Major C. E. N. Lomax (Welch Regt.) till Sept. 1918 (Battalion left Division).

22nd Battalion the Manchester Regiment :
Lieut.-Colonel P. Whetham, till Feb. 11th, 1917.
Major F. W. Woodward (Loyal North Lancs), till Dec. 20th, 1917.
Major B. G. Atkin, till Jan. 14th, 1918.
Major H. G. Harrison, till April 11th, 1918.
Major G. O. Ramsbotham, till Armistice.

24th Battalion the Manchester Regiment :
Lieut.-Colonel J. B. Batten, till Nov. 12th, 1916.
Lieut.-Colonel J. H. Chadwick, till May 3rd, 1916 (killed).
Lieut.-Colonel F. S. Pountney, till Armistice.

2nd Battalion the Gordon Highlanders :
Lieut.-Colonel H. P. Uniacke, till Oct. 30th, 1914 (wounded).
Captain J. R. E. Stansfeld, till Nov. 2nd, 1914 (wounded).
Lieut. J. M. Hamilton, till Dec. 5th, 1914.
Captain B. G. R. Gordon, till Dec. 17th, 1914.
Captain J. R. E. Stansfeld, till Jan. 29th, 1915.
Lieut.-Colonel H. P. Uniacke, till March 13th, 1915 (killed).
Major J. M. Hamilton, till April 4th, 1915.
Lieut.-Colonel A. F. Gordon, till May 16th, 1915 (wounded).
Major J. R. E. Stansfeld, till Sept. 25th, 1915 (killed).
Captain L. Carr, till Oct. 26th, 1915.
Major B. G. R. Gordon, till July 20th, 1915 (killed).
Lieut.-Colonel H. A. Ross, till Sept. 3rd, 1916.
Major R. D. Oxley, till Sept. 6th, 1916 (killed).
Major D. R. Turnbull, till Oct. 1st, 1916.

Lieut.-Colonel R. N. Tytler, till Dec. 27th, 1916.
Major D. R. Turnbull, till Feb. 4th, 1917.
Major P. W. Brown, till Aug. 17th, 1917.
Lieut.-Colonel F. L. M. C. Maitland, till Sept. 1st, 1918.
Lieut.-Colonel H. A. Ross, till Oct. 27th, 1918 (killed).
Major W. Gordon, till Armistice.

6th Battalion the Gordon Highlanders :
Lieut.-Colonel C. MacLean, till March 13th, 1915 (killed).
Major P. W. Brown, till July 8th, 1915.
Lieut.-Colonel J. E. MacQueen, till Sept. 26th, 1915
(killed).
Major J. Dawson, till Jan. 1916 (Battalion left Division).

4th Battalion the Cameron Highlanders :
Lieut.-Colonel A. Fraser, till May 17th, 1915 (killed).
Lieut.-Colonel H. Fraser, till Jan. 1916 (Battalion left
Division).

2/1st Battalion the Honourable Artillery Company :
Lieut.-Colonel A. Lambert Ward, till June 2nd, 1917.
Lieut.-Colonel R. N. O'Connor (Scottish Rifles), till
Armistice.

Divisional Train :
Lieut.-Colonel C. M. Ryan, till Nov. 7th, 1914.
Major H. G. Burrard, till April 1st, 1915.
Lieut.-Colonel G. Vawdrey, till Sept. 1918.
Major A. M. R. Whittington, till Armistice.

7th Battalion Machine-Gun Corps (formed April 1st, 1918) :
Lieut.-Colonel R. M. Birkett, till Armistice.

APPENDIX V

Victoria Crosses :

Lieutenant J. A. O. Brooke, Gordon Highlanders, Oct. 1914.

Drummer W. Kenny, Gordon Highlanders, Oct. 1914.

Captain J. M. Vallentin, South Staffordshires, Nov. 1914.

Private J. Mackenzie, Scots Guards, Dec. 1914.

Private A. Acton, Border Regiment, Dec. 1914.

Private J. Smith, Border Regiment, Dec. 1914.

Captain C. C. Foss, Bedfordshires, March 1915.

Corporal W. Anderson, Yorkshires, March 1915.

Private E. Barber, Grenadier Guards, March 1915.

L.-Cpl. W. D. Fuller, Grenadier Guards, March 1915.

C.-S.-M. F. Barter, R. Welch Fusiliers, May 1915.

Private W. Angus, H.L.I. (attached Royal Scots), June 1915.

Private A. Vickers, R. Warwickshires, Sept. 1915.

Private T. Veale, Devonshires, July 1916.

MAP 36.

INDEX OF BATTLES AND ACTIONS

The names printed in heavier type are of those actions for which Battle Honours have been awarded to units which served in the Division.

---

[1] The battle honour " Delville Wood " was awarded for the operations in that area of the period July 15th–Sept. 3rd.

[1] The battle honour " Polygon
Wood " was given for the operations
in that area of Sept. 26th–Oct. 3rd,
1917.

INDEX OF PERSONS

Capper, Maj.-Gen. Sir T., 3, 5, 8, 19, 23, 24, 39, 43, 48–51, 55, 65, 70, 80, 82, 93, 94, 100, 101, 107, 112, 117 123, 131, 138, 141, 150, 152, 182, 196, 198, 216, 221–3, 276, 403, 413, 492, 499
Carden, Maj. H. C., 207
Carlton, Maj. H. D., 406, 508
Carr, Capt. L., 242, 503, 512
Cartwright, Capt., 208
Cator, Maj. A. B. E., 101, 159, 493, 502, 507
Cavan, Br.-Gen. Lord, 87, 94, 100–105 (Gen.), 459
Cavendish, Capt. H. C., 492, 501
Chads, Capt. H. F., 238, 503
Chadwick, Lt.-Col. J. H., 393, 396, 512
Chauncey, Capt. W. A. A., 218
Chichester, Maj. A. C. S., 403, 500
Christie, Maj. H. W. A., 83
Clark, Maj. C. J., 506
Cleaver, 2nd Lt., A. E. T., 176
Clifford, Lt. E. H. M., 502 (Maj.), 507
Colam, Lt. S. d'E., 396 (Maj.), 504
Colby, Maj. L. R. V., 52
Coles, Lt.-Col. M. C., 92, 493, 508
Congreve, Lt.-Gen. Sir W. N., 246
Connaught, H.R.H. the Duke of, 448
Connell, Capt. A. H., 224, 231, 510
Cookson, Lt.-Col. P. B., 492, 505
Cooper, Lt. W., 208
Corkran, Maj. C. E., 112 (Lt.-Col.), 159, 171, 191, 507
Cottrell, Capt. J., 434
Crewdson, Capt. E., 506
Crofts, Maj. L. M., 92, 505
Crossman, Capt. G. L., 159, 503
Cumberlege, Capt. C. B., 147, 509
Cumberlege, Capt. G. F. J., 503
Cumming, Br.-Gen. H. R., 323, 335, 344, 345, 350, 387, 388, 504

D

Dalrymple, Maj. Lord, 60, 63
Daly, Maj. A. C., 112, 500
Darby, Lt. M. A., 157
Darell, Maj. W. H. V., 197, 492, 500
Darwell, Maj. G., 511
Davies, Maj.-Gen. Sir F. J., 165
Davies, Col. T. A. H., 509
Dawson, Maj. J. (Gordons), 54
Dawson, Capt. J. M., 434
Deane, Lt. C. H., 511
Dempster, Capt. D. B., 428
Dendy, Capt. M. H., 500
Denne, Maj. W. H., 112, 147, 509
De Trafford, Capt. H. J., 208

Deverell, Br.-Gen. C. J., 237, 249, 258, 301, 502
Dibben, Lt. W. L., 226
Dickson, Maj. G. F. H., 510
Dillon, Maj. E. FitzG., 499
Dobson, Maj. G. C., 266, 507
Dooner, Lt. A. E. C. T., 40 (Capt.), 84
Douglas, Gen. Sir C., 9
Douglas, Capt. W. S., 101, 492, 500
Drake-Brockman, Capt. P. L., 500
Draper, Capt. W. B. T., 506
Dresser, Maj. P. B., 506
Driver, Maj. B. H., 417, 421, 508
Drysdale, Maj. W., 493, 503
Duckworth, Capt. R., 505, 511
Duff, Lt. S. H., 263 (Capt.), 366, 369
Dugan, Lt.-Col. W. J., 271, 287, 509
Duguid, Capt. C. F., 359
Duke, Capt. J. P., 208, 504
Duncan, Sergt., 475
Dunlop, Capt. J. S., 47, 49, 51
Du Port, Lt.-Col. O. C., 505

E

Earle, Lt.-Col. M., 71, 72, 96, 493, 507
English-Murphy, Lt.-Col. W. R., 453, 511
Evans, C.-S.-M., 58

F

Fabeck, Gen. von, 70–86
Fairlie, Capt. F., 44, 58
Faithfull, Capt. T. J., 501
Fanshawe, Lt.-Gen. E. A., 341
Fanshawe, Maj.-Gen. R., 441
Fasson, Lt.-Col. D. J. M., 493, 505
Fearon, Capt. P. J., 122
Fellowes, Capt. R. T., 504
Finckenstein, Gen. von, 412
Finlay, Capt. T. P., 212
Finlayson, Maj. R. G., 501
Fisher-Rowe, Lt.-Col. L. R., 143, 150, 507
FitzWygram, Capt. Sir F. L., 507
Fleetwood, Capt. G. C., 85
Fletcher, Capt. A. H., 502
Foch, Gen. F., 183, 201, 202
Forbes, Maj. A. H. M., 510
Forbes, Lt.-Col. J. F., 96, 493, 511
Forsyth, Maj. C. G., 193, 225, 511
Foss, Capt. C. C., 147, 148, 220, 323, 502, 509, 514
Foster, Maj. G. M. B., 508
Foster, Capt. R. C. G., 350
Fox, Capt. C. V., 60, 63
Fraser, Lt.-Col. A., 513
Fraser, Lt.-Col. H., 513
Fraser, Maj. the Hon. H., 21, 43, 60
French, F.-M. Sir J., 7, 29, 30, 41, 70, 119, 133, 154, 166, 183

34

INDEX OF UNITS

GERMAN INFANTRY